# YOUNG LAWYER FOR THE NEW DEAL

## An Insider's Memoir of the Roosevelt Years

Thomas I. Emerson

Edited and with a Foreword by
**Joan P. Emerson**

with a Preface by
**Charles A. Reich**

Rowman & Littlefield Publishers, Inc.

**ROWMAN & LITTLEFIELD PUBLISHERS, INC.**

Published in the United States of America
by Rowman & Littlefield Publishers, Inc.
8705 Bollman Place, Savage, Maryland 20763

**Library of Congress Cataloging-in-Publication Data**

Emerson, Thomas Irwin, 1907-
Young lawyer for the New Deal : an insider's memoir of the
Roosevelt years / Thomas I. Emerson ; edited and with a foreword
by Joan Emerson ; with a preface by Charles A. Reich.
p.   cm.
Includes index.
1.  Emerson, Thomas Irwin, 1907-
2.  Government attorneys—United States—Biography.
3.  United States—Officials and employees—Biography.
4.  New Deal, 1933-1939.   5.  United States—Politics and
government—1933-1945.   I. Emerson, Joan.   II. Title.
KF373.E47A3   1991   973.917'092—dc20   [B]   91-13838 CIP

ISBN 0–8476–7626–9  (alk. paper)

Printed in the United States of America

 ™ The paper used in this publication meets the minimum requirements of
American National Standard for Information Sciences—Permanence of
Paper for Printed Library Materials, ANSI Z39.48–1984.

# CONTENTS

# PREFACE

# An Institution Man

Thomas I. Emerson would have made a truly remarkable journalist. In this extraordinary book we are able to enjoy him in that role. We get to experience Washington, D.C. at its most exciting, the years of the New Deal. Our vantage point is on the inside, among the most creative spirits of this experiment in activist government, and our guide possesses a discerning eye for what is happening, always getting to the essentials and never losing his wonderfully understated sense of humor.

Professor Emerson served as a government lawyer and eventually a top administrator during one of the most precarious and innovative times in our history. It was a time of idealism, of intellectual ferment, of top-notch people in government. He was an insider's insider. Yet he retained so much objectivity that his account always offers an independent point of view, as if he had been at the same time both a participant and a person stationed as an outside observer.

This book is far superior to most Washington journalism in several ways. First, for each of the succession of important agencies where he worked, Professor Emerson provides us with a clear and concise explanation of what the agency's mission was, how it operated, what problems and issues were encountered, the underlying politics, and finally, a penetrating appraisal of the agency's success or failure.

Second, whenever possible Emerson gives us an account—firsthand, in the case of the National Labor Relations Board (NLRB)—of the conditions and people outside of Washington that the agency was trying to deal with. Thus in the early days of the NLRB he was a field attorney in the South, and he describes the workers, their meetings, their working conditions, and the frequent intimidation to which they were subjected.

Third, the book is full of sparkling thumbnail portraits of the often fascinating individuals who held key government positions. These quick, vivid and searching sketches are far bolder than anything we see from the Washington journalists of today. Emerson gives us an honest appraisal of each person's *ability*, high or low. This is radical journalism indeed.

Professor Emerson's book goes beyond day-to-day journalism, however. Underlying the story there is a basic inquiry. Emerson served in Washington during our first and only major experiment with activist national government, an experiment undertaken when the nation's problems became very urgent. Today there is once again great urgency, and consequently debate about the need for activist government is heard again. Did the earlier experiment succeed for fail? Was it sabotaged and cut short? What were the crucial factors in success or failure? Were policies or people more important?

Today we can see that the New Deal agencies called for the services of a hitherto unknown type of professional. The agencies required people who could engage in long-range strategic planning, formulate policy to deal with immediate action, make decisions on the basis of expert knowledge while adhering to principle, reject improper outside influences while being responsive to the needs of the community, and set aside personal interests to pursue a mission in the public interest. In order to administer agencies with unprecedented powers and vast discretion, a most uncommon type of individual was thus required—one with a most uncommon combination of ability and integrity.

The questions that underlie this book are whether activist government can find the people it requires, what characteristics such people must possess, and why government all too frequently excludes the very people who could best serve it. As an eager young recruit, then a high-level administrator, and finally a man of principle at odds with the system, Thomas Emerson's New Deal experience well illustrates the paradoxes of government service.

At the very beginning of the New Deal, the atmosphere was one of idealistic commitment plus intense pressure to get on with the job of government. Professor Emerson recalls that for the first week or so of his employment in Washington, he didn't even have time to find a place to live. "I just kept moving, staying where I was when the day's work was over, or with the person with whom I was working when the day came to an end." One night he "merely went to bed in a hotel room that the office had hired for a conference when the conference was over."

He was alive to the excitement of unlimited possibilities:

New agencies were being created and new policies determined.... Anyone with ability could very nearly create his own job within an agency.... The times were astoundingly enlivening, in a way never since equalled in the government.

The chairman of the NLRB, J. Warren Madden, had many of the qualities necessary for government administration. Although without extensive experience in the labor field, Madden possessed a keen sense of social reality and was "quite objective in his point of view, always open-minded, always searching conscientiously to get to the bottom of a situation." But to Emerson, Madden's most important quality was his character: "He was also a person of overpowering integrity, a man of genuine moral principles and faith, completely honest and courageous." There was room in the agencies for the person of vision. For example, Leon Henderson of the Office of Price Administration had "a clairvoyant ability to predict economic trends and problems of the near future. Always in the forefront, he advocated moves for some months before they took place, anticipating what was about to occur, urging action." David Ginsburg, one of Henderson's chief assistants, "was always three or six months ahead of everybody else as to what the next developments and problems were going to be."

But people of exceptional ability also made enemies, aroused suspicions. The best people in government were easy targets for political attacks in Congress, where intellectuals were equated with nonconformity, and nonconformity was equated with disloyalty. The people brought in by the New Deal gradually lost ground to conservative forces that were also opposed to the underlying programs and goals. Emerson himself was investigated more than once by congressional committees for alleged "Communist" activities. Although nothing came of it in his case, we can see already in the 1930s and 1940s how the tendency to question the "loyalty" of government employees grew into a shameful national obsession a few years later.

When Truman replaced FDR as president, a complete reversal of the previous high standards for government jobs occurred. Professor Emerson gives as examples two of the highest officials concerned with planning for the nation's postwar economic future. One was John Caskie Collett, director of the Office of Economic Stabilization:

A typical Truman appointee, Collett was utterly unsuited for the job.... Although he was a pleasant person, he had no competence in economics, administration, or even in law. He had no idea what the issues were–they were totally beyond anything he had ever thought about before. He was completely lost in the job, never knew what he was doing, and operated purely as a figurehead.

The second official, the top official of the Office of War Mobilization and Reconversion, John W. Snyder:

His outstanding characteristic was narrowness. He was completely uneducated, with no interest in intellectual or cultural issues.... His point of view was almost entirely that of a small-town banker.... He had no respect for the feelings or dignity of his subordinates. He would fly into a rage without justification and give a tongue lashing to a subordinate.

Professor Emerson's book offers a strong case for the proposition that activist government did not fail, it was abandoned once the immediate crisis of the Depression was over. Americans found unity in the imperative for economic recovery, but there was no such unanimity with respect to any permanent change in the economic structure of our democracy. The nation was not ready for a government that would engage in long-range planning with the goal of economic security for every individual. Even if a large number of people wanted those reforms, a powerful business-oriented group was able to block further progress.

Emerson knew it was time to resign when the concept of planning was so precipitously and totally rejected with the return to a civilian economy following the end of World War II. But the lesson of this book is an affirmation of activist government, should it be called for again. The brilliant young lawyers who worked together for the public welfare proved that national social and economic vision is indeed possible.

I particularly hope that the present generation of young lawyers and lawyers-to-be will read Thomas Emerson's Washington memoirs. He shows how a career in law can be based on public service, idealism and integrity, and how fulfilling such a career can be. Today the pressure to make money in the big firms is so great, I am not sure if young lawyers are giving themselves a fair choice between economic success and the Thomas Emerson kind of success, participating in the great public challenges on one's times and preserving a vision of the law "as an instrument for attaining political justice and maintaining democratic values."

Thomas Emerson once described himself to me as an "institution man." We had just finished having lunch at Mory's, and as we emerged onto York Street and saw the Yale Law School building across the street, Tom turned to me and said with unusual emphasis, "I'm an institution man. Individuals depart, but the institution keeps on going. The work you do is carried forward by others." I remember a feeling of surprise, because Tom has so often been a dissenter. But later I realized that his idea of the institution man or woman was very different from the version we all too often accept.

We have wrongly become accustomed to associating "bureaucrats" with mediocrity and conformity, or with self-serving and empire building. By contrast, Professor Emerson's idea of the institution person includes innovation, imagination, idealism, and dissent. During the New Deal, many of those who served in government approached this ideal. It is a model of service we need to restore today.

For Thomas Emerson the reward was fun in the best sense of the word. He was a witness to history, caught unforgettable glimpses of FDR, watched in the Supreme Court as Chief Justice Hughes delivered his *Jones v. Laughlin* opinion changing the course of American constitutional history. He remembers, "I was astonished when Hughes thundered out his famous opinion with an air of complete conviction, as if the outcome had never been in doubt. An amazing performance!" Emerson was a participant in the strategic thinking of a society looking for new answers. He took his reward in experience, in the discovery of how things really work. By those standards, the rewards were great.

This book would not have been possible without the dedicated work of Joan Emerson, Tom's daughter, whose fine job of editing turned an oral history project into a well-organized and fast-moving narrative. I should add that, as one who has often enjoyed hearing Tom's Washington experiences in the comfort of his living room, I can vouch for the fact that this book captures his essence. It has always been a pleasure and a privilege to listen to Tom Emerson's recollections. We are fortunate that they can now be shared with the reader.

Charles A. Reich

# FOREWORD

In 1953 my father, Professor Thomas I. Emerson, dictated an oral history to Dr. Harlan B. Phillips of Columbia University's Oral History Research Department. Twice a week Dr. Phillips would come to New Haven and Professor Emerson would speak into a tape recorder from prepared notes, prompted by an occasional question from Dr. Phillips. The result was a transcript of some 2600 pages.

Starting from his New England antecedents, Professor Emerson spoke briefly about influences on his career from his childhood, his undergraduate days at Yale, at Yale Law School, and his two years in Walter Pollak's New York law firm, where he assisted on, among other cases, the Scottsboro Case.[1] The bulk of this "oral history," however, concerned his career in Washington from 1933 to 1946, first as a lawyer present at the inception of the Roosevelt administration and the New Deal, later with several of the New Deal's executive agencies as the United States carried out its part in World War II. Following World War II and the final dissolution of the New Deal, Professor Emerson joined the faculty of the Yale Law School, where he remained from 1946 until his retirement in 1976. The transcript was set aside, much as, some might say, happened to the New Deal.

Thirty years after those pages were dictated, I found my father's transcript and began to organize and edit it into this book. Reading my father's recollections provided me with a map on which to pinpoint fragmented childhood memories. Most of the names mentioned were familiar. Some were long-time family friends. A few were the parents of my friends. Most were names I had heard in the interminable political talk that surrounded me as I was growing up. As a child I wanted to be part of my father's world and I tried to make conversation about the people he knew because the people were easier to comprehend than the nature of his work. Some of those people came to our house. I remember my father sitting at the head of the dining room table, talking excitedly and laughing with his articulate, spoiling-for-debate colleagues

---

[1] The Scottsboro case, involving the prosecution of nine young blacks in Alabama on charges of rape, became a landmark decision of the U.S. Supreme Court on the right of defendants in criminal proceedings to a fair trial.

and their wives. Some of those people played tennis with him on Sunday mornings at the Friends' School; others participated in the Sunday touch football games. As I read my father's narrative, I learned who these people had been, how they had come into our lives, who had been "senior" and who had been "junior," and to whom. . . . I remember my Dad in his blue V-necked sweater with a white shirt collar or dressed in white shirt and white ducks to play tennis or mow the lawn. I remember a trip to the Luray Caverns in Virginia, walking across a swinging foot bridge over the Potomac River, a Sunday excursion to Falls Church, Virginia, to visit Judge Madden. I always had a sense my father's friends were important people, but Judge Madden I knew was particularly significant to my father because my brother, Robert Madden Emerson, had been named for him. I remember the cocktail hour before dinner—my father mixing drinks and serving each one with a flourish, including the children's glasses of grape juice and ginger ale. When I was sick in bed he would come to my room in the evening and read newspapers. When I fell on the concrete steps at age three and cut my eyebrow, he read Raggedy Ann to me until it was time to go to the doctor for stitches. When I had my tonsils removed at age two and a half, he appeared at the door of my hospital room with a red cocker spaniel puppy for me. And one Sunday morning, as he washed his convertible in the driveway, he was justifiably annoyed when I climbed on the car roof and fell through the canvas into the back seat.

I remember standing on the porch of our Washington house on Quebec Street, where rose tendrils entwined around the iron railing, listening with surprise as both my parents came in the front door about four o'clock on a weekday afternoon in April . . . at first delighted at the prospect of extra time in their company, then realizing something must be wrong because my father never came home as early as four o'clock . . . and when told, "The President died," realizing it was a momentous occasion.

Roosevelt was the only president I had ever known. People around my house always referred to him as "The President." "The President" meant Roosevelt. At the time I revered Roosevelt as a hero. Now, reading my father's transcript all these years later, I was surprised to see the criticism of the Roosevelt administration that he recalls as being current even then among his colleagues and associates.

I remember my father as an early, fervent supporter of the New Deal, albeit critical of Roosevelt for not going far enough. Here, however, I find he speaks from a more mellow point of view. It is the voice of someone capable of considering the New Deal, assessing its inadequacies and failures, but immersed for a lifetime in its ideals. As a result, instead of an assemblage of evidence compiled centuries after the fact by laborious research, affording only the most tentative of generalizations, here we get a day-to-day, "this is what we were doing" kind of understanding, from someone who was present, involved, responsible, and (perhaps it goes without saying for a good lawyer) possessed of an excellent memory for detail.

A chronology of the various New Deal and wartime agencies where my father worked may be helpful:

National Recovery Administration
Assistant Counsel, August 1933–July 1934

National Labor Relations Board
Principal Attorney, August 1934–July 1936

Social Security Board
Principal Attorney, August 1936–August 1937

National Labor Relations Board
Assistant General Counsel,
Associate General Counsel,
September 1937–October 1940

Department of Justice
Special Assistant to the Attorney General,
December 1940–May 1941

Office of Price Administration
Associate General Counsel,
June 1941–October 1942
Deputy Administrator for Enforcement,
November 1942–March 1945

Office of Economic Stabilization
General Counsel, April 1945–August 1945

Office of War Mobilization and Reconversion
General Counsel, August 1945–June 1946

The New Deal, my father's career, and this book open together in a chapter on the National Recovery Administration, where we see the fervor of the early New Deal and can understand immediately why young lawyers, flooding into our nation's capital, had an inordinate influence on that agency. Five chapters describe the National Labor Relations Board: how business interests failed to mobilize to stop the legislation because they assumed it would be declared unconstitutional, how employers ignored the law, and how the law was eventually upheld and enforced. Seven chapters detail the activities of the Office of Price Administration, which administered price control, rent control, and consumer rationing during World War II: how voluntary compliance was encouraged, how widespread violations tended to escalate, how the regulations were formulated, publicized, and enforced. The two concluding chapters then offer accounts of the Office of Economic Stabilization and the Office of War Mobilization and Reconversion, two World War II super-coordinating agencies that were responsible for establishing top level economic policy and coordinating all the governmental agencies dealing with the U.S. economy.

The first three of these agencies had only recently been created at the time that my father signed on. For the people recruited to work in them this meant participating in the process of formulating the very goals of the New Deal: stabilization and revitalization of the economy, establishing our nation's economic "safety net," writing the rules of modern labor/management relations–and translating these ideals into specific administrative agenda. Many of the people involved were enthusiastic at the possibility of putting our democratic government to work to effect social change.

As World War II engulfed the nation, the Roosevelt administration entered a second phase, and the last three agencies where my father worked were wartime agencies concerned with promoting the United States war effort, by controlling and stabilizing the economy and then smoothing the transition to peacetime. The crisis of the Great Depression merged into the crisis of mobilizing the extra effort to win the war, and as people believed winning the war would mean the triumph of freedom and justice, the two phases of the Roosevelt administration were unified by those values. From promoting freedom and justice within the country, the administration turned to promoting it internationally. Throughout both crises, the Roosevelt administration saw management of the economy as crucial to the success of the New Deal and the prosecution of the war, and thus my father's account of the wartime administration of the Office of Price Administration provides well-placed insight into one of the most important agencies of that time.

To appreciate the context in which this oral history was recorded, we should try to think back to the hopes and ideals that dominated the 1930s. With the increase in homelessness and economic uncertainty we see around us as I write today, it seems that we still haven't answered the central question of that time: Is the power of government to be used to safeguard established interests, or to counterbalance them in the interests of the less advantaged? The near collapse of the economic system in the early 1930s temporarily frightened the established interests into cooperating with governmental measures to effect change. As evident in my father's narrative as well as other accounts of the New Deal, however, as soon as the crisis faded the established interests became concerned about the implications of widespread governmental control over the economy–especially if that control might be dominated by persons who lacked a proper appreciation of the absolute inviolability of the profit motive. When the established interests struck back, they struck a death blow to much of the New Deal. They managed either to turn back the governmental regulations or to put crucial decisions in the hands of representatives of the establishment so that in the end the controls actually worked against social change.

This book takes us back to the inception of many of the day-to-day practices that we now take for granted. When we realize that many of the contemporary issues and struggles in our society are influenced by decisions, programs, and ideals that originated with the Roosevelt administration, perhaps those who are frustrated by all the "government regulations" in our lives today will give consideration to the atmosphere in which this "active" government originated: in the context of a make-or-break struggle to save a nation from economic collapse, assure a better life for the citizenry as a whole, and "save the world for democracy."

Those who complain about the heartlessness of present-day bureaucrats may be interested to read about a bureaucracy as it was being born, as opposed to ossifying; about a time when talented young people with boundless energy flocked to serve their country. Now disillusioned experts claim that if an official remains in a Washington agency for more than five (eight?) years, he (or she) becomes dead wood, incapable of new growth, with his primary occupation being simply holding onto his job. Bureaucracy, we are told, is the haven for those seeking to retire from active professional life. How interesting to see that under the New Deal it was quite the opposite. The bureaucracy was intended as an instrument of change, to provide leadership toward a better society. This book provides insight into how change can be–was–carried out by bureaucracy, and into what happened when idealists attempted to use democratic government to make humanitarian changes and in particular to create a broader, more equitable distribution of wealth and power.

In the end we see Professor Emerson bewailing, as he recounts his participation in the New Deal, the unfortunate predominance of private interest and the incredible difficulty in motivating people to act for the collective good–*even in wartime.* The New Dealers were operating with a strong measure of collective interest. Today many people, young and old, view as the crucial issue of our time whether we can learn to put our collective interest ahead of private gain, in order to survive as a civilization–and we can appreciate that the profit motive, personal career success, and other forms of private interest are less restrained today than they were in 1933, when my father begins his account. All the more timely, then, the memoirs of a young lawyer in Washington. . . .

Finally, as Professor Emerson's daughter, I would ask the reader to recall that this book is in effect an edited transcript of an "oral history" that was recorded in 1953, a few years after my father left government service. Out of respect for its spoken nature, its subjectivity and in particular certain habits of speech that could have as easily been "updated" have instead been maintained. I feel obliged to add, however, that New Deal Washington through the eyes of my father was a world of men, where women were "wives" and rarely colleagues. I honor those New Deal professional women who must have had to steel themselves against unwelcome and derogatory attitudes and work without the easy-flowing collegial assistance that the men took for granted.

My father speaks from knowledge gained from holding certain positions in the agencies where he was required to take action on a day-to-day basis. His position meant that he was knowledgeable about certain aspects of those agencies and not others. Some matters were important for his job and others were not. Like anyone, he has constructed a view of the past for himself that is consistent with and reinforces his present concerns and world views. As a fair-minded and even-handed reporter, and an idealist, he has given us a clear-sighted glimpse of the New Deal, from the inside out. And that surely is what an oral history is supposed to do.

Joan P. Emerson

# ACKNOWLEDGMENTS

This book had its origins in the Columbia University Oral History Project. We are greatly indebted to Dr. Harlan B. Phillips for his hours of patient listening, astute questioning, and overall guidance of the oral history to completion.

To my secretary, Diane Hart, we offer thanks for years of loyal service and, in particular, for her laborious word-processing of this manuscript with its reams of corrections.

Mary Calvin, my sister-in-law, gave a labor of love in preparing the edited copy for word-processing. Instructions such as "see asterisk on page 131" and other obscure notations did not faze her. Mary shared with us her excitement at the birth of each new chapter. As the first person to see the emerging manuscript in draft, her enthusiasm meant much to us. She was an integral part of the production of this manuscript. We acknowledge both her intangible and her concrete contributions.

We were very fortunate to find David Good. We want to thank him for his sensitive editing and general assistance. His enthusiasm and commitment to the project, and his effortless understanding of material that was for him only history, far exceeded the bounds of any formal arrangement.

To my wife, Ruth Calvin Emerson, we wish to express our deep appreciation for her constant interest and support throughout this enterprise.

# NEW DEAL ABBREVIATIONS

| | |
|---|---|
| ABA | American Bar Association |
| AFL | American Federation of Labor (*see* CIO) |
| CIO | Congress of Industrial Organizations (*see* AFL) |
| CPI | Consumer Price Index |
| FCC | Federal Communications Commission |
| FEPC | Fair Employment Practices Committee |
| FTC | Federal Trade Commission |
| NDAC | National Defense Advisory Commission |
| NLRB | National Labor Relations Board |
| NRA | National Recovery Administration |
| OES | Office of Economic Stabilization |
| OPA | Office of Price Administration |
| OPACS | Office of Price Administration and Civilian Supply |
| OPM | Office of Production Management |
| OWMR | Office of War Mobilization and Reconversion |
| PAB | Petroleum Administrative Board |
| RFC | Reconstruction Finance Corporation |
| SEC | Securities and Exchange Commission |
| TNEC | Temporary National Economic Committee |
| TVA | Tennessee Valley Authority |
| UNRRA | United Nations Relief and Rehabilitation Administration |
| WLB | War Labor Board |
| WPB | War Production Board |

# NEW DEAL ABBREVIATIONS

# 1

# A YOUNG LAWYER
# FROM YALE

*Growing up and going for a career in the 1930s meant going to
Washington.*

Both my parents were brought up in late-nineteenth century Brooklyn,
New York. The third of five sons, I was born in 1907 and raised in
Demarest, New Jersey.

My father's family came from New England; my mother's parents were
born in Germany. At home we were continuously steeped in stories about
my father's family. Pictures around the house displayed many of my
ancestors, all of them rather grim-looking New Englanders. All my
paternal ancestors were farmers, school teachers, or ministers, until my
grandfather broke with tradition to become a lawyer. My relatives were
leaders in small-town America, upholding conservative traditions. Strong
traces of New England sternness and emphasis on work, thrift, progress,
and education, with particular emphasis on never being idle, pervaded my
family atmosphere and had a significant impact on me.

My father, an electrical engineer for the firm of Clark, McMullen &
Riley (101 Park Avenue, New York), was a reserved man with a stern
outlook on life, but at the same time with a certain deviltry in his make-
up. He definitely laid down the law for the family. His unconventional
streak was revealed in his instructions to us as to what marks we were to
get in school: "A" in everything except deportment, in which we were to get
"B". His sympathy for people out of the ordinary was surprising in view of
his general reserve and sternness. He took an interest in the one Jewish
and the one Negro family in town. A Republican Party voter in the days
when it was still thought of as the party founded by Abraham Lincoln, he
took part in community affairs and served for many years on the Demarest
Board of Education. Most of his leisure time was spent working around
the house and garden, rather than on intellectual pursuits such as reading.
But he read to us extensively from Charles Dickens, Walter Scott, Mark
Twain, James Fenimore Cooper, and Robert Louis Stevenson. (A good
many books were around the house, although some had never been read,

1

as I discovered later when I got around to reading every book in the house.) He was not very vocal about his ideas. He would explain things to us at times, but little verbal communication occurred in our family at an intellectual level, despite the assumed intellectual background. He pushed us to compete and improve ourselves, particularly to improve our minds, and to read good books. The most important things in life were intellectual and obtained through education. Although religion played a minor part in my family, we were imbued with a moral responsibility to prepare ourselves to contribute to the social progress of the country. My father played baseball and football with us and took us ice skating. Particularly in our younger days there was an undercurrent of tenderness, but family affection was to be taken for granted rather than demonstrated outwardly. If we did our duty right, then we were entitled to relax to a certain extent.

My mother was a softening influence in the household; she would make sure that we had done our chores so that we didn't get in trouble when our father came home, and she would comfort us. Even now I find it hard to strike a proper balance between work and relaxation; I do not feel comfortable unless I am doing something constructive. However, this family background generated independence and resourcefulness in me.

When I was two years old I contracted a severe case of infantile paralysis. For many years after that my father would massage the muscles in my right leg and arm every day; he also taught me exercises to strengthen the muscles. In the end the infantile paralysis left no serious effect.

I used to go next door when my grandfather returned home about 4:30 from his law practice in New York City and read newspapers with him. That is mainly how I learned to read. At first I was intensely interested in the Boston Red Sox; I felt this was terribly important because I saw it in print. Then I gradually started to read other parts of the newspaper. When I read the political news I had the same feeling of its importance; I wanted to get into politics and become a senator. My interest in political matters stems to a large extent from that experience of reading newspapers at my grandfather's house. Although we enjoyed each other, my grandfather and I were not terribly communicative. My decision to enter the law probably was made initially because my grandfather was a lawyer. I was excited when he showed me clippings of cases he had handled; he had a general practice with extensive courtroom work. My first ideas about a career, as soon as they had progressed beyond the stage of being an engineer on a train, came from that source. My grandfather used to give me lessons in public speaking; he made me practice four minute speeches urging the purchase of Liberty Bonds. I realized that a good entry into politics was through law–that many legislators, presidents, cabinet officers, and public officials were lawyers. So I envisioned a legal career leading into politics. My father encouraged this.

I had the record, which I have always held up as an example to my children, that I was never absent or tardy through twelve years of elementary and high school. My success in school was due primarily to the fact that I had a good memory, was precise in my thinking, and could concentrate on what I was doing. I had no intellectual flair; I was a rather unimaginative pupil. In school I assumed that what was given to us was what one learned, and was uncritical of anything that went on. I am not sure that I lived up to my father's suggestion of getting a "B" in deportment. Occasionally, I would be disciplined to the extent of being kept after school, but on the whole I behaved quite well. Boys who liked school were considered sissies, so I carefully concealed how much I enjoyed it. In particular, my high school Latin teacher took an interest in me. I remember her as imparting her feeling for the form and organization of the language as our class explored use of words to express precisely defined meanings.

I was quite shy in school. By the time I graduated from grammar school I was still quite small in stature, and all through high school I was definitely smaller than most of the other students. At full growth I barely measured 5 feet 5 inches. This contributed to my shyness.

I spent enormous amounts of time in the Englewood Public Library, reading almost exclusively literature. We would find a book on the open shelves and conceal it behind some other books so no one else would find it and check it out when we were halfway through.

I went out for the high school debating team on the theory that if I were going to be a lawyer or politician I must be able to speak publicly. The debating coach kept urging me to relax, to let myself go and speak with more determination and fire, but the harder I tried to do that, the less I could. My strong point was in organizing material. I was not aggressive in debating and I could not easily make up my mind as to what my position was that I was supposed to take so strongly. I always saw several sides to an argument and consequently I could speak with equal conviction on either side.

When I was in high school my mother became ill and a good deal of the housework fell to us children. All of us became fairly adequate cooks.

My mother died when I was nineteen.

## BECOMING A LAWYER

By the end of high school I had not deviated from the plan that I had conceived at such an early age of becoming a lawyer. I automatically assumed that I would go to Cornell, where my father had gone and my older brother was. At the last moment my Latin teacher got me interested in going to Yale. She persuaded the Yale Alumni Association of Bergen County (New Jersey) to give me a scholarship.

### Yale
Formal courses at Yale had a minor impact on me. I majored in English, probably because almost everyone else did and the English Department was one of the strongest at Yale–but government and

psychology attracted me more. My course work was aimed more at developing the technique of getting good grades than toward expansion of my intellectual capacities. One of my strategies was to turn in my examination book so the books before and after mine would be those of the worst members of the class; when the examination books were piled on the desk I would search through the stack and put mine after that of the lowest man in the class. I made Phi Beta Kappa in my junior year.

The main influences of my college days were other students. After my first week or so as a freshman I noticed a fellow in several of my classes whose mind attracted me: Thomas Copeland. Copeland had an intellectual capacity far above anything I had seen at close range. By criticizing everything in terms of his high standards, he taught me to be critical and question authority. However, the topics of his critiques were largely the subject matter of courses and the behavior of teachers and students, rather than social, political, or economic matters. In retrospect one of the most striking things about my whole college experience was my fellow students' complete lack of interest in political, economic, or social problems.

Following graduation with honors, I continued on my chosen path and was accepted to Yale Law School. Contrary to my experience as an undergraduate, I found law school competitive and intellectually stimulating. The faculty were engaged in a crusade to replace the traditional approach–logical reasoning from abstract legal principles–with an emphasis on the function of law and realistic factors that influenced legal decisions. I did some individual research for William O. Douglas. I was the top student in my class and editor-in-chief of the *Yale Law Journal*. On a trip to Washington I and some other members of the editorial board conversed with Justices Holmes and Brandeis.

**After Yale**

Upon graduating with my new law degree, I started looking for a job with only two basic ideas. One was that I wanted to practice in New York City, because I considered it to be the center of the universe. Second, I had a rather vague feeling that I was not too keen on going into one of the large New York City law firms. I had absorbed sufficiently liberal views by that time that I objected to their conservatism and had an inclination to use my talents in another direction. The three top New York law firms and two others made me offers, but I took a job in a small firm as assistant to Walter Pollak, who was known for his work on civil liberties cases.

The major cases I worked on with Pollak were intensely interesting. He took the civil liberties cases as a public service, because of his concern with justice through legal process, particularly freedom of speech and fair trials. Pollak was extremely meticulous; he would weigh every word and every comma, then change it in galley, and then change it again in page proof. Even in my careful work on the *Yale Law Journal*, which was a rigorous training in precision, accuracy, and choice of words, I had not run into such high standards. (Later, when I worked for the government, I found that I had to shift to the opposite extreme, because we never had time to do anything properly.)

## The Scottsboro Case

One of the first cases I worked on was the first Scottsboro case, which Pollak was then taking before the U.S. Supreme Court. The Scottsboro case involved seven Negroes who had been convicted in Alabama of raping two white girls on a freight train. The case resulted in a landmark Supreme Court decision on the right to counsel under the Fourteenth Amendment.[1]

I was with Pollak's law firm for two years, during which I did not have any responsibility of my own or do any court work, except once in a while when Pollak would let me argue an insignificant motion. The first time I was in court on my own, the matter involved only postponing a trial. Two impressive attorneys representing the other parties each made a little speech explaining that we had all agreed that the matter should be postponed. The judge then turned to me and said, "And what were you told to say, sonny?" I was still rather youthful in appearance and he apparently thought I was the officeboy.

Many lawyers that I came in contact with looked on law simply as a means of making a living. Others, including some of my classmates who were getting along well in the large law firms, seemed to view the law as a technique of facilitating their corporate clients' business activities. A much smaller group, which included Pollak, viewed law as an instrument for attaining political justice and maintaining democratic values, without thinking in terms of using law for controlling the economic system or securing economic justice.

These questions had come to have a very real importance in our lives, as America had just fallen into the grips of the Great Depression. My friends and I talked animatedly about the current economic and political scene. We were skeptical about the Democratic presidential candidate, Franklin Roosevelt. We were not convinced there would be any substantial difference if he won the 1932 election, and we doubted he had the capacity to run the country in a time of crisis.

---

1 A few years later when my wife and I were on our honeymoon we drove to Scottsboro to see the famous town. We arrived toward dusk and went to see the court house. As we entered I naively asked some functionary sitting with his feet on a desk, "Which is the courtroom where the Scottsboro case was tried?" An unbelievable tension immediately filled the air. The fellow spat out a long tirade about people coming down from the North sightseeing, that we had no business in the matter, that the Yankees ought to stay out of it. He ended by saying, "The best thing for you to do is to get out of town and get out quick." I got a sinking feeling then for the first time of what the trial must have been like. However we did not "get out of town." Refusing to admit we were intimidated, we stayed overnight at a fifth-rate hotel there. After dinner we went for a walk and again we felt shattered by the overpowering reality of the conditions under which Negroes were falsely accused as well as the conditions under which Negroes generally lived there.

## DAWN OF THE NEW DEAL
*In the crusading spirit of the time, I move to Washington...see Tom Corcoran...land a job at NRA...*

In the end I cannot remember whether I voted for Roosevelt or Norman Thomas [the Socialist candidate]. I do remember avid discussions about whether capitalism should be reformed or abolished. We knew that something drastic had to be done, particularly for the relief of unemployment. I felt that an underestimation of the crisis prevailed among most of the people I knew.

Immediately after Roosevelt was inaugurated in March 1933 he moved rapidly and made a series of legislative proposals. For those of us who counted ourselves in the liberal wing, it was tremendously exhilarating to see Roosevelt move as rapidly as he did. We believed he should be supported and we itched to become engaged ourselves in dealing with the national crisis.

By June 1933 I was definitely beginning to think of moving to Washington. My initial idea was to take a leave of absence from Pollak's office for six months or a year, to help out for a while in the national emergency and then to return. My interest in the operation of government and politics was heightened now that the government was actually attempting some regulation of the economic structure. I was greatly excited by that. My interest in all the solutions that had been suggested to solve the economic crisis and the proposals that now were being embodied in legislation continued to increase. I was eager to work for an agency that was handling the New Deal legislation. Other people I knew around New York were thinking about joining the influx to Washington, too. A crusading spirit was in the air.

About the end of June I finally made up my mind to go to Washington for six months. When I asked Pollak for leave he raised no objection. Pollak contacted Justice Frankfurter on my behalf. Frankfurter replied that I should see Tom Corcoran in Washington. In early July I did so. Corcoran was rushing around frantically. He only had about 30 seconds to spare. He did not do much more than send me over to see Donald Richberg, then the general counsel of the National Recovery Administration (NRA), which had just been created.

I saw Richberg for maybe 30 seconds as well. He referred me to Blackwell Smith, who was his chief assistant in the Legal Division of the NRA. Smith interviewed me for the job. Smith himself was so busy that he was interviewing in pairs. I was paired with Ernest Gross, who had finished law school the year before I did and was working in the State Department. Smith told us that things were very uncertain, that they were moving ahead and needed lawyers, but that they did not know how fast they could take them on. He said he was pretty sure that he would be able to take on additional lawyers very soon. He was interested in us and without making a definite offer said he would get in touch with us. I assumed that I had the job.

6

While I was in Washington, I also went around to see Charles Wyzanski, who was then solicitor of the Department of Labor. I had an introduction to him from David Niles [a presidential assistant]. I did not know which agency I wanted to work for. I had some feeling that the NRA was the place, since that seemed to be the agency that was dealing most directly with the economic controls, the aspect that interested me the most, but I was not sure. I had thought about the Department of Labor and the Agricultural Adjustment Administration, which was just being considered by Congress. I talked with Wyzanski at some length about what was happening in Washington and what the different agencies were doing. Wyzanski could not offer any hope that the Labor Department would expand to any degree (and he turned out to be right). He encouraged me—and his advice proved to be excellent—to work for one of the new agencies that was just in the process of being established and that would move very rapidly. Wyzanski's point was that anyone in on the ground floor of such an outfit would have considerable responsibility fairly soon, much more than in a old-line department, even under the new administration. As a result of that conversation I came to the conclusion that the NRA was the place for me. I then returned to Tom Corcoran, as he had requested, and told him what I planned to do.

About one week later I received a formal offer from the NRA. The salary, as I recall, was $3600, which was a little more than the law firm was paying me. I accepted, wound up my affairs in New York, went to Washington on July 31, and reported for work on August 1, 1933.

## A Young Lawyer in Washington, 1933

Washington was in tremendous tumult. Everyone was working excessively hard in a spirit of great fervor; they were in a great hurry and excited beyond measure. All sorts of ideas were floating around as to what should be done. For instance, shortly after I arrived Jacob Baker, who held an important job with one of the relief agencies, proposed that the government build factories and put unemployed workers to work in its own factories. This proposal had tremendous economic and political implications, as I could see at the time, even with my slight acquaintance with such matters, for it would have put the government in competition with private industry. Baker was starting slowly with some mattress factories and furniture factories. The project was quite out of character with the basic thinking of most of those in important posts in the Roosevelt administration. Nevertheless, the idea was seriously considered.

The situation was unusually fluid, with very little red tape. New agencies were being created and new policies determined. New enterprises were springing up all over. Anyone with ability could very nearly create his own job within an agency, or at least assume as much responsibility as he could take on. The times were astoundingly enlivening, in a way never since equaled in the government. Even World War II did not quite arouse the last ounce of energy as did the early New Deal.

7

An indication of the pressure was that when I arrived in Washington, I did not have time to find a place to live for a week or ten days. The first night I stayed on the living room couch of a fellow employee, Milton Katz, whom I had known only slightly before. The next night I merely went to bed in a hotel room that the office had hired for a conference. The following night I stayed with Blackwell Smith. I just kept moving, staying where I was when the day's work was over, or with the person with whom I was working when the day came to an end.

I moved into an apartment with Blackwell Smith's brother and another lawyer for a month or six weeks. Then I went to live in a house with four other lawyers, including Leon Keyserling, then secretary to Sen. Robert Wagner; Howard Westwood, who worked in the government; and Ambrose Doskow, a law clerk to Justice Cardozo. James Allen, who was working in NRA, also lived in this rented house. We paid a maid to cook and clean. Later we were joined by Abe Fortas, who graduated from Yale Law School in 1933 and came to Washington to work in the Agricultural Adjustment Administration. The house members changed slightly from time to time.

Almost everybody in a policy position at NRA, and many stenographers, worked evenings on a regular basis. By Labor Day weekend, 1933, Gen. Hugh Johnson felt it necessary to close the building and forbid anybody to enter, insisting that a three-day holiday was essential for the physical and mental health of the staff. He did the same thing the following Thanksgiving.

My own routine was to work until about midnight or 1 AM, go home, fall into bed, and be back in the office again by 9 AM. This continued through Saturday afternoon. Then, unless something was exceptionally urgent, I would knock off at 5 or 6 o'clock Saturday, relax Saturday evening, sleep until 1 or 2 o'clock Sunday afternoon, relax the rest of Sunday, and start again Monday morning. I kept up that routine for six or eight months. My schedule was not particularly unusual; many people worked those hours or even longer. The atmosphere gradually calmed down, but especially at first everybody threw himself into the work with extraordinary zeal.

## THE NATIONAL INDUSTRIAL RECOVERY ACT
*"A floor under wages, a ceiling over hours"*

The National Industrial Recovery Act, setting up the NRA, became effective June 16, 1933. When I joined NRA on August 1st, it had been in operation only about six weeks–in fact, less than that, because it had taken some time to get the first administrator on the job and moved into offices in the Commerce Department building. As I recall, I was about the 150th member of the staff. Later the staff increased to thousands. I will outline the provisions of the act and give a general picture of the operation of NRA before I discuss my own experience there.

**Section 7(a)**

The objective of the National Industrial Recovery Act was to establish a floor under wages and a ceiling over hours, hoping by raising wages to increase purchasing power and by reducing hours to spread employment. The wage and hour provisions benefited labor. In order to obtain the cooperation of industry the statute contained provisions for elimination of unfair methods of competition. The most important part of the act ultimately turned out to be the collective bargaining provisions in section 7(a). Under this provision each NRA code had to include a clause guaranteeing that employees had a right to organize and bargain collectively, free from interference, restraint, or coercion on the part of their employers. Section 7(a) also eliminated company-dominated unions and "yellow dog" contracts (whereby the employee agreed not to join a union). To implement the statute, each industry was to formulate a "code of fair competition," which would include wage and hour provisions, trade practice provisions, and the collective bargaining provision. The code would then be submitted to the NRA, revised to the extent necessary for approval, and then submitted for approval by the president. To merit the president's approval the industry group presenting the code had to be representative of the industry, the code could not be designed to promote monopolies or to eliminate or oppress small enterprises, or to discriminate against them, and a collective bargaining provision had to be included. The president could impose a code upon any industry that did not develop a code of its own. When approved, the code became law and was enforceable by an injunction, by a criminal prosecution resulting in a fine (although no jail sentence), and by the enforcement procedures of the Federal Trade Commission Act.

Between 500 and 600 codes were eventually issued, covering all the basic industries, such as cotton textiles, automobiles, steel, and many minor ones. The definition of what was an industry was in confusion. We used to joke about codes that covered such exotic areas as the "hog ring industry."

Under the National Industrial Recovery Act an industry was supposed to formulate the applicable code, but in practice the NRA legal staff drafted most of the codes, in consultation with the relevant industry group. What actually happened was that the professional personnel of the trade associations were most likely to take the initiative by requesting a code; they often had some specific ideas about what they wanted in the code. If no trade association existed, the leaders of the industry frequently would form one. An NRA attorney working with the industry group and with the NRA official who had been assigned to that code would prepare a draft. We inquired as to whether the group proposing the code was representative of the industry and decided to what extent other groups within the industry would have to be given a place on the committee that was proposing the code. A hearing date was announced in trade papers and the general press. Anyone could come to the hearing and present ideas supporting or criticizing the proposals. The hearing was conducted on a rather formal basis, somewhat like a congressional legislative hearing. NRA officials studied the transcript of the hearing and a second period of negotiation with the industry group followed. The final code was then submitted to the head of the NRA section and division, and sent up for signature by the administrator. In the process the Legal Division had to approve the code. Approvals by the Industry Advisory Board, Labor Advisory Board, and the Consumer Advisory Board were necessary too, but rather pro forma. (I will discuss these boards shortly.)

**The Codes**

The codes consisted of four parts.

The *first* part was the wages and hours provisions, which soon came to be framed in standard language. There was usually considerable negotiation about setting the minimum wage. Often differences arose within the industry, with the high-wage portion of the industry attempting to bring wages up, and the low-wage portion resisting. In industries where labor was organized, union representatives played an important role. Normally, however, not much of a struggle occurred over the wages and hours provisions.

The *second* part of the codes was the collective bargaining provisions. Industry was usually not too happy about the collective bargaining provisions, but agreed to include them because it was required.

The *third* part of the codes, and the part in which the industries were by far the most interested, included the trade practice provisions. These became more elaborate as time went on, and ended by covering an enormous variety of problems that came to be called unfair trade practices. Most of the provisions related to prices, including provisions prohibiting sales below cost or prohibiting discrimination in prices between different kinds of buyers. Price reporting provisions required industry members to report to the code authority the prices at which sales were made. The code authorities collected this material and published it, or distributed it to the members of the industry. Although this was theoretically only a reporting arrangement, these provisions facilitated price-fixing and usually had that effect. Other trade practice provisions dealt with advertising practices. For instance, a Macy's department store ad stating that Macy's sold 6 percent below any other store was prohibited under the retail code. Various provisions applied to practices that were attacked as unfair trade practices, but which tended to be the practices used by the more efficient and aggressive elements in the industry. One-cent sales were prohibited, for instance. To some extent, the provisions did relate to what everyone would agree were bona fide unfair trade practices, but more and more they tended to embrace prohibitions against the merchandising practices of a store such as Macy's, which was an extremely intelligent, hard-hitting, forward-moving outfit that made life uncomfortable for its competitors. So the trade practice provisions became very elaborate, covered a wide area of business practices, and, on the whole, tended strongly toward monopolistic devices detrimental to consumer interests.

10

The *fourth* and final part of the codes created a code authority, for administration of the codes. The code authority normally was composed of a representative group of members of the industry, usually appointed by the NRA administrator. Some effort was made to have the trade associations function as code authorities, but this was consistently resisted by NRA. Actually, however, the trade associations usually constituted the dominant element in the code authority. The function of the code authority was to be a clearinghouse for information about the code, attempt to educate the members of the industry with respect to the code provisions, receive complaints from the industry concerning defects in the code, make studies of how things were going, propose code amendments to NRA, and in general supervise the activities of the industry under the code. Some code authorities had more enforcement powers than others.

Controversy surrounded the relationship of NRA officials to these code authorities. Some code authorities wanted to meet in secret, but NRA insisted that an NRA official could be present at all meetings. Although it was disorganized at first, later NRA designated certain officials to follow what the code authorities were doing. In many instances my division, the Legal Division, would send the lawyer who was working on that code to the code authority meeting.

A major issue, and the one which first indicated to me the power structure in the organization, was whether labor should be represented on the code authorities. Industry resisted representatives of both labor and consumers extremely hard. Labor's failure to undertake any fight on behalf of this proposal indicated the absence of any strong labor influence.

**Administering the Codes**

The codes were undergoing continual revision. An important code might be amended several times a month. This was less true as time went on, but still a code might have as many as 60 amendments. This raised difficult legal problems, because after the first few amendments, it became difficult for anyone to figure out what the code stipulated. At that time there was no *Federal Register* in which the amendments could be published, so NRA was repeatedly reissuing codes to include all the amendments. A major task, in which the code authorities assisted us, was to place in the hands of the industry members the various versions of the code. (The Office of Price Administration, dealing with the same problem later, provided a loose leaf service for its regulations; I will discuss OPA later.)

Little effort was made to decentralize the NRA operation. The principal job of code formulation would almost necessarily have to be done in Washington. A small amount of decentralization occurred in the area of enforcement and to some extent in the interpretation of the codes.

NRA had some success in persuading state governments, and in some cases city governments, to pass legislation making it a state or local offense to violate the NRA codes. Such legislation would bring into the enforcement picture the state and local apparatus for investigating and prosecuting violations. But a number of constitutional problems arose.

11

One was the question of delegation of power by the states, since they had delegated power to the federal government to make laws that would become crimes in the states. Also, technical problems arose with those state constitutions that prohibited the device of incorporation by reference; anything that was made a violation of the state law had to be spelled out in the statute or ordinance. So the state or city could not incorporate the NRA codes by referring to them, and they could not spell out verbatim 600 of these codes–that in any case were changing every day! This was a difficult problem.

In addition to problems with the legislation, there were problems in the administration of the codes. In the course of NRA operations, factionalism within an industry was discernible in many instances. The industries I dealt with (I will detail these later) had complicated conflicts. I did not deal with any of the great monopolies or the quasi-monopolistic groups. The NRA representative was usually someone from the industry and often represented the viewpoint of only one segment of the industry. Sooner or later conflicting factions in the industry would appear. To prevent later challenges, we made considerable effort at the very beginning to bring the major factions into the open and to reconcile their views. Most NRA representatives made a genuine attempt to do this.

Most industries gradually became aware of the possibilities of using NRA to advance the interests of the dominant faction. The trade association personnel often were the first to see the potential. With little advance planning on the part of industry, the political thrust of NRA developed in a haphazard way.

The code authorities usually ended up being dominated by the majority group, although there was often minority representation. Without any careful advance plan, the administration of NRA was carried out under circumstances and in an environment such that it inevitably spread out to permeate enormous areas of industry, and to give industry groups a sizable piece of governmental power with which to control their own industry.

A good deal of the initiative that did come from the industries seemed to come from the professional trade association secretaries and others who had spent more time considering the broader aspects of their industry's problems, rather than the direct management of the industry itself. The business leaders were rather rigid in their outlook, unfamiliar with law and government, and had not contemplated what role the government should play or what the distinction between private power and government power might be. I was particularly surprised at the representatives of the banking industry who came to Washington to have codes drafted. They seemed remarkably helpless people, with an almost complete lack of knowledge of how our democratic government operated. They did not know what they wanted or have much idea of what was going on. In fact, my general impression of the businessmen who came to Washington concerning all these codes was the exceedingly narrow scope of both their interests and their capacities. They seemed lost in the Washington environment, unable to grasp what was necessary in formulating a code or what might be done with respect to problems in their industries.

**The NRA Advisory Boards**

One of the innovations of the New Deal was the idea of an "advisory board," to provide direct input from the citizenry to the administrative agencies being created by the New Deal. The enabling act set up NRA to include three advisory boards: the Industry Advisory Board, Labor Advisory Board, and the Consumers Advisory Board. The Industry Advisory Board was composed of top people in business. They were not particularly influential, simply because it did not seem to be necessary; the regular administrators carried out their interests without any help. The Labor Advisory Board was headed by Leo Wolman. At that time he had the reputation of being a very able, very liberal, hard-hitting person. It was somewhat of a surprise when he did not fight very hard for the labor position on the various issues that came up, such as whether the automobile industry could modify Section 7(a) when it formulated its code. The NRA administrator, General Johnson, compromised and permitted them to do this, because he wanted the automobile code out in a hurry. Later there was sufficient protest from labor as a whole that the modifications were rescinded, and no other code was permitted to be framed in that way.

One issue that I spoke to Wolman about, and urged him informally to do something about, was the question of labor representatives on the code authorities. The code authority was a committee that represented the industry in administering the relevant code. In terms of increasing its prestige, and in terms of a legitimate interest in the wage and hour and collective bargaining provisions in the codes, I would have thought that labor would have made strenuous efforts to be represented on the code authorities. Wolman refused to press this at all. So with the exception of a few well-organized industries in the garment trades, there were no labor representatives on the code authorities.

Almost from the beginning, therefore, Wolman did not press what many of us thought was labor's legitimate point of view. The Labor Advisory Board never achieved much influence. In view of the business background of the staff, it would have been a difficult struggle, anyway, but Wolman never attempted it. He claimed that he was working effectively behind the scenes and did not want to bring issues into the open to antagonize people. I did not know enough about what happened "behind the scenes" to judge that fully, but from what I could see, he was pulling his punches and not exploiting his position to the fullest. It was rather incomprehensible to me and to some of the others. Later Wolman turned out to be conservative. Others have told me he was conservative from the beginning and that I had misjudged him in thinking that he was a fiery liberal. In any event, the labor position did not carry much weight in NRA.

The third board, the Consumers Advisory Board, was headed by Harriet ("Miss") Elliott, from North Carolina. Supported by Mrs. Roosevelt, she was a nice lady who meant well, but she was not very effective. The Consumers Advisory Board was in a hopelessly difficult position anyway, because they had no organized force behind them. Miss Elliott was assisted by Dexter M. Keezer, who operated fairly effectively at the time.

13

They did have some effect, but by and large they were without much influence, either.

## The Blue Eagle

Before I had arrived on the scene, the NRA had undertaken to promulgate a temporary measure known as the President's Reemployment Agreement. The National Industrial Recovery Act had provided that the president could enter into voluntary agreements and approve voluntary agreements between industry groups. Under this provision of the statute, NRA had issued, with great ballyhoo, a proposed voluntary agreement that it asked all industrial and trade enterprises to enter into. The agreement contained provisions primarily dealing with wages and hours. The collective bargaining provisions were in there also. The effort was to boost wages and reduce hours as quickly as possible, without waiting for the necessity of framing codes, through voluntary participation by large numbers of business enterprises.

A great number of business firms did sign up. The agreement was not enforceable by any court sanction. It was enforceable only through the device of the "Blue Eagle." The symbol of the Blue Eagle was central to NRA publicity. Business firms, if they complied with the voluntary agreement, would be permitted to display the Blue Eagle in their shop window, attach it as a label to their products, use it in their advertising, or in any other that they wanted to. The only enforcement of the voluntary agreement was the disgrace of removing the Blue Eagle. Policing the President's Reemployment Agreement–checking up on which shops had the right to use the Blue Eagle–was done on a haphazard and informal basis. NRA was hardly organized at the time and had no enforcement staff. Most of the formal removals of Blue Eagles came under the codes after the voluntary agreements had been superseded.

This was one of the first government campaigns in publicity of this sort. The crusading spirit of the times at first ensured a substantial degree of compliance with this purely voluntary arrangement. There was great excitement throughout the country. Parades in various cities celebrated the Blue Eagle and the Blue Eagle soon became famous. Removal of the Blue Eagle was considered an important deprivation, particularly to industries that relied on consumer demand. Law suits were instituted to enjoin the removal of the Blue Eagle by NRA.

Most industries had considerable incentive to secure the approval of a code to replace the voluntary agreement. Under the code they could establish various provisions relating to trade practices that they were interested in. Also, since the code was more formal, it was less likely that certain parts of the industry would be out of compliance with the wages and hours provisions.

After the codes were formulated, they were enforceable by court sanction, but the device of removing the Blue Eagle still continued. The Blue Eagle was also used in certain codes as the equivalent of a licensing device. This was done in the garment industry, for instance, which was highly organized, with a strong labor influence and a tradition of union labels. Under the garment codes a business could not operate unless it sewed the Blue Eagle label into its products and it could not do that if the Blue Eagle had been taken away. This unauthorized licensing system operated with considerable effectiveness, although it had a dubious legal base.

Gradually, however, the crusading spirit faded and the Blue Eagle tended not to be respected any more. Still, the voluntary agreement and the Blue Eagle lasted quite a period of time.

### Enforcing the Codes

No real thought was devoted to the problem of enforcement until the matter became acute. Finally, when it could not be dodged any longer, an Enforcement section was created as part of the Legal Division of NRA. One of the attorneys who had done code drafting became head of the Enforcement section. From then on efforts were made to work out an organization and a staff to handle the enforcement job.

NRA staff could investigate violations and prepare the cases for trial, but any actual court proceedings had to be brought by the Department of Justice. The theory was that action by the Enforcement section through court proceedings was the last resort. The initial effort was to obtain compliance with the codes on a voluntary basis, originally through patriotic propaganda and the device of the Blue Eagle, and later through the efforts of the code authorities and through education by NRA. Under the rulings of some codes, the code authorities had the power to settle or compromise complaints of violation. Even after cases were referred to the Enforcement staff, only the more significant ones would be prosecuted.

Gradually the code authorities began to investigate violations and to use pressure to bring about compliance. The extent to which the code authority engaged in enforcement varied, but it was primarily in the garment industry that the code authorities were most active. From the viewpoint of sound government administration, the enforcement role of the code authorities was dubious. It was impossible to make code authorities truly representative if a division existed in the industry, and most industries had conflicting factions. Yet this group would investigate a competitor, examine his books and records, make a decision as to whether he had violated, attempt to put pressure on him to comply and make some recompense for his violation, and, if he did not conform, threaten to use economic pressure or to refer him to NRA for criminal prosecution.

The enforcement job turned out to be impossible. By the time the Enforcement section was organized, the situation was already getting out of hand. Voluntary compliance under the Blue Eagle had definitely eroded. The code authorities were not able to handle the growing number of violations. If violations reached a certain level and became fairly widespread, then simply as a matter of competitive self-protection the entire industry would tend to violate also. So a small group in an industry could start a chain reaction that accelerated into widespread noncompliance. Furthermore, the codes were so complex and yet remained so vague in some ways–for instance, the provisions against selling below cost were so imprecise in their terms–that enforcement of many provisions was hardly feasible.

The Enforcement staff, never very large, had no experience in enforcement techniques, and did not function at all effectively. It operated with a growing lack of public support, and no effort by NRA to obtain support from the public in its behalf.

One of the first court cases brought by NRA involved a small battery manufacturer in Pennsylvania. He successfully challenged the enforcement process and won public support for his position that the code was unfair to him, that he was being made a martyr, and that he was a small businessman who was being shabbily treated by the government. In the end, as I recall, the case was dismissed. The Enforcement staff and the whole NRA suffered a resounding public defeat. Incidents of that sort made the enforcement job even more difficult.

It became clear to those in Enforcement, sooner than it did to others in NRA, that a test of the constitutional issues was necessary. Unless a ruling by the U.S. Supreme Court on the constitutionality of the act were obtained, it would be impossible to establish conditions under which effective enforcement could be undertaken. This was true not only because there was doubt about the act's legitimacy, but also because the prestige of the Supreme Court and the whole judicial system behind a favorable decision, whether or not on constitutional grounds, would have conferred a legitimacy to enforcement efforts that NRA could hardly have obtained in any other way.

## THE NATIONAL RECOVERY ADMINISTRATION

### NRA Administrators
*General Hugh "Iron Pants" Johnson, Donald Richberg...*

The first administrator of NRA was Gen. Hugh Johnson. General Johnson was a protege of Bernard Baruch, who had been a consultant in the preparation of the NRA legislation and who had delegated to Johnson the power to represent him in the actual work of drafting. General Johnson was an enormously vigorous man, outspoken, blunt, with considerable ability to coin a phrase. He was a salty and effective speaker, with a good sense of publicity. Having great confidence in himself, he did not appear to be bothered by doubts of any sort. He could make decisions rapidly and make reasonably intelligent ones on the basis of the information he had, but it was on a level of unthinking action, and therefore was usually in terms of the unexpressed assumptions of the heads of the NRA staff, who were largely businessmen. He had little notion of policy formulation. His main drive was to get things done, and he did not consider too deeply what might be the policy behind what he was doing, or plan too carefully. His interest was in getting the NRA codes out, rather than in formulating very clearly the principles on which they should be based. He was willing to compromise a good deal to get action. He was more pliable than he appeared on the surface. To a certain extent his gruffness and abruptness would disappear if he were opposed and saw that it was necessary to sit down and negotiate. He was open to reason—more so at the beginning than toward the end of his regime. General Johnson was often called "Old Ironpants," and to a large extent that was an appellation of affection. At least at the beginning General Johnson was popular with his staff and with many people around Washington, including the newspapermen. He was a colorful figure.

General Johnson was largely oriented toward business. He was somewhat hostile to labor and not much concerned with the consumer. He was quite different from Harold Ickes, or Henry Wallace in Agriculture, who proceeded much more cautiously, from a point of view that was non-business but pro-liberal and pro-labor. They planned things very carefully and were shocked at the way General Johnson just sort of charged into the china shop, usually on behalf of business. I think he was aware of the magnitude, although not the complications, of the task. He worked excessively hard. Later on he became groggy from fatigue. He also began to drink heavily. Eventually it was necessary to ease him out of the post. He was replaced by a board, headed by Donald Richberg.

The other main figure in NRA at the beginning was Donald Richberg. He was a Chicago lawyer, with the reputation of being an excellent attorney and a liberal, one of the few seasoned lawyers who came to Washington in the New Deal. He had worked with Harold Ickes on various liberal projects, had been counsel for some of the Railroad Brotherhoods, and had been active in the preparation of the Railway Labor Act.

Richberg was supposed to give a liberal balance to Hugh Johnson's business approach. As it turned out, Richberg moved more and more into the business camp. That was displayed fairly early in NRA. I recall taking several issues to him for decision, on which he definitely took the business rather than the liberal point of view. He used to joke about it guiltily, but every time I would come into his office, he would say, "Oh, what's the trouble now?" as though to discourage me from raising issues of this sort at all.

Blackwell Smith, Richberg's chief assistant, was an extremely able lawyer, keen, acute, skilled at negotiation and compromise, resourceful in thinking up ideas. He was not a torch-bearer and not adept in initiating policy. But in terms of carrying out policy and adjusting differences he showed unusual ability. Smith actually ran the Legal Division. Richberg was engaged on high policy issues and we seldom saw him.

As I recall, all of the major division heads, who handled the formulation and operation of the NRA codes, came directly from the business world. The person I worked with particularly was Arthur Whiteside, who was head of Dun and Bradstreet, an extremely able, although somewhat

17

eccentric, individual. I also worked with a vice-president of International Business Machines who was incredibly stupid. Another one of the division heads was Malcolm Muir, of McGraw-Hill [publishers]. Another was Henry King, an executive from a large copper company. Some of these businessmen were first-rate; others, particularly later on, seemed to be business misfits that the business organizations must have wished on the government. There was some turnover because many were on leave and returned to their corporate jobs after a short time in Washington. A group of younger people, often assistants to the division heads, were also on their way up in the business world. These people were associated with business, but did not hold any significant position as yet. Some of them were very able, some less so. Practically the entire operating staff, outside of the Legal Division, was recruited from business.

NRA operated in accordance with the policies of General Johnson and his immediate assistants. The Legal Division played a fairly important part; it was substantially more liberal and less business oriented, but not enough to change the general drift. General Johnson supported his staff unless he got some outside pressure. The labor and consumer groups had a peripheral influence because they were not present at key meetings when the chips were down. There was not much friction between the advisory groups and the staff, simply because the advisory boards could not raise an issue in a way that made negotiation necessary. Cloaked by the spirit of emergency and good will, controversy was relatively mild and subterranean.

The attitude of many in the Legal Division was different from the attitude of General Johnson and his division heads, but everybody was so busy that we did not have much time to thrash out general policy issues. It was not clear where everything was going or what the implications were. The staff was still composed of novices who did not understand the necessity of maintaining a position from the very beginning or the strategy of balancing political forces. Those of us who were on the liberal side were youngsters who did not carry much weight. There was not as much open difference of opinion as one might have supposed–partly because nobody really knew what he was doing!

### LAWYERS IN NRA

Donald Richberg, head of the Legal Division, confined himself to important policy issues and allowed his chief assistant, Blackwell Smith, to run the division. At first there was little organization. Lawyers were assigned to various codes and worked with the relevant industry group on formulating the codes. But not long after I arrived the Legal Division was organized into four or five sections, according to the various types of industries being brought under the codes. As the organization continued to expand, a section on legal research and a separate section on enforcement were created. When I left in August 1934, I believe there were about 125 lawyers.

At least two-thirds, or probably three-quarters, of the lawyers were bright young men recently out of law school who were attracted by the crusading atmosphere of the New Deal. The older lawyers were either in the very top positions, like Richberg and Blackwell Smith, or they were likely to be misfits who had not thrived in private practice–and tended not to do well in government either. On the whole, however, the NRA attorneys were an extremely able group. Many stayed in government for a number of years, played important roles in the later New Deal, and became well-known in other connections. Ernest Gross later became an ambassador. Milton Katz also became an ambassador and then [1953] went to the Ford Foundation. Bernice Lotwin became assistant general counsel of the Social Security Board.

**My First Assignment at NRA**
My first assignment for NRA was to attend a hearing on a proposed code for the silk industry. This hearing was to occur at 10 AM on the same day that I reported for work, at 9 AM. I had no training of any sort, nor had I time to do much more than read over the statute, before I was sent to represent NRA as legal counsel at this hearing where lawyers who had been in practice for twenty or thirty years were representing important segments of the industry. I had no idea what would happen or what I was supposed to do. Actually, I did not do very much. I postponed any problems that arose until I had a chance to ask other people about them. My task was facilitated by the fact that the cotton textile code had been formulated prior to my arrival and could be used to some extent as a model. In any event, the hearing was completed in a day. Then my job was to negotiate the exact provisions, draft the final code, and obtain approval.

So, purely as an accident of arriving at NRA on the morning when the silk industry hearing was scheduled and no one else was available, I became the Legal Division's textile expert. I was also assigned the cotton textile code, as well as the other textile codes, hosiery, and so on. I started off as legal counsel for half a dozen of these textile codes.

Of the codes that I handled, the textile codes were, on the whole, comparatively simple. The textile industries were quite competitive, but tended to be dominated by relatively few of the larger and more efficient mills. This was particularly true of the silk and rayon mills. The major problem grew out of the differences between the northern and southern mills in the cotton textile industry. The industry was in the midst of a movement from the North to the South. The northern mills were greatly concerned because of the lower wage scale in the South and attributed the movement in a large part to that wage differential. I am not sure that the wage differential was the sole cause of the movement, but at least it was the cause of a good deal of friction. The major problem of the code was whether there should be a southern differential in the minimum wage scale. We finally provided for one, but the differential was fairly narrow. Labor had little influence in any of the textile industries. One possible exception was the hosiery workers, who were fairly well organized at that time and as a result had much more to say about their code.

19

The garment industries were highly competitive, afflicted with various seasonal problems, and engaged in cut-throat competition. Their situation was much more hectic than the textile industry and called for more complicated code provisions. The industry was split between those groups who operated out of the major garment centers in a half dozen of the major cities and those who were gradually locating in more rural or smaller city areas and were attempting to get rid of the union, or to avoid having a union organize their plants. Serious conflicts arose between these groups, although the city groups were by far the most numerous and were still the most important segment of the industry. Labor was also much more influential in the garment industries, particularly the Amalgamated Clothing Workers led by Sidney Hillman and the International Ladies Garment Workers under David Dubinsky. I had some contact with Hillman and Dubinsky. Hillman struck me as an extremely able and forceful man, although I was surprised by his apparent lack of facility in dealing with problems on paper. Occasionally issues would be presented to him in the form of a document, and I thought he was rather inadequate in analyzing the language and comprehending the implications. When he did perceive them, he was resourceful in his ideas and an extremely skillful negotiator, although he did not actually press too hard on many issues. Perhaps he was spending his force and influence in other fields rather than on codes.

When the first major organization of the Legal Division of NRA took place, I was put in charge of the section which included the textile codes, garment codes, distribution codes and banking codes, plus certain other miscellaneous codes. It was a strange assortment deriving from the historical accident of what needed to be done at the time I happened to be available. The other sections were heavy industry, light industry, mining and lumbering. Later the sections were formulated along somewhat different lines.

### The Power of Young Lawyers

You can see that I was given important responsibility from the very first moment. That was characteristic of the operations of NRA. Young and inexperienced lawyers were immediately placed into positions of responsibility, where they found themselves face to face with well-established lawyers who had been working for some years as representatives of important business interests. I received rapid salary increases, so that in less than a year I was earning $6000. That was a tremendous salary at that time for a person who had been out of law school less than three years, either in private practice or in the government. I was earning much more in this government job than were any of my classmates who were in private practice at the time. I do not know to what extent the financial rewards influenced lawyers to come to Washington, but I think probably very little. The greater attraction was that the government gave a young lawyer responsibility that was tenfold above what he would receive outside. So quite apart from the ideological attraction of the New Deal and purely in terms of one's own career there were great inducements for the young lawyer in Washington. A great many very able young lawyers came at that time.

The major task of the lawyers was to prepare drafts of the codes. We were given data upon which to base the draft, but the data often were so vague, confused, uncertain, and subject to differing interpretations that we had considerable latitude. This was less true of the wage and hour provisions, which tended to become standardized, and the collective bargaining provisions, which were entirely standardized. It was mainly the unfair trade practice provisions where lawyers could be creative. This meant that the lawyer working with an industry had to have detailed and concrete knowledge about that industry. The industry representatives generally knew what bothered them and they had background information on the industry, most of it unorganized, but they did not know how to accomplish what they wanted, especially without doing other things that they did not want to do or should not be allowed to do. So the lawyer had to explore in depth the organization of the industry, methods of operation, very often technical problems, relations with employees, the competitive situation, and relations with other industries–all in order to formulate the exact end that the industry wanted to accomplish with a particular provision that it was proposing.

The drafting work involved considerably more than using technical means to achieve the industry's aim; it required, first of all, a decision as to whether what was being sought by the industry was within the administrator's policy guidelines. In consultation with the NRA official assigned to that code, we lawyers considered the major policy issues involved. NRA lawyers inevitably tended to engage in negotiations with the industry representatives, negotiating between NRA and the industry or between different factions within the industry. Often everyone finally agreed on general and hazy proposals, but it was the lawyers who took the responsibility for formulating their exact provisions. The drafting task also extended to considering the public relations effect of the code provisions.

Few statistics or other data pertaining to any given industry were available. By questioning a group of men who had been in the business all their lives, we familiarized ourselves with the technological, economic, political, and labor relations structure of the industry. Some statistical material available through the Bureau of Census or the Bureau of Labor Statistics was useful in drafting the wage and hour provisions, but as no organized data pertained to problems of the unfair trade practices, our efforts were far more primitive than they would be later [in OPA].

Lawyers were important also because they dealt directly with the code authorities. Like the main administrative branch of NRA, the Legal Division usually had a representative who was responsible for keeping in touch with what the code authorities were doing. Particularly if code authorities handled interpretation or enforcement matters, the lawyers had a good deal to say about it. Plus, interpretation of the codes, once they were formulated, was a legal matter.  This gave lawyers tremendous power and put them in the position of serving as coordinators.  Finally, as many of the more difficult problems arose at a later stage and were handled as amendments, the constant need for amendment and revision caused the need for lawyers' drafting abilities to extend long beyond the initial formulation of the code,

In addition to drafting specific codes, the lawyers offered general counseling to other sections of NRA.  They participated in practically every meeting between NRA and industry officials and in advisory board sessions.  Other NRA officials frequently turned to them for advice and to negotiate compromises.  The distinction between legal advice and general advice was blurred.  Since the lawyers themselves determined what was a legal issue, they had the opportunity of framing many issues as legal that under a narrower interpretation might not have been so defined.  The lawyers tended to use obscure technical jargon as a weapon in negotiation and consultations.  Further, the lawyers frequently were called upon for advice on matters that obviously had no legal import, simply because they were intelligent people with a disciplined way of thinking and imagination as to how problems might be solved.  Lawyers played a useful role in assisting an NRA section chief who was involved in negotiations for formulating a code.  So lawyers exercised considerable *policy* influence.

The lawyers were also in a position to exercise a *coordinating* function.  The Legal Division held its own staff meetings, had considerable esprit de corps, and functioned as a unit unto itself.  Every operating section of an agency had a lawyer.  Since the Legal Division had sources of information with respect to everything that was happening in the agency and since it was relatively small as compared with the agency as a whole, and well organized, the Legal Division exercised a coordinating influence. A report would come in from a certain section that a particular question was arising.  It would then turn out that the same question was coming up in a different area and was being decided in a different way.  The Legal Division would spot issues like that and resolve them on a consistent basis or bring the question to a higher level.  This put the lawyers in a strategic position.  It was a matter of some significance because other types of coordination were lacking.

Lawyers also were responsible for most procedural questions, such as what constituted a hearing, how much notice had to be given in advance, what the procedure should be at the hearing, and whether the industry group was a truly representative group or should include other factions.  Numerous questions of that sort gave the lawyers considerable authority to determine what happened.

Finally, NRA used lawyers in a variety of other ways.  They drafted letters and wrote speeches.  When congressional criticism arose, an administrative section head usually asked a lawyer's advice about how to deal with the congressman, how to answer the letter, or how to give the information.  Minority groups in industry would raise a row sometimes, and the administrative head often would turn to the respective lawyer for advice on what to do, whether to pay attention or ignore it, whether to try to work something out and, if so, what.

Lawyers played an exceedingly active and important part in the work of NRA. Most of us were not businessmen's lawyers. To some extent we exerted an ameliorating influence on the business control. But most of us were youngsters, not powerful enough to tilt the organization in another direction–and I think we never attempted to do so. In other words, the lawyers' influence was exercised within the broad limitations of the agency's business orientation.

Perhaps the lawyers' influence is explained by the fact that the lawyers were one of the few groups who had any training whatever that was relevant to NRA's mandate. Certainly the businessmen's experience and training was far removed from questions of drafting, interpreting, and administering legal codes and regulations. No other university experience was relevant with the possible exception of the political science departments, and they did not supply many people, at least to NRA, with training relevant to the problems of government administration. The lawyers had training in the careful use of words, in making decisions through the application of a general principle (rather than on an ad hoc basis without consideration of other cases), in the concept of a government of laws and not of men, and in drafting documents. So although the lawyers' training did not precisely fit the job, they tended to feel comfortable with the tasks and to take over beyond the strictly legal aspects. The pattern of pervasive influence by lawyers continued throughout the New Deal period and still continues in government operation, at least in the regulatory agencies [1953].

Another important factor in the lawyers' influence was that a large number of outstanding lawyers were attracted to Washington. Some entered nonlegal jobs, such as Jerome Frank in the Securities and Exchange Commission (SEC), or Dean James Landis of the Harvard Law School, first in the Federal Trade Commission and then the SEC, or Lloyd Garrison, who was later chairman of the National Labor Relations Board. The legal influence on the New Deal was reflected also in the Tom Corcoran-Ben Cohen team at the White House, and had ramifications throughout all the agencies–the Triple-A where Jerome Frank was with his people, the Labor Department, and others. A cadre of young lawyers saw a good deal of each other informally and influenced many of the important agencies. They maintained significant influence throughout the whole development of the New Deal in Washington. Their influence extended, to some degree, even to Congress.

## TESTING THE CONSTITUTIONAL ISSUES
*The Schechter case and the change from NRA to the NLRB*

In view of past decisions handed down by the U.S. Supreme Court under the commerce clause, the Legal Division had foreseen the constitutional issues raised by NRA from the beginning. But the direction

NRA took was not influenced by fear of constitutional challenges. For the first year we assumed that, in the emergency of the Great Depression, with a public demand that something be done and the unanimous support of all groups, the Supreme Court would have to accept the situation. Hence, although we realized that many undecided constitutional problems existed, particularly those relating to the commerce power, the agency made no effort to conform its operations to any strategy for testing the constitutional issue. It would have been much easier to sustain the basic statute had there been a much narrower and more effective administration instead of this tremendous expansion throughout the economy.

After the issue of enforcement began to loom, the problem of a constitutional test came to the fore. One strategy, advocated by Felix Frankfurter, was to delay the constitutional test for as long as possible; the longer NRA remained in operation, the more it would become an integral part of the governmental machinery in control of the economic system and as a practical matter the Supreme Court would feel bound to support the act. An opposing strategy was that the sooner a test was made the better, based in part on the practical consequences of the failure of enforcement and in part on the theory that as the economic emergency tended to fade into the distance, the courts would feel freer to declare the act invalid on constitutional grounds. Those ideas were debated with the Justice Department from time to time and the Frankfurter view prevailed. Several cases arising in the winter of 1934–35 could have become test cases, such as the Smith case, involving the oil industry; but some technical problem stood in the way, so that the decision not to proceed with it may have been justified.

Fairly early in 1935 the Belcher case, arising out of the southern pine lumber industry, could have been used as a test case. The Department of Justice, favoring the Frankfurter point of view out of caution, opposed use of the Belcher case on the ground that the case did not raise an issue under the commerce clause, which pertained to goods moved from one state into a manufacturing plant in a second state, and then from there into a third state. NRA's Legal Department believed that the main constitutional basis for the statute was the *Stafford v. Wallace* decision, which had upheld regulation of the stockyards at the central point in a flow of commerce that began in the states where the cattle were bred and raised, moved into the stockyards, and then moved out through the packing plants to the consumers. The Belcher case did not involve the flow of commerce, which the *Stafford v. Wallace* decision had stressed; although most of the lumber moved out to the North, it had originated in the same state where the activities to be regulated took place. Persuaded to drop the case, the government disposed of the Belcher case on some ground that prevented it from getting into the Supreme Court.

**The Schechter Case**

Our hopes that the constitutional issues might be avoided altogether or wait until the following term of the Court—when our position might be buttressed by modifications to the renewed National Industrial Recovery Act that would eliminate some of the opposition and provide a second congressional mandate—were not realized. A few weeks after our decision to drop the Belcher case, we faced a constitutional test anyway because the Second Circuit in New York had decided the Schechter case. The government in Washington was either ignorant of the existence of the Schechter case or did not know that it was likely to be decided so rapidly. Consequently, Washington was taken by surprise when it turned out that a case would reach the Supreme Court that spring. Since the circuit court had decided most of the issues in favor of the government and a petition for *certiorari* had been filed by the company, we could not get out of it. If the decision had gone against the government in the lower court, we could have let the case ride and not applied for *certiorari*, or perhaps we could have pressed for a rehearing and so manipulated the case that it would have gone over into the next term.

The Schechter case was among the worst of all possible cases that could have been brought to raise the constitutional issues, mainly because it did not raise the commerce issue in a favorable form. The case did not involve a major industry or a "flow of commerce," because although the commerce in question, chickens, was coming into New York, it was sold and disposed of in that state. In addition, some of the provisions of the code upon which the indictment had been brought were among the most exotic and far-reaching of the NRA provisions. One in particular provided that a buyer purchasing chickens for slaughter, if he took less than the whole coop, could not pick out the better ones, but had to take a random selection of the chickens in the coop. This was a price-stabilizing arrangement because it meant that the coops could be sold for more, since if half a coop of the worst grade were left, it would have had to be sold for less. This detailed regulation did not appear to be entirely fair or to be accomplishing any major social purpose. Consequently, some issues raised by the regulation itself were no good for test purposes.

In any event, the government was stuck with the case. It came up to the Supreme Court for argument. Donald Richberg and Stanley Reed, then solicitor general, argued for the government. The argument for the company was handled by two lawyers, the regular lawyer for the Schechter Company and Frederick Wood of Cravath, de Gersdorff, Swaine and Wood. Just what interests paid the fees for Frederick Wood, I am not sure, except that clearly he was representing big business; his participation indicates that by that time one segment of big business was interested in having the National Industrial Recovery Act overturned.

The unknown lawyer for the Schechter Company, Joseph Heller, was remarkably vivid in his presentation. With great flare he described to the Court how, if you wanted to buy half a coop, you had to close your eyes, stick your hand in the coop, and pull out the first leg that you caught hold of. Familiar with the industry, he effectively conveyed that an exceedingly stupid and unfair regulation reached down to the most minute aspects of a business, in which all interstate commerce had long since ceased. His vivid description of the NRA's administration of the codes was more effective than the more abstract and eloquent pleas of Richberg and Wood.

The main argument was over the commerce issue. Our opponents also contended that there was an invalid delegation of legislative power in the broad grant of authority to the president under the statute, without sufficient standards or criteria for exercising it. No case had thus far been decided in which the Supreme Court had held an act of Congress unconstitutional on the ground of invalid delegation of power. Many vague and general statutes, such as the Federal Radio Act with its standard of "public interest, convenience, and necessity," and the "reasonable rates" of the Interstate Commerce Commission Act had been upheld. The government believed that that argument would not be taken seriously by the Supreme Court.

After the argument in the Schechter case, but before the decision was handed down, the Court decided the Panama Refining Case, in which it held invalid one section of NRA as an invalid delegation of power, a clear warning that the Schechter case also might turn on that issue. But practically no attention was paid to that aspect of the case at the time of the argument. Of the several hundred pages in the government brief, no more than two or three pages were devoted to it. My recollection is that it was passed over lightly in oral argument as well.

The Schechter decision came down on May 27, 1935, and held whole NRA code to be unconstitutional, on both the delegation and the commerce grounds. The decision was sufficiently sweeping that, in effect, it invalidated the entire National Industrial Recovery Act. From that time on, NRA regulations were off the books.

**Opposition Begins to Build**

While the Schechter case was pending in the courts the question of whether NRA should be renewed had arisen. The statute itself was to continue in effect only for two years, but we had no thought that the whole operation was merely temporary. Those who administered NRA, at least during the first year, as well as those from industry who were working with the issues, looked upon this as an indefinite arrangement. It was assumed that the act would be renewed. By the beginning of 1935 [just prior to the ruling in the Schechter case], however, opposition began to develop toward various aspects of NRA, particularly the way it was administered. Much of the original opposition came from the anti-trust forces in Congress and elsewhere who believed that the act tended to create strong business monopolies.

The first sign of opposition was the investigation by a Senate committee—I believe under Sen. Gerald Nye early in 1934—into the effect of NRA on small business. Clarence Darrow was counsel to this committee. The committee held hearings in Washington at which persons opposed to the development of the codes up to that date testified. One of the major issues that the committee delved into was the treatment of Macy's [the New York City department store mentioned earlier]. Macy's was hardly small business, but it was a minority so far as the department stores were concerned. It was contended that Macy's had been mauled by the opposition with the connivance of NRA. Since I was NRA counsel in the retail field, I went over to the hearing. I made some remarks attempting to correct factual misstatements made by some of the witnesses. I found myself in the position of defending the monopolists. It was my first experience with congressional committees. I was astonished by the difficulty of getting what I took to be the facts of the case before the committee and how witnesses distorted facts susceptible to varying interpretation. The committee received quite an erroneous impression of what had happened. In the end, however, nothing much came of this particular investigation.

However, opposition mounted as time went on. Some of it came from small business, supported by liberal midwestern senators who were strong anti-monopolists. For them NRA had grown too fast, too loosely, and too haphazardly, and its administration was seriously defective. Substantial opposition developed from big business, as well, particularly as the fear of economic collapse wore off and business conditions improved. The opposition essentially was to government interference in business, even though big business had taken over the administration of the agency and dominated governmental policy in the matter. Another factor was that enforcement was steadily deteriorating. The more disreputable sectors of business, called the "chiselers," initiated many violations, but the more respectable elements of business began to think their position was untenable because competitors were violating without adequate punishment. More and more respectable businesses joined the violators. The collective bargaining provisions generated strong opposition from big business. Realizing the implications of these provisions far more than they realized the implications of most other aspects, big business was determined to jettison government support for labor organizations. Although the collective bargaining provisions were not being enforced, they were having an important effect in terms of morale, as the official governmental support they symbolized was a key aspect of the organization of labor that was taking place in response to all the economic factors that had led to the New Deal.

Senate and House committees held renewal hearings, and they were still in progress or had just finished when the Supreme Court handed down the Schechter decision. Congress probably would have continued the act, perhaps with further changes to prevent any monopolistic tendencies, but following the Schechter decision no further effort was made to reenact the NRA statute.

## AFTER NRA, THE NLRB
*With the demise of NRA following the Schechter case, the act's collective bargaining provisions are recreated within the purview of the NLRB*

I was not with NRA at the time of the Schechter decision. I had left NRA several months earlier, on August 1, 1934, to work at the first

27

[original] National Labor Relations Board (NLRB). After I left NRA I maintained rather close connections, both officially and unofficially. My duties at the NLRB related to enforcement problems and other legal problems with which NRA was also concerned. Both agencies were concerned with the constitutional issue. I had many friends, including some people whom I saw practically every day, who remained in NRA, from whom I learned what was happening. Since I was actually on leave from NRA, on loan to the NLRB with the intention of returning to NRA, I had reason to keep in touch with what transpired. But I obviously did not have the kind of firsthand knowledge I gained while I worked there.

However, after the Schechter decision my official connection with NRA ended and I lost touch. I know little about the details of the liquidation of NRA. I think it was liquidated rather rapidly. Practically all the attorneys I knew who were interested in staying in Washington landed other government jobs. Many joined me at the [new] NLRB, which was reestablished under a new statute shortly after the end of NRA. Others went to the new Bituminous Coal Administration and the Social Security Board, which was just starting at that time. Most of the businessmen returned home to their businesses, but many of the clerical staff and miscellaneous functionaries remained in Washington and were absorbed elsewhere in government.

The Schechter decision did not end all efforts at enactment of legislation of the NRA variety. The coal industry, which was in particular trouble, had been toying for some time with a statute of its own. In spite of the Schechter decision, it went ahead with the Bituminous Coal Act. President Roosevelt supported this, saying, "Although there are doubts about the constitutionality, that should be left to the courts to decide." Both the industry and the union were pressing heavily for this special legislation to handle the coal problem. In this case, all important segments of the industry agreed. There was a strong drive from the coal state senators and little opposition. The coal act passed later in 1935.

Labor made efforts to draw up a special act for the textile industry. I participated with some of the American Federation of Labor (AFL) groups in drawing up a special statute that Rep. Henry Ellenbogen of Pennsylvania introduced. Here, however, there was considerable opposition within the industry and the bill made no headway.

Jet Lauck and the AFL group that was later to become the CIO continued to press for a general statute that would impose federal regulation of business. Their scheme was to develop a system for federal incorporation of business firms, attaching conditions to the charters of incorporation that would require minimum wages and maximum hours, guarantee the right of self-organization and collective bargaining, and impose other restrictions on the operation of the corporation. I participated with this group in drafting a bill, which was introduced by Senator O'Mahoney. But the old-line AFL group was lukewarm and the bill received little attention. This was my first close contact with the AFL leadership. I was astonished by the incompetence, narrowness, and stupidity of the AFL traditionalists. The CIO group was incomparably more alert, intelligent, and aggressive.

The most significant effort was to reenact as separate legislation the collective bargaining provisions of NRA. An attempt to establish a separate collective bargaining act in 1934 had been defeated in Congress, largely through big business opposition, but a compromise was adopted, in what was called Public Resolution No. 44, that reestablished the NLRB with authority to handle the administration of Section 7(a) of the National Industrial Recovery Act, thus removing the collective bargaining provisions from NRA. This was a substantial victory for labor because administration of the collective bargaining provisions was withdrawn from an organization largely dominated by business. There had been no enforcement of Section 7(a), with the exception of one or two cases, prior to the passage of Public Resolution No. 44. To place the interpretation of that section, as well as the pressure to obtain compliance with it, in a separate agency where labor had considerably more influence was a major victory. However, Resolution No. 44 was due to expire in the summer of 1935.

The Schechter case threw considerable doubt on the possibility that Congress would enact a comprehensive National Labor Relations Act embodying the collective bargaining provisions, but despite the opposition it passed without much difficulty in 1935, shortly after the Schechter decision was handed down by the Supreme Court. Ironically, the Schechter decision may have facilitated passage of the act, because the opposition was so confident the legislation was unconstitutional that little effort was made to defeat it in Congress.

Little agreement existed in the administration as to what should be done about NRA, prior to the Schechter decision. The administration was pressing for its renewal. Many people feared, even at the time of the Schechter decision, that the country would fall apart without NRA. On the other hand, the administration had a bear by the tail. The administrative problems had gotten out of hand. The monopoly aspect of NRA operations was increasing to a point where it was interfering with the basic recovery program. Until John M. Keynes' book, *The General Theory of Employment, Interest, and Money*, was published in 1936, supplying an ideological basis for New Deal economic development, no overall theory about the type of economic controls necessary for economic recovery existed.

**NRA: AN ASSESSMENT**

In 1935 I belonged to an informal group that met to discuss basic economic problems. Many such groups were meeting around Washington at the time. This one included Leon Henderson, Blackwell Smith, Milton Katz, two or three others, and myself. We talked in some detail about measures that would be necessary to achieve full recovery, what the impact of NRA was, whether wage scales should go up or down in order to promote recovery, and so on. We were amateurs, uncertain, and had no consistent program in mind. Our confusion reflected the state of the Roosevelt administration at that time.

NRA operated under several basic conditions. One was the need for speed. Everyone believed that the safety of the country depended on our getting every industry operating under a code within the next few weeks. We worked in tremendous haste amidst constant activity.

A second factor was the almost complete lack of experience in dealing with the problems NRA faced. No area in the government had the kind of experience that would have been valuable here. The nearest would have been the Federal Trade Commission (FTC), or possibly the Interstate Commerce Commission. But by the time I arrived in Washington, the FTC was suffering from an advanced stage of bureaucratic rot. I recall going over to see the chief counsel of the FTC on some problem and being astounded to find that he was out having afternoon coffee at 3:00! To us that was a most surprising performance. It is much more common in government and other organizations today [1953], but at that time it was a sign of decay. The FTC did not have the talent or the spirit that was necessary in NRA. Its experience was of no help in the situation, nor was that of the Interstate Commerce Commission. So NRA had to operate practically a virgin field without recourse to the prior experience of other agencies.

Third, NRA lacked any clear policy. Most things happened on the spur of the moment and not in response to any overall plan. There was little coordination. The domination of the agency by big business personnel was about the only thing that introduced and coordinated policy. Nothing was crystallized; the situation could have turned in many directions.

At the beginning we had no idea how complex the economic system was. We concentrated primarily on wages and hours. The unfair trade practices provisions were considered secondary through the early stages of formulation. The statutory provisions were sufficiently vague so that almost anything might have happened. Action could have been entirely confined to wages and hours and collective bargaining. But, as it turned out, the National Industrial Recovery Act was carried to an extreme. Its administration took the course of spreading out all over the place, attempting to deal with innumerable problems without sufficient factual grounds for doing so. NRA responded readily to the desires of industry groups. There was some concern for the minority in industry, but not too much.

NRA started off as a scheme for achieving industrial recovery by pegging minimum wages and maximum hours. Support from business groups was won by including provisions to eliminate cut-throat competition. A labor group managed to have the collective bargaining provisions included. The legislation was a mixture of dissimilar ingredients. The system had few safeguards against abuse by private individuals seeking private advantage. I had left NRA by the time this system became fully established and did not have much contact with it. But this was certainly one of the most serious flaws in the whole NRA operation and the target of much criticism. I think it caused serious decline in respect for the administration of NRA and thus a decline in the effectiveness of NRA as a whole.

As the administration of the statute was taken over by the major business interests, its sense of purpose faltered, and many from the business world began to oppose it. However, business was primarily repudiating all government interference, rather than attempting to take over government operation itself. In fact, the number of people who grasped the possibility of representatives of the business world moving into governmental positions and exercising control through governmental administration was small. They included Averell Harriman [later governor of New York], incidentally. He was on the NRA Industry Advisory Board and I used to see a fair amount of him. He was an exceedingly keen person who saw many of the broader implications that most of the others missed. At the time he was toying with the idea that business should grasp this opportunity of operating as part of the government.

Considerable opposition to NRA existed within the Roosevelt administration itself. The Department of Agriculture under Henry Wallace spearheaded the opposition; Rex Tugwell, Jerome Frank, and others over there backed Wallace. They contended that NRA was not accomplishing the purpose of the wage and hour provisions to any great degree, but in any event was tremendously encouraging monopoly. They also believed that government had withdrawn in favor of business control. Secretary Ickes and his staff also opposed the monopoly element of NRA; they preferred to achieve recovery through the public works program and similar methods, rather than through this pseudo-economic control over business.

Nevertheless, the prevailing opinion within NRA and within a large part of the Roosevelt administration was that the mission of the NRA was still essential. Perhaps those too close to the problem were blind or bogged down in inertia. In retrospect, it seems clear that the Supreme Court served the country well by disposing of NRA. It had become unmanageable and was plainly heading nowhere, except perhaps to a corporate state. It did not fit into the rest of the New Deal program. After the Schechter case, as the Keynesian theories gained popularity, this was the evaluation of NRA that emerged in New Deal circles.

# 2

# THE EARLY DAYS
# OF THE NEW DEAL

*NRA was unconstitutional. The New Deal comes back with the NLRB.*

Around the first of August 1934, after I had been at NRA for about a year, I transferred to the [original] National Labor Relations Board. This was the board created under Public Resolution No. 44. It functioned during the period of about a year before the National Labor Relations Act was passed [to replace NRA, as this chapter details], establishing the permanent National Labor Relations Board (NLRB). When the new board was created it kept the same name as the old one.

One of my colleagues in the Legal Division of NRA asked me to come along on a luncheon date with Lloyd Garrison, who was then chairman of the NLRB, saying that Garrison was looking for lawyers to join his staff. I went to lunch, was impressed with Lloyd Garrison, and received an offer of a job on the spot. After thinking about it for some time, I decided to accept. I transferred in part because of my interest in labor problems and the more liberal aspects of the New Deal, and in part because I was excited at the prospect of participating in the creation of a new agency. This transfer was typical of the mobility of lawyers, particularly young lawyers, in Washington in those days. Newly formed agencies would pick up some of their personnel from the "older agencies," i.e., agencies that had been operating for a year or two. Most of the younger New Deal attorneys probably served in four or five agencies during ten or twelve years in Washington.

## SEVERING LABOR RELATIONS FROM THE NRA

Under the National Industrial Recovery Act there had been a board called the National Labor Board, also known as the Wagner Board because Sen. Robert Wagner was its chairman. This board was set up to handle labor disputes that arose in connection with NRA and the protection of collective bargaining under Section 7(a). It also attempted to settle disputes over wages and hours and disputes relating to working conditions generally. Composed of representatives from labor, industry, and the public, this board functioned somewhat separately from NRA in that Senator Wagner maintained an autonomous position and from the beginning would not recognize the jurisdiction of General ("Iron Pants") Johnson. This board had its own staff. William M. Leiserson, I believe, was the executive director and the main staff member. Milton Handler was the general counsel. Other staff members included Benedict Wolf, later the first Secretary of the NLRB, and Paul Herzog, who later became chairman of the NLRB.

### Drafting a Labor Relations Statute

In part as a development of this board and in part because of the labor interest that had resulted in Section 7(a) of the original act, a movement to draft a separate Labor Relations Act began. The idea was to separate labor relations from the primarily business-oriented NRA. In part the plan arose out of Senator Wagner's inclination toward separation and his unwillingness to operate under General Johnson or anyone else. Senator Wagner did not want to take responsibility for all that NRA was doing by associating his group with NRA. Also, people wanted an agency that would maintain a special responsibility for labor problems and not be merged into the general administration of the NRA. If Section 7(a) was to be administered efficiently, an administrative procedure modeled on the Federal Trade Commission procedure was essential for enforcement purposes. The sanctions available for enforcement of Section 7(a)–namely, the injunction proceeding in a court or a criminal proceeding, also in a court–were too cumbersome and ineffective and, particularly as they depended on the cooperation of the Department of Justice, were unlikely to result in aggressive enforcement of Section 7(a).

The Department of Justice was then at its lowest ebb of any time during the New Deal period, in terms of the capacity of its personnel. Under Homer Cummings it was a patronage agency. The lawyers, at least the ones we dealt with, were very limited in their abilities, highly political in their backgrounds, and hardly interested or capable of carrying on an effective enforcement program, particularly of Section 7(a). The solicitor general, James C. Biggs, a lawyer from North Carolina, was an outstanding example of incompetency. At that time I lived with the law clerk to Justice Cardozo and heard constant reports that the members of the Supreme Court were extremely dissatisfied with the government arguments in the cases, and particularly with the arguments of Mr. Biggs himself.

The drafting of a separate statute was undertaken by a group headed by Leon Keyserling, who was then Senator Wagner's secretary. Leiserson was in from the beginning, although he was not a lawyer (and, in fact, was very anti-lawyer in his point of view). He later withdrew when the group refused to adopt some of his pet theories. Charles Wyzanski, solicitor of the Department of Labor, was an active member of the group. I believe that his assistant, Tom Eliot, also participated. I think that Milton Handler was in it, although he was not one of the most active members. Busy with my NRA work, I was on the fringes of this group, but I attended one or two of the meetings and knew what was going on because Leon Keyserling was one of my housemates. As I recall, the AFL did not participate directly in the drafting conferences, although they were interested and followed it, primarily, I believe, through Joseph Padway, who was their general counsel. The dominant spirit in this group was Keyserling. He was in a key position as secretary to Senator Wagner, who would introduce the bill and lobby for its passage. The major part of the actual drafting was done by Keyserling and the ultimate product was primarily his, although the others contributed substantially to it.

Senator Wagner introduced the bill in the Senate. It was also introduced in the House and was pressed for passage through the first half of 1934. The attitude of the administration toward the bill surprised me at the time. The president seemed to take no great interest in it one way or the other. He seemed to have a hands-off or neutral attitude. He told Wagner privately that he favored the bill and he was willing to let Wagner get the bill through if he could, but he was not willing to make it an administration measure, or to put it on his list of "must" bills. We were quite upset with Roosevelt about this. I, of course, had no direct contact with the president. My information came largely through Keyserling, Wyzanski, or other people in secondary positions. But certainly the president never sent a message to Congress, or even, as far as I can remember, endorsed the bill in a press conference. While he was unwilling to oppose his good friend Bob Wagner, he did not seem to be committed to it or to understand the implications.

Miss Frances Perkins, as Secretary of Labor, took a similar position, almost one of neutrality. She was interested in the question of whether or not the new National Labor Relations Board created under the bill would be part of the Department of Labor, but beyond that she made no real effort to back the bill. Senator Wagner was a kind gentleman who did not like to offend anybody and he was never openly on the outs with Miss Perkins, but he did not really like her nor was he convinced that she understood the labor problem. Originally the bill did put the board in the Department of Labor. But when other elements in Congress wanted it made separate, Senator Wagner quickly yielded to the pressure and agreed to take it out of the Labor Department. Miss Perkins was quite unpopular in Congress at the time. Ickes was friendly to the bill, but not active in support. As near as I could tell, only the group around Wagner and no one else in the administration saw the political advantages of the bill: that there might be a potential mass labor vote for the administration that passed it.

So Senator Wagner, a group around him, and some factions of the AFL lobbied for the bill. One group in the AFL understood the importance of obtaining special legislation of this nature. This was the same group who had spearheaded the insertion of Section 7(a) in NRA from the beginning and included Jett Lauck, John L. Lewis, Sidney Hillman, and some more.

This group, which largely coincided with the group that later formed the CIO, was pressing for organization of the mass production industries, with intellectual leadership on this issue coming, to a large extent, from Lauck. Padway was working with them. On the other hand, William Green's support seemed rather nominal, although that might have been true of everything he did. He was a man of very limited ability, certainly without the capacity to visualize many of the implications.

There was no mass campaign at this time on the part of the labor movement for the bill. To a surprising extent the whole thing was carried on behind the scenes, by inside maneuvering. I was astonished at the time that the bill came as close as it did to passage, because it seemed almost as if Senator Wagner and Leon Keyserling were getting this bill, with such far-reaching implications, through by themselves. The labor movement was friendly but not really hitting for it. It was astonishing and indicated the complete fluidity in the situation at the time. The issues were not clear, economic forces had not crystallized, the battalions had not lined up yet, and nobody knew exactly what was happening. Here was one Senator, or one small group, pressing for legislation and no substantial opposition, and if the Senator was one in the position of influence that Wagner was, it had a fair chance to go through.

As I recall, brief hearings were held. Industry was very much opposed to the bill, but the opposition hardly crystallized and barely made itself felt on Congress in any coherent way. Although in retrospect the legislation was one of the most significant of the New Deal, people treated it rather casually at the time. As a result of the press of other legislation to which the administration leaders in the Senate and the House gave priority, and perhaps legitimately so, the Wagner Bill did not come up for a vote until the very last part of the session, shortly prior to adjournment. Enough opposition developed, particularly from the steel industry, so that it looked unlikely that Senator Wagner would be able to get the bill through before adjournment. As a result a compromise was made in which it was agreed to lay the bill over until the next year and to pass in the meantime a resolution that became known as Public Resolution No. 44, which was to be a stopgap measure. Public Resolution No. 44 created the first National Labor Relations Board, but did not confer powers in addition to what was already in Section 7(a). It was merely created administrative machinery, in the form of a labor board, for the administration of Section 7(a).

## THE FIRST NATIONAL LABOR RELATIONS BOARD
*Starting with a clean slate to write the rules of the American workplace*

The original National Labor Relations Board (NLRB) appointed by President Roosevelt consisted of Lloyd Garrison as the first chairman, with Harry A. Millis and Edwin Smith as members. In September 1934 Garrison left to return to labor law teaching and Francis Biddle replaced him. I do not know how Biddle happened to be appointed; so far as I know, he had no background in the labor field. Sometime after I came to the board, Calvert Magruder was appointed general counsel. He then functioned as general counsel until this original board was replaced by the new NLRB.

The original NLRB lacked the power to carry into effect the rights theoretically protected by Section 7(a). On the other hand, it started with almost a clean slate on which to write a theory of labor relations and a basis for federal control over the right of collective bargaining. In the interim period in which it functioned it had the opportunity to test and build the foundations for a permanent labor relations policy and machinery to deal with this problem. While the old Wagner Board had had some of the same problems, it had been a loose tripartite group that tended to exercise its functions within the framework of mediation. The new NLRB, on the other hand, consisted of three board members, all representing the public, which established a much tighter, more effective, more systematic policy and organization.

## NLRB Functions

The major part of the board's work was to decide on whether there had been a violation of Section 7(a). The board had nothing to do with wage and hour problems or mediation of similar disputes. It was devoted entirely to protecting the rights of labor to organize under Section 7(a), and to regulating the relationship between employers and employees in the area of organization and collective bargaining. The board decided a number of these cases, and eventually published two volumes of its decisions. Section 7(a) was stated in very broad terms and numerous questions of interpretation arose. The board was building a series of decisions that elaborated and specified the general policy stated in Section 7(a). In addition, the board was deciding factual issues, i.e., whether or not certain conduct had taken place in violation of Section 7(a). But in view of its lack of enforcement powers, the mere decisions as to whether an employer was violating Section 7(a) were of less significance than the formulation of the detailed principles that the board found to underwrite the broad guarantees embodied in Section 7(a).

The board made little progress in the area of enforcement. Before the board was created there had been very little enforcement of Section 7(a). One criminal prosecution was brought by the Department of Justice against the Weirton Steel Company in West Virginia. I believe the case went to trial and the defendant was acquitted, or the case was dismissed by the judge. I cannot recall exactly, but the government suffered an inglorious defeat. But cases which the Wagner Board had referred to the Department of Justice had not been acted upon, with the exception of the Weirton case. The Department of Justice was an obstacle partly because it had no interest in enforcing Section 7(a) and partly because, even if it had able and interested lawyers, it would not have had the kind of experience in labor problems that was necessary to carry on successful litigation. Moreover, at the beginning of the New Deal the judiciary was largely Republican-appointed and most of them were unfriendly to the New Deal. Certainly I remember the judge in the Weirton Steel case was very unfriendly.

So the possibility of bringing enforcement cases to court seemed remote. The board would hold a hearing, make its decision, and attempt to obtain voluntary compliance. It had some luck in getting voluntary compliance, but that became more difficult as time went on. In the early days, if the employer remained recalcitrant, the board would refer the case to the NRA for withdrawal of the Blue Eagle. After that became ineffective the board would refer the case to the Department of Justice for prosecution. A substantial number of cases were referred to the Department of Justice, but nothing more happened. It was amazing how the Department of Justice could always find some technicality or some possible doubt about cases sent over there. Thousands of violations were taking place. The board had many cases before it and issued decisions in several hundred, but every time a case was sent over to the Department of Justice, the lawyers there were able to find some issue that persuaded them that it would be a bad case to test.

**The Houde Case**

The NLRB succeeded in pressing the Department of Justice into commencing only one case, the Houde case. My first assignment after my move to the original NLRB was to draft the board's decision in the Houde case. The issue was whether or not a union that represented a majority of the employees in a collective bargaining unit should be the spokesman for all the employees in that unit. This issue of majority rule was important because if it were to be held that the union could represent only those employees who were members, or who voted for it, then it would be possible to have an employer bargaining with two, or perhaps even more, unions, and playing one off against the other. From labor's point of view it was imperative that they be permitted to bargain with respect to all members of the unit. On the other hand, it was argued that it was unfair to require an employee to accept representation from a union he did not want. The question had not been officially decided by the board before and this was the first case in which the problem arose. After considerable discussion the board decided in favor of majority rule–that is, that the majority representative would represent all the employees in collective bargaining negotiations. Our chairman, Lloyd Garrison, worked closely with me in drafting the decision. The final draft was substantially his own work, but I spent a good deal of my time for the first couple of weeks at the board on that problem.

The company failed to comply and the board, I guess after removing the company's Blue Eagle, referred the matter to the Department of Justice. The Blue Eagle was not of any concern to the company since it was a machine tool company that supplied other manufacturers and did not have to please the general public. The board pressed the Department of Justice strongly to bring an injunction proceeding that would test the validity of majority rule and also the whole constitutionality of the Section 7(a) provisions. After a long while the Department of Justice gave their consent. The board then undertook to draft the complaint that was to be filed in the case. The board's associate general counsel, Robert Watts, who was a New York lawyer with some litigation experience, was in charge of the litigation for the board and I worked with him. Under his direction I drafted a complaint that we took over to the Department of Justice and finally got cleared. The Department of Justice notified the United States attorney at Buffalo, where the company was located, that the case should be filed. The complaint was sent up to Buffalo and filed by the United States attorney in a court.

The company then instituted a series of delaying motions: a motion to dismiss, a motion for a bill of particulars, and one or two other motions. The judge set those motions down for argument. Watts, an attorney from the Department of Justice, and I went to Buffalo to participate in the argument of those motions. We went to see the United States attorney, a fairly able man who had been in the office for some years. He was totally ignorant of the particular issue involved in this case, had no experience in labor relations, and no concept of the issues that would be involved in the majority rule issue, or of the basic constitutional issues. He was, however, quite willing to cooperate with us, perhaps because he figured prominently in numerous newspaper photos and long newspaper accounts of the case. The matter was argued before the judge. As I recall, the Department of Justice attorney and Watts shared the argument. It took one morning in court. The company was represented by lawyers from Buffalo, but the main part of their case was handled by lawyers from Detroit who had been brought in to assist them. The main lawyer was a well-known Detroit lawyer who represented financial and business interests in Detroit. After the argument the judge reserved decision and we returned to Washington. We heard nothing more about the case for some weeks. Finally, the judge granted the company's motion for a bill of particulars and we then prepared a bill of particulars to be filed in the case. We had just about filed that when the Schechter decision came down and the whole case therefore could no longer be pressed.

Although the Houde case was the first case that I had worked on when I came to the original NLRB in August 1934, and the board had decided it in August or early September, by May 1935 when the Schechter decision came down there had been no progress in the case, the only case that the board had succeeded in getting into court during all that period. So the lack of adequate enforcement mechanisms was abundantly clear by that time.

### I Successfully Defend the Blue Eagle

The board did have some defensive litigation arising from efforts to prevent the board from functioning. In the two major cases, the Firestone Rubber Company and the Goodrich Rubber Company were suing to enjoin the board and NRA from taking away their Blue Eagles. The issue seems ridiculous now. I worked on both those cases, which were important because they raised the issue of the constitutionality of Section 7(a). In preparing the briefs and arguments in those cases it became necessary for the first time for the board to concentrate on the development of the basic legal argument for constitutionality under the commerce clause.

The cases, when I was assigned to them, were in the Circuit Court of Appeals for the 6th Circuit and my assignment was to prepare the draft of the brief. I worked under supervision of Watts again, and in cooperation with the Department of Justice attorney, Wendell Berge. He and one of his assistants took a good deal of interest in the cases and pressed them in a competent and effective manner.

In working out the brief, I was forced to develop for the first time the details of the legal theory. Certain aspects of this had already been covered by Donald Richberg in a case that had been decided prior to the New Deal where he had represented the Railroad Brotherhoods. This was the Texas and New Orleans case, in which the Railroad Brotherhoods had obtained an injunction under the Railway Labor Act enjoining a railroad from interfering with the organization of its employees and from refusing to bargain collectively with them. The substantive provisions were pretty much the same, except they had applied to the railroads under the Railway Labor Act. The constitutional issue in those cases was easier because an instrumentality of interstate commerce was involved. By reading the Richberg brief, I got the nucleus of the argument that had to be developed as to areas involving manufacturing rather than railroads. I undertook to prepare what amounted to a Brandeis brief in support of the constitutional points. I went over to the Department of Labor library and collected material showing the actual impact of strikes upon interstate commerce. I used strike statistics, reports on strikes (such as a report which had been prepared on the steel strike of 1919), and other material dealing with the strikes that occurred in the open shop period of the early 1920s, to show in concrete detail how by stopping production the strike had stopped the movement of goods across state lines. The point was fairly obvious, but the material had not been assembled before. I also collected material to show the extent to which strikes, and hence the stoppage of interstate commerce, had been caused by disputes over the right to organize and bargain. I demonstrated that the policy of the act, in undertaking to eliminate causes of labor disputes by prohibiting the employer from refusing to deal with the union, had a direct bearing on the number of strikes, and hence on the movement of commerce across state lines. Here again I went through the official and semi-official reports of earlier strikes as well as statistical material to demonstrate that a substantial proportion—in those days well over half—of the worker-days lost through strikes arose out of disputes over the basic issues of collective bargaining, rather than over wage and hour provisions or matters pertaining to conditions of work. I prepared a brief in the form of an economic brief according to the Brandeis style. This was the first time that the full theory and supporting data for the constitutionality of collective bargaining legislation had been elaborated and submitted to a court.

The case came up for argument. Berge and his assistant, Watts, and I went before the Sixth Circuit. Again, the newspapers were watching and commenting on the case in considerable detail. Berge and Watts argued the case. I no longer recall much about the reaction of the court, except that they reserved judgment and the issue was not decided before the Schechter case brought an end to the controversy.

### Another Victory for the Original NLRB

At the beginning a constant struggle occurred with NRA over the autonomy of the board and other issues. The dispute came to a head in a case involving alleged violation of Section 7(a) by a newspaper. The American Newspaper Association was active in fighting the case on behalf of the newspaper. Elisha Hanson, their counsel in Washington, was very much in the middle of the matter. It was argued that the question was under the jurisdiction of NRA and that the NLRB had no authority. Francis Biddle put up a considerable fight and finally won, establishing jurisdiction of the board over this area and at the same time the independence of the board from the general business atmosphere of NRA. As the matter received considerable publicity it was also useful in keeping alive in the public mind the importance of having a board that would protect the right of labor to organize and bargain collectively. In fact, as time went on public relations became perhaps the main function of the board. The board's effort to secure adherence to Section 7(a) was constantly losing ground as a result of the failure of the Blue Eagle and the failure of any enforcement. But the board was demonstrating through its decisions, its reasoning, and the workmanlike character of its performance that the whole plan could operate.

Finally, this original Board played an important part in the formulation of the legislation that later became the National Labor Relations Act, both in the redrafting stage and when it came before Congress in the spring of 1935, establishing the "new" NLRB.

### THE TEXTILE STRIKE OF 1934

My second major assignment at the original NLRB was as counsel and staff member for the mediating board appointed by President Roosevelt to attempt settlement of the textile strike of 1934. The textile workers had been trying to organize the textile industry, particularly the cotton textile industry, ever since the beginning of NRA. Few employees from the textile industry were unionized in 1933. Practically the entire South and large parts of the North were unorganized. Stimulated by the election of 1932, the New Deal, Section 7(a), and other factors, the textile unions, as did many unions at that time, made extensive efforts to organize the mills, including a major campaign in the South. They were partially successful in this period, at least in that their membership increased rapidly. In parts of the South the movement to join the unions had the aspect of a religious revival. The employers apparently were caught off guard and at first did not oppose it as strongly as they had in the past.

In the beginning it looked as if the textile union might achieve success. However, the new members did not really understand what they were getting into. Partly because the organizing drive was more in the nature of a revival than a steady, workmanlike, down-to-earth job of union organizing, and partly because of the evangelical character of the movement, the union found itself in the position where it became necessary to show some positive achievements or it would be likely to lose substantial membership. By the summer of 1934 the union was attempting to obtain concessions from employers and the employers were resisting. The basic issue was union recognition. The union wanted to deal with the cotton textile trade association–the Cotton Textile Institute–on an industry-wide basis, but in addition it wanted recognition by individual employers. There was no firm recognition of the union in any of the new parts of the industry and the union had been unable to obtain any new contracts. Another issue was increased wages, which the industry opposed on the ground that the NRA code established wages and the industry had no further obligation. A third issue was the so-called "stretch-out," a term the union applied to the effort by the industry to increase the workload of the individual employee. There had been substantial improvements in machinery in recent years and with the installation of this new machinery had come a steady increase in the workload. In addition, some plants, trying to keep up with plants that had the new machinery, were increasing the workload without the additional machinery.

As a result of these grievances the union threatened to strike unless concessions were made. The employers refused to make any concessions and about the first of September 1934, the union went out on strike. The strike seemed fairly successful at the beginning; the union claimed 500,000 workers were out. Altogether it was one of the most dramatic strikes in recent years. The president of the union was an older person overwhelmed by the situation who did not participate much. The actual conduct of the strike was delegated to the vice president, Francis Gorman, who had a flair for the dramatic. He announced when the strike was to begin through a special radio broadcast, heard in meetings of all the locals throughout the South; this was the first use of the radio for directing operations of a large strike. The union gave prizes to the first locals to have all members out on strike and made much use of publicity. Gorman was quite good at publicity and at making a fighting speech over the radio or at a union meeting, but he had little of the solid organizational ability that Hillman or Dubinsky or others had. For a few brief months his star rose on the labor horizon and he was well known; after the strike he passed into relative obscurity again. Industry leadership was in the hands of George Sloane, who at that time was president of the Cotton Textile Institute. Sloane was an intelligent, very handsome, well-mannered man with an intransigent core. He held firmly his own point of view and was unwilling to make any concessions. I had known him in NRA in connection with work on the cotton textile code.

When the strike occurred, President Roosevelt appointed a board to mediate, with John Winant as chairman. I think Winant came to the president's attention through the NLRB chairman, Lloyd Garrison. Winant, a friend of Garrison, asked Garrison to assign someone to assist the board. Garrison assigned me. I spent all of my time for the three weeks that the strike was in progress with the board, mostly with Winant himself.

Winant was a very unusual person–tall, thin, and gaunt-looking. He had been a Republican governor of New Hampshire, campaigning by systematically visiting every one of his constituents in the state, passing from farm to farm and talking to people individually. He, or his wife, was wealthy but he apparently never carried any money with him. When he and I used to go home after working until late at night, we would often stop for a hamburger and cup of coffee, and he never had any money to pay. I always had to pay the bill on those occasions.

Winant was in many ways an excellent man for this task, although he was not an expert in labor. He was very intelligent, extremely conscientious, and very decent in his relations with everybody. A man of the utmost integrity, he made an almost agonizing effort to discover the right thing to do and to do it regardless of the consequences. Very sensitive, he was terribly tense at all times, and very inarticulate in private conversation, although more articulate in writing. Working closely with Winant for three or four weeks, I became extremely impressed by him on the whole. Quite the opposite from a sophisticated, polished government administrator, he was a most refreshing person because of his basic integrity. He dominated the board. The other two members, whose names I cannot even recall now, did not figure significantly.

The president had asked Winant to begin by consulting Frances Perkins, secretary of labor. As a preliminary briefing by the highest governmental official responsible for labor problems, the purpose was to give to the board its basic lines of authority and the broad administration policy under which the board was expected to carry out its functions. Thereafter, Miss Perkins did not figure in the strike or in the actions of the board at all. That was the first time I had met Miss Perkins. I was surprised by her attitude on the issue. Here was the first major strike in the New Deal administration, clearly involving the question of the extent labor would be successful in organizing new areas. It was testing the effectiveness of Section 7(a) in guaranteeing the right to organize without employer interference. Miss Perkins seemed to have no notion of the more fundamental questions at stake. Her entire attention was focused on "How can we get these men back to work and earning wages again?" In contrast, Winant saw the broader implications.

The mediating board held hearings at which the union and employers each presented its case separately. The Textile Institute group refused to meet or deal with the union leaders directly, on the ground that they did not represent the employees. Each side presented material on the wage scale, the "stretch-out," and the issue of union recognition. The mediating board then attempted to get an agreement between the parties for settlement of the strike, but the parties were so far apart that agreement was impossible. Sloane and his group would not make any concessions on the crucial point of dealing with the union. The industry was aware that it was unlikely the strike could last long or be very successful. The union would have been willing to make substantial concessions, but it could not concede everything. Also Gorman was not adept at handling this kind of negotiation and he came up with no suggestion as a basis for settlement. Even if he had, it would not have dissolved the impasse because the industry, knowing it was in a commanding position, was unwilling to yield anything of importance. In fact, the industry was interested only in a complete defeat for the union.

When this became clear by the second week of the strike, Winant telephoned President Roosevelt at Hyde Park to report the situation. I was allowed to listen on the extension in the other office when Winant put through this call and I heard the conversation. Winant told the president that the mediation board had been unable to reach any kind of settlement, that the employers would not make any concessions at all, and that there seemed no hope of settlement. The president's reply was, "Oh" in a very concerned tone, but with no indication that he had any ideas of his own on what to do. Obviously very worried about the situation, he was at a loss as to what steps might be taken. After further conversation they agreed that the board would make another effort and if that failed issue a fact-finding report. That report would be published and as a result of publication we hoped that public opinion would be aroused to a point where the employers would be forced to accept the board's recommendations for settlement.

So the board made further efforts to settle the strike, but without success. The board then prepared a report which was intended to outline the issues, summarize the basic facts, and make recommendations for a settlement. I did the major work on drafting the report and Winant worked quite intensely on it. After five or seven days we had the report ready and the board had approved it.

The report recommended that a special board devoted entirely to the textile industry be established. This board would hold hearings and make decisions on the enforcement of Section 7(a) and would also attempt to make adjustments with respect to anyone who claimed to be discriminated against when the strike was over. That was the most important recommendation because it would have set up the machinery by which the worst effects of the strike on the union's rights to organize could be eliminated. I cannot remember how the wage question was handled, but it was postponed in some way.

The "stretch-out" issue had been delegated to a special committee of engineers appointed by Winant. Morris Llewellyn Cooke was one and the others included some company engineers familiar with the textile business. They were supposed to come up with some solution or recommendations. I naively thought that this was a scientific problem on which scientists would produce results. I had been consistently disillusioned by the businessmen and the bankers, and now I placed great faith on the engineers. We hoped that the committee would produce some sort of a mathematical engineering formula as to how much the work load should be, on the basis of which the "stretch-out" problem could be settled. In their preliminary conversations the committee members talked in those terms. It seemed a little difficult to me at the time, but in any event they

came up with nothing at all. I suppose it was impossible. The board finally had to bypass the "stretch-out" issue with the recommendation that further study be made by a group of engineers.

The union did not gain much immediate advantage from the recommendations. Still, if the report had been accepted the union would have received sufficient advantages to save face. But on the whole the problem was insoluble. The "stretch-out" and wages were issues that differed so much from plant to plant that there was no real possibility, acting under the data then available, for any solution to those two problems. The only feasible strategy was to protect the union's right to organize and enable it to work out these other issues through negotiation over a period of time. That is what the board's report provided for, so far as it could.

After the report had been prepared and approved by the board I was dispatched as a courier to deliver it to President Roosevelt. He was at Newport watching the International Yacht Races. So I took a train for Newport and arrived there in the morning. The first thing I did was to purchase a hat, the first hat I ever owned, as the occasion struck me as demanding a hat. Then I went to the hotel where the White House staff was stationed and reported to Marvin McIntyre, the president's general secretary. McIntyre was expecting me, accepted the report, and said we would deliver it to the president on his yacht. We boarded a cutter in the harbor, along with a crowd of newsmen, and we went out and anchored near the president's yacht. The president held an informal press conference from one boat to the other. He recognized many of the reporters on our boat and shouted to them. They shouted questions over to him and he had a glorious time waving and shouting and answering questions between the two boats. The report was delivered by a small boat to the president's yacht, but neither McIntyre nor I went over. The president was to look over the report and meet to discuss it with Winant and Miss Perkins in Poughkeepsie that evening after the races were over.

So I rode back to shore with McIntyre. Then I drove with McIntyre and a couple of others to Poughkeepsie so as to be available for the president's meeting with Winant and Miss Perkins. McIntyre struck me as the stereotype of the newspaper man, easygoing, free-thinking, with the flair you often find in newspaper reporters. He was constantly joking, never taking anything seriously, always skeptical. As attractive as he was, I judged him at the time as superficial and I doubted he was helping the president very much. On the other hand, he obviously knew his job and the newspaper field, and since that was his job, as I look back I suppose he was carrying on pretty effectively.

I stayed overnight in Poughkeepsie and the conference took place the next day. I was not present, but after the conference Winant and Miss Perkins picked me up and we all rode down to New York. I gathered from what they said that the president had read the entire report word for word, and the three of them, agreeing the recommendations were the best possible under the circumstances, decided to release the report.

By the time the report was released the strike was nearly over. A good many of the strikers had returned to work. Those who were still out were making no progress. The report did not give the union any great impetus to continue the strike. If the strikers could have held out a little longer, they might possibly have mobilized some public opinion, but the strike was practically washed up by this time. When the report came out, the union called off the strike on the basis of the report and proclaimed it a great victory. Actually, it was a great failure, because the employers had made no commitment to accept the terms of the report.

After the report was published and the strike was over, the board disbanded, leaving the union without any government agency responsible for taking care of the aftermath of the strike. No one officially was assigned to implement the recommendations of the report, or to protect the strikers' jobs.

I continued on, however, attempting to get this done, although I had no official status. All this time I was on the staff of the NLRB and just loaned to the textile board.

### The "Textile Labor Relations Board"
The major job was to prepare an executive order that would set up a textile labor relations board, as recommended, and which would follow through on the proposals for a study of the "stretch-out" system. I prepared such an order and checked it with Charles Wyzanski, solicitor of the Department of Labor. I then met with the employers in the industry to give them an opportunity to state their position on the draft order. No representatives of labor were present. It was a peculiar situation, in which the heads of the industry, meeting in the luxury of the Union League Club in New York, were attempting to resist my efforts, and I was merely an unattached federal employee in a minor and ambiguous position. The discussion was interesting, but I did not wring any concessions from them at all. I told them that the administration had prepared and was committed to the issuance of the order setting up the board and establishing a study of the "stretch-out" and wage systems. They were not in a position to prevent that, but they were still unwilling to do anything to assist the union or to relieve the union from the effects of the strike.

I took the order to Wyzanski; he put it through channels and it was signed by the president. The textile board was established as a special board under Public Resolution No. 44. It was intended to function as the large board did, confining its activities to the textile field, and in addition, to mediate in getting strikers back to work, as well as to set up the study of the "stretch-out" and wage systems. President Roosevelt appointed the board and I stayed with them for several hectic weeks, attempting to get them working. Complaints poured in from all over the country that union leaders had been excluded from the plants after the strike had been declared over. The board attempted to get field representatives to look into these situations and straighten them out as rapidly as possible. Actually, little was accomplished since the board lacked effective enforcement procedures and the law was uncertain on whether the strikers had any legal right to reinstatement. The question of the status of strikers after a strike, when they were seeking to return to employment, had really not been decided at that time and was in a state of considerable uncertainty.

In any event, many of the leaders of the abortive strike were deprived of their jobs and were still out of work when the new National Labor Relations Board was established in 1935. When I went to the Atlanta regional office under that board and visited a number of mills, the scars of the strike were still very much in evidence. There was some evidence of a blacklist of the leaders. In other words, the aftermath of the strike was a definite further defeat for the union. Union membership had fallen away to a very small percentage of what it had been at its peak. There still remained, however, a group in which a nucleus of the union continued. Since union organization generally was expanding throughout the United States, the union had moral support from other places and continued to function in a number of areas where it had not existed before. To that extent, the union held some gains, but not very many, and certainly the losses from their inability to protect their local members left an impact for some time to come.

The textile board functioned similarly to the larger board, holding hearings and looking into alleged violations of Section 7(a) of the textile codes. It suffered from the same lack of power and the same frustration with the Department of Justice. Although it specialized in the field, it was even less effective than the larger board because it had less prestige. The inquiry into the "stretch-out" came to nothing; the engineers did not do any better the second time around.

### The Textile Strike of 1934 and the "Textile Labor Relations Board": An Assessment

In retrospect, the textile strike of 1934 probably did not have as much effect as it appeared to have when it started. As the first major strike in the New Deal period, at least for purposes of organizing a large industry that had previously been unorganized, this strike if successful would have increased tremendously the tempo of organization all over the country. But the defeat did not seriously obstruct the trend toward labor organization. Organization in steel, automobiles, rubber, and other mass production industries that had not previously been organized continued, despite this temporary setback.

This episode of the textile strike seemed to me fairly typical of the attitude of the Roosevelt administration. The president and secretary of labor were far more interested in the wage and hour issues than with the basic question of the organization of labor. It has been asserted that the administration strenuously encouraged the organization of labor from the beginnings of the New Deal. My impression was that that was not correct. The forces that encouraged the organization of labor were forces that operated in the country at large, but were not reflected in the specific actions of the administration at this time. That is to say, the forces at work at the time were the whole impact of the Depression, and the political excitement of the New Deal election, and the extremely important fact that Section 7(a) was included in an official piece of legislation and therefore represented an official policy on the part of the government as a whole to encourage and safeguard the organization of labor. The labor movement itself was stirring, both those elements of the AFL leadership that later became the CIO as well as some of the other leadership of the AFL, and there was also activity in many local areas. But I could discern no policy in the executive branch of the government that deliberately or aggressively encouraged the organization of labor.

About a month after the textile board began to function I left to return to the [original] NLRB. I could have stayed with the textile board, but I decided that it was operating in a narrower sphere than the larger board and that I would prefer to assist there.

## PASSAGE OF THE NEW NATIONAL LABOR RELATIONS ACT
*To replace NRA, renew the NLRB, govern the workplace*

Before discussing the new legislation that was passed to establish the second NLRB, I will appraise the accomplishments of the first NLRB. The first board formulated the basic propositions of policy with respect to collective bargaining in substantial detail, not only in the majority rule case, but in other cases involving company domination of unions, discharge of employees, various types of interference in union organizing, and other aspects of refusal to bargain. By spelling out these principles in reasoned decisions the board kept alive the federal guarantee of the right to organize and bargain collectively. The board had established its independence from NRA and some had justification for operating as a separate agency. It had built up the nucleus of an experienced staff both in Washington and in the field. Inheriting from the Wagner Board about a dozen regional offices, the board had consolidated the staff, establishing a regional director, regional attorney, and some staff in each office. Finally, the board rendered considerable assistance on the new legislation, supplying much of the manpower and expertise essential to the passage of any piece of legislation. Actually, this first NLRB, in cooperation with Keyserling from Senator Wagner's office, spearheaded the move for the National Labor Relations Act. Calvert Magruder, general counsel of the board, worked diligently on the preparation of the legislation and the hearings. After the decision in the Schechter case in May, the board had no function in regard to specific cases. The original bill was re-drafted and re-introduced in February 1935. Again, Keyserling carried the major responsibility for the re-drafting. This time he was helped primarily by Magruder. Wyzanski did not figure much in the picture any more, although he kept in touch with the situation. I did not have any close connection with the inside legislative work on the bill. I attended some of the hearings and rendered some help in getting witnesses and matters of that sort. I was still sharing lodgings with Keyserling, so I heard day-to-day reports on what was happening. Most of the work with the committees was done by Magruder, and I think Philip Levy, who was assisting him and later became Wagner's secretary worked on it a good deal.

The Senate Committee on Education and Labor and the House Labor Committee held elaborate hearings in March and April 1935. The board supplied much of the data and favorable testimony. Biddle testified before the committees on behalf of the board. The board staff, together with Keyserling, rounded up a number of other witnesses who testified on behalf of the bill. Some opposition emerged at the hearings, but not as much as one might have expected. The committees voted to report the bill out favorably. The bill was submitted, together with reports actually written largely by Calvert Magruder, with some help from Keyserling. The committees themselves had little staff at that time and it was not unusual for committee reports to be written outside the staff. The bill came up for debate in May 1935.

### Passing the Bill Establishing the New NLRB

When industry discovered that the bill was moving along, they had little hope of defeating it in committee, but nevertheless did oppose it. Also a group within the administration, largely the NRA business group, undertook to modify the bill drastically. Donald Richberg submitted to the president an alternative bill that would have drastically curtailed the powers and effectiveness of the board. It was never generally known that Richberg had prepared an actual draft of a very weak measure, which, for example, permitted employers considerable leeway to set up company unions and did not accept the majority rule principle. Richberg could see the president almost any time he wanted to and was on reasonably good terms with him. Richberg attempted to sell this bill to the president, but the president said he would consider it and then referred the matter to Wagner who, of course, ditched it. Wagner found out about it only when the president gave him a copy of the Richberg bill and said, "Richberg thinks this is the way it should be. What do you think?" This indicates how Richberg had moved much closer to the business viewpoint than anybody had realized at the time.

The Department of Justice objected to a provision in the bill that permitted the NLRB attorneys to appear in court. This was a key provision because of our previous experience with the Department of Justice. However, the Department of Justice understandably had the basic policy that any court work should be handled by Department of Justice attorneys. The committees drafting the bill did not accede to the Justice Department's request so the attorney general appealed to the president. The president agreed and spoke with Wagner. Wagner said he would not object if an amendment were proposed, inserting this provision. It was then arranged that Sen. Joe Robinson would propose an amendment on behalf of the administration, but when the debate came, Senator Robinson was off the floor or forgot, so that he never proposed it. Apparently by accident the bill passed with the original provision concerning NLRB attorneys appearing in court.

By the time the bill came up for debate the Schechter decision had come down, so industry deemed the legislation unconstitutional and expected the courts would throw it out. Thus either for that reason or for lack of organization, they made no full-scale attack on the bill, even though they certainly opposed it.

Of course, Senator Wagner was the chief proponent of the measure, but since it had been reported out by the Labor Committee, the control of the debate in the Senate was assured by the chairman of that committee, Sen. David Walsh of Massachusetts. Senator Walsh supported the bill, but he did not understand the ins and outs of what was behind the various provisions. Consequently, in the course of debate, when he was engaged in colloquies with other Senators and attempted to explain the provisions, he made some statements that would have caused serious difficulty in later interpretation of the Act. However, Calvert Magruder was able to get the typewritten copy of the transcript of the debate, which each Senator has a right to correct, and by taking great liberties to correct the statements of Senator Walsh, he succeeded in removing this unfavorable legislative history from the debate. So the *Congressional Record* does not reflect the compromises that Senator Walsh made on the floor. Of course, Magruder could not change what any other Senator had said. He could only alter Walsh's remarks, but by doing so he did manage to change the legislative history rather substantially.

Sen. Millard Tydings of Maryland submitted two amendments that would have seriously weakened the bill. The amendments obtained some support, but were defeated rather easily, receiving only twenty to twenty-five [out of ninety-six possible] votes.

This was my first intimate experience watching legislative machinery in action. The Senate debate was reasonably impressive, in the sense that ideas were exchanged and the discussion was to the point. The bill passed the Senate by an overwhelming vote. Very few were against it at the end. More supported the Tydings amendments than voted against the bill as a whole.

The bill then came up for debate in the House. There was a general debate on the bill for a couple of hours–which did not throw much light on the subject–and then a reading of the bill with opportunity for amendments. There was some questioning back and forth of the supporters of the measure. Little objection to the measure was manifest. The chairman of the House Labor Committee, Rep. William P. Connery of Massachusetts, comprehended the bill better than Walsh did. Although not an intellectual, Connery was highly intelligent and understood the labor problems involved. So he handled himself very effectively, both in the general debate and when amendments were proposed. The amendments were subject to the five minute rule whereby no congressman could speak more than five minutes on any one amendment. So it was difficult for the congressman proposing the amendment to explain in that brief time what he had in mind. Those congressmen present did not listen carefully anyway. Connery, who had been a former vaudeville actor, was extremely effective in his role as a supporter of the legislation and excellent at answering questions in a few words or sentences. The vote followed party lines with the administration being supported on all amendments so far as

I can recollect. It was fairly clear that the congressmen did not understand the import of many of them, but they followed Connery's leadership and he was sufficiently impressive as a debater so that he maintained the confidence of his colleagues and was able to ward off all amendments so far as I can recall—at any event, all major ones. The final vote in the House was overwhelmingly in support of the measure.

## ESTABLISHING THE "NEW" NLRB
*Establishing legitimacy and an agenda*

The National Labor Relations Act contained two main substantive provisions. These provisions were similar to those in Section 7(a) of the NRA. One provided that employees had the right to organize and bargain collectively and to engage in concerted activity. A specific provision stated that it was an unfair labor practice for an employer to interfere with this right of self-organization and collective bargaining. Five specific unfair labor practices were enumerated.

- The most general prohibited interference with, restraint of, or coercion against the rights guaranteed to employees under the act.
- The second made it an unfair labor practice for an employer to create a union of his own, or to dominate or control a union.
- The third provision prohibited an employer from discharging or disciplining an employee because of his union activity.
- The fourth prevented an employer from punishing or disciplining an employee who gave testimony under the act.
- The fifth made it an unfair labor practice for an employer to refuse to bargain collectively with the representatives of his employees.

The second major substantive feature was a provision that the NLRB had power to certify the representatives of a majority of the employees as a designated collective bargaining unit. In other words, the board determined both what the collective bargaining unit was and who the representatives of the employees in that unit were.

The rest of the act consisted almost entirely of procedural provisions: methods for administration and enforcement. The NLRB was created with authority to administer and carry out the provisions of the act. Thus an administrative agency was created whose only function was to administer the provisions of this legislation.

In addition, the procedural provisions set up an administrative procedure based on the procedures in the Federal Trade Commission Act for enforcement of the provisions of that act. Reliance was not placed upon criminal, or even ordinary civil, enforcement provisions; the enforcement was to be done through a system whereby the board issued a complaint against an employer charged with having engaged in unfair labor practices. A hearing was held. The board made findings and if it

51

found the employer had engaged in unfair labor practices it then issued a "cease and desist" order. In effect the "cease and desist" order was like an injunction requiring the employer to cease from engaging in unfair labor practices. The board also could order employers to take affirmative action, such as reinstating employees who had been discharged for union activity. The "cease and desist" order could be enforced only if taken to a federal circuit court of appeals. Either the board or the employer could take the case to the circuit court of appeals. The court of appeals then had a limited review. It had to accept the findings of the board if they were supported by evidence, but could review entirely questions of law. If the court supported the board, it issued an order enforcing the board's order. Once the court had issued an order, violation of that order became a contempt of court and was punishable as such. Parties could appeal the decision of the circuit court to the Supreme Court by way of *certiorari*–that is, if the Supreme Court decided to accept the appeal, it could hear the case.

This procedure was somewhat unusual in that it resulted in what amounted to a court injunction, but achieved it through an administrative process–that is, through a hearing held by an administrative board and findings and decision made by the administrative board. It subsequently was challenged as a violation of the basic principle of separation of powers: that judicial functions were being performed by an executive agency. It so happened, however, that this procedure had been incorporated in the Federal Trade Commission Act, which was passed in 1914 and had never seriously been challenged on these grounds. It was an application of the procedure used in the attempt to control monopoly to a situation involving labor relations. The main reason for turning to the administrative procedure was our experience of a complete lack of enforcement under the older methods of criminal prosecution and civil injunction proceedings through the Department of Justice.

The drafting of the National Labor Relations Act was an exceedingly fine job. Leon Keyserling had considerable experience in drafting. The statute used no excessive language, but language that permitted the board to cover most of the problems that came up in the next few years. In short, the statute stood up under formidable attack extremely well. For a period of more than ten years, or until the Taft-Hartley Act was passed, there was no need even for clarifying amendments. Proposals for many substantive amendments were hotly disputed, but clarifying or amplifying amendments daily or weekly, as in NRA and OPA, was not necessary. The National Labor Relations Act was one of the best-drafted pieces of New Deal Legislation.

The bill passed in June or July 1935, but I believe that the board was not finally appointed until the end of August because of difficulty in finding a satisfactory chairman. As a result of the Schechter decision, most lawyers were convinced that the statute was unconstitutional, so the job of chairman was not appealing. Procuring the chairman was delegated to Miss Perkins, who delegated it largely to Wyzanski. He sounded out a number of people, including William O. Douglas, all of whom turned it down. (Bill Douglas called me up to talk about it after it had been offered to him.) Finally, J. Warren Madden was selected for a five year term. Nobody had heard of him. Madden had been a professor of law throughout most of his life, and an expert in domestic relations; most recently he had been teaching at the University of Pittsburgh Law School. He had been a member of a board of arbitration, and so he came to be considered for the job as chairman of the National Labor Relations Board.

Edwin S. Smith, who had served on the old board, was appointed to the board for the one year term. He was a protege of Edward Filene of the Filene stores in Boston and I believe had worked as his assistant for some time. He had been interested in labor problems. I guess he was probably also known to Felix Frankfurter and was a friend of Walsh and to some extent of Connery. The third member was John Carmody. Carmody was an engineer–a very attractive Irishman, an extrovert with an unlimited supply of stories. A person of integrity, he understood and was friendly toward labor. At the same time, he had his own ideas and was not easily persuaded. He had had some experience on labor issues as an engineer. Carmody retired after a year and was replaced by Donald Smith. Madden and the two Smiths conducted the board for about four or five years after that.

The major problem that the board faced as it came into office was establishing the constitutionality of the act. As a result of the Schechter decision there was considerable doubt as to the validity of the act. It was clear that the board could not function effectively until a Supreme Court decision had been obtained. Agreeing that the constitutional test had to be obtained as quickly as possible, the board focused on what strategy to use in bringing up cases that would test the constitutional points. The board could influence what cases would get to court because an issue could not come before the courts until it had gone through the administrative process, and the board could select which cases to decide and in which cases to issue a complaint. By moving as quickly as possible in those fields where the best test cases could be secured and delaying in other areas the board could ripen a series of promising cases that would test various aspects of constitutional validity.

At the same time the board had to establish regulations implementing the provisions of the legislation. The regulations dealt primarily with procedure: the manner in which hearings would be held and other procedures the board would use to conduct its business. Even before and especially after the passage of the act, and before the appointment of the board, the staff had prepared a draft of procedural regulations and tentative recommendations with respect to various organizational problems, such as where regional offices should be located, and what the relationship of the regional offices to the national office should be, and what the organization of the board should be. When the board came into office, it examined these plans and regulations and made some changes, but as a result of this preliminary work, it was able to begin its routine functions fairly quickly.

The board also had the problem of maintaining its prestige and enforcing the legislation, or at least holding the situation together as well as it could until the constitutional issues could be decided. Shortly after the act passed, the Liberty League issued a legal-type brief, in which it argued strongly that the act was unconstitutional. Organized primarily for the purpose of opposing the New Deal, the Liberty League was a group of lawyers who regularly represented the largest industries in the country. This brief, in effect advising industry that it would not suffer if it did not comply with the terms of the act, compounded the board's difficulties in obtaining compliance.

After a few weeks of intensive effort on organization, adoption of regulations and discussion of basic policy, the board assigned a substantial part of the Washington staff, particularly the lawyers, to the regional offices on a temporary basis. These Washington representatives were to reorganize the regional offices. In certain cases the regional directors, appointed in some instances by the old Wagner Board, did not seem qualified for the new operation and they had to be replaced. In other areas new offices had to be set up. In all areas a much larger staff had to be recruited. The job of revitalizing and reorganizing the regional offices was entrusted, in most cases, to representatives from Washington.

The lawyers also were to search for suitable test cases in which to start board proceedings in accordance with the master plan for testing the constitutionality. The master plan was to bring up first a case involving interstate transportation. The railroads were not subject to the act, but bus and trucking companies that carried passengers or freight in interstate commerce were. This area was chosen as the one to begin with because it would be clearest under the commerce clause, particularly in view of the decision in the Texas and New Orleans case. Following the establishment of the constitutionality of the act as a whole, as applied to interstate transportation, the next project was to bring a case involving a major industry, such as steel or automobiles, and a major plant within that industry, to present the most favorable case involving manufacturing employees. We then planned to bring a case involving a small concern that had manufacturing employees but where the materials came into the state from another state and then a considerable proportion of materials were shipped out. From then on we would test various other areas of increasing doubtfulness as to the constitutionality, such as industries where all materials originated in the state, but a substantial portion were shipped out, or industries where little or nothing was shipped out, but a good deal came in, and so on down into the distribution trades, hotels, and other areas. We had not worked it out in complete detail, but we were definitely agreed on the three major steps–interstate transportation, large, and then the small, manufacturing companies–as the order in which the cases should come up to the Supreme Court.

The board could choose from virtually an unlimited supply of cases because Section 7(a) had been violated widely and similar violations of the National Labor Relations Act continued. Compliance was unusual, particularly as a result of the Schechter case and the Liberty League brief. Employers felt safe in disregarding the act and at the same time labor was in such a ferment that issues were bound to arise. So it appeared feasible to carry out this scheme.

# 3

# WASHINGTON BUREAUCRAT IN THE FIELD

*Taking the New Deal to the Old South.*

As I have said, the renewed NLRB began carrying out its new mandate by dispatching many of its legal staff to regional offices on a temporary basis. I was the Washington representative sent to reorganize the southern region, with headquarters in Atlanta and including Georgia, Alabama, South Carolina, North Carolina, Florida, and Tennessee. I went to the Atlanta office in September 1935 and stayed until February 1936. My assignment was to organize the office under the new National Labor Relations Act and to establish the operational procedures; these included assessing personnel, making recommendations for change, and hiring new personnel when necessary. In addition, and perhaps this was the reason a lawyer was assigned the task, I was to initiate cases that would test the constitutionality of the act. An early test was clearly essential, both because of increasing opposition to the act and because of the notion circulating in the brief of the Liberty League (Chapter 2) that the act was unconstitutional. Also, from a public relations point of view we needed to commence legal proceedings as soon as possible so as to give the impression that the board was engaged in effective action. Consequently, the Washington representatives to each region were instructed to concentrate primarily on finding cases that would present the constitutional issues.

## THE SOUTHERN REGIONAL OFFICE IN ATLANTA

Frank Coffee was the head of the Atlanta office at that time. A public relations man, Coffee had served as regional officer for the old Wagner Board and had continued on when the original National Labor Relations Board superseded. A pleasant person, rather easy-going and lackadaisical, Coffee was not intellectually astute and was not aware of, or interested in, labor problems. He was better suited to the mediation of labor disputes called for under the Wagner Board than as an administrator of a tightly drawn law demanding a carefully framed and executed administration. I recommended that he be replaced. Charles Feidelson became regional director for the South and remained in that post for a number of years. A native of Birmingham, Alabama, Feidelson had been a practicing lawyer and then had moved into the field of journalism and was the editorial writer of a Birmingham newspaper. Although not strong as a person or administrator, he was very intelligent, sympathetic with the point of view of the framers of the act, and would conduct the office on a considerably higher level than it seemed likely that Coffee would have.

The appointment raised the question of whether or not it was advisable for the board to appoint a staff from the locality in which the regional, or local, office was situated. On the one hand, only a local person would be familiar with local problems and have the local connections necessary for a successful administration. On the other hand, local persons were subject to greater pressures from the area in which they operated. The board had discussed this from time to time and concluded that a mixed group of persons from the locality and persons from outside the locality would work best. We tended to place local people in the top job of regional director, and to some extent as regional attorney, the second job in the office, but to ensure that some of the staff working on lower levels was not subject to the local pressure inevitable in the administration of the law.

Frank Coffee had a general assistant named Gene Curtis from Douglas, Georgia. Curtis was a rough, rather blunt country boy-type, not an intellectual but shrewd in his handling of people. He had been a mediator in the United States Conciliation Service and had joined the Atlanta office of the Wagner Board. Curtis knew his business; he had a capacity for bringing two sides together in a rather rough, practical, warm-hearted, jovial style, which made him a valuable employee. He was completely familiar with the territory, understood the problems, and his heart was entirely in the right place. He turned out to be very effective during my period in Atlanta.

Coffee and Curtis had run the office themselves with perhaps a couple of others and clerical assistance. In establishing the new office under Feidelson, I was acting regional attorney, Curtis was the main field examiner or general investigator who settled cases, and we hired several other investigators and two other attorneys. One of the attorneys, who later succeeded me as regional attorney and stayed for several years, was Mortimer Kollender. A Northerner, Kollender had attended Williams College, New York University Law School, and had practiced law in the North. He had worked with Charles Fahy on the Petroleum Board in the Department of Interior during NRA days. Fahy, as general counsel of the NLRB, had brought him over and sent him to Atlanta to help me. Like myself, Kollender was an outsider in Atlanta. Able, jovial, decidedly independent in his ideas and stubborn in many respects, Kollender got along well with people; he was constantly cheerful, an excellent companion, and became one of my best friends. I had not known him before, but we became very close in Atlanta and our close friendship continued when he returned to Washington. Walter Cooper, the other attorney, had been to law school in the South and was a native of Atlanta, where he was practicing law. Rather young, as were Kollender and myself, Cooper was the intellectual type, reasonably able, and modern in his ideas and approaches to problems. He subsequently went on to teach at Emory Law School.

The new staff was more intellectual than political, except for Curtis. In general, the personnel were neither employer-oriented nor did they have a background in the labor movement. To some extent this characterized the other regional offices, although they varied substantially. A number of men retained from the old board were operators rather than intellectuals.

I had practically no contact with employers or employer groups in Atlanta, except in connection with specific cases. They made no effort to contact our office and we made no effort to establish a relationship with them. The lines already were clearly drawn by the time I arrived in Atlanta. The manufacturers' associations and other organized groups of employers had declared war on the act and the board. Relying on the courts to declare the act unconstitutional, they were determined to make no concessions, and were not even bothering much with the administration of the act.

In contrast, we had frequent contact with labor groups, both in individual cases and generally. The two chief labor leaders, George Googe and Steve Nance, dominated the labor picture in the Southeast. Both were southerners. Nance was the chief official of the Georgia Federation of Labor and Googe was the representative of the AFL in the southeast. Googe was an extremely able, clever, skillful, smooth operator. I was always a little uncertain about him and suspicious of his lack of principles, but there was no doubt that he was a very shrewd and careful manipulator, and a person of considerable ability. Highly regarded by the AFL in Washington, he furnished most of the brain power to the Southeast labor movement. Nance was a hearty, bluff man of considerable ability, much more straightforward than Googe, much less devious and not quite as able, but nevertheless very superior in his abilities. The rest of the labor group were not in his class at all. Most of the organizers were far inferior to Googe and Nance in ability, experience, ideas, background, and education. Some were conscientious, hard-working, reliable people. Others were unreliable and might not show up at a meeting that they had agreed to attend. Some losers who had not been able to make a living at other things. However, all of them had considerable courage, because it took real courage to be a labor organizer in that territory, at least outside the big cities.

As the CIO did not yet exist, the conflict between the AFL and CIO that later dominated the labor scene had not begun. The main strength of the AFL was in the building trades and craft unions of the major southern

59

cities such as Atlanta, Birmingham, and Jacksonville. That organization was reasonably respectable by then. Googe was accepted in major political circles, for instance. Beyond that, labor had little organization. The United Mine Workers had some organization in the coal area of Alabama. There was practically no organization in the lumber industry, which was one of the toughest areas, as it was far out in the country and away from any protection of law and order. Foundries, pipe shops and smaller industrial plants of that sort had a smattering of unions. There was practically no newer industry that was burgeoning in the South then. Several automobile plants previously had been started there, as well as a couple of rubber mills and some plants in the rayon field; these new, highly efficient plants, sporting the latest technology, had practically no labor organization at all.

The major activity had been in textiles, where labor organization had spread quite rapidly and then had met severe defeat in the strike of 1934, following which it had lost most of its strength. The textile union still persisted in many areas, although often their leadership had been discharged and was unemployed, and nothing much had been accomplished since the strike. The scars of the strike were still evident. Most labor action, and thus most of the board's activity, related to the textile field, because the effort at organization, the counterattack by the employers, the aftermath of the strike and the continuing resistance of employers all created problems arising under the Act. Considerable agitation, interest, and turmoil were present. Labor had not been, by any means, defeated. Despite the severe setback in the textile strike, labor was optimistic. We had plenty of cases. There was no sign of compliance with the National Labor Relations Act on any voluntary basis. The only reason that we did not have more cases was that labor had so little organization, but the legislation had not restrained employers from opposing the union and fighting it through discharging employees and other now illegal practices.

## THE GATE CITY COTTON MILL CASE

Our first case was the Gate City Cotton Mill case. The Gate City Cotton Mill was a small mill, employing 150-200 workers, located on the outskirts of Atlanta. We started a proceeding to determine who would be the representatives for collective bargaining and to make a certification of representatives. In other words, it was not an unfair labor practice case, but simply a determination of whether the union represented a majority and was therefore entitled to bargain collectively with the employer. We chose to start with this case not only because it was conveniently located near our office and a small plant that could be handled easily, but also because it presented a fairly clear-cut picture of a group attempting to bargain collectively under the procedures of the act. The union organized at this spinning mill had 80-90 percent of the employees signed up as members when they joined the 1934 strike. The strike was a failure and the mill hands returned to work. The president of the union and perhaps one of the other officers were not taken back. However, the president of the union had other means of support; he had a small truck and a little farm and did handyman work such as small carpentry jobs. So he was not dependent on the mill, although he had worked in it as a loom-fixer from time to time. Although he had been fired from his job, he continued to live on his farm and be president of the union. He held the union together. After the employer had refused to bargain on the ground, among others, that the union no longer had the support of the majority of employees, the union had circulated a petition, which many had signed, requesting an election under the National Labor Relations Act to determine whether they were collective bargaining representatives. We thought that the matter could proceed rapidly and would be a sign that the board was moving into action.

Curtis and I interviewed the president of the union at his farm. A man with an independent personality, he was glad to give us the details. We obtained a good deal of the information that we needed from him, especially the names of persons who might be willing to testify in the case. As we soon learned, one of our major problems was to find witnesses who would be willing to expose themselves by testifying in NLRB proceedings. At that time and under those conditions, workers were understandably reluctant to do so.

To track down persons who had significant information, I attended a union meeting a few nights later on the outskirts of Atlanta in a one-room shack. The meeting had a religious atmosphere, opening and closing with a prayer, but was rather pathetic in the obvious incapacity of the union to cope with the present situation in which it found itself. I explained the National Labor Relations Act and the nature of the proceeding that was to be instituted, and indicated what information I wanted with respect to persons who had attended union meetings and could testify as to how many were present and other questions of that sort. I asked all those who were interested or who had information to stay after the meeting and talk to me individually. A number of them did stay. Choosing two or three people who seemed to know most about it and would hold up best in an open hearing, I discussed with them what sort of questions would be asked. It later turned out that the company had an informer at the meeting. At the hearing the next day it was clear that the company knew exactly what had taken place. Several years later someone testifying before a congressional committee investigating the NLRB distorted my evening appearance into the charge that I spoke at a union rally on behalf of the union outside my role as a government official.

The hearing was the first proceeding of the board in that territory, one of the first proceedings in the country, and consequently received notable publicity in the newspapers. Organized labor also took a good deal of interest in it. Even the employers must have been paying some attention to it because they sent an attorney named Scott Russell, a very effective, smooth-operating lawyer from Macon, Georgia, who was counsel for the

Georgia Manufacturers Association, to help out the local lawyer for the company. So the company was represented by their regular attorney, who was a mediocre lawyer from Atlanta, plus Scott Russell. The hearing officer, Dick Wolf, was supplied by the board from Washington. My job, as attorney for the board, was to establish two major points. One was to show that the company's business operations affected interstate commerce so as to come within the constitutional doctrines applicable under the commerce clause of the Constitution. The other was to establish that a question had arisen concerning representation of employees and to establish the proper collective bargaining unit.

The part of the hearing related to interstate commerce went reasonably well. I had subpoenaed the president of the company and from his testimony drew out information respecting where he got his materials and where he sent his products. I scrutinized every possible product used in the course of his business, even the paper and ink he used in the office and the grease used on the machines. Although most of the cotton, the major raw material, came from Georgia, some came from outside Georgia. Most of the product was shipped out of the state to northern mills: Gate City Cotton Mill was a spinning operation that supplied northern weaving mills and other places outside the state. So our case was fairly strong on material moving out of the state, but not so convincing on material moving into the state. The president responded to my questions reluctantly, but did not conceal the facts at all so far as we were able to check. His attorney from Atlanta obviously did not grasp the significance of this line of questioning, but Mr. Russell had a much clearer understanding of the case.

The statute required demonstration of the existence of a question concerning representation, before the board could hold an election or certify a representative. This was tricky. I had to produce testimony that the union was active, that the union group included a substantial number, though not necessarily a majority, of the workers at the mill, and that the workers were asking for a certification in order to bargain collectively. I had in my possession the union membership records from the peak period. The records actually were out of date. I also had the signed petition asking for an election by the board. The union was unwilling to have their membership or the names on the petition made public for fear of recrimination. The company most likely knew the union membership through its undercover people, but the union thought the company might not have a complete list and in any event was unwilling to disclose the names of its backers. So I introduced testimony from the union president and other witnesses to show that the union was an active, functioning organization in the plant in which it was asking for recognition. We had testimony as to the number of persons present at meetings, and so on, although no names were divulged. The company objected strongly and tried to cross-examine and ask names, but the trial examiner ruled all that out, despite the company attorney's vigorous protests. The company's defense was primarily that there was no question concerning representation, as proved by a third petition that they had in their possession. The third petition stated that everybody was satisfied with conditions as they were and did not wish to bargain collectively.

Lola Eckles, one of the women in the plant, had circulated the petition. Lola Eckles had been a member of the union, gone out on strike, and then had shifted over and become rather strongly anti-union. The story was told that she had gone to the management and had asked the management what she could do to show that the employees had abandoned the union. They suggested to her that she get up a petition. The company attorney put Lola Eckles on the witness stand and she produced this petition, signed by a large proportion of the employees, saying that they were perfectly satisfied, did not want an election, and did not want the union, or anyone else, to represent them. This was the first time I had ever attempted to cross-examine anybody on a witness stand. I met far more than my match in Lola Eckles. I made no headway at all. Convinced that the petition had been signed by many employees under considerable duress from foremen and under company pressure, I attempted to worm this out of her by various questions, but with absolutely no success. This sharp-tongued millhand, earning $14 per week, left me looking rather foolish in exchange after exchange.

The hearing lasted about a day and a half. The record was then sent to Washington; the board considered it and made a decision to order an election. In their view there was enough information to show that a substantial group of employees had raised the question. Even the third petition, if taken at face value, did not indicate that there was no desire, or no substantial question left. The Gate City Cotton Mill Case must have been one of the first two or three cases that came before the board. We hoped that they would be able to move quickly and were disappointed that it took about three weeks for the board to make a decision. This was our first contact with a really difficult problem that pursued the board throughout its history: the delay in making decisions.

We announced that an election would be held. The day was set and my direct participation was to end because I delegated to Curtis the responsibility for conducting the details of the election, including obtaining the payroll and being there to check off the names. I was merely to offer general advice. About a week before the election was scheduled I was in another hearing we had started when I received word that the company had filed a suit for an injunction in the Fulton County Court of Georgia to enjoin the board from holding the election and that the judge wanted me to come immediately and argue the case. The company had filed a request for an *ex parte* restraining order, but the judge seems to have insisted that he wanted to hear the attorney for the NLRB before he took any action. I had thought a good deal about the constitutional and other issues, but I had no argument officially prepared and had to appear before the judge with scarcely time to collect my thoughts. I argued mainly on the constitutional issues, as did the company. I also explained the statutory provisions and procedure. Both judge and opposing attorney were quite ignorant of the issues that were being advanced; it was something completely outside their normal area of operations. To my great astonishment the judge ruled in my favor and would not grant an injunction. I must have convinced him that an argument could be made that the statute was constitutional. The judge, I think, was influenced to a large extent by a belief that state courts should not interfere with the enforcement of federal law. That was the first injunction proceeding brought against any board action throughout the country and the first decision upholding the constitutionality of the statute.

Several days later the company brought an injunction proceeding in the federal court of the District of Columbia to enjoin the members of the board from holding the election. The suit was brought in behalf of Lola Eckles. The complaint alleged that she was being deprived of her liberty of contract contrary to the Constitution in that the board was forcing her to bargain collectively, whereas she preferred to bargain for herself as an individual. This time Lola Eckles was represented by Cravath, de Gersdorff, Swaine & Wood, as the firm was then known. The federal judge granted a temporary restraining order preventing the board from holding the election on the scheduled day. The argument on a further motion was postponed for some weeks, and ultimately for several months; by the time it was argued, I was back in Washington.

Several cases involving the same issue of an effort to enjoin the board from carrying on its activities were argued at the same time. I participated in the argument before the judge in the District of Columbia court, contending with a considerable array of legal talent, including Mr. Frederick Wood, who had been successful in the Schechter case. The judge was Jesse C. Adkins, who as a prosecuting official had brought *Adkins v. Children's Hospital*, a famous minimum wage case. A kindly and patient man, he listened to all of us with great consideration. He heard arguments over the course of about two days and finally rendered a decision in which he also denied an injunction. The company immediately appealed and meanwhile asked for a stay of the decision. Although he had denied the injunction, the federal judge granted a stay of his order denying the injunction until the company attorneys could complete their appeal. That stay remained in effect until the case went through the court of appeals. The result was that although the judge had technically decided in our favor, by granting the stay he had cut the ground from under us. That legal obstacle remained in effect until the ultimate decision on the constitutionality of the entire National Labor Relations Act in the Jones & Laughlin case. The election at the Gate City Cotton Mill never took place and the union soon disappeared from the scene.

## Two Other Typical Cases

The second case that I undertook as regional attorney was an unfair labor practice case involving the Clinton Cotton Mills in Clinton, South Carolina, a relatively small town–I believe the county seat–in a central South Carolina county. The mill was moderately sized, with about 400-500 employees. After the union struck in the Textile Strike of 1934 the union president and several other union leaders had not been rehired. Still out of work, they engaged in farming. Despite the loss of leadership, the union held together to some extent. The company had formed a company union known as the Good Will Club. So the issues in the case were an interference with union activities, the discharge of union employees for union activity, and the establishment and control of the alleged company-dominated union. An organizer for the textile union in whose territory this mill was located had filed a charge under the National Labor Relations Act, alleging a violation of the law.

I went to Clinton to investigate the matter and determine whether it presented a case we should bring at this stage. The cotton mill was the only industry in that area. Although the town was not entirely dependent on the company–as it was a center for the surrounding agricultural area–the company dominated the town. While Clinton had nice residential areas and a small college, it was a sleepy town, with a small, third-rate hotel, a bank, grocery stores, drug stores, but not much of a business center. The employees lived in extremely dilapidated company houses. Clinton struck me as desolate. The town was run by the mill and the bank, with little objection by employees, union, or anyone else. The frail union had no meeting place in town; most of their meetings were held in open fields. There was no place in town where the board could hold a hearing; the hearing had to be held in Greenville. The union people were frightened; they believed that they were closely watched and that the community bosses strongly disapproved of their actions. I spent two or three day talking with members of the union. I made no attempt to contact the company or to obtain a settlement; we assumed that would have been useless because the companies were sitting tight and planning to raise constitutional issues. Since we were looking for test cases, we deliberately did not undertake any informal settlement prior to bringing the case to hearing. Otherwise, our policy was to make every effort to adjust each case on the basis of an informal agreement or possibly a formal consent order.

We held a hearing and again I recommended the case to the NLRB in Washington for a decision. Again there was a long delay–in this instance three months or more–before a decision was rendered. The union was in a precarious state, hanging on by the skin of its teeth after its defeat in the 1934 strike, and the delay had serious consequences. Delayed decisions became an extremely serious problem for the board despite a diligent effort to work efficiently. When a finding against the company was finally rendered, the decision had little effect because the company did not comply with it and further NLRB action awaited decisions on the constitutional cases that were then pending. Several years later there was a settlement based on the board's order, but by that time the union had pretty well disappeared.

Labor did not always play the role of the meek. Elsewhere labor groups were pressing much harder than in Clinton; considerable agitation was occurring and there seemed some possibility that labor might be able to hold its own. As it turned out, when the efforts to organize were pressed vigorously, they were met with considerable resistance, and later in 1936 and in early 1937 considerable rioting and violence accompanied labor organization drives.

But still, the South was the South. I recall a later case, the Dwight Manufacturing Company case in Gadsden, Alabama. Here too there was considerable violence at union drives at the local steel mill and particularly the Goodyear rubber plant. A militant employer group fought to keep the unions out, but the unions had a sufficient base in the town that once they got a foothold, they could hang on and play an effective role. This situation was just beginning to develop at the time I went there to conduct a hearing. The unions and workers from other plants showed much more interest in this hearing than in the others I've mentioned. So the hearing, held in the federal court room, was very crowded. People overflowed into the corridors and outside the building. It was one of the best attended hearings that we had. The trial examiner opened the proceedings with this statement:

> I want to call the attention of the audience to the fact that we're meeting in the federal court room. The janitor of the building has asked me to please call to your attention that it's prohibited to spit on the walls. Please refrain from doing so.

## GENERAL IMPRESSIONS OF LABOR AND LAW IN THE SOUTH

During my five or six months in the South I covered a large portion of South Carolina, Georgia, Alabama, and Tennessee. My general impression was that there was no doubt about the general anti-union atmosphere of the whole territory. The atmosphere outside the major cities was openly anti-labor. Even in the major cities it was essentially the same, although of somewhat different character. The company-town/company-house syndrome was pervasive, as well as a strong feeling that if the companies operated on a paternalistic basis, the workers ought to be satisfied and there was no point in bringing in outsiders. A widespread feeling of threat overhung the picture, at least outside the large cities. Union organizers were chased out of town, occasionally beaten up or subjected to other violence. It required impressive courage to be a union organizer. Several organizers were former preachers. They used an evangelical style, but even they were not exempt from being mistreated physically. Physical violence against the local people, those who worked in the mill and became union leaders, seemed to be considerably less, although the local leaders lived in the shadow of violence and contended with constant antagonism from the people who ran the town.

I was never personally threatened, but company spies seemed to be present at all my dealings with the unions that involved any large gathering. This was true at Gate City, the Clinton case, and the Dwight Manufacturing Company. As I could tell from the development of the hearing, as well as from later indications, the company knew everything that was going on. I was consistently followed in those mill towns. My District of Columbia license plates made my car conspicuous. On several occasions when I drove around at night a car's lights followed me in and out wherever I went. I am sure that the company received a report on whose houses I visited.

Curtis ran into a threat of violence when I was there. He went to a mill in Dalton, Georgia, identified himself at the gate, and a guard with a rifle came out and escorted him to the office of the president. The president then proceeded to tell him that the act was unconstitutional, that he would not have anything to do with it, and told the guard to escort Curtis back to the plant gate at rifle-point. He warned Curtis not to show up again. (I'll return to this story shortly.)

I was impressed by the poverty, particularly in the rural sections of northern Alabama and southern Tennessee. (Driving through that part of the country several years later, after the TVA had been established, I was amazed at the enormous change.) The company houses, except in the most modern and newest mills, were usually deteriorating, badly in need of paint, very drab and desolate. During the wintertime they had no central heating. I never had been so cold as I was sitting in some of those houses without cellars; a damp chill that lasted for days seemed to permeate the whole place. Women worked in the mills about as much as the men. People seemed to be washed out at an early age. Women in their early thirties seemed to have lost all zest for life; I would learn that they had toiled in the mill for fifteen years already. Many of the men also had worked in the mills since they were children. The drudgery seemed to have a very depressing effect. The wages were extremely low at the time. Not only that, but they were constantly subject to deductions. Although the typical worker might be paid at the rate of $12-$15 a week, the amount of money he actually took home would be considerably less, because there would be deductions for rent of the company house, deductions for loans, for groceries charged at the company store, and so on. I saw pay envelopes for three cents, twenty-seven cents. . . .

Labor had no press that I was aware of. There may have been an AFL paper in Atlanta, but it did not figure much. Although labor had no support in the press, the reports of the hearings were fairly objective.

There was no organized opposition to what we were doing in the various towns, other than from the parties involved in the case. The labor movement had not reached a potency where it was necessary to organize counter-organizations. Labor lacked any power outside the large cities; a handful of people–the mill (which could hand out jobs), the bank, and maybe the stores–completely dominated, largely because of their economic position. I suppose the major organization in most of these places was the church. It was an amorphous, fluid, uncrystallized situation, and very gloomy in the small town areas.

The paternalistic philosophy prevalent in that area did not recognize any possible place for labor organization and opponents were willing to use violence to prevent it. How those episodes were arranged, I do not know, nor who the people were, nor what relation they had to the mills, but vigilante groups turned back organizers, or kidnapped them, or beat them up. There seemed to be no solution outside the major cities.

Racial issues were surprisingly absent in our work. I was shocked when I first arrived in the South at the obvious signs of racial discrimination: waiting rooms, drinking fountains, toilet facilities—segregated for colored and white. Negroes were not allowed to work in any of the industries I dealt with except as loaders or unloaders outside the plant; even the janitors were white. Negroes also were excluded from the steel mills and rubber plants, but not from the coal mines. I understand that even at that time the United Mine Workers had a desegregated local in Alabama. I do not remember discussing the race problem with the union leaders except on one occasion with Googe; we discussed the situation in the United Mine Workers, which he approved and supported. Overwhelmed with other issues, the unions were not thinking about creating employment for Negroes in the plants.

I was fascinated by this experience in the South. I used to be quite nervous during many of those arguments, but once I became immersed the strain would tend to disappear and I would get a kick from matching wits, trying to develop a record, out-thinking the other lawyers and witnesses. I look back on it as one of the most significant periods in my whole career, partly because I was engaged in dramatic legal work such as trials and hearings, but also because I had contact with the grassroots as trends and procedures were developing. It was quite a contrast with the life of a Washington lawyer who is so far removed from the daily concerns of ordinary people. Dealing with this down-to-earth reality was stimulating and enlightening. It also gave me a sense of the labor picture and contact with the actual operations of unions, individual workers, plants, and relationships.

Law in the South was practiced more informally, less from an abstract, intellectual point of view; but the persons involved had closer personal relationships than those found in New York or Washington. I had the impression that politics hovered prominently over the courts. I also had the impression that federal officials had considerable prestige throughout the South. Federal officials were outside this network of personal relationships. They dealt with somewhat different problems than arise in state courts and had more public prestige.

My experience in the South gave me a sense of how the National Labor Relations Act operated and the importance of swift decisions. In handling certain legal issues I had a more finely tuned knowledge of the practical situation, which enabled me to weigh the advantages and disadvantages of various outcomes and translate the intent of the act into concrete terms more effectively than could Frederick Wood, for example, a Wall Street lawyer who had never immersed himself in the nitty-gritty. For example, our main legal argument on the injunction motion in the Gate City Cotton Mill case in federal court was that one could not enjoin the operations of the NLRB or raise the constitutional issues except by going through the procedure established by the statute, and then raising it in accordance with the statutory method for raising legal questions. In other words, it was necessary to exhaust administrative remedies before bringing matters into court. The company argument was that it would suffer irreparable injury if it were forced to go through elections, hearings, and procedures, and that therefore it should be allowed to attack the issues right away. My argument was strengthened because I could bring my firsthand experience in the South to bear on the issue of whether the company was suffering irreparable harm. As a matter of fact, I used the episode of Curtis at the Dalton plant as an argument, stretching the facts somewhat. Section 12 of the National Labor Relations Act stated that it was a crime, subject to criminal prosecution, for anyone to interfere with agents of the NLRB in the performance of their function. The company made a major issue out of this Section 12, arguing, "Look, we're subject to criminal prosecution here if we don't hold this election, or if we should interfere with the operation of the board's agents in any way." Our argument was that the company was suffering no criminal penalty, and would suffer no penalty at all, until they had gone through the procedure, so the usual rules about going through the procedure before raising the issue should apply. The judge at first seemed concerned that the company might be subject to criminal prosecution before the proceedings. In explaining to him what Section 12 meant, I said, "So far as I know it has been invoked in only one case." The judge pricked up his ears and then I told the story about Curtis entering the plant at Dalton and facing a man with a gun, then being escorted out with a gun at his back. I said, "Curtis called me on the phone and asked me what to do. I replied, 'You go right back in there. You're fully protected by Section 12.'" The judge was very much amused at my story: it illustrated my point that Section 12 was meant for extraordinary circumstances like that, so it was not realistic for the company to claim they were subject to criminal prosecution if they behaved reasonably. So my grounding in what the act was meant to do and how it operated in practice was extremely helpful to me in arguments that appeared to be legal technicalities. I used this grounding repeatedly in connection with NLRB issues and later with OPA issues.

# 4

# THE CONSTITUTIONAL ISSUE COMES TO A HEAD

*FDR tries to pack the Court...but then the Supreme Court decides.*

Following completion of my mission as regional representative of the NLRB in the South, I returned to Washington, to the headquarters of the [new] National Labor Relations Board, in February 1936. My main task was to assist on the cases testing the constitutionality of the National Labor Relations Act.

## PREPARING TEST CASES FOR NLRB HEARINGS

Pursuing the basic strategy of raising first an issue in transportation, then in a large manufacturing concern, and then others, the board had deliberately held its first hearing in a case concerning the Pennsylvania Greyhound Lines, an interstate transportation company. In fact, the record shows that the union filed its charge with the NLRB on October 8, 1935, and the board issued its complaint the next day. Under ordinary circumstances the staff would have taken considerable time to prepare the complaint, conduct an investigation, and attempt settlement. But in this test case the board was aware of the alleged unfair labor practice before the charge was filed, had already investigated, and so the filing of the charge was merely a formality. Although our standard procedure was to attempt to settle cases, we made no attempt in this deliberately selected test case. Another unusual factor was that the board held the hearing itself. Under normal circumstances, trial examiners appointed by the board conducted the hearings. Based on the trial examiner's intermediate report the board prepared the findings of fact and a decision. But the board conducted this hearing itself for the sake of speed and in order to learn what kind of issues would arise and gain a general sense of the nature of such hearings. The board's decision, issued in the first part of December 1935, found that the evidence sustained the allegations of unfair labor practices. So the first case was then ready for court action.

Another early transportation case involved the Delaware-New Jersey Ferry Company. Since the company transported passengers between points in Delaware and New Jersey, the case clearly raised interstate commerce issues. In the event that something went wrong with the Pennsylvania Greyhound case, another case would be standing by to test the validity of the act in a situation that was definitely a case of interstate transportation. A trial examiner conducted the ferry case and the board rendered a decision at a very early date, making it available for a test case. As events turned out, it was not needed as a test case, so it was not brought to court decision, but was settled in another manner.

The major case for the next stage in the strategy, namely, a large industrial corporation with ramifications in many states, started out to be the Fruehauf Trailer case. The Fruehauf Trailer Manufacturing Company produced trailers that were attached to trucks. It had a large business and was closely integrated with the whole automobile and truck industry. Here again the board held the hearing itself. As I have indicated, the board could control the strategy of the test cases because it had the latitude to decide when to bring the proceeding, when to make its decision, and to some extent when to take the case into court. The plan was to have the Pennsylvania Greyhound case precede the others so a court decision would be rendered there first, and to bring the manufacturing case along somewhat later. So there was not as much of a rush about the Fruehauf case, but it was to be prepared as the leading case to come along after the Greyhound case had been decided. The board's hearing was held in November 1935, and the decision came later in December, after the Greyhound case. We did not appeal to the circuit court until after the Greyhound case had been in court for a while.

### The NLRB v. Jones & Laughlin Steel Company
Subsequently, another case arose that looked more promising than the Fruehauf case. The Jones & Laughlin Steel Company case was better because it was a substantially larger concern and the ramifications of the steel industry were even more interstate in character than the truck–trailer industry. The case centered around the discharge of about a dozen employees who had been active leaders in the union. (Of course, in each case the board had to use a situation in which the unfair labor practices had occurred after the act was passed. It had to have made an investigation and determined that there was substance to the charges that unfair labor practices had taken place.) The Jones & Laughlin case was not called to the board's attention until some time in December 1935, when it came to the notice of the board through a report from one of the regional offices. The board realized that it was an important case and decided to bring it along after the Greyhound case and in tandem with the Fruehauf case as the leading case to test the manufacturing point. So the board took the case over from the regional office. Normally, the whole matter would have been handled by the regional office through the hearing stage.

Consequently, the board issued the complaint in January 1936, and early in March conducted the hearing in Pennsylvania where the main Jones & Laughlin plant was located. The associate general counsel of the board, Robert Watts, presented the material dealing with the interstate operations of the company, as well as the material dealing with the unfair labor practices. The record came to Washington for consideration and decision by the board.

It was then decided that it would be well to include in the record of this case as much material as possible dealing with the economic issues underlying the constitutional problem. As I have mentioned, our basic constitutional argument was to be that labor disputes were caused mainly by controversies over recognition of the union as the collective bargaining agent, or the discharge of union leaders, or the struggles of the union to exist, and that the act prohibiting these unfair labor practices would thereby eliminate the causes of a substantial amount of industrial unrest, which in turn would promote the free flow of interstate commerce.

Following the precedent of the Brandeis brief, we wanted a substantial amount of economic, statistical, and other material substantiating our argument. The Brandeis brief had used the material simply in the brief as presented to the court. We decided to extend the concept of the Brandeis brief by putting this material into the record so that there would be no question about the court having taken judicial notice of it. We therefore decided to reopen the hearing before the NLRB in Washington to present this material. I was designated as the attorney to collect the material and another attorney, Al Wirin, assisted me. We collected a lot of statistical material, but more important, we interviewed and prepared as witnesses a number of experts on this topic.

### The NLRB Hearing

The board's hearing lasted for four or five days in the beginning of April 1936. Confident that the act was unconstitutional, Jones & Laughlin refused to participate in the hearing, although the company did have its lawyers sitting in the room as observers. The only official representative of the parties, aside from the board's representative, was Edmund Toland, who was representing the company unions. However, he did nothing more than sit at the hearing. He made no objections and did not participate actively, except incidentally as certain facts with respect to the unfair labor practices came up at this hearing. (Toland was later appointed chief counsel of the Smith Committee when it began investigating the NLRB; see Chapter 6.) We were grateful to be able to present our testimony not only without objections, but without interruption of any kind. Whatever we wished to put in the record could go in. We had the field to ourselves and could relax. No struggles between lawyers occurred and the witnesses were permitted to say what they had in mind. The only restriction was the board's view of what might be relevant.

A major witness we called was Edward Berman, the leading authority in the country at that time on the government's role in labor disputes. He was an associate professor of economics at the University of Illinois. His book, *Labor Disputes and the President of the United States,* was a history of the various incidents in which the federal government had intervened in labor disputes, primarily through the use of troops. Our point was that labor disputes did create problems of national concern, including problems that directly affected interstate commerce, and that the federal government had in the past frequently intervened. The National Labor Relations Act followed this precedent, although a different method of intervention was employed, in that the act attempted to eliminate the *causes* of the disputes after they had occurred.

We also called Hugh Kerwin, who was then chief of the conciliation service in the federal government. Professor Sumner Shlichter of Harvard, who had been a member of the committee of the Twentieth Century Fund, which had made a special study of labor problems, also testified. His book, *Labor and the Government,* was a history and discussion of the role that the government had played in labor disputes. We also called William Leiserson, chairman of the National Mediation Board, which administered the somewhat similar provisions of the Railway Labor Act. He testified generally on the role that the government played in labor disputes and the extent to which the prevention of unfair labor practices would stop disputes from arising.

Along the same lines, we called Miss Charlotte Carr, an expert on labor problems who had been an assistant to Governor Gifford Pinchot and was familiar with the role of the Pennsylvania coal and iron police in the labor disputes in Pennsylvania, mainly in the 1920s. John A. Fitch, John Lapp, Otto Beyer, and a number of other experts in the labor field were called. All testified as to the causes of labor disputes and the extent to which they interrupted interstate commerce.

We also had witnesses dealing specifically with the steel industry. The first hearing had put into the record material dealing with the Jones & Laughlin Steel Company and had established in great detail the movement of raw materials into the major plant at Aliquippa, Pennsylvania, from various sections of the country, and the movement of products from the plant into other states. This material had covered the participation by Jones & Laughlin in activity clearly affecting interstate commerce. To establish the fact that the steel industry as a whole had numerous interstate ramifications, we had Professor Abraham Berglund (who had prepared a study of the economics of the steel industry) testify generally as to the economic structure and the interstate ramifications of the steel industry. We called Heber Blankenhorn who had prepared much of the Interchurch World Movement report on the steel strike of 1919. He testified on the causes of the steel strike of 1919, demonstrating that the strike had arisen from efforts of the company to destroy a union. This tied in closely with our case where we had a steel company attempting to prevent the union from organizing. Blankenhorn also showed in great detail how the strike had interrupted the flow of goods across state lines.

Finally, we called David Saposs, who was the head of the economic division of the NLRB, to put into evidence reams of statistical material from the Bureau of Labor Statistics showing the number of strikes occurring each year, the number of employees involved, and the causes of the strike.

In this way we included in the record without contradiction an enormous amount of factual material establishing the foundation of our legal argument. How much this material influenced the Supreme Court in the final decision cannot be determined, but it certainly was helpful. Of course, many other factors came into play at the time of the Supreme Court's decision.

The board issued its decision in the Jones & Laughlin Steel Company case on April 9, 1936, the day after we had finished the presentation of this economic material. Actually, the board had prepared the decision based on the first hearing while we were preparing this economic hearing. The board decided not to include in its decision the material that we were now putting into the record, but simply to have that available for the court proceedings. The case was ready for court action in the early part of April.

## BRINGING TEST CASES TO COURT

### The Pennsylvania Greyhound Case

We had filed the Pennsylvania Greyhound case in the Court of Appeals for the Third Circuit in Philadelphia shortly after the NLRB's decision was issued in December 1935. One of my first assignments on my return from Atlanta was to work on the brief in the court of appeals in that case. It did not take me long because I already had developed a similar argument in the Blue Eagle cases under the NRA. Pressing as hard as we could, we filed the brief early in March 1936 and the case was scheduled for argument in late March.

Charles Fahy, general counsel of the NLRB, argued the case and I attended the argument in Philadelphia with him. The court sat in a large room of the Federal Court House with a great roaring fire in the fireplace at the rear. It was the only time I had seen that in a courtroom. The atmosphere was informal, pleasant, and somewhat relaxed, although the case generated tremendous excitement because it was recognized as being a first case. Considerable newspaper publicity focused on it and quite a crowd, mostly lawyers, gathered in the courtroom to listen to the argument.

The combined ages of the three judges must have made this the oldest bench that ever heard an argument in almost any court in the United States. Judge Joseph Buffington was in his eighties. Judge J. Witaker Thompson and Judge J. Warren Davis were both in their seventies. I believe that the baby of the court was about seventy-five. They were well on their way toward retirement and not as alert as judges should have been in this situation. It seems surprising, even in retrospect, that they had so little awareness of the basic constitutional issues involved.

I remember Fahy's argument. After he had indicated what the issues were and was launching into the basic constitutional argument, a colloquy with the court went something like this: Judge Buffington asked, "Now, what provision of the Constitution are you relying on?"

Fahy replied, "The commerce clause."

Buffington said, "What clause is that?"

Fahy said, "It's Article I, section 8, clause 3 of the Constitution."

There was a long pause while the court found a copy of the Constitution and looked for Article I, section 8, clause 3. Buffington then put his finger on the clause and read it slowly, "Congress shall have the power to regulate commerce with foreign nations and among the several states, and with the Indian tribes." He asked Fahy, "You don't contend that this is a regulation of commerce with foreign nations?"

Fahy answered, "No."

"You don't say that it's a regulation of commerce with the Indian tribes?"

Fahy answered, "No."

Judge Buffington then said, "Well then it must be that you're contending that it's to regulate commerce among the several states."

Fahy replied, "That's exactly it."

You can understand, from that exchange, the level on which the argument was conducted. All the subtleties buzzing in the legal world for several years had not penetrated this courtroom. The court was capable of comprehending only a much more elementary argument. To add to our frustration, the judges had advanced hearing impairments and Fahy was a soft-spoken person anyway. The argument ran through the morning and was to have resumed after the lunch recess, but one of the judges became ill and fainted during the lunch period, so the argument had to be postponed until the next day when he had recovered.

We were discouraged with this reception. We had to bring the proceeding in the circuit where the company did business or where the unfair labor practice occurred. In this case we probably could have brought it somewhere else, but the headquarters of Pennsylvania Greyhound were in Pennsylvania and this was the normal court in which to bring the case. We were not sufficiently familiar with the operations of the Third Circuit at that time to anticipate the frustrating conditions.

The Third Circuit Court upset our test strategy because it did not make any decision in the Pennsylvania Greyhound case. We urged them to make a decision promptly so we could take the case to the Supreme Court and get it on the docket that term before the court adjourned in June. We planned for the Jones & Laughlin and Fruehauf cases to come before the Supreme Court in the fall in the new term so we would have those decisions in late 1936. But we waited days and days, then weeks and weeks, then months and months, and no decision came. The court did not issue a decision until June 1937, *after* the Jones & Laughlin decision in the Supreme Court. Since we were unable to get the Pennsylvania Greyhound case before the Supreme Court, we had to change our strategy.

**The Carter Coal Case**

Meanwhile, the Supreme Court decision in the Carter Coal case came down in April or May, 1936. The Carter Coal case, even more than the Schechter case [which had seen NRA declared unconstitutional, in May 1935], seemed to indicate that the Court would hold the National Labor Relations Act unconstitutional. The case involved the Bituminous Coal Act, which fixed minimum wages and maximum hours for the industry ["a floor under wages, a ceiling over hours"], regulated prices, and also contained provisions protecting collective bargaining that were almost identical with the provisions of the National Labor Relations Act. Although the issues in the coal case did not involve specifically the collective bargaining provisions, they were in the statute that was declared unconstitutional. Furthermore, the Court's decision, which did address itself very specifically to the wage and hours provision of the Bituminous Coal Act, held very definitely that the fixing of wages and hours in the bituminous coal industry was a local matter and that, although it had some repercussions on interstate commerce, nevertheless it always had been a question of manufacturing and remained a local problem. The Court completely refused to consider the ramifications of cutting wages throughout the coal industry.

The argument in the coal case was that as a result of cut-throat competition in cutting wages, the movement of coal across state lines was affected because the lower the wages the more business that mine did, and therefore the coal moved from that mine across state lines rather than from a local mine that had not cut wages. Hence, there was a dislocation of interstate commerce. That and similar arguments were rejected.

The physical interruption by strikes was not presented as an argument in the Carter Coal case. We were making an argument of the same general nature, but not exactly the same argument. Nevertheless, the decision was so sweeping and so clear-cut, since in a local matter with interstate ramifications the Supreme Court chose to disregard the interstate ramifications, that the possibility of the Court upholding the National Labor Relations Act seemed extremely remote.

Virtually every lawyer in Washington who followed the Supreme Court's actions believed that the Carter Coal case foreclosed the constitutionality of the National Labor Relations Act.

**The Injunction Problem**
*Still pending a decision in the Jones & Laughlin case...*

As a result of the Carter Coal decision, the injunction problem worsened. I also did some work on this other major legal problem: resisting industry's efforts to enjoin the NLRB from holding hearings. After the Gate City Cotton Mills first used this maneuver, in an increasing number of cases the company would respond to the board's initial complaint by going to court to obtain an injunction, enjoining the board from holding a hearing, on the ground that the act was unconstitutional.

If this tactic had been adopted earlier and had succeeded a little earlier, the board would not have been able to hold any hearings or bring to the Supreme Court an actual case in which there was testimony about an unfair labor practice as a test case. We would have had to raise the constitutional issue in the injunction proceedings which would have been a much more abstract problem. But fortunately for us, the board had had an opportunity to conduct a number of hearings before injunctions blocked us, and some of the cases were on their way to a court test on the basic issues.

But applications for injunction started almost from the beginning, and kept increasing and getting more successful. For a while we were able to defeat the injunction proceeding. Our argument was that the statute had presented a method of raising the constitutional issues that was exclusive. That is, the statute provided for full review of both the constitutional issues and the issues of a particular case by the court. That method was the only method by which the issues could be raised. One could not enjoin the government from proceeding to hold a hearing, even though constitutional issues were involved. There was no damage done as a result of the hearing to give the court equitable jurisdiction to grant an injunction. We therefore said that the constitutional issues were irrelevant in the injunction cases, but if we lost that argument, we sometimes also argued the constitutional issues. The constitutional issues were not normally decided. All the court needed to decide was whether it should issue an injunction or not, assuming there was some question, as there undoubtedly was, about the constitutional issue. The board tried desperately to defend itself against these injunction proceedings. We persuaded a number of district courts and several of the circuit courts of appeal not to grant the injunctions. But other district courts did grant them. The result of the delay in the appeal, or the affirmance of the injunction by the circuit courts, was that in some parts of the country it was impossible to hold a hearing, because if we scheduled a hearing the company could get an injunction automatically in view of the precedent.

So, by about the middle of 1936 it was almost impossible for the NLRB to hold hearings at all. Sometimes we could get agreement on a union election and in a few cases the court decision was in our favor and it was possible to go ahead with the proceedings. But the harassment of defending against the injunction suits, plus the fact that the courts had ruled against us in a number of areas, meant that the hearings gradually came to almost a complete stop. By the fall of 1936 practically no new hearings were taking place.

### Back to the Jones & Laughlin Case
*I prepare the brief...*

We were waiting for a decision in the Pennsylvania Greyhound case and when it did not happen we decided that we would have to move in another area. The Jones & Laughlin Steel Company case normally would have been filed in the same court as the Greyhound case because the unfair labor practices had occurred in Aliquippa (Pennsylvania) and the main plant and headquarters of the company were there. But we did not want our best case lost in *that* circuit, so we looked around to see where else we could get a court decision. We filed in the Fifth Circuit, which comprises Louisiana and the southeastern states. This court technically had jurisdiction because the Jones & Laughlin Steel Company had a warehouse in New Orleans from which they distributed steel products and did a little bit of fabricating.

We had other choices because the company did business in other places, but the Fifth Circuit had decided the Texas & New Orleans Case upholding the validity of the Railway Labor Act. That was perhaps the leading decision in support of our position. Although it referred to the Railway Labor Act, the opinion seemed to be stated in a sufficiently sympathetic manner that we thought the court would look with some favor upon the National Labor Relations Act.

I was assigned the preparation of the brief. I used substantial portions of the economic material we had put into the record and developed in the fullest detail so far the constitutional argument. The oral argument was set for May. It was finally decided that I would argue the case. Fahy, the General Counsel, assigned me despite the skepticism of some members who thought I was too young or inexperienced. The board asked me to give a summary of how I intended to argue the case. So I attended a board meeting and rehearsed my argument before the board, Fahy, and Associate General Counsel Watts. I experienced more stress about the rehearsal than the actual argument. Each one wanted his ideas made available to the court. So we discussed my presentation. As I remember, the main thing that they induced me to change was my pronunciation from "New Orleens" to "New Orlins," which is how the natives say it.

I went to New Orleans and argued the case. The court listened with great interest and spent a great deal of time questioning me. In fact, I spent most of my time answering questions of the court. It was a rather lively argument. They seemed reasonably sympathetic, or at least I was convinced that they understood what the argument was about. It was a much different experience than that in the Third Circuit.

I did not have any real hope of winning. While it was not that consequential, because the Supreme Court ultimately would decide, it would have been heartening to have a favorable decision. However, the Carter Coal case was very difficult to distinguish, particularly for a lower court. To persuade a lower court that our case was different from what the Supreme Court had declared just a few weeks earlier in the Carter Coal case was almost impossible. My argument on the Carter Coal case was that the collective bargaining provisions had not been directly involved, that they were only incidental to the wage and hour provisions in that legislation, and that the Supreme Court had not really considered the line of argument that we were presenting. However, the Fifth Circuit Court was skeptical about that, because the main thing that the Carter Coal case had hammered home was that the regulation of labor relations was a local matter.

I returned to Washington. A month or so later the court, without even writing an opinion, decided against us. It was a *per curiam* decision, in which they stated the facts briefly, quoted at length from the Carter Coal case, and ruled that that case controlled this one. We were then ready to appeal to the Supreme Court with Jones & Laughlin.

## WERE THE NLRB'S DAYS NUMBERED?
*I transfer briefly to the Social Security Administration, but follow the National Labor Relations Act test cases through to their sweeping conclusion...*

At this point I decided to transfer to the Social Security Board. Governor Winant, who was then chairman of the Social Security Board, had been urging me for some months to join his staff. I preferred to stay with the NLRB, but when the Carter Coal case came down I (along with most of the rest of the lawyers in Washington) thought that the decision so clearly covered the National Labor Relations Act, and that it was so unlikely that the National Labor Relations Act would be sustained, that I might as well assist with establishing Social Security, as that agency had only recently been established. So, about August 1936, I transferred to the Social Security Board without too much of a guilty conscience. By that time the NLRB's functions were almost entirely suspended because of the aforementioned injunction proceedings. The job remaining was the presentation to the Supreme Court of cases testing constitutionality. On that I was to be available to render whatever assistance I could.

The NLRB members and staff felt discouraged, but they had by no means given up. The lawyers recognized that the outcome was uncertain until the issue was officially decided, and other factors beside the legal doctrine might affect the situation. But only Charles Fahy consistently refused to concede that the matter was, in terms of legal doctrine, decided. He could not be persuaded of that, and that was one reason that he was as successful as he was as the NLRB's general counsel. He refused to admit to himself or anyone else that the Carter Coal case controlled the problem. This was more an emotional reaction than a rational assessment. But except for Fahy, the general view was that, legally, the matter was virtually closed.

Outside the NLRB people also believed that the Carter Coal case definitely meant that the board was unconstitutional. So when John Carmody resigned from the NLRB at about this time, it became almost impossible to find a successor. No one was interested in the job. It was under these circumstances that Donald Wakefield Smith was appointed as the third member of the board. He had neither the background, nor the ability, nor the stature for such a position. He normally would have been appointed to a subordinate job in the Department of Labor, but no one of any capacity would take the opening on the NLRB. His appointment, which was so contrary to the high character of the board up to that point, illustrated the extent to which the community of Washington surmised that the board's days were numbered.

To my knowledge, the Roosevelt administration at that time was undertaking no effort at further legislation to protect labor, should the NLRB be declared unconstitutional. We believed that there was a good chance that the act would be sustained as to interstate transportation and therefore in that narrow area the board would continue. With that limited mandate we contemplated gradually expanding case by case into other areas.

### The La Follette Committee
*What you may find when you raid wastebaskets*

Many of the board's staff turned their attention in another direction: the La Follette Committee. It appears that some of the major tacticians around Washington—although I'm not sure who they were—came to the conclusion that in this period of stress, when the board was tied up with injunctions and its constitutionality was in doubt, the next move should be a congressional investigation. This was similar to the situation in 1934, when Public Resolution No. 44 was in effect, a period of suspension on legislation protecting collective bargaining. There was no guarantee that the way would be clear for the government to move ahead in terms of legislative protections as it had before. Some agitational activity might be useful to maintain a positive focus on the issue; a legislative investigation would supply this and perhaps generate favorable public opinion that would help the board become established on a legal basis. The La Follette Committee got underway in the early part of 1936. By the middle of 1936 (following the Carter Coal decision) the board's staff had more free time than they knew what to do with. The available tasks were the constitutional cases, on which a relatively few people could work, and the remnants of fighting the injunction cases, which also could use only a few people. Since the La Follette Committee did not have much money, they turned to the board as a source of manpower, as was customary for congressional committees at the time.

It was a lively period. Robert Watts, Fahy's assistant, who was less the intellectual type and more the trial lawyer type (and hence was not deeply involved in the constitutional problems any more since they were in the appellate stages) worked with the La Follette Committee. It was he who conceived the idea of obtaining the contents of the wastepaper baskets of the various agencies that supplied strikebreakers. The committee served a subpoena on one of the leading agencies to have them produce all their material dealing with strikes and "oppressive labor practices," which is the term that was used. Watts calculated that this would frighten everybody else into destroying records. So he devised an elaborate plot with the board's regional offices whereby they would make an agreement with the janitors to collect the contents of the wastepaper baskets of these agencies two or three days following the announcement of this subpoena. As I look back on it, I am concerned about the legality and ethics of this scheme, but at the time it was very effective because the wastepaper baskets provided a tremendous amount of material that had been destroyed, most of it torn into pieces. For days and days members of our clerical staff who had nothing else to do were patching these pieces together. A number of the retrieved documents were used in the committee hearings and provided important material. That event reflects the atmosphere of that period.

To some extent the board enlisted the labor organizations on its side. The labor leadership understood that there would have to be a constitutional decision before the board could really proceed. They were aware of the problem and generally sympathetic. But the labor movement as a whole could not understand the legal technicalities, delays, injunctions, the fact that nothing ever happened, and particularly that the board could issue decisions and they were not complied with. The membership were thoroughly mystified. To them, a law was a law. The labor movement was definitely restless and approaching the point of dismissing the NLRB as useless and a fake.

Labor during this period was organizing rapidly. The movement led by the CIO–namely, a vigorous effort to organize the mass production industries and a tremendous response by the workers in those industries–was getting underway all through 1936. Unions in the steel industry, rubber industry, automobiles, coal, and all the major industries where there had been little or no organization before, were beginning to boom. The employers were resisting strongly. The National Labor Relations Act, which theoretically would have mediated this situation, was for practical purposes in abeyance (following the Carter Coal case in the spring of 1936). The outcome was an increasing number of strikes–and on the whole fairly bitter strikes. This was the beginning of the sit-down strike period, which developed through the fall of 1936 and reached a crisis point in the spring of 1937, when the celebrated automobile industry sit-down strike occurred at a General Motors assembly plant in Flint, Michigan. The labor situation was in a state of uncertainty. Violence was common. Many people were frightened as to how far it was going and where it might end.

The presidential election in the fall of 1936 returned the New Deal to Washington with an overwhelming mandate. This was the election in which only Maine and Vermont went Republican. This added to the rising spirit and backing that labor had. The context of these momentous events undoubtedly affected the Supreme Court as much as anything else.

## Roosevelt's Court-Packing Plan

In January or February 1937 President Roosevelt announced his court-packing plan. It was a surprise to everyone. The story in Washington was that he had not discussed it with his cabinet and that only the attorney general, Tom Corcoran, Ben Cohen, and a few intimate friends of the president were aware that he was about to announce it. The plan apparently was devised by Tom Corcoran, Ben Cohen, and the attorney general.

The reaction of many of us New Deal lawyers at the time was two-fold. First, we felt that the plan could not have been more insulting in its details if that had been the total objective. The proposal was that any federal judge who had reached the age of seventy and had been on the bench for ten years could retire, and that if he did not retire the president would appoint another judge as a counterpart to help him make decisions. Second, many of us believed that a constitutional amendment was a better way to obtain the same goal. The success of the 1936 election should be crystallized and the momentum continued around an attempt to obtain a constitutional amendment. Until the Carter Coal case, I had hoped that the Supreme Court might be persuaded to adjust its decisions so as to uphold the basic elements of the New Deal legislation. But the Carter Coal case convinced me that that expectation was unrealistic. The Supreme Court would continue its opposition; it was necessary to do something and it was better to act on a clear-cut basis, as by a constitutional amendment. The proposal I had in mind was one that primarily expanded the powers of the federal government under the commerce clause. There were several other proposals for a constitutional amendment at the time that were much more far-reaching. One was that the Supreme Court be denied power to pass on the constitutionality of any federal legislation. There was a modification of that, to the effect that the Supreme Court could deal only with subjects involving civil liberties and the protections under the Bill of Rights. Another proposal required that a declaration of unconstitutionality be by a two-thirds vote. No consensus jelled on which constitutional amendment to advance. But no one in the Roosevelt administration supported this solution, regardless of the form of the amendment.

Of course, among the New Deal lawyers there was great dissatisfaction with the Supreme Court. Lawyers outside the government who represented business interests thoroughly supported the Supreme Court and considered it the last bastion against the radical New Deal. However, liberal lawyers within the government and many enlightened conservative lawyers, although I did not meet many of those, regarded the Supreme Court as completely wrong in its approach to these problems and anticipated some kind of explosion.

I remember discussing this with Justice Benjamin Cardozo once. The law clerk to Justice Cardozo lived in our house and Cardozo used to come for dinner fairly frequently. Although we never discussed pending cases, and barely discussed cases that had been decided, we did discuss the general problem. I expressed the view of many people at the time when I suggested to Cardozo that the Supreme Court had put itself in a hopeless position and probably had damaged its prestige for many years to come. About this time Edward Corwin published a book called *The Twilight of the Supreme Court*, a title suggested to Corwin by Charles Clark (dean of Yale Law School), expressing the attitude that many of us held then. Our idea was that the Supreme Court had to adjust to the basic forces moving throughout the nation, particularly as evidenced in the 1936 election, and if it tried to resist, it would in one way or another be swamped and lose its effectiveness. The Supreme Court did not have the power, political backing, or prestige to survive as an obstacle to these irresistible social forces. Cardozo did not dispute that. He was quite cautious in the conversation, but I gathered that he accepted our point of view that the Supreme Court was bent on suicide if it continued its present policies.

The entire country had to be sold on the court-packing plan in order to obtain the necessary legislation. That task was undertaken largely by Tom Corcoran and Ben Cohen, who prepared most of the materials and assembled witnesses to testify before congressional committees.

Tom Corcoran was eager to have the National Lawyers Guild, which had just been formed, express a favorable opinion on the plan. Since the American Bar Association was vehemently opposed, Corcoran wanted some organization of lawyers to lend its support. The National Lawyers Guild, formed precisely because many lawyers opposed the American Bar Association point of view, was the logical association to support the president on New Deal legislation and on legal issues arising out of the New Deal. Robert W. Kenny, later Attorney General of California and one of the leading figures in the Guild, testified on behalf of the Guild in support of the plan. A few other lawyers testified in support to the plan, but not many. Charles Clark testified in support, as did Henry Edgerton of Cornell. Those were the leading figures from the legal profession who supported the president. Corcoran had to scratch around to find as much legal support as he did. I had nothing to do with the fight over the court plan; I simply watched it from the sidelines.

## THE SUPREME COURT DECIDES
*The fate of the National Labor Relations Act is decided*

It was in this atmosphere [early in the new year following Roosevelt's triumphant reelection in 1936] that the Supreme Court considered the cases raising the constitutional issues. Five NLRB cases reached the Supreme Court at the same time:

- The Washington-Maryland Bus Company case involving the transportation of passengers from the District of Columbia to another state, and therefore in a legal sense an interstate

84

transportation case. This had been filed as a substitute for the Greyhound case. The board had won in the Court of Appeals for the District of Columbia.
- The Jones & Laughlin Steel Company case.
- The Fruehauf Trailer case, which had also been decided in the Sixth Circuit. As in Jones & Laughlin, the court had simply issued a *per curiam* opinion, without a formal opinion by any member of the court, holding that the statute was unconstitutional.
- The Friedman-Harry Marks Company case, concerning a small garment manufacturing firm with about 700-800 employees. This case had moved faster than expected and had been decided by the Fourth Circuit Court, against the NLRB.
- The Associated Press case, which the NLRB had won in the Second Circuit.

All five cases were argued before the Supreme Court in February 1937. The argument for the board's position was made by Stanley Reed, who was then Solicitor General; Charles Wyzanski, who was then in the Solicitor General's office, representing the Department of Justice; Warren Madden, chairman of the NLRB; and Charles Fahy, general counsel of the NLRB. Wyzanski and Fahy carried the main burden of the argument. Reed and Madden also participated extensively, but on issues that were somewhat broader than the specific issues on which the Supreme Court would decide the case. The main position of the board was that labor disputes interrupted production and hence interstate commerce. The government also put considerable stress upon the stream of commerce theory, as set forth in *Stafford v. Wallace*. The strike theory would apply equally well whether there was a stream of commerce flowing from one state into a central point and then out again, as in *Stafford v. Wallace*, or whether the stream of commerce began in the state and simply flowed out, or whether it came into the state and never went out. But the government was desperately trying to provide a theory that the Supreme Court could rely upon without accepting the strike theory. A good deal of the argument also concerned the Schechter (May 1935) and Carter Coal (May 1936) cases, and the attempt to show how the five NLRB cases could be distinguished from them.

The justices, who were much interested in the argument, asked a great many questions, and there was considerable colloquy between the justices and counsel throughout. The argument lasted two days, as I remember, or even part of a third day. It was hard to tell from the attitude of the justices how they would decide. We were left quite up in the air as to what the outcome would be. We did have a definite sense that some of the members of the Court were looking for a method of deciding the cases that would uphold the act at least in part. But it was impossible to predict from the way the justices expressed themselves as to what they would do.

The attorney representing the Washington-Maryland Bus Company had a difficult task because of the Texas & New Orleans decision. We did expect to win at least the bus case, because the justices did not seem sympathetic to the argument that the labor relations of an interstate transportation company did not relate to interstate commerce. In other words, there was no indication that they would repudiate the Texas & New Orleans case. John W. Davis argued the Associated Press case. He was excellent in presenting factual material, but he got into hot water when he broached the First Amendment. He argued that the Associated Press, as an organization of newspapers, was protected by the First Amendment from government regulation of the sort that the National Labor Relations Act involved. That was a desperate argument to make, because it would have meant that newspapers were not subject to wage and hour legislation, or child labor legislation, or anything of the sort. He did not get very far with it.

The main interest in the argument was over the three manufacturing cases. The main argument for the manufacturing companies was conducted by Earl F. Reed of Pittsburgh, who was counsel for the Jones & Laughlin Steel Company. The argument was presented adequately but not particularly brilliantly by counsel for the companies. They did not have to do much as they were representing a point of view that had been clearly expressed in the Schechter and Carter Coal cases. The burden was on the government to convince the Court otherwise. Thus many fewer questions were addressed to counsel, with the justices seeking most of their enlightenment from the government and the counsel for the companies playing a secondary role.

The decision came down on April 12, 1937. Since the presentation of the cases before the Court in February, tension had mounted. The number of strikes had increased. The automobile industry was in the midst of the famous sit-down strikes. The political battle over the court plan was being waged furiously.

**The Decision: The National Labor Relations Act**

I was in court on the day the decisions came down and heard Hughes deliver his opinion orally. I was astonished when Hughes thundered out his famous opinion with an air of complete conviction, as if the outcome had never been in doubt. An amazing performance! He stated his position so firmly that no one would have thought that there could have been any question as to what the law on the subject had been. It sounded as if he were simply stating elementary principles that always had been recognized. Actually, the decision was a spectacular reversal of direction for the Supreme Court. Hughes used the Schechter case in support of many of the general principles that he invoked, which were preliminary to the more precise issues on which the case turned. Turning to the precise issues, he simply recited the facts of the Schechter case and said it was not applicable in these cases. As I recall, he mentioned the Carter case only to distinguish it and say that it was not applicable. Making no effort at any kind of subtle distinction, he simply waved the Schechter and Carter cases aside.

He then went on to report the Supreme Court's historic 5 to 4 decision upholding the National Labor Relations Act and upholding the NLRB on all the manufacturing cases. The implications were far reaching, because it opened the way for federal regulation of manufacturing and greatly extended the scope of the commerce power. In legal terms, *The NLRB v. Jones & Laughlin Steel Company* has proven to be a major case in the development of the commerce power.

Even more important, the decisions had widespread political implications. The court-packing plan no longer was necessary. By making clear the possibility of effective government protection of the right to organize, and transforming labor's struggle from organizing the basic industries to one over working conditions, wages and hours, and other specific issues in the context of a recognized right to organize, an entirely new phase of labor relations was initiated. (I do not mean to say that this transformation occurred immediately as a result of the decision. Rather, over a period of time it became clear that this was the result of the Supreme Court's decision.)

As it turns out, the Court had intimated a change in position two weeks before the NLRB decisions, with a decision reversing themselves on state minimum wage legislation and upholding the New York State minimum wage law. Although the commerce issue was not raised, because state legislation was involved, two key members of the Court, Hughes and Roberts, indicated a different approach toward New Deal social legislation, and the Supreme Court hinted at more sympathy than had been evident in prior decisions. Nevertheless, we were tremendously surprised when the decisions were announced. Lawyers around Washington who followed the work of the Supreme Court concluded that the justices definitely had reversed themselves as a means of protecting the Court from the effects of the court plan and adjusting the Court's position to New Deal developments.

After the Jones & Laughlin decision, the NLRB operated from a position of strength. Henceforth industrial plants were clearly to be subject to the provisions of the act. Since the constitutional issues had been settled, all the injunction suits based on those issues were nullified and not much basis remained for granting injunctions against hearings by the board. A company might use an injunction suit to stop NLRB hearings where they had other questions of a constitutional or statutory nature, but the *Myers v. Bethlehem Shipbuilding Corporation* decision the following year (1938) settled the matter by prohibiting courts from granting injunctions even where constitutional issues were raised. Employers were required to raise all issues, including constitutional issues, by going through the administrative proceeding of the board before raising the issues in court. They could not challenge any issue by an injunction proceeding to prevent the board from holding a hearing. From that time on the use of the injunction completely disappeared.

The Pennsylvania Greyhound case was decided two months later, in June 1937, by the Third Circuit Court of Appeals, against the NLRB, not on the constitutional issues but on the grounds that the board had not given notice to the company-dominated union that was involved in the case. Subsequently, the Supreme Court reversed the Third Circuit on this point.

Some constitutional questions remained, but they were decided shortly afterwards. For instance, the Santa Cruz case, decided in 1938, settled the problem of whether the act applied to a situation where the raw materials originated in the state of manufacture and the products were then shipped out of the state. The Santa Cruz Company canned fruits and vegetables grown in California and shipped 38 percent of the product outside the state. The Court upheld the application of the act in that situation, thus making clear that a stream of commerce flowing into the state and then out again was not necessary. Similarly, in another case the Court held that goods brought into the state, worked on, and sold within the state, even if the company that did the work had no transactions outside the state, were still under the provisions of the act. Gradually, even small amounts of commerce between the states were held to be under the jurisdiction of the act, so that the NLRB eventually extended its purview over virtually every area of industry, and those aspects of the constitutional issues on the commerce power not decided by the Jones & Laughlin decision were rather quickly resolved.

The Jones & Laughlin decision marked the end of an era for the NLRB and a turning point in the board's history. The primary task now became enforcing the rights guaranteed by the statute.

# 5

# THE RENEWED, EXPANDED NLRB

*The NLRB rewrites the rules of the American workplace.*

I left the Social Security Administration after only a brief stint and returned in September 1937 to the NLRB, which had been regalvanized by the Supreme Court's historic decision upholding the constitutionality of the National Labor Relations Act. Since the Jones & Laughlin Steel Company decision in April, a great many cases had accumulated and the board was swamped with work. When I joined in September the board still was in the process of building its organization to handle its new mandate, and as a result I participated in the expansion of the renewed NLRB.

## THE COURT REVIEW SECTION AND THE REVIEW DIVISION
*The NLRB was back in business, and I head a division*

### NLRB Staff
I returned to the board in September 1937, as head of the Court Review Section, the legal staff which handled the cases in the circuit courts of appeal. I had a staff of about six lawyers who prepared briefs in these cases. Argument was spread over a wider group; in addition to members of my section, Charles Fahy and Robert Watts argued cases, and I myself argued a number of cases in the circuit courts, including the Third, Fourth, and Seventh Circuits.

Before describing the components of the NLRB where I worked, I will mention the other important sections. My boss when I ran the Review Division was Charles Fahy, head of the General Counsel's Office. A lawyer who had practiced for his health in Arizona, Fahy had recently returned to Washington as head of the Petroleum Administrative Board in the Department of the Interior under Ickes during the NRA period. He was appointed General Counsel of the NLRB shortly after the board was established in 1935. He had a keen and analytical mind, but did not have broad interests; he was more the narrow lawyer type than the lawyer who was interested in the broad economic, social and political aspects of the law. He was a person of strong conviction, very loyal to his associates and demanding loyalty from them. (He never quite forgave me for leaving the original NLRB to work at Social Security.) Born in Rome, Georgia, he resented any criticism of the South very strongly. Although he intellectually accepted the arguments against racial discrimination, he could not face the issues that arose out of the Negro problem in the South except on an emotional basis. You could feel his tension with respect to southern attitudes and activities. He also was extremely emotional in regard to communism and radical activity. Fahy had a jesuitical mind in many ways. He could convince himself of his position and then argue most ingeniously and forcefully, with complete inability to see the other side of the case. Of great value to him in court, that quality made it somewhat difficult to work with him at times. On the whole he did an excellent job. He was highly respected and his judgment valued by the board's staff. He was not a keen student of labor relations, but he was a keen student of law and the reaction of the courts to the situation. He made a very important contribution.

The associate general counsel, Robert Watts, was in charge of all of the General Counsel's Office except for the Review Division. He was a good technical lawyer, but with little interest or principles outside the law. He had no understanding of or sympathy for the labor problem. His contribution was entirely in the field of legal technicalities in the narrow aspects of a case. A somewhat remote technician, older than most of us and about the same age as Fahy, he was in no sense one of the New Deal group on the board's staff. He was not as able as Fahy, but he handled himself quite well and was competent in litigation.

The Legal Division included mostly people of considerable ability. Aside from the Review Division and the Court Review Division where I worked, a major section was the Trial Examiner's Section, headed by George Pratt, a lawyer of considerable ability. There was also a small section whose job it was to obtain compliance with the board's decisions.

The agency had an Information Division, which was not too active in attempting to sell the board but confined itself mostly to publicizing the board's decisions.

Finally, there was the Economics Division headed by David Saposs, who had written extensively on labor problems. In the past he had been somewhat of a radical and a Socialist and had written a number of books in that field. He may have been the cause of the stories about Communists on the staff. A congressman testified before the Smith Committee that Saposs had told him that there were a number of people on the staff who were Communists, or who were following the Communist Party line. He mentioned me as one who had followed the Communist Party line. Saposs denied having stated this, but there was some indication that Saposs had sent material to people outside NLRB critical of the board's operations. Ironically, the first victim of the attack on the board was Saposs, who was forced off the NLRB by the House Appropriations Committee, which apparently thought that he was a serious radical (as he had been in his early days, but was no longer). They attached a rider to the Appropriations Act in 1938 saying that no money should be expended in appropriations to the Economics Division. It was intended that the board construe this as a mandate to discharge Saposs. The board defended him and abolished the Economics Division while retaining Saposs and some of his staff as economic consultants, technically complying with the Appropriations Committee rider. The following year when the Appropriations Committee passed a further rider stating in effect that no money could be used for purposes of paying economic consultants, the board had no choice but to let Saposs go.

I did not stay with the Court Review Section for more than a few months. In November or December of 1937 the secretary of the board, Benedict Wolf, left. Nathan Witt, who was then in charge of the Review Division, was appointed secretary of the board. I became assistant general counsel in charge of the Review Division. The rest of my work with the board was as head of the Review Division, where I remained until the very end of 1940.

## HOW PERSONALITIES AND INTERACTIONS AFFECTED THE BLUEPRINT
*J. Warren Madden, the Smiths, Leiserson...*

The original NLRB had consisted of J. Warren Madden as chairman, appointed for a five year term; John Carmody, appointed for a three year term; and Edwin Smith, appointed for a one year term. When Edwin Smith's term expired he was reappointed for a five year term. Carmody resigned at the end of about a year and was succeeded by Donald Wakefield Smith, who filled out the rest of his term, so that through most of this period the board consisted of Madden and the Smiths. When Donald Smith's term expired in 1938, William N. Leiserson was appointed in his place. Leiserson functioned until 1940, when I left the NLRB.

Madden must have been in his early forties when he was appointed chairman. His experience in labor relations had not been extensive. In some ways it was surprising, in fact, that a person who had not had any real experience in the labor field, and had been engaged in an academic job all his life, should have had as keen a sense of the realities of the labor situation as Madden did. He was quite objective in his point of view, always open-minded, always searching conscientiously to get to the bottom of a situation.

He was also a person of overpowering integrity, a man of genuine moral principles and faith, completely honest and courageous. He was mild-spoken, but with fire underneath, not in support of any partisan cause but in support of the general principles of the National Labor Relations Act, in which he fully believed. He had a rather keen sense of humor. He had a twinkle in his eye a good deal of the time, and a very kindly and sympathetic approach to people. All the members of the staff had the highest respect for him. Even those who disagreed with his point of view at times were nevertheless impressed with his ability and his sincerity, and his genuine interest in carrying out the objectives of of the act. Even his worst enemies among the employers and the AFL conceded his basic honesty and sincerity. Only the congressional investigators missed, or probably deliberately ignored, this characteristic of Madden's.

Because of all these factors Madden dominated the board. It was his point of view and his policies that were essentially followed by the board's staff, partly because Donald Smith agreed with him on most things–in fact, there was not much disagreement among all three board members–and partly because of the sheer effect of his personality on the board. He did as courageous and effective a job as any government servant I have seen.

Edwin Smith had considerably less native ability than Madden, although he was able. He was not a lawyer, although eventually he picked up a good deal of the legal approach in deciding cases. He was not as objective or judicious in his decisions as Madden. Smith leaned toward the labor side of issues, more likely to come out on the CIO side. His judgment seemed to some extent an emotional one–at least, much more so than Madden's, which was keenly intellectual. His judgment as to basic fairness, what in the total situation would be considered by the public as the fairest result, was not as sound as Madden's was. Later, after Edwin Smith left the board, he served in various capacities with left-wing unions for a while and engaged in various sorts of left-wing activity. To what extent he was influenced by these at the time he served as a board member I do not know. His effort was, I am sure, to be objective.

The briefest member of the original NLRB was John Carmody. Energetic and jovial, Carmody had a rather keen, shrewd mind, not an intellectual in any sense, but a practical operator with a good sense of the realities of the situation and a pretty good judge of people. During the time he was with the board the development of the legal principles with the Review Division had not taken place, so he did not figure in that aspect.

Donald Wakefield Smith, mentioned earlier, was in an entirely different class from the other three. A lawyer from Pennsylvania, he was a person of no real ability and very limited capacity. Generally, he followed Madden in his decisions, but as a person of very small physical stature he apparently felt on occasion that he had to show his independence. This tended to cause difficulty because usually the two more reasonable points of view were taken by Madden and Edwin Smith, or else they agreed, and when Donald Smith occasionally had to show that he was not controlled by any of the other board members, he usually lit upon a solution to the problem that seemed rather out of place.

As I have said, Smith was not reappointed. There was a story, possibly apocryphal, in Washington that the reason that he was opposed by the AFL was a mistake–they had thought he was *Edwin* Smith. Both Madden's and Donald Smith's decisions on questions such as bargaining units went far toward giving the AFL all that was reasonable. It was Edwin Smith's decisions on the bargaining units that particularly aroused the antagonism of the AFL, and they would have been particularly anxious to get *Edwin* Smith out. Whether AFL President William Green really confused the two, I do not know. Possibly it was just that Roosevelt had received reports that Donald Smith did not measure up to the job.

Donald Smith's term expired in August 1938. There followed a considerable delay before his successor, William N. Leiserson, was appointed to the NLRB in June 1939. Leiserson's background was almost entirely in the labor field as an economist and labor relations expert. His service with the government had been primarily with the National Mediation Board under the Railway Labor Act. His point of view was almost entirely that of a mediator, rather than that of an official enforcing a statute requiring certain obligations and granting certain rights. He believed that a good mediator compromised issues and gave a little to both sides and that this approach should inform the administration of the NLRB. He believed it was wrong to decide consistently in favor of one party, and that in order to keep a system functioning, one would have to award decisions to some extent to both sides. Leiserson always indicated that he was unhappy on the board. From what he said he preferred the Railway Labor Board and the National Mediation Board type of work.

Not a lawyer himself, Leiserson was extremely anti-lawyer in his point of view. He had no respect for the legal profession, believed that we had no business in the labor relations field, and was outspokenly anti-legal in his views. He rejected entirely any theory of *stare decisis*. Each case should be decided upon its individual facts, he insisted, without any regard for precedent or legal principles. I used to argue with him repeatedly about this. I would point out that whether you recognized or did not recognize the fact, every decision was governed by certain principles, expressed or implied, and it was impossible to disregard precedent. I also argued that it would be entirely unfair to decide similar cases in different ways. His answer was that every case was unique, that one had to decide on the basis of the facts of that case, and that only. He never recognized the principle of precedent.

In many discussions with Leiserson he seemed to indulge in flat inconsistencies, and he was the kind of person with whom I had no intellectual relationship. Our minds were in two entirely different worlds. He was not concerned with being inconsistent. He would take each position separately, saying, "This is a different situation. You can't argue that under another rule." He was a very frustrating person to deal with. There was no doubt, as I frequently pointed out to him, that he was operating on the basis of principles underlying these different cases, but he would never concede that.

Leiserson's views were so contrary to our ideas of legal thinking that we were quite at a loss in dealing with him and considered his point of view extremely irrational. On the other hand, he was by far the most experienced member of the board in terms of labor relations, having worked in that area practically all his life. A keen observer of the labor field, he was shrewd in judging situations. He had considerable insight into how far people were really willing to stand on their position, where they would compromise, what they would be willing to accept, and for what they would fight to the last ditch. That ability was of some use on the board, and his background and experience could have been of great value.

Leiserson came with a mandate, either from President Roosevelt or on his own, to "clean up" the NLRB. He was appointed at a time when there was considerable criticism of the board on the ground that it was pro-labor and pro-CIO. With his announced objective of cleaning up the board, the result was that he was almost immediately precipitated into a bitter conflict with Madden and Smith, and with a large part of the board's staff. Leiserson destroyed the unity with which the board had operated previously. He split the board and gradually split the staff. His potential value to the NLRB was completely overshadowed by his deliberate effort to change the it, change its direction, and change many of its personnel. It became a clear-cut showdown between him and Madden. When Madden's term expired in 1940, Madden was not reappointed. This was not to be the last time I would run into William Leiserson.

### The Record

Despite the fact that Donald Smith was not of much use and Leiserson was extremely erratic, I was greatly impressed with the value of a multiple-headed agency in making judicial determinations. The three members of the board supplemented each other no matter which three they were. Madden and Edwin Smith supplemented each other well and the third member made some contribution. The issues were tossed back and forth between the three experts in a way that presented all angles. The net result in almost every case was far better than it would have been if a single individual had undertaken to make the decision. In other words, a process of deliberation in which there was a cooperative result brought about a notable better conclusion than would have been possible under any single administrator.

Generally the board's decisions, although sharply criticized, were on the whole fair and reasonable within the terms of what the National Labor Relations Act was intending to accomplish. Where there was a conflict of testimony in the record between a union witness and a company witness, the discrepancy was usually resolved in favor of the union witness. There was very little way of being sure as to who was correct. To some extent the issue could receive some light from corroborating evidence from other sources, but very often there was a flat conflict. The board was inclined to take the view that the employee was telling the truth, or nearer to it, than the employer's witness. I suppose that the fact that the union or employee had brought the charge at all and the case had been pressed indicated some slight presumption. That was a very difficult aspect of the decisions, and I think the board did as well as could be done.

The legal interpretations of the act, sharply criticized as carrying the act far beyond what was intended, were completely sound in my opinion. The board took a courageous and sound position. The same can be said of their decisions of general policy, which necessarily involved quasi-legal principles, a certain amount of decision as to fact, and a certain amount of judgment. The board's decisions were subject to checks by the courts, and anything that was clearly out of place could be corrected by the courts. It is true that the scope of review by the courts was limited, but actually one cannot limit the courts by a mere formula. Where the courts believed that something was wrong, they never hesitated to reverse the board. The fact that the board's record in the courts was so successful is a very strong indication that it was never very far off track.

One major criticism frequently heard was that the NLRB so often decided cases against the employer. This was true, but the statistics were misleading because the cases that the board decided in favor of employers rarely reached a formal hearing. Those cases that reached the board after a hearing were a select group where the board's regional staff had thought that a case was quite clear. Hence it was inevitable that the preponderant number of decisions would be against the employer, because the ones in his favor had been weeded out. Actually, only 8 percent of the many thousands of cases ever reached the stage of a formal complaint. Many of the remaining 92 percent were resolved in the employer's favor. I cannot believe that after the full process of the board's procedure had been followed, and the courts had taken a look at the record, there could have been more than an isolated case or two where an employer was unjustly found guilty of unfair labor practices.

In all my time with the NLRB it never adequately solved the problem of delay. At one time we were more than a year behind in many of our decisions. The elapsed time from the filing of the charge until the board's formal decision probably ran about two years at this time. This defect in the operation of the act was not fatal throughout this period because of rising business activity, increasing scarcity of labor (particularly as World War II approached), and also because of expanding union organization. If the reverse had been true and there had been a period of unemployment and more effort by employers to destroy unions, the situation would have been quite different, and the delay might have meant that the act would have been rendered relatively ineffective. The worst delay came in the years immediately after 1937, when a huge backlog of cases was up for decision and employers were in their most obstructive frame of mind and dragging out the hearings. Gradually the timeliness of decisions improved, but even now [1953] it takes a year on the average between the filing of the complaint and the decision.

The board's record in the courts throughout this time was extraordinary. In fact, one of the board's strongest rebuttals to criticism was that its court record was far better than that of most of the other New

Deal administrative agencies. Of the first 25 cases that the board took before the Supreme Court, the board was overruled completely in only two. Its position was modified in perhaps three or four more. In the remaining cases its position was fully sustained. Compare this with the Federal Trade Commission, which had been unable to win any of its cases before the Supreme Court over a period of many years. In fact the NLRB's record before the Supreme Court was unparalleled compared with its sister agencies.

This record was largely because of the quality of the legal drafting work turned out by the NLRB. Typically, the level of craftsmanship was high. I think the Supreme Court rather quickly began to have confidence in the board's work in contrast to some of the other administrative agencies.

On the other hand, when it came to interpretation of the law, as to letter and to intent, the courts were quite set on deciding for themselves. I recall one case that I had in the Fourth Circuit, involving a section of the act that I myself had drafted when I was working with Leon Keyserling. The provision was that the board had authority to order the reinstatement of employees with or without backpay, and to order such other affirmative relief as might seem to be required under the circumstances. In this case the employer had not fired employees already on his payroll, but had refused to hire workers because of their prior union activities at a different plant. The board had ordered the company to hire them under this provision. There was no doubt in the minds of those who drafted the act that the act was intended to cover this. In fact, it was the major example of "other affirmative relief" that the board could order that the draftsmen had had in mind when they used that term. However, I was unable to persuade the Fourth Circuit that this was what Congress had intended. In spite of the fact that I was the person in the best position to interpret the language of the provision (although I did not let on that I had written it) the court disagreed with me and held that the board had no power to order the employment of persons who had not worked for an employer before, and that Congress had not intended that it should have this power. Later the issue was resolved the other way by the Supreme Court. I was amused that I could not convince the judges that the language meant what I had intended it to mean when I wrote it!

## Opposition

By now we were halfway through Roosevelt's second term and opposition to the New Deal had begun to coalesce. Originally it centered in Congress. The turning point came after the congressional elections of 1938. Until then the New Deal had been advancing at full force; as late as 1938 headway was still being made. But after that the executive branch split into a group that wanted to cooperate with business and those who wanted to move more in the anti-monopoly direction. The first general opposition to the New Deal came into focus in the fight over the court-packing plan in 1937, even though that opposition was rendered moot, along with the plan, when the April 1937 decision suggested that perhaps even the Supreme Court was affected by the extremely pro-New Deal tenor of the time. But the Fair Labor Standards Act, passed in 1938, was the last significant New Deal measure that passed on Capitol Hill. After that the opposition had regrouped and began mounting a counterattack, largely through Congress. It is significant that the Dies Committee (to be discussed below) began operations sometime in 1938.

The Roosevelt administration, sensing this growing opposition in Congress and believing that it still maintained the support of the public at large, took the occasion of the national congressional elections to attempt the purge of 1938, to eliminate those congressmen who were not friendly to the New Deal point of view. The purge was badly organized and backfired, except in one New York district where a Democrat who opposed the administration was defeated. Otherwise, the members of Congress whom the administration had targeted for defeat were reelected. Actually the administration defeat went considerably beyond that, because the liberal wing of the party was seriously weakened, with the most vocal liberals–and some who could even be described as left-wingers, such as John Bernard of Minnesota, John Coffee of Washington, and perhaps Maury Maverick of Texas–practically wiped out in the House of Representatives.

This fact did not pass unnoticed, and the opponents of the New Deal pressed their advantage. Throughout 1939–40 the Dies Committee continued to grow more active. The most important New Deal accomplishment in 1939–40 was a study, by the Temporary National Economic Committee (TNEC), and not legislation. The New Deal was now weakened to a point where it was forced to make studies in an attempt to arouse public opinion; it no longer had enough votes to pass further measures in Congress. What might have happened if World War II had not intervened is impossible to say. Whether the opposition would have increased or whether the Roosevelt administration would have regained its mandate with a more carefully planned campaign during the presidential election of 1940 is hard to say.

That the New Deal was not advancing left the NLRB vulnerable to attack, particularly from Congress. And the attack came, both in the form of congressional investigations and in the form of proposed amendments to the labor relations statute.

## LEISERSON ON THE RAMPAGE

As background to Leiserson's campaign to oust Nathan Witt as secretary of the NLRB, I will outline the history of the Secretary's Office. The Secretary's Office supervised most operations of the regional offices and the work of handling the cases up to the point where they became formal complaint cases, or where they went to formal hearing.

## Personnel

The first Secretary of the NLRB was Benedict Wolf. He had been attached to the old Wagner Board as assistant secretary. He was a lawyer of considerable ability, tough-minded, and rather brusque in his relations with people. He antagonized many people he came in touch with, but he knew a good deal about the board's operations, had seen the development of the board from the beginning, and functioned, on the whole, very effectively.

Wolf left the board to return to law practice in New York late in 1937 and was succeeded by Nathan Witt, who had been head of the Review Division. Witt's background was basically, I suppose, the streets of New York. He had operated a taxicab for a while before going to law school. He graduated from Harvard Law School in 1930 or 1931. Witt had exceptional ability. He was a person of broad interests, although not of what is generally considered of an intellectual character. He was very shrewd and practical in his thinking and quite imaginative, too. He had a good comprehension of the labor movement. Not brought up in middle-class fashion, he had an underlying contempt for middle-class virtues, although he worked hard. Exceedingly tough-minded, he also was not at all smooth in his handling of people and readily made enemies. In his personal relations he was an unusually interesting person. Beneath a happy, kidding exterior he was fundamentally serious and had obviously made up his mind as to basic issues and where he was going. He was very effective in his work when he was dealing on a personal basis with people who were generally sympathetic to what he was trying to do. He was not good in his public relations or in his relations with people on the staff. I suppose he had a basic feeling of insecurity which came out in an emotional manner so that he tended to antagonize people. He seemed well aware of his deficiencies in his public appearances and confined them to as few as possible. He simply was not a person who could adjust himself to other people in a public situation. I suppose that was his chief weakness in his job as Secretary.

I had a very close association with Witt. I knew him extremely well, worked with him closely, and saw a good deal of him socially. Strangely enough, we had few political discussions. We discussed the Washington scene extensively, as two people in Washington would, but I cannot recall any conversations with him that dealt with broad political issues. I have no recollection of ever having talked with him about the Nazi-Soviet Pact, although that was taking place at a time that I saw him daily. I have practically no recollection of any discussion of foreign policy, except of a limited kind, such as the Popular Front in France around 1936.

Later there was testimony that he was a member of a Communist cell with Alger Hiss, Lee Pressman, and several others throughout this period. I had no indication of that at all. As I look back on it, I can trace no improper influence in the handling of his job. I agreed with him on most issues, although not all, in connection with his work. We had some difference of opinion about whether workers who had gone out on strike over a wage issue rather than an unfair labor practice, and who had been replaced, were entitled to get their jobs back. Witt went much further than I did in insisting that the board should order the employers to rehire the strikers in that situation. Other differences of opinion of that sort occurred, but by and large I agreed with his position on most issues that arose and we discussed practically all of them. I think he did an exceedingly competent and reliable job. Judging purely by the results of his actions in connection with his job, I would not make any exception.

Witt's assistant was Beatrice Stern. She was the wife of Max Stern, who was a reporter for the Scripps-Howard newspapers. Of considerably less ability than Witt or Wolf, she realized her limitations and was relatively insecure and immature with respect to her position, acting pleasant to her superiors and nasty to her subordinates. Although she was Witt's chief assistant, she carried little prestige with the board. She immediately got into difficulties when a union was formed among the board's staff. Her reactions were almost those of a typical employer. The board had to watch carefully so that she did not put them into a position where they would be accused of unfair labor practices with respect to their own employees.

Another assistant whom Witt brought in later was an attorney named Alexander Hawes. He was a Harvard Law School graduate from the class of 1931, a lawyer of considerable ability, from a very respectable family. Rather quiet and reserved, he engaged in the elite social life of Washington. He was an extremely honest and straightforward person who looked at the labor movement from a middle-class point of view.

Witt also had several other assistants, most of them people whom Witt had chosen because they got along better with some of the regional offices than he did. They were used primarily as liaison officers with the regional offices.

## Procedures

The Secretary's Office handled cases prior to the hearing. A large part of this took place through the regional offices in election cases. After petitions for elections were filed through the regional offices, the first step was to assess the situation, then to try to settle the issue informally through a conference between employer and union; if necessary, to hold a consent election—in short, to dispose of the case through informal procedures if possible. If not, an application was made to hold a hearing. Similarly, in unfair labor practices cases the first step was to investigate. In many of those cases it turned out that no violation of the act had taken place so the complaint would be dismissed. If there was a violation, the regional office made an effort to settle the case, and those negotiations were often long and difficult, but in most cases they were successful. If the employer would not settle, the matter was then presented as a formal complaint.

At the beginning all or most settlements were transmitted to Washington for approval. The Secretary's Office would present the facts to the board on the basis of the regional office report and the board would approve the settlement. Later there was more decentralization. If a formal complaint was to be filed, the regional offices would request authority from the Washington office. The Secretary's Office would present the case to the board, explaining what the facts were in investigation. If the board thought there was a prima facie case of an unfair labor practice, they would authorize the issuance of a formal complaint. The Secretary's Office also supervised the regional offices in the holding of elections. Staff from the Secretary's Office would travel to the regional offices, and fairly frequent conferences of representatives of the regional offices were held on matters of policy and procedure. So both the supervision of the field activities of the regional offices and those matters from the regional offices which came before the board for approval were handled through the Secretary's Office.

The Secretary's Office functioned under close supervision from the board members. All the major decisions, including all settlements at first, were made by the board itself after a presentation of the issues and discussion, usually by the full board. For a long time all complaints were considered by the board. Later there was some decentralization of that, although the important ones continued to be presented to the board. All personnel decisions were decided by the board, including all the positions in the regional offices. The board even passed on the appointment of clerical and stenographic personnel, and approved all salary increases and changes of classification. Instead of a review attorney, the Secretary, or a representative of his office, would present the matter to the board.

On the whole, this highly centralized arrangement operated fairly effectively, except that it was far too centralized for swift decisions. Perhaps the centralization was justified at the beginning when policies were being formulated in this exceptionally sensitive situation. Possibly the board could have delegated more from the beginning, but I can understand why they held the reins tightly in view of the potential trouble that one apparently minor mistake could cause.

## Leiserson's Campaign

Immediately following his appointment to the NLRB in June 1939, Leiserson undertook a campaign of criticism of the Secretary's Office, culminating in a motion to the board that Nat Witt be dismissed as secretary. The campaign took the form of a series of memoranda that Leiserson wrote to other board members. As one of his opening moves, when a tentative decision was presented to him for consideration, he refused to participate and wrote a memorandum saying, this case is "too old, and there are the usual irregularities of procedure characteristic of the Secretary's Office." Madden was exceedingly upset by this charge of irregularity and immediately sent a memorandum to Leiserson asking him to state what he meant by "the usual irregularities of procedure characteristic of the Secretary's Office." Leiserson replied by listing half a dozen cases in which he claimed there had been irregularities. Madden wrote back asking him to state what the irregularities were. Leiserson then replied:

> I have nothing to add to my memorandum of July 26, except to say that I agree with your statement at the conference Wednesday afternoon that the Universal Pictures case smells. I think it is time that we look around for a Secretary who understands the administrative duties of the job and sticks to them.

Unable to extract more details from Leiserson, Madden asked Charles Fahy to make an investigation of these cases and to report back whether there were irregularities. Fahy made the investigation and reported back that in his judgment the charge of irregularities could not be sustained.

Nothing could be substantiated in Leiserson's criticisms, but they kept coming and his memoranda usually were sharply worded. For instance, another one stated,

> If you think immediate action is needed on this, you can leave me out of the case entirely. I would rather not participate in it. I think this is another one of those cases into which the Secretary has put his fingers and bawled it up, and I suspect that this telegram from Brackett was inspired.

The suggestion was that the secretary was going behind the board's back in asking some labor organizer to send a telegram to the board. There was absolutely no evidence of that.

Leiserson had no bill of particulars against Witt. Apparently, he was referring to either the long delays or to judgments that had been made as to whether a case should be sent back to the regional office for further evidence before the board took action, or matters of that sort. Many of the cases tended to become complicated and lengthy. For instance, a case might include both an unfair labor practice charge and also a request for an election. Should we handle the unfair labor practice first and then hold the election, or should we hold the election first and then deal with the unfair labor practice? After the unfair labor practice was disposed of, would there be any union left to want an election? A multitude of minor decisions would be made in intricate cases, often after consultation with the board, which usually could have made either way. Occasionally Leiserson would make insinuations such as that the Brackett telegram was inspired, but he never had any proof. Insofar as we could pin him down to anything, he was referring to judgments that had been made in cases that could have gone, presumably, either way. By using terms such as "irregularities" and other dramatic and colorful words, he made these judgment calls sound as though they were an intentionally improper procedure. But no evidence of improper procedure came forth.

The board considered Leiserson's motion to remove Witt, discussed it at some length with Fahy, and rejected it. Witt stayed on until Madden left, at which time Witt also left.

Leiserson kept bombarding the board with these memoranda, making general accusations, but never being at all specific as to what his objection was. At the time it seemed completely irrational and I found it impossible to account for. In the light of later events, I suppose that Leiserson thought that it was essential to clean up the board so the board would be able to survive the attack from outside conservative forces. He honestly believed that the board had interpreted the act and administered the act in such a way that it had created a sufficient degree of opposition so that unless the board modified its administration it would be an easy victim for its enemies, in the sense of Congress cutting off appropriations, making amendments, launching investigations, and so forth. Unable to find any specific criticism that would stand up, he chose this irrational way of pressing the issue. Perhaps he had information that convinced him that Nat Witt was a member of the Communist Party and, determined to get rid of Witt and some members of his staff, he thought that his methods were of less concern than the ultimate objective. If so, so far as I know, he never passed this word on to Madden. Certainly he never convinced Madden that Witt was incompetent or should be discharged.

All these memoranda later appeared in the congressional investigation and were perhaps the most serious criticism of the board that the investigating committee developed. Probably Leiserson realized that any memorandum he was writing would provide evidence in a congressional investigation and he was writing them with that in mind. Congress voted to investigate the NLRB on July 20, 1939; the first of Leiserson's memoranda severely critical of the Secretary's Office appeared on July 26th. Although Leiserson had been with the board for nearly two months, he previously had not indulged in such tactics. Why he undertook an approach that completely disrupted the unity of the board and staff, and that exposed the NLRB to the most serious attack by its opponents, I do not understand.

I never knew what had gone on behind the scenes in the administration with regard to this whole matter. Had the administration, specifically the secretary of labor and the White House group, concluded that the board had gone too far and was so far out on a limb that the whole thing would be cut off unless it was checked, and had put Leiserson in to accomplish that? I think that most likely they had some such judgment, possibly from Miss Perkins who had not fully recovered from the fact that the board had not been put in the Labor Department, and who never had achieved a sympathetic relationship with the board. A number of people in the administration regarded the board as a political liability that had become too pro-labor and pro-CIO. Even a person such as Dave Niles [a presidential assistant], I believe, somewhat shared that opinion. Consequently the board was somewhat isolated. So far as I know the

Roosevelt administration never approached the board directly with suggestions that it modify its approach; however, nor was there was any strong effort to support the board, either.

All this conflict was entirely out of character; nothing like this had ever happened to the board before. There had been a close unity, a real esprit de corps among the board's staff. Particularly for this to happen to Madden, who was the essence of open-mindedness and integrity, was most ironic, not to say frustrating and agonizing. As Madden's term neared its expiration date and it looked as though Leiserson might gain control of the NLRB, the split tended to widen. Bea Stern and others tended to join the Leiserson camp so as to get on the winning side. The whole atmosphere deteriorated in the latter part of 1940.

# 6

# ON THE DEFENSIVE

*Resistance to the New Deal...return to the old...?*

From the Jones & Laughlin Steel Company decision in April 1937, through 1940, the NLRB was under constant attack from employers, the AFL, and other sources. Beginning in June 1939, when William N. Leiserson was appointed one of the three board members, the board was also subject to attack from within, and all these attacks were reflected in Congress. A disheartening amount of the agency's time, energy, and resources was devoted to defending itself against attacks and investigations. A large percentage of the time of the board members and staff was devoted, not to administering the National Labor Relations Act, but to the NLRB's survival, answering charges that were made and dealing with proposals to amend the act. For many months in the winter of 1939–40 I was spending practically full time on the investigation conducted by the Smith Committee. Prior to that, in the early part of 1939, I spent practically full time for two or three months on proposed amendments to the act. Other members of the staff had to spend their time the same way.

## CRITICISM OF THE NLRB

*Internal reports.* First of all, the board investigated various aspects of its own operations. I have mentioned the appointment of General Counsel Fahy to investigate the charges that Leiserson had made with respect to the Secretary's Office. About the same time the NLRB decided to appoint a committee of our regional directors to make a study of the board's operations and to recommend methods by which operations could be improved. This group made a rather intensive study, mostly of the Secretary's Office and the relationship of the Secretary's Office to the regional offices, but also including all aspects of the board's activity. The study did not result in any recommendations for major changes, but a number of significant recommendations were made, many of which the board implemented. One change was that authority was granted to the regional offices to handle more cases on their own without requesting approval of Washington. The committee also recommended that the

NLRB trial examiner's report be used to a greater extent in the making of board decisions. In order to accomplish this, the caliber of that report needed improvement; a supervisory system, by which the reports were read, criticized, and revised by supervisors on the chief trial examiner's staff, was established. Both these changes improved the central board's operation.

*Appropriations.* The board was required to obtain a budget appropriation from Congress each year, and in that connection sent people to testify before the House and Senate Appropriations Committees for purposes of justifying its budget. The main appropriations hearing was before the House Committee, as the Senate Committee's deliberation was more superficial. The hearings usually lasted a day, or sometimes a day-and-a-half or two days. During that time various members of the House Appropriations Committee would interrogate the board in detail about policy issues, board decisions, and other matters that were not directly related to the appropriations. The committee used this as an occasion to have the board justify certain positions and to influence the board on certain policies.

The Republican members of the subcommittee of the Appropriations Committee, strongly opposing the NLRB, were eager to limit its effectiveness by cutting its appropriation. In addition, the subcommittee contained a number of southern Democrats who also were rather strongly opposed to many of the board's activities. The result was that the board usually took a cut from the House Appropriations Committee.

For example, following the Jones & Laughlin decision, the House Appropriations Committee allotted the NLRB an inadequate appropriation. With the expansion that the NLRB was undertaking, it was quite clear that we would require more money and later we obtained some additional funds for the end of that fiscal year. I was not present at that session, but every year from 1938 through 1940 I was present at the House appropriations hearings, at least in part because my division was expanding so much and was in particular need of funds.

We routinely ended up attempting to have the funds restored on the floor of the House. The board usually let the labor organizations, its principal backers, know that the question was up for consideration. The board's supporters would then lobby heavily in favor of the board's appropriations. Sometimes we got some of the funds restored. Usually, nothing much could be accomplished on the floor of the House but on one or two occasions funds were restored, at least in part, through the Senate Appropriations Committee. Each year a considerable controversy arose over the board's funding, and the board was apprehensive as to whether it would be granted adequate funds or even be cut below its current level. In the end the board did not receive as much as it wanted, but it was not crippled by the action on the appropriations.

In addition to the funding limits, the Appropriations Committee started the practice of attaching riders to the appropriations bills, limiting the board's activities, such as the one that attempted to block retention of

David Saposs as head of the Economics Division (mentioned in Chapter 5). We were always nervous lest restrictions of that sort would be imposed upon the board through the Appropriations Committee.

*Investigations*. A second source of congressional investigation came as early as January 1938, from a resolution introduced by Senator Burke (Nebraska) calling for a full investigation of the board. Senator Burke was among the most conservative, not to say the most reactionary, members of the Senate. A group of employers instigated his move. It was said that it was the coal operators who were backing him up.

The Senate Judiciary Committee held preliminary hearings to consider whether or not to report a resolution calling for a full-scale investigation. Senator Burke presented his charges and the committee called various members of the board's staff to answer them. The principal charges were generally that the act was not fulfilling its purpose, that it was not a method of lessening labor disputes, and there was a general and rather vague attack that the act was not accomplishing anything and was unnecessarily restricting the rights of both employer and employee. Senator Burke attacked the majority rule principle of the act, saying that it was unfair to the minority group among the employees. There was also a rather personal attack on the board's administration of the act, and upon the board members themselves, particularly Edwin Smith. Senator Burke brought out material published in some magazine with respect to a trip that Edwin Smith had made to Mexico. It was one of those examples of yellow journalism, in which the magazine had, for instance, printed a picture of Smith at some occasion sitting under a Soviet flag, without explaining that this was an occasion in which flags of many nations had been displayed and that Edwin Smith was sitting next to the American ambassador. The article was a completely distorted and vicious piece of journalism.

The leading testimony by the board came from our chairman, Warren Madden, who put on one of the best performances that I have seen before a congressional committee–hard-hitting, earnest, very eloquent. He answered all the charges and convinced the committee that there was no substance to the allegations of Senator Burke. As a result, after two or three days of hearings the committee either took no action or affirmatively decided not to report out the resolution. That was the end of Senator Burke's attempt, which had alarmed the board and staff, but on this occasion the board came off relatively unscathed and without having to spend much time or energy on the defense.

An article by Walter Gellhorn and Seymour Linfield, published in the *Columbia Law Review* for March 1939, reported a rather exhaustive study of the board's operations from a scholarly point of view. The authors addressed themselves to various criticisms of the board:

*First*, the board stirs up labor strife by bringing in unwarranted charges against employers.
*Second*, the board doesn't give respondents fair notice of the charges

against them so that they cannot properly prepare their defense.

*Third*, the board's hearings are conducted in an arbitrary and disorderly fashion.

*Fourth*, the board does not observe the rules of evidence and decides cases without any support in the record.

*Fifth*, the board does not do its own work, but passes on to inconspicuous subordinates, or to complete outsiders, the duty of deciding controversies.

*Sixth*, there is too much confusion in the roles of judge and prosecutor in the board's work, so that it cannot objectively appraise the cases before it.

Gellhorn and Linfield then examined each of those issues and analyzed the board's work. On each criticism they supported the board's position, method of operation, and activities. The authors concluded:

> The authors are satisfied that the denunciations find no support in fact. Government agencies are rarely popular when they control and command; new government agencies which control and command are even more rarely popular; and a new government agency which controls and commands in situations so surcharged with emotion, as have been those committed to the NLRB, would be a latter day miracle if it were popular with all whom its operations affect.

That was one of the few public vindications of the board.

## ATTEMPTS TO AMEND THE NATIONAL LABOR RELATIONS ACT

A series of amendments to the National Labor Relations Act were introduced in the new Congress that met in January 1939. The most significant bill embodied a series of amendments introduced by the chairman of the Labor Committee, Sen. David Walsh (Massachusetts), on behalf of the AFL. Another bill incorporated proposals supported by employer groups, principally the Chamber of Commerce. In addition, half a dozen other bills were of relatively minor importance.

*AFL amendments.* The AFL bill, which would have emasculated the act, was particularly startling to us and experts in the labor field because the AFL, in a spirit of intense bitterness, seemed to be cutting its own throat. First of all, a series of amendments would have prevented the board from interfering with the AFL. The amendments were designed to eliminate company unions so far as possible, but to permit various kinds of employer favoritism toward unions with national affiliations. The proposals eliminated from the act the general prohibition against interference, restraint, or coercion of any kind with efforts at self-organization and substituted a much more restricted prohibition, which would simply prohibit discrimination that took the form of dismissal or refusal to hire, or interference that took the form of financing a labor organization, compensating anyone for services performed in its behalf, or contributing money, services, or materials. In other words, under these amendments the employer would not have been prohibited from giving the AFL unions considerable advantages over CIO unions.

Another proposal designed to accomplish the same purpose was a proviso that any expression of opinion on the part of employers should not be prohibited, "provided that such expressions of opinion are not accompanied by acts of discrimination, or threats thereof." In other words, the employers were permitted under this to argue with their employees on behalf of the AFL, so long as it did not go to the extent of being an act of discrimination or a threat of an act of discrimination.

Another amendment would have permitted employers to make collective agreements, including closed shop agreements, with a union that had been assisted by the company. Here again an effort was made to prevent an employer from entering into such contracts with a company-dominated union. But this would have overruled a series of cases in which the board had invalidated AFL contracts made after the employer had substantially assisted the AFL to organize the employees, and had discriminated against the CIO.

Another provision was that supervisory employees should mean only foremen who were regularly employed in supervising the work of others and who had the power to hire and fire. This provision would have meant that no supervisory employee could be prevented from interfering with union activity unless he had power to hire and fire. In many plants only the very top foremen, or even the general manager, had the power to hire and fire, so a large number of subsidiary supervisory employees would have been fully entitled to participate in the organization of the workers in the plant and to throw their weight in behalf of one union or another. Again, it was designed to permit the AFL to receive support from employers, while attempting to eliminate complete company domination.

Other changes related to the bargaining unit and the position of craft unions. The AFL proposed that "whenever a craft exists composed of one or more employees, then such craft shall constitute a unit appropriate for the purpose of collective bargaining, and a majority of such craft employees may designate a representative for that unit." It also provided that the appropriate unit could not include the employees of more than one employer. That was designed to reverse an NLRB decision that had ruled to include in a single bargaining unit all the longshoremen on the Pacific Coast. The AFL, who had organized small organizations in one or two ports, had protested that decision with particular bitterness.

Also in connection with the bargaining units, the AFL proposed that the courts be given authority to review certificates of representation. The board had successfully established that there should be no judicial review of its certificate that a particular unit represented a particular group of employees. If the employer refused to bargain with the representative certified, then an unfair labor practice case could be instituted and there would be review of that proceeding, including at this point a review of whether the certificate was properly granted. The board considered this a matter of considerable importance, because if prior review had been permitted, it would have been possible for any employer to hold up an election in the plant almost indefinitely while the matter was considered by the circuit court of appeals, or perhaps even by the district court first, and ultimately by the Supreme Court.

Another provision authorized employers to file petitions for elections. The board had decided that only employees, or representatives of employees, could file a petition for an election. Its viewpoint was that the employer had no legitimate business to force an election, that the employer's only obligation was to bargain if the union presented itself and asked to bargain, and that therefore the employer had no interest that would permit him to file a petition and obtain an election or a certification of representation. This was one of the issues most hotly debated, and perhaps was one of the most questionable positions that the board had taken. When two unions asked for bargaining recognition, the employer might have a legitimate interest in having the Labor board decide which one, if either, represented the employees. There was also an amendment that increased the scope of court review over the board's decisions on unfair labor practices cases.

The AFL bill proposed a board of five members instead of three. This would have permitted the appointment of two additional members and was designed to change the administration of the act by injecting new personnel.

Later a well-founded report circulated that these amendments had been devised by the General Counsel for the AFL, Joseph Padway, with the assistance of attorneys representing the Chamber of Commerce. In substantiation, the proposals included items in which the AFL could not have had much interest, and the revisions seemed beyond the capacities of Padway, a lawyer of limited abilities.

*Chamber of Commerce amendments.* Also introduced was a Chamber of Commerce bill, proposing to alter the personnel of the board by increasing it to five members. Bills with other sponsors would have abolished the existing board and appointed a tripartite board with one member representing employers, another employees, and the third the general public. The purpose was to oust the present board members or at least to obtain a different majority favoring a more conservative policy.

Like the AFL bill, the Chamber of Commerce bill broadly increased the scope of judicial review and permitted judicial review of certificates of representation. The proposed bill would have completely changed the administrative process by separating the function of prosecuting cases from the function of deciding cases. It proposed the establishment of a commissioner in the Department of Labor who would file complaints and prosecute cases at the hearing; the board's duties would be confined to adjudication of the issues. This combination of prosecuting and adjudicating functions in the same agency was another major controversy about the board's operations. The bargaining unit provisions were changed along the same lines as the AFL bill proposed. The large farmers from California had a provision extending further the exemption of agricultural employees from the act. A provision required that a majority of any bargaining committee consist of employees in the plant rather than union representatives not employed by that particular employer. One provision added a statute of limitations.

Note the close resemblance of this bill to the Taft-Hartley Act passed in 1947. The provisions of the Taft-Hartley Act are much more refined, but many of them accomplish the same purposes: the inclusion of the employee unfair labor practices; the separation of functions; the extension of judicial review; the relaxation of the provision against interference, restraint or coercion; and the statute of limitations.

*Employer amendments.* A final set of amendments, in effect an employer bill, also relaxed the flat prohibition against interference, restraint, or coercion with the right to self-organization by providing that nothing should interfere with the employer's right to advise his employees with respect to any matter of mutual concern. This bill created a category of unfair labor practices on the part of employees. This was a response to a major criticism of the original legislation as one-sided because it controlled only the actions of employers and did not impose any limitations on employees. The bill declared that it would be an unfair labor practice for an employee to interfere, restrain, or coerce other employees in the exercise of their rights to self-organization, to threaten or intimidate other employees, to engage in any unlawful act during a labor dispute, to interfere with the orderly conduct of employer business where such interference grew out of a labor dispute, to strike except in pursuance to a majority vote, or to strike in violation of a contract. These prohibitions, if literally enforced, probably would have prevented any union organization at all, because if you prohibit an employee from interfering with another employee in his rights to organize, it presumably means that he cannot even ask him to join a union. These prohibitions were not to be enforced by a cease and desist order the way the unfair labor practices of employers were; if the board found that employees had engaged in these unfair labor practices, then the protections of the act were to be denied to such employees. In other words, an employer could invoke as a defense to his own unfair labor practice that the employee had engaged in an unfair labor practice. In effect, the act would not be operative at all in a case when any one of these prohibited actions could be found. Another provision of this bill would have abolished the majority rule decision–that the union representing the majority could bargain for all employees.

## Response

The CIO generally supported the board and resisted all amendments. At this time the CIO wielded considerably more political power than it does now [1953] and was not undermined by accusations of "Communism."

The Roosevelt administration's point of view was somewhat equivocal. While it did not openly support the board, neither the White House nor the Department of Labor had any desire that the amendments pass. The administration inclined to the point of view that the act was all right, but that the board had gone a little too far in administering it; that perhaps it would have been willing to see the board increased to five members so that there would be a reshuffling of personnel. However, they were not in a position to advocate this because any defender of the act had to take the position that no amendments at all should be allowed, since if the act were once opened to amendment, Congress would undoubtedly carry the amendment process very far and the NLRB might be totally crippled. The administration played a rather silent role in the fight, although they threw their weight definitely against the amendments. The board's greatest source of strength was the fact that both the House and Senate Labor Committees were quite friendly toward labor. The majority of the members of both committees were opposed to any substantial amendment of the act and were confused by the AFL attack.

The board's two-pronged strategy was to argue on the merits and to delay the consideration until Congress would adjourn without taking action. Our argument on the merits was assisted by the fact that both the AFL and the Chamber of Commerce had overplayed their hands on the amendments. Both sets of amendments were so far-reaching that they clearly would have destroyed the act in anything like its present form. They were crude in conception and in proposed execution. The AFL amendments to permit company favoritism, for instance, would have wrecked any action by the board to stop employers from destroying a union or establishing a company union. The Chamber of Commerce amendments would have gone so far toward destroying the act that it was possible for the board to make a powerful case that appealed to those who supported the basic ideas of the act, even though they thought the board had gone too far. The board made the most of its case. It prepared an elaborate document discussing each amendment in great detail and pointing out what the effect would be. Several reporters predicted that this would "stop the passage of the amendments this year"–and they were right. The board and staff testified before the Labor Committees along the same line. The board had an opportunity to make a very effective presentation, and they made the most of it.

The second prong of the strategy was to drag out the hearings so nothing could be done that session. The House and Senate Labor Committees cooperated in this. They would hold hearings two or three days a week, usually only in the morning. Altogether between the House and Senate committees 175 witnesses testified on those amendments. The sessions dragged on for three months. The board spent a good deal of energy digging up witnesses who would testify, and the committee staffs brought in more witnesses. Congress was hoping to end its term as soon as it became dreadfully hot in Washington–there was much less air conditioning then–and they were eager to leave town.

As July approached and the strategy of the board apparently had worked, as the hearings were still in session, the opposition turned to another tactic. Deciding that it was impossible to get satisfactory amendments through the Labor Committees of either the Senate or House, they had a resolution introduced by Rep. Howard Smith (Democrat, Virginia) to investigate the NLRB over the coming year and to report on the administration of the act as well as upon the various proposed amendments. This resolution was introduced on July 13, 1938, passed by the Rules Committee on July 19th and passed by the House on July 20th by a vote of 254 to 134. The 134 votes represented approximately the basic New Deal strength at that time, indicating the extent to which it had slipped from prior Congresses.

## THE SMITH COMMITTEE INVESTIGATES

The House resolution established a committee of five members to investigate the NLRB. They were authorized to investigate whether the board had been fair and impartial in its conduct, decisions, interpretation of the law, and in dealings between different labor organizations and between employer and employee. Also, they were to determine what effect, if any, the National Labor Relations Act had upon increasing or decreasing labor disputes. The committee was further authorized to recommend amendments, which would, however, have to go through the regular Labor Committee before they could reach the floor of the House.

### The Committee

The chairman of the committee, Howard Smith, was author of the famous Smith Act. He was hard-bitten, dour, and rather shrewd, although not of any great intellectual competence. He was an able politician. A strong conservative, he was one of the most effective leaders of the southern Democrats in opposition to the New Deal. Not a demagogue like Martin Dies or Joseph McCarthy, Smith was not seeking publicity. He was a person whose mind was thoroughly made up; he definitely knew what he wanted, but he operated more behind the scenes than as a person who attracted noteworthy public attention.

The two other Democrats on the committee were pro-New Deal. Rep. Arthur Healey (Massachusetts) was one of the authors of the Walsh–Healey Act, regulating wages paid under government contracts. Healey was a typical Irish politician: well-meaning, rather strongly supporting the New Deal, but not a person of any great intellectual capacity. He was a fairly good politician, I assume, but not a man of any great stature. He was a lawyer and later was appointed a district judge in Massachusetts. Rep. Abe Murdock (Utah) also was not a person of any great intellectual ability, but was fundamentally decent and honest. Of all the members of the committee, he was the most useful to the NLRB. Murdock later became a senator and, when he failed to win reelection, was appointed a member of the NLRB.

One of the two Republicans was Charles Halleck from Indiana. Halleck possessed considerable intellectual attainments. He was extremely fluent, made excellent speeches in the House, rapidly understood the point of things, and was a fairly decent person, but he was also very politically ambitious. He was clearly on his way up in the Republican Party and had committed himself by and large to the conservative viewpoint in Congress. He was more receptive than Smith or the fifth member, Routzohn, to the board's arguments, but ended by putting them aside and joining the other two in their strongly anti-New Deal position. Halleck later became majority leader of the House when the Republicans won with Eisenhower [1952]. The other Republican, Routzohn, formerly had been an attorney for one or several AFL craft unions in Ohio. Extremely conservative, not to say reactionary, he was brusque and irascible, functioning as a prosecuting attorney more than any other member of the committee.

The line-up was typical of Congress from that period on: a coalition of southern Democrats and Republicans controlling New Deal Democrats. Smith and the two Republicans cooperated from the beginning in a common cause. Healey and Murdock supported the board, at times with a few misgivings, but generally rather thoroughly attempting to protect the Roosevelt administration, and to some extent to protect the board itself.

The committee appointed as counsel an attorney from the District of Columbia named Edmund Toland. It will be recalled that Toland had been attorney for the company union involved in the Jones & Laughlin case and had participated in that case before the board, and in several other cases representing employers or company unions. Toland was a rather flashy type, not a person of any scholarly ability but of considerable shrewdness. He had the talents of a pretty good prosecuting attorney. We underestimated his understanding of public relations and the appeal that certain types of evidence would make to the press and public. For three or four months Toland and his staff of five or six young attorneys investigated the files of the NLRB. Their staff members actually took offices in the board's office building. They examined all the individual files of the board members and the chief members of the staff, a number of files in cases, and some of the files in half a dozen of the regional offices. In short, they spent an enormous amount of time combing through the board's files looking for derogatory material.

There is no question that the principal aims of the committee were to show that the board was unfair in its approach and to secure passage of amendments to the act. Apart from searching the board's files, the only other preparation the committee made for the hearing was to send questionnaires to all the parties who had appeared in board proceedings and to the attorneys who had appeared before the board, as well as to a number of labor relations experts, professors of administrative law, and so forth. The committee reported that those questionnaires were tabulated, but the results were never disclosed. Apparently, the answers were used primarily as leads for material in the board's files. The committee did not call as witnesses persons who had participated in the board's hearings. They relied almost exclusively upon material from the board's files and testimony of members of the board's staff.

**The Hearings**

The hearings opened on December 11, 1939, and in their initial stage ran through February 28, 1940, taking place on 37 days during that period. The board was permitted to reply to the case that the committee's counsel had made only in the period from January 29 to February 5. Although the committee indicated it had not finished its hearings, it decided to issue an intermediate report so as to get before Congress, at a date sufficiently early so that action could be taken, various amendments that the committee was proposing. On March 30, 1940, the committee issued an intermediate report that severely castigated the NLRB and proposed a series of amendments to the National Labor Relations Act.

Many of the techniques used by the Smith Committee were those that were later developed by the House Committee on Un-American Activities and other committees investigating subversive activities. The outstanding characteristic of the hearings, which seems to me to be characteristic of a number of congressional investigations, was that the hearings were extremely one-sided. The committee's legal staff had collected all the possible derogatory information that they could from the board's files, and this was put in evidence day after day by the counsel for the committee. This material included memoranda in which a staff member had expressed himself rather frankly about the AFL, indiscretions that appeared in the files in inter-office communications, efforts to show that board members had stimulated boycotts of employers and attempted to deny government contracts to employers who were not complying with the act, efforts to show that particular staff members were incompetent, or that the board had discharged staff for improper reasons. Nothing favorable to the board was permitted to get into the record. There was no reference at all to the board's accomplishments, to the number of cases it had handled, to the success of its court proceedings, to its accomplishments in carrying out the purposes of the act. Furthermore, there was no opportunity to explain the incidents as the committee was inserting them into the record. Leiserson was called as one of the first witnesses to record his criticism and charges against the Secretary's Office, but the opportunity for Madden, Edwin Smith, and Witt to answer this testimony was delayed two months.

Another example of biased testimony arose because the NLRB was operating under a decision issued by the comptroller-general in NRA days, which stated that government agencies were forbidden to enter into contracts with violators of the NRA or of the president's voluntary agreement. This was a clear precedent for how the NLRB was to proceed, but no reference was made to it when material was presented showing that in three cases the board had asked procurement agencies to deny contracts to employers who had violated the act.

A third example was a memorandum that Nat Witt had written to a regional office with respect to the hearings on the 1939 amendments, saying, "We understand that [a particular person] is coming in to testify on the amendments. It might be that if he has cases pending before the

115

board for oral argument he will want to come in at a time when he can handle both matters. Therefore we could set the oral argument at a time that will be convenient to him." The committee put this memorandum into the record without indicating that this memorandum had never been sent because Witt had changed his mind and decided it was improper as it tied too closely the person's opportunity to assist the board by his testimony to the outcome of his cases before the board.

There were many examples of this kind of treatment of the material that the Smith Committee had found in the NLRB files. It was extremely one-sided, inaccurate, and often deliberately misleading. Of course, some of the material that the committee dug up reflected improper actions. These were isolated instances and by themselves could not give an accurate picture of the board's operations. Most of the committee's evidence had no substance if all the facts were known.

The second major aspect of the hearings was a rather substantial lack of consideration of issues on the merits. Many of the questions raised by the proposed amendments should have been considered–such as the issue of the bargaining unit, the rights of AFL and CIO unions in that situation, the right of an employer to petition for an election, and the separation of prosecution and adjudication functions. Instead, the emphasis was on dramatic but isolated instances of agency actions. The committee attempted to create a sensation by disclosing abnormal events that created the impression of partisanship by the board, and in some cases there was evidence of partisanship by individual staff members. For instance, a letter from Francis Biddle, formerly chairman of the NLRB, recommended an attorney for employment in the Review Division, commenting that this attorney was "unusually able, with a liberal point of view (I should say turned left)." The committee would produce a document of that sort, dramatize the alleged implications, and that would receive newspaper headlines. I was constantly astonished at the newspaper headlines that disclosed these matters. In my innocence, I had thought that they were of no particular value to a committee. I naively had thought that public issues were decided more on a serious basis than was apparent from the success of the Smith Committee in using this sort of material.

A final aspect was the skillful use of publicity in this committee presentation. The committee's counsel, Toland, would make sure that he had a sensational document available for the press shortly before noon, when the reporters filed their stories to make the afternoon papers. Again, sometime just before four o'clock, which was the deadline for most of the stories to get into the next morning's papers, he would do the same thing. He parcelled out the material in such a way that he sustained a continuous flow of spicy headlines about the board.

When Toland was presenting material with respect to the Review Division, he called as witnesses all the women attorneys employed in the Review Division. At that time women professionals were looked upon with considerable skepticism by Congress and perhaps the general public. He exploited that negative attitude by calling the ten or eleven women, one after another, to testify. In fact, these were practically the only witnesses he called to explain the work of the Review Division. He did not call any of the top people of the division. Of course, some of these witnesses did not understand the general position of the board on many points; others were inarticulate or frightened. The effect that testifying before a hostile congressional committee can have on a witness who is not used to public appearances was disclosed to me then. A witness can practically black out before a committee. I remember at the time thinking that hereafter I would not blame anybody for how they performed before a congressional committee. But the net effect was not favorable to the Review Division.

To counter this testimony the board was confined to two measures. First, we could check as rapidly as possible, when the testimony came out, on the full background of any "disclosures," and at times we could supply the friendly members of the committee, Healey and Murdock, with material or with questions they could ask. Generally, a member of the NLRB staff sat fairly close to Healey or Murdock and was able to pass questions to them. At times they could even inject an isolated bit of material. So there was a chance of making the record more complete in this way, but on the whole it was ineffective. Most of the time we were surprised by the testimony and our rebuttal depended on a search of the board's files. Second, the board had a week allocated for a defense. We carefully prepared a detailed analysis of the hearing record and the full facts with respect to all the incidents developed. Madden, Edwin Smith, and the staff entered much of this into the record. Surfacing so many weeks after the original material, it received little or no publicity and had practically no effect in counteracting the reaction to the earlier testimony. The board also was able to put in considerable material on what its operations had consisted of, what it had been able to accomplish, some of the difficulties under which it functioned, and some explanation of its court record, but this testimony did not attract much public attention either. The board's rebuttal tended to get lost in the newspapers and had little or no influence in counteracting the effect of Toland's presentation.

I might mention one incident that gave us comic relief. Some months previously J. Edgar Hoover had written a letter to Madden about one of the board employees. This letter in full was as follows:

I wish to advise you information has been received by this Bureau to the effect that Mr. Cannon, a field examiner connected with the National Labor Relations board at St. Louis, is known to have radical tendencies leading toward communism. It is further reported that Cannon has studied anthropology and has been affiliated with the National Labor Relations board for three years. It was also reported that Cannon visited Mexico City, Mexico to observe the presidential election in that country in July 1940. The above information is submitted for your consideration and whatever action you deem appropriate.

(Signed) J. Edgar Hoover

The letter had seemed to us so absurd and dangerous in terms of what was then beginning to be a loyalty movement that we were itching to make the letter public. We thought it would look well in some column and would have the effect of showing some of the absurdities of the early loyalty program, but we did not feel free to reveal the letter or leak it to the press since it was sent by Hoover in the course of regular government correspondence. Toland, on the other hand, when he discovered this letter in the files immediately placed it into the record. So, despite our scruples, we were finally able to get this letter made a matter of public record, thanks to Toland's lack of scruples.

The barrage of criticism and exposés emanating daily from the committee naturally affected the board's staff. The effect of the hearings was tremendous damage to the board's public reputation. The publicity, day after day, of this kind of material undoubtedly gave the public the impression that the board and its staff were a thoroughly one-sided, biased group who were totally oblivious to any canons of fair play or fair procedure. Our friends in Congress and the administration were put in a difficult position about publicly defending the board. It would have been so difficult to have answered all the minutia, and to some there was no direct answer, and the public had become so convinced that the board had gone too far in the administration of the act, that a person who fully defended the board would have become a laughingstock. So even our friends were put into the position where the most that they could say was, "Well, these are isolated instances, not of any great importance, and the major accomplishments of the board are "'so and so.'" Many would not even go that far. They now tended to take the position, "Well, the board has made mistakes and perhaps some infusion of new personnel by the addition of members to the board would be the best way of handling it." The hearings left the public with an impression that I think is unfair to the board and its staff. Of course, I am biased on the subject, but even as I look back at it from this distance, I think that there are many people who, if they had had time to make a close study of the situation, would have concluded that the board was doing a courageous and sound job—but due to the hearings they either judged otherwise or did not think that they could defend the board. The board's subsequent reputation for partisanship was created by the publicity of these hearings and has never since been changed.

### The Smith Committee Intermediate Report

The intermediate report of the Smith Committee was issued in March 1940. It began with a recital of charges that had been made against various members of the board. The second part dealt with the performance of the various divisions of the NLRB. Based largely on the Leiserson memoranda, it severely attacked the Secretary's Office. It criticized the personnel policies of the Review Division, and specifically two of the least competent attorneys with some justification, but neglected to appraise the other 103 attorneys in the division. The report then went on to allege that the review attorneys had considered facts outside the record in making their recommendations to the board and had discussed cases with trial examiners, general counsel, and litigation division and regional directors. This allegation was totally without foundation.

The next part of the report discussed the board's policies and interpretations.

The final portion dealt with recommendations for amendments to the act, although the content of the hearings had not directly related to these issues. First of all, the committee recommended the abolition of the existing board and the creation of a new board, which would have involved the appointment of totally new personnel. Secondly, they recommended the modification of the prohibition against interference, restraint, or coercion, advocating the AFL amendment with respect to expressions of opinions by employers. They also proposed that the obligation to bargain collectively should be modified so as to make it clear that it was not an obligation to make an agreement, but simply an obligation to discuss differences. Next, they had an amendment with respect to the authority of the board to designate the collective bargaining unit, which went considerably beyond the AFL proposal. The committee proposal was that where there was a controversy as to what the unit should be, the board had no authority to make any determination. They also came out in favor of the separation of functions, recommending the creation of an administrator to handle the investigating and prosecuting functions; the new board would be limited to adjudicating functions. The committee proposed an amendment requiring application of the rules of evidence "insofar as it is practical to apply them." The scope of court review would be extended. The committee recommended that employers be permitted to petition for election in the event that more than one union was petitioning to represent the workers. Other amendments imposed a statute of limitations and excluded a substantial group of agricultural laborers.

Representatives Healey and Murdock filed a minority report. Two attorneys in the Department of Labor were largely responsible for drafting this minority report based on the NLRB's analysis of the hearing record and the majority report. The majority would not postpone the issuance of the majority report until the minority had had time to prepare its report in response, so the publicity was all related to the majority report. When the minority report came out about two weeks later no one paid much attention.

The minority report was firmly critical of the majority:

> What the majority report fails to state, however, is that the committee made little effort to follow out the mandate of the House that it "investigate and ascertain the facts" which might point the way to desirable changes in the National Labor Relations Act. Rather, under the guidance of the general counsel, this committee spent many weeks listening to charges and counter-charges of unrelated instances of alleged

indiscretions on the part of various employees of the board, rather than focusing its attention on the manner which the board was dealing with the administration of the Act, and the extent to which the board, or the provisions of the present statute, fell short of achieving the objectives so clearly set forth in the preamble of the Act.

The minority then immediately went into an analysis of the amendments. Healey and Murdock chose to emphasize their objection to the amendments proposed by the majority and to subordinate their rebuttal to the attack on the board. The fact that they thought it was more important, and more likely of success, to hit directly at the amendments rather than to first defend the board reflected the effectiveness of the attack. The minority proposed that the board be increased to five members, but retaining the existing three members. They said this would serve to bring a fresh viewpoint to the problems of the board, whether of policy or personnel, and "help to resolve fairly and equitably any disputed problem without sacrificing the advantage of continuity in the administration of the Act." That also was a recognition of the effectiveness of the committee hearings. They proposed to grant employers the right to petition for elections in the event that two unions were demanding bargaining rights. The rest of the report contained a survey of the board's accomplishments and an analysis of the detailed charges made by the majority.

## WORLD WAR II

The amendments proposed by the Smith Committee were referred to the House Labor Committee. The House passed a series of amendments similar to those recommended by the Smith Committee, but the amendments did not come to a vote in the Senate. At about this time the war in Europe began to assume serious proportions. The Nazis burst through into France at the beginning of May 1940 and the attention of the country was directed in large part to the European war and its implications for the United States. It was also the beginning of the defense program, the acceleration of the program of aid to the Allies, and the controversy over the Selective Service Act. These preoccupations prevented the opponents of the National Labor Relations Act from obtaining enough momentum to get the amendments through the Senate in 1940. The amendments were postponed for another year. By the following year the war effort had assumed such proportions that further amendment of the act was not taken up until after World War II.

Ultimately, the culmination of all these efforts were the Taft-Hartley amendments, passed in 1947.

But these events lay in the future. At the time, the Smith Committee's report was damaging to the board's public reputation and made our daily business more difficult. We found it more difficult to negotiate settlements. It added to the intensity of the opposition to the board by individual employers and to some extent by the AFL. It had some effect on the courts, but it is hard to measure that. The courts saw a particular piece of the board's work, knew the details of that, and were guided to a large extent by what the board had done in that particular case. So the board's success with the courts on the whole continued unimpaired. Since the board was performing an effective job, the basic fairness of the board's procedures tended to offset the general implications of the Smith Committee's hearings. The damage was substantial, but perhaps not as great as might have been expected.

Warren Madden's term as chairman expired in August 1940. After a long delay it was decided in December 1940 that he would not be reappointed and Professor Millis was appointed as chairman. The following year Edwin Smith's term expired and he was not reappointed. Thus by August 1941 the board had been effectively reconstituted, and the new members functioned more cautiously than had the prior members.

The war changed the whole atmosphere. The tremendous upsurge in economic activity, rising prices, the ability to pay higher wages, the heightened motivation to solve strikes and settle labor disputes—all this resulted in much conflict between labor and management. By 1941 unions had become widely established and were in a much stronger position than they had been at the beginning of the New Deal. NLRB cases tended to deal with more minor issues rather than those of basic significance to organized labor. So the act was not as necessary to labor. The controversy over the NLRB receded from public focus.

The close of 1940 marked the end of a definite era in the history of the NLRB. The main task that the board had been given to perform had been accomplished. The revision of the board's composition eliminated some of the public criticism, merely because it was a change in personnel, and also because the new members modified some of the board's positions, so that management and the public had less about which to raise controversy.

Employer opposition continued and blossomed immediately after World War II. The hangover from this earlier prewar period undoubtedly affected the drive for the Taft-Hartley Act. Considerable impetus was also given to the Taft-Hartley Act by the economic and political situation after the war. In the face of postwar unemployment, labor was pressing for higher wage rates. An intensification of the conflict between labor and management in the immediate postwar period revived the incentive that management had for amendments that would take some of the steam out of labor. The postwar reaction against the New Deal and the Democratic losses in the 1946 congressional elections gave a political impetus to this. Employers now thought that they could accomplish what they could not accomplish before the war and they sought to take advantage of it.

## THE FINAL REPORT OF THE SMITH COMMITTEE

After issuing the intermediate report in March, the Smith Committee continued its hearings through most of the rest of 1940. Not as spectacular as the earlier hearings, they trained a consistent fire on the NLRB and perpetuated the impact of the original hearings on public opinion. The Smith Committee issued its final report on December 28, 1940. Healey and Murdock issued a statement charging that the majority, eager to issue its report before the end of the year (when the session of Congress and the committee's authority expired), had compiled it hurriedly and had not made it available to the minority even to look at, much less to prepare a minority report.

### Smearing the NLRB with the Red Paintbrush

The emphasis in the final report turned much more toward the "red" issue. The first part of the report was an elaborate attempt to smear the whole board and its personnel as being motivated by un-American ideals and activities. In the introduction to the report the majority for the committee stated its four major conclusions as to the defects in the present situation with the act administered by the present board. The first two conclusions related to the Communist problem. First, it was alleged, there was "the existence of a large group among the board's personnel motivated by a social concept of an employer-employee relationship based upon class conflict rather than cooperative enterprise." Second, the report saw:

a complete lack of loyalty and belief in democratic institutions and processes, demonstrated at times by an open or half-concealed allegiance to alien and subversive doctrines, and by affiliations with or sympathies for un-American organizations advocating the overthrow of our political and economic system; and others, by a bold defiance of the people of the United States.

The third point the report found was a flagrant disregard of constitutional rights and procedural safeguards.

The fourth and final point was that the interpretation of the law by the board and its staff was in a way that was not intended by the framers of the legislation. The report goes on:

Examples from the record are presented to show how members and employees of the board were profoundly influenced by the doctrines and teachings of the leftist philosophy which the committee believes incompatible with a truly democratic system of government. Fraternizing with Communist sympathizers, attending meetings of societies behind whose innocuous names lurks the Communist incubus, accepting suggestions and instructions from Communists and near-Communists—all these and many other instances of improper associations and activities have convinced the committee that many of the employees of the board are unfit for the task of fair and impartial administration of the act. Amid such a luxuriant growth of alien philosophy, no democratic process would long have a chance to survive.

That was the conclusion of the Smith Committee and what they attempted to convey to the public. The report did not give any substantial evidence for those conclusions. Most of the objections focused on Edwin Smith. His trip to Mexico was referred to at great length. It was pointed out that he had participated in a meeting, or series of meetings, sponsored by the Confederation of Workers of Mexico, which was alleged to be a Communist-dominated organization. The report likewise attempted to make a great deal out of various contacts that Smith had had with Harry Bridges [head of the Longshoreman's Union on the West Coast and "reputed" to be left-wing]. These contacts were all matters relating to issues before the Labor Board, and so far as the record discloses there was nothing that could be considered improper about them. Nevertheless, the committee attempted to build them up as showing a sort of collusion between Smith and Bridges.

The committee also made a good deal out of the fact that late in 1940, after Chairman Madden had not been reappointed and the board was attempting to function with only Smith and Leiserson as board members, the board had received a letter stating that one of the stenographers was a member of the Communist Party. Another letter had been received from the Civil Service Commission stating that they had information that another stenographer at the board was either a member of the party or interested in Communist activities. The question had come before the board as to what should be done about these two charges. Leiserson took the position that the matter should be referred to the Department of Justice for investigation by the FBI. Edwin Smith took the position that the charges did not show any violation of law, were general in their nature and unsupported by any factual detail, and were therefore too vague to refer to the Department of Justice for any action and no action should be taken on the matter. As there was no third member of the board present, the conflict remained unresolved.

There was also an effort to show that Madden shared this support for "alien ideologies." This was done entirely by pointing out that Madden had supported Al Wirin for a position on the board's staff. Wirin had been active in the American Civil Liberties Union. At one time, in attempting to represent an individual in Gallup, New Mexico, he had been seized, beaten, and thrown out of town. There was considerable publicity about that incident. He had applied and been accepted for a position on the board's staff. There was then considerable opposition to him from several sources, including Sen. William G. McAdoo of California. Madden supported Wirin and refused to discharge him. The committee used this as the principal reason for its charge that Madden "demonstrated decidedly zealous favoritism for radicals and radical movements." The other episode zealous favoritism for radicals and radical movements." The other episode that they advanced in support of that generalization was that Madden did not dismiss David Saposs after the House Appropriations Committee had recommended the abolition of the Economic Division. The committee's report also contains a section on Saposs.

The remainder of the section on Communist influences on the board related to various employees. The committee emphasized that the union of board employees was an industrial type of union, implying that the board employees were favorable to the CIO. A congressman who was a member of the Subcommittee on Appropriations that was considering the board's appropriations testified that Saposs and one of his assistants, George Brooks, had both stated that there was a substantial group of employees at the board who followed the Communist Party line. These included myself, Shad Polier, and Margaret Porter (all of us in the Review Division) and Aaron Warner. Saposs and Brooks both denied having made this statement when they were called before the committee.

This was the first time that I had been charged in any substantial or official way with following the Communist Party line. I had already testified before the committee, so I wrote a letter, in which I said:

> While I assume that the committee would not base any conclusions regarding my political affiliations upon such remote hearsay, in order that there may be no doubt on the matter I wish to state that I am not now and never have been a member of the Communist Party; that I do not now and never had "hued to the Communist Party line"; and that I do not now and never have belonged to any organization dominated or controlled by the Communist Party. I request that this letter be printed in the proceedings of your committee. I am quite willing to appear before your committee at any time to testify regarding the foregoing matter.

That was my first public denial of Communist Party membership and curiously enough seems to be expressed in the language that later became famous: "I am not now and never have been. . . . " The committee acknowledged that the charges had been denied by me and the others.

The report also contained statements by three or four board employees in letters indicating some sympathy with the Soviet Union. One of them, for instance, was by an attorney who was as far from being a Communist as anyone could be, but who had been to the World's Fair and was enthusiastic about the Soviet exhibit at the World's Fair. He had ended his rather fatuous letter praising the perisphere by saying,

> Just seeing this exhibit might work up an interest in you not only to see the country, but also to become a citizen of Russia.

It was a rather stupid remark that the committee, of course, played up a good deal.

The report quoted an article written by one of the trial examiners referring in uncomplimentary terms to the role of the FBI and the Department of Justice in the Palmer raids; it also referred to a particular state's police system as having "because of their activities against labor and radical groups become known as American cossacks." The report then states, "When the extent of this expressed contempt for cherished American institutions is realized, it is not surprising that such leftist doctrines should find their way into the very decisions of the board itself."

Finally, there was a long section on an NLRB case involving a secretary at the *New York Times* who alleged that she had been discharged for union activity. Her employer's defense was that he had discharged her because she was connected with a "communistic group." The issue in the case was a simple one under the act of whether or not she had been discharged for union activity, or for some other reason. If she had been discharged for union activity and that was the dominant cause in her discharge, then clearly she was entitled to reinstatement. If she had not been discharged for union activity, but for any other cause—including Communism—she was not entitled to reinstatement. Madden and Smith both agreed that the facts showed that the secretary had been discharged for union activity. Leiserson had not addressed himself to the factual issue of the cause of the discharge, but had assumed that the discharge was because of Communist activity.

I have described in some detail this part of the report on the alleged Communist sympathies of the board and its staff because it illustrates the atmosphere of the period. The committee undoubtedly had been influenced in focusing its attack in the final report on the alleged radicalism of the board by the success of the Dies Committee, which had been functioning since 1938 and apparently had been effective in making an impact on the public. [The Dies Committee later evolved into the House Committee on Un-American Activities.]

The Smith Committee took an extremely irrational and distorted position on this matter, one that offended the sense of decency and honesty of any person who might read the record and examine the details. On the other hand, the report indicates the extent to which the board members and staff thought that issues of communism were relatively unimportant and should not be permitted to distract attention from the merits of the issues involved. Thus, the fact that Al Wirin had been attacked as a radical made no difference to Madden so long as Wirin's work for the board was competent. It was the same way with respect to the question of whether a stenographer who was a member of the Communist Party should be discharged or not. Edwin Smith took the position that it was relatively immaterial, that no harm could be done if she were a member of the Communist Party. Another example is the *New York Times* case, where the fact that a person was alleged to be engaged in Communist activities was held by the board to be quite irrelevant on the issue before it, which was whether the individual had been discharged for union activity.

This reveals the two opposing views on Communist activity in government. The board's view was that no serious danger was involved, that certainly there was no cause for emotion or irrational acts; they discriminated between different types of liberal and radical views. This still seems to me to be a sound approach to the problem. On the other hand, there was the highly emotional approach of the Smith Committee and the attempt to prejudice the entire work of the NLRB on the basis of allegations that some of the board staff and members held radical views; this seems to me a complete distortion of the picture and an attempt to create prejudice rather than to throw any light on the situation.

This was the first time that I had seen at close range the use of charges of radicalism in this way. The Dies Committee had not struck home to me as much as the Smith Committee. I think the attack tarnished the reputation of the board further.

Edmund Toland, the committee counsel, was undoubtedly responsible for a large part of this report. The intermediate report had been replete with isolated incidents used to prove generalizations that were not warranted by the facts. The only thing that was new in this final report was the emphasis on the Communist issue. Toland was very conservative, a member of the Catholic Church, subject to Catholic influences on the Communist issue. My impression of Toland when he appeared before the board was that he was not a good lawyer, that he was happy-go-lucky, superficial, and not well trained or disciplined in technical legal work, nor skillful at dealing with legal issues or writing briefs. He might have been an adequate trial lawyer in the sense that he was an extrovert and probably adept at handling people. The extent to which he had a keen sense of drama and publicity surprised us; we had not seen that potential in him.

The remainder of the final report of the majority of the Smith Committee to a large extent reiterated the charges made in the intermediate report, mostly without acknowledging the answer that the minority had made to the intermediate report. The final report delved into more detail. It spent more time attacking the board's interpretation of the National Labor Relations Act as expressed in various cases, without any analysis of the judicial decisions that had affirmed the board's position in many cases. The final report also contained more material on the work of the regional offices.

Concerning my own bailiwick, the Review Division, the report again reiterated charges, without any consideration of the answer to them, and went further, charging that the review attorneys "pretty well decided what [any] decision should be." There was no documentary or testimonial support for this charge in the report.

By the time of the final report Leiserson was no longer using the Review Division for his information in reaching a decision. In his original testimony before the committee he had stated that the Review Division was working adequately. In fact, he tended to praise the work of the Review Division, comparing it favorably with the work of the Secretary's Office. But later he took the position that he would not sit in the board meetings at which the Review Division reported on cases, but would make his own examination of the records. The Review Division thought that his reason was that he did not want to work such long hours as the other board members did in hearing the reports. He claimed that it was quite unnecessary, that he could tell by reading the trial examiner's report and the briefs how the case should be decided. Sometime toward the middle of 1940 he ceased coming to board meetings. Consequently, the cases were decided by Madden and Edwin Smith, drafted and prepared, and then Leiserson would make his decision. We never knew how fully he was acquainted with the record. It seemed to us that he could not possibly have had any real grasp of the material in the record, because the records were so long and much of the evidence was in conflict.

In the final report of the Smith Committee, Leiserson's position was noted and used as evidence that Leiserson no longer believed that the Review Division was performing a necessary function.

The intermediate report had spelled out in great detail the committee's proposals with respect to amendments and no changes were made at the time of the final report. Since the House had already passed the Smith Committee amendments, they merely expressed the hope that the Senate would take similar action. Consequently, the recommendations in the final report related to the board itself. Their main recommendation was complete reorganization of the board and its personnel.

The minority members of the committee declared in a press statement:

> In our future informal report, the minority members of this committee will show that the blanket charges against employees of the National Labor Relations board are entirely unwarranted. If there be employees of the board unfit to hold a government position, we are confident that the present board is able and willing to take any necessary action. It should be observed also that any individual instances of irregularity should be measured against the genuine and important accomplishments of the act and the board's administration.

The minority never prepared this promised report.

The Smith Committee had succeeded in getting across to Congress, the public, and even to a fair proportion of the administration that the board was exceedingly biased, partisan and prejudiced in its handling of the National Labor Relations Act, and that it was prejudiced against both employers and the AFL. The committee also succeeded in getting across the notion that the board included a number of Communists on its staff, was influenced by and sympathetic to Communist notions, and generally was filled with radicals and radical sympathizers.

I should note that throughout this period the House Dies Committee had continued hearings, and had been attacking many figures in the administration as being un-American: Harry Hopkins, Frances Perkins, Leon Henderson, and many of the leading figures of the New Deal. President Roosevelt's reaction had been a complete disdain for the committee, refusing to yield to its accusations and dismissing it as the work of a lunatic fringe. The president made sharp attacks on the committee in press conferences. The spirit of the administration was to treat accusations of radicalism as insignificant flea bites bound to occur in our system of government, which should not be taken too seriously.

My view of the Smith Committee's legal procedures was one of contempt and unconcern. It did not occur to me that this sort of material, unsupported and distorted, without substance, would ever be effective. I completely missed the portent about the Communist issue. My point of view was shared by most of the younger New Deal lawyers. They tended to treat the whole thing as a laughing matter. Most of them did not hesitate any more than before in expressing radical views or participating in radical organizations.

That attitude, shared by many young lawyers and ardent New Dealers around Washington, gradually changed. The implications became more serious and the position of the committees became stronger. All along many members of Congress had taken the alleged "Communist" threat seriously and pretty much at face value, or at least they voted that way, because the committees always received strong support from Congress. Apparently the public at large took it seriously, too, but as the 1930s–with the Depression, the New Deal, and all we had accomplished–drew to a close and the new decade opened with the ominous rumblings of World War II, I did not foresee how the "Communist" issue would develop.

## AFTERMATH

Although many people around Washington did not take the charges of radical activity seriously, subsequent events indicate that the attack on the NLRB was quite effective. Undoubtedly, Congress would have passed debilitating amendments except that the war issue had diverted attention elsewhere, and the failure to reappoint Madden and the resignations of some key members of the board's staff had provided an opportunity for reorganization of personnel and policies. The Roosevelt administration was urging strongly that no further action be taken until the effects of these personnel changes could be assessed.

The Attorney General's Committee had made a detailed survey of the board's operations in connection with its general survey of administrative procedure in the federal government during this period. In its final report and in a separate monograph on the NLRB, it had discussed the board's procedures. Unlike the Smith Committee, the attorney general's committee attempted to give a picture of the normal operations of the board. The focus was on procedures rather than policy. Conducted by people from a more objective and scholarly point of view, and by people more friendly to the objectives of the National Labor Relations Act, the report vindicated the board. It recommended some changes in the board's procedures, as it did in the procedures of most of the agencies it studied. These changes, however, were not of a major character. It urged that the trial examiner's function be strengthened through creation of an Office of Hearing Commissioners, and that the intermediate reports filed by trial examiners be improved and used much more as the basis of the board's decisions. In this way it would be possible, the committee thought, to make reliance on review attorneys unnecessary. Actually, I do not think that review attorneys could have been entirely eliminated, but the recommendation to make more use of the trial examiner and to avoid some of the duplication between what the trial examiners did and what the review attorneys did was a change toward which the board itself had been working.

The other recommendations were even more minor. The committee thought that the board ought to specify more details of the charges in its complaints, that uncontested issues that were admitted should not have to be tried, and that a uniform method in obtaining subpoenas for attorneys from both sides was needed because the board's practice with respect to subpoenas permitted the board attorneys to obtain subpoenas somewhat more readily than attorneys for other parties, a criticism that I think was justified. The committee also urged that the board's attorneys participate in the post-hearing process by preparing briefs and making oral arguments in matters after the trial examiner had rendered his report, a practice that the board would have liked to incorporate but did not have the funds, staff, or time to do.

The board's crisis deepened because of the failure to reappoint Chairman Madden. When his term expired in August 1940, Madden stopped functioning as a board member, as no section of the act provided for a member to continue until his successor was appointed. It was uncertain between August and December whether or not Madden would be reappointed. Considerable pressures from employers, Congress, and the AFL opposed him. The CIO was his main advocate. The administration was uncertain what to do. The president and Miss Perkins realized that Madden was a highly incorruptible public servant who had performed in a most effective manner. At the same time they thought he had not shown sufficient resiliency in adapting to the pressures surrounding the board and that he had carried things too far and therefore was a serious political liability. It soon became clear that no decision would be announced before the election of 1940. No matter what the president did he would have antagonized an important wing of the labor movement.

The board could not accomplish much with only two board members. During this period labor was fortunate that it did not need the National Labor Relations Act as much as it had in previous years. The organization of the mass production industries had been consolidated. The opposition of employers had not only decreased by 1940, but no longer challenged the basic elements of the National Labor Relations Act, at least openly. Yet labor suffered substantially from the conflict within the board and particularly from the delay in the appointment of a chairman. Although a good deal of the board's work could proceed almost automatically by this time, a number of important decisions could not be made and labor protested. But the board's major work had been accomplished by 1940.

Finally, in November or December the president announced that Professor Millis would be appointed to take Madden's place. Madden was appointed to a judgeship on the court of claims. Those of us who knew him have sensed that he felt that life on the court was rather dull in comparison with his work on the NLRB, and that he was not fully reconciled to the quasi-retirement that the new post entailed.

Some of us felt a keen sense of outrage that the administration had not reappointed Madden. We believed it was a serious injustice because Madden had demonstrated his complete devotion to the objectives for which he was appointed and in his official capacity as administrator had done an excellent job. We realized that opposition to him had developed, but most of us on the board's staff thought that the opposition was completely arbitrary and short-sighted and the administration should not have given it the weight that it did. Consequently, there was considerable talk of resignation.

Nat Witt obviously had made up his mind to resign if Madden was not appointed. Perhaps he would have resigned anyway. He was eager to return to New York and to leave the government. He felt somewhat stifled, as he expressed it, from the turn of events that he foresaw as coming and those that were then taking place. He also realized that as long as Leiserson remained at the board, his position was untenable. It was impossible for a board to function with even one member refusing for all practical purposes to deal with him and expressing lack of confidence in the Secretary's Office.

The other members of the staff were in a somewhat different position. I was myself, in that Leiserson's criticism had not been directed to any extent against me or the Review Division. If Millis had agreed with Leiserson, the work of the Review Division would have been seriously curtailed; nevertheless, I could have continued my job with Leiserson there. However, I believed that we should protest publicly the president's action in refusing to reappoint Madden. I felt deeply that Madden had been wronged in the matter. I talked with Alexander Hawes, Witt's chief assistant, and some of the others about resigning. Witt, who had decided to resign himself, took a completely neutral position as to whether anyone else should or not. He refused to urge us to, and, if anything, rather urged us not to. However, Hawes and I finally decided that we would resign. Consequently, the day following the announcement that Madden would not be appointed, Witt, Hawes and I all resigned. Our resignations created quite a stir. Many people interpreted our action as rats quitting the sinking ship. At the same time our resignations were welcomed as an opportunity for the board to answer some of its critics by appointing new personnel.

So my association with the NLRB came to an end. This was a turning point not only in my career, but in the Washington scene. It marked the final curtain on any aggressive New Dealism. In fact, the board had survived beyond its time.  In many New Deal agencies talented people had left and been replaced by less able persons: the New Deal spirit was eroding and the board had persisted along the old lines in the new atmosphere.  Its downfall was probably inevitable.

## Assessment

I never enjoyed any period of my career more than my five years with the NLRB.  I felt a sense of mission, a sense of active struggle against opposition, and a sense of accomplishment.  I believed that the work the board was doing was extremely important.  I had believed from the very beginning that the National Labor Relations Act was the key piece of legislation in the New Deal.  By establishing the power of labor to organize into associations, the act was creating an institutional force that would support the liberal measures that the New Deal advocated.  This would be the most significant organized force in support of the New Deal and in support of the change in the social, political, and economic structure of the country—which I thought was necessary.

I also believed that the job was performed more in accordance with the principles of sound government and more efficiently than had been true in NRA, for instance.  Here we had time to assess the situation and gradually work out procedures that were reasonably well-balanced between the government's interest in efficient operation of the law and the individual's interest in a fair chance to present his viewpoint and be treated fairly.  I believe the board was doing a fine job.  Despite opinions that the board's position was too intransigent, I am convinced that the board's interpretations of the act and the board's aggressive enforcement of the act was what was needed.  I was not willing to make any substantial concessions to the practical politics of the situation.

I sensed more unity at NLRB than in any other organization in my experience, before or since.  The harmony that existed among the various factions at the NLRB is rare.  There were differences of opinion, but the staff had sufficient goodwill toward each other and sufficient devotion to the ultimate objectives that concessions were made willingly.  We negotiated decisions that were satisfactory to everyone.  The result was a tremendous esprit de corps.  I attribute a good deal of it to the leadership of Chairman Madden.  His integrity generated such respect, his ability to compromise and his perspicacity about people and their viewpoints promoted such resourcefulness that he towered above the situation and was largely responsible for the remarkable harmony.

This unity was shattered when Leiserson came.  I was astonished at the way Leiserson broke down a structure that had functioned so harmoniously.  He not only made relationships among the board members almost impossible, but his position created various factions within the staff.

The NLRB of my time became a legend among government lawyers.  As young lawyers arrived in Washington, they would hear tales of an agency that was characterized by tremendous courage, great ability to resist pressure, and great tenacity for its positions.  Some look back with longing at the way the board backed up its subordinates who basically were performing well, but who had got into some immediate difficulty. Even now [1953] it is regarded as an unusual government agency, with which young idealists could be happily associated, but alas, it no longer exists in that form.

I learned an inordinate amount at the NLRB. I had held the naive assumption that careful, scholarly, objective work would win out in the end, and was by itself sufficient. The antics of the Smith Committee investigation and of Leiserson did not turn me into a cynic, although I concluded that under certain conditions the obscurantism, distortion, and prejudice of a Smith Committee would make an impact, and that one would have to take those factors into account. I did not toss overboard all the previous values that I had held with respect to government work. It did open my eyes, however, to other aspects of government operation in a way that I had certainly not visualized before.

# 7

# WORLD WAR II
# INTERVENES

*Before Pearl Harbor...*

Before embarking on my account of the Office of Price Administration, I would like to mention a few matters with respect to the political atmosphere in Washington in the years just before the United States entered World War II.

## THE POLITICAL ATMOSPHERE
*The Dies Committee, the Hatch Act....*

The presidential election of 1938 marked the turning point in the New Deal. After that it no longer continued to advance and became instead a holding and consolidating operation. The failure of Roosevelt's attempted purge in the 1938 election and the loss of a substantial group of liberals were signs of the turning temper of the times. From that time on, support for the administration in both the House and Senate declined substantially—and presumably Congress reflected the sentiments of the country.

At the same time, increasing attention was paid to "Communist infiltration" in the government and the issue of loyalty. Beginning in 1938, when the House Committee on Un-American Activities ( known then as the Dies Committee) started functioning, more and more attention focused on problems of "Communist subversion." The attacks became increasingly shrill, and the assumption that the problem in the government was a serious one, requiring firm measures, became more accepted. The Dies Committee was the main institution creating this atmosphere. Perhaps other groups originated the issue, but the Dies Committee fostered it and pressed it most vigorously in the beginning. Rep. Martin Dies (Democrat, Texas), from the start of his committee in 1938, was constantly preaching the necessity of ridding the government of subversive employees. He made broad charges that numerous employees in the government were subversive and disloyal. When the Roosevelt administration refused to dismiss employees he had mentioned, he would attack the administration for continuing to harbor subversives.

Dies himself was quite important in creating what became the standard procedure: extreme over-generalization, extreme charges, lack of any substantial evidence to back up most of the charges, use of the doctrine of guilt by association, denial of adequate opportunity for those accused to rebut the accusation, and repeated public assertions of the serious nature of the problem. These were all characteristic of the beginning of the Dies Committee.

It was clear from the beginning that this attack by Dies was mainly a political attack on the New Deal. Many of the individuals that Dies singled out as the objects of his charges were important New Deal officials. He demanded the resignation of Secretary Ickes and Secretary Perkins, as well as Harry Hopkins, on the ground that they all espoused the philosophy of class hatred. One committee member attacked a series of forums that he claimed had been organized by Communist front organizations and listed as government officials who were sponsoring the forums William O. Douglas, Jerome Frank, Edwin Smith (of the NLRB), Corrington Gill (who was then assistant WPA administrator), and Nathan Margold (the solicitor of the Department of the Interior). The motivation for the anti-Communist campaign was made clear by Rep. J. Parnell Thomas, who was then a member and subsequently became chairman of the committee, when he said, "In some respects it [referring to the "fifth column"] is synonymous to the New Deal, so the surest way of removing the fifth column from our shores is to remove the New Deal from the seat of government." Another indication of the political nature of the issue was the attack on the Tennessee Valley Authority (TVA), resulting from the accusation that twelve subordinate employees out of 3500 employed by TVA were members of the Communist Party.

The administration declined to fight the Dies Committee hand-to-hand in this early stage. It took the position that these charges were the product of a fanatical mind and did not deserve serious attention; the charges were either ignored or flatly denied. For instance, in October 1939 Representative Dies made public a list of over 500 federal employees who were charged with membership in the American League for Peace and Democracy, an organization the Dies Committee had already accused of being a Communist front. While it probably was true that the American League for Peace and Democracy was rather strongly influenced by the Communist Party, many of the persons on Dies' list had never belonged to the organization. His list apparently included a mailing list as well as a membership list. None of those charged had been given a chance to appear before the committee or to indicate in any way whether they were members or not. On this occasion President Roosevelt attacked the committee, charging that the publication of the list was a "sordid procedure."

However, as time went on it became clear that the Dies Committee had considerable support in Congress. Despite efforts of the administration to defeat the committee or restrict its appropriations, it always succeeded in obtaining a substantial vote from the House. Until 1946 the committee was a select committee; consequently its life had to be extended at every new Congress, so the issue came up every two years as to whether the committee should be extended. Also, the question of how much money should be allocated to the committee's work arose every year. The committee consistently won these repeated tests of its popularity by increasingly large margins.

Anti-Communist pressure from Congress also arose from other sources. As I have indicated, the Smith Committee's investigation of the NLRB delved into this area in the second series of hearings in 1940. In addition, Congress passed the Hatch Act in 1939, which included a provision that no member of the federal government could belong to any organization that "advocates the overthrow of our constitutional form of government." No criminal penalty was attached to the Hatch Act; the sanction was that any such person should be removed from office and that no funds should be used to pay him. Beginning in 1941, a provision was inserted in all appropriations acts directing that none of the funds could be used to pay the salary of a person who "advocates, or who is a member of an organization that advocates, the overthrow of the government of the United States by force and violence." In 1940 passage of the Smith Act made it a criminal offense to advocate, or conspire to advocate, overthrow of the government by force or violence. So throughout this period Congress was passing a series of enactments directed against the problem of subversion.

The early period when the administration could afford to ignore or blast the criticism coming from congressional committees gradually passed into a situation in which the administration acknowledged that some action was necessary. Also, certain persons in the administration who were more sympathetic with the committees' viewpoint than others began moving more vigorously in accordance with the general point of view that the committees represented. In 1941 Dies sent a list of 1121 federal employees to the attorney general, charging that they were either Communists or affiliated with subversive organizations. The administration apparently believed that these charges should be investigated and therefore they did not oppose an appropriation of $100,000 for the FBI to check this list and other groups of alleged subversives. In 1941 and early 1942 the FBI used this appropriation to make an extensive check of the employees named by Dies and other persons. In September 1942 the attorney general reported back to Congress that with most of the investigation completed, the evidence uncovered by the FBI had resulted in the dismissal of two employees out of the 1121 and disciplinary action against one other. However, in spite of the lack of evidence for the Dies charges, substantial support for increasingly more restrictive measures was generated.

In 1941 Helen Miller, an employee of the Department of Labor, became the first person discharged on loyalty grounds. Charged with subversive acts, she was discharged under general provisions of the civil service laws that permitted discharge for such cause as would promote the efficiency of the service. This was the first public and clear-cut loyalty case. Subsequently, special provisions, beginning with the Hatch Act (which had already been passed) and other specific provisions including those of the appropriations acts, were relied upon. In April 1942 the attorney general appointed an interdepartmental committee on investigations to attempt to coordinate loyalty investigations. That committee issued a list of subversive organizations that was circulated privately to the government agencies. The Civil Service Commission was also rather active in pressing early loyalty investigations. Shortly after the passage of the Hatch Act, operating under its mandate to investigate and approve the appointment of employees, the commission established procedures to implement the Hatch Act that involved, in effect, loyalty clearance.

All these developments expanded the concept and machinery for a loyalty program. Many governmental employees regarded it as foolishness and were not seriously affected by it, but a proliferating group began to consider more carefully their associations and the ideas they were expressing on governmental policies; they were particularly concerned with the persons they were responsible for employing. The standards for government employment with respect to persons reputed to hold radical views gradually tightened and government employees became increasingly cautious about radical associations and opinions.

Another element in the political atmosphere was the influence of the war. The Nazi breakthrough in France in May and June 1940 had a dramatic effect on Washington; from that time on the war was the major issue in Washington and affected everything that was done. The war made an economic impact as the defense program expanded and a political impact as the war issues began to assume major importance in the Washington scene. The focus on war increased throughout 1941, particularly as the economic picture began to change. The development of the defense program created numerous problems that began to absorb most of the attention of the administration as 1941 progressed.

### Attack on New Deal Administrative Procedures

While the political atmosphere put the New Deal on the defensive, one thrust of the attack is particularly relevant to the following discussion of the Office of Price Administration (OPA): the attack on New Deal administrative procedures. The attack on the NLRB, including its procedures and administration, was only the most dramatic thrust of a general attack on the administration of most of the New Deal agencies. Agencies such as the Securities and Exchange Commission (SEC), the Federal Communications Commission (FCC), sections of the Department of Agriculture, and other key agencies in the New Deal also were frequently attacked for the manner in which they were administering New Deal legislation and with respect to their administrative procedures.

Until the shift in the Supreme Court's position in 1937, the New Deal had faced opposition mainly on the substantive issues and on the basic constitutional validity of the legislation. After 1937, however, it appeared that the substantive positions were rather firmly entrenched and that the constitutional attack no longer was a route to success. Attacks on administration had occurred all along, but the legitimation of existing New Deal programs shifted the focus from 1937 up until the war to various aspects of how the New Deal was being carried out. Since the opposition had succeeded in producing a stalemate whereby no significant new legislation passed after 1938, the focus of controversy shifted to the administration of the existing legislation.

Although many of the basic procedures had been established in connection with the Interstate Commerce Commission and the Federal Trade Commission (FTC) at a much earlier period, there had been no comprehensive attack on the fundamental procedures of either agency. Considerable and in many respects successful opposition had developed to both agencies, but the opposition focused on issues rather than on procedures. So the FTC procedure, which was a serious modification of prior methods and theories of separation of powers and the role of the judicial function, had never been challenged as unconstitutional in Supreme Court decisions. This is further evidence that the controversy over procedure arose in part from opposition to New Deal measures and was a concealed attack upon the substance of the provisions, although in part it was a genuine concern over the developments in administrative law. Many people with a liberal point of view were honestly concerned that the developments in administrative procedure were tending to undermine traditional judicial procedures and that the whole situation needed review and some modification.

The sources of the opposition were varied. A substantial part centered in Congress, representing both good faith concern and opposition to the New Deal. Even within the administration some viewed the procedural developments with alarm. It was not clear how the current situation would evolve.

Another source of challenge was the courts. Even before 1937 the courts had shown a concern about New Deal administrative procedures. The case of *Jones v. SEC* illustrates the attitude of the conservative members of the old Supreme Court toward administrative procedures. In this case the Court opinion strongly attacked the SEC for a situation in which the SEC position was at the very least reasonable.

All these decisions were rather cumbersome attempts, without full understanding of the administrative process, to impose some sort of restrictions, but none of the decisions could stand the test of reality. All were rather quickly forgotten (although none has ever been expressly overruled). The Court demonstrated no particular skill in seizing the weakest points of the administrative process. Of course, the Court was confined to those cases which came before it. The Court obviously was fearful that the administrative process was getting out of bounds and wanted to impose some court restrictions, but the justices either did not know enough or the proper case did not come before them so that they could impose restrictions that as a practical matter would stand up.

A third source of opposition was the legal profession, as represented by the American Bar Association (ABA). The leading lawyers of the country, representing primarily the major business interests, were the natural spokesmen for industrial groups in opposition to New Deal legislation and in particular to New Deal administrative procedures. Procedural issues mainly involved constitutional problems of due process; it was natural that since the issues were expressed in legal terms, lawyers should take the lead. Administrative law was emerging as a whole new body of law. As early as 1933 the ABA had appointed a committee on administrative law to investigate the new developments in administrative law and make recommendations. The committee's first report in 1934 was quite critical of the developments in the administrative process. From then on it functioned as the spearhead in the opposition to New Deal administrative procedure.

A fourth source of opposition was growing in academia. Prominent among the scholars protesting developments in administrative procedure was Dean Roscoe Pound of Harvard Law School. Others in the legal profession and some political scientists were equally critical. As a substantial part of the academic profession tended to defend the New Deal, the academic world was swept by the political controversy of the era.

Critics attacked the administrative process on numerous grounds. First, political scientists in particular expressed concern at the independence of the regulatory agencies, the fact that they were created as independent units and functioned without direct supervision of either the president or a cabinet officer. Once a number of independent agencies had been established, the governmental structure became a nightmare from a political scientist's point of view, in the sense that the cabinet, which was supposed to report directly to the president, represented only one part of the government. Many governmental operations were carried on entirely outside the cabinet department structure, resulting not only in lack of control by the president or by any department head, or of any centralized control, but also in considerable variation in the procedures of the different agencies and in differences of policy.

A second rebuke was directed against the failure of the administrative agencies to give full information to the public on what actions they had taken. This criticism was particularly acute during the NRA period, when hundreds of regulations, and perhaps thousands of amendments, were being issued and there was no systematic method of making the regulations available to the citizens who were supposed to comply with them. The issue had been dramatically focused in the argument of the Panama Refining case, where the actual regulation had accidentally failed to include a key paragraph that everybody had supposed was still in it. Informing the public presented a genuine problem, as did the independence of the regulatory agencies.

A third line of attack was that the agencies were exceeding their authority, that they were acting *ultra vires*. This was the focus of a large part of the Smith Committee's attention. Later in 1942 another Smith committee was appointed, also under the chairmanship of Howard Smith, whose express function was to investigate the abuses by executive agencies exceeding their statutory authority. Those choosing this objection were less pure in their motives than proponents of the preceding two; the issue often concealed an attack on the merits of the legislation. The objection was made also in connection with the sanctions applied by administrative agencies. The accumulation of economic controls had given the government extra powers in addition to their official powers to exercise economic pressure. In some instances these extra powers were being used to bring pressure upon individuals and corporations beyond the express sanctions formally provided in the legislation. The controversy over the question, for instance, of whether government contracts should be awarded to a firm that was in violation of the National Labor Relations Act, or any other federal law, raised this issue. The sanction aspect of the issue raised a serious matter that needed attention. Except for that, most of this objection was another form of opposition to the substance of the legislation, and in any event was subject to control by the court process. The question of interpretation of statutes was subject to judicial review in practically all questions of that sort. But developments in regard to the use of extra sanctions were not always subject to judicial review. Such methods often were exercised informally and presented a problem of growing concern as the complexity of economic regulation increased.

A fourth criticism was the lack of formal judicial procedure in making an essentially judicial decision, or sometimes the lack of any formal procedure in making a decision. The agencies exercised rather extensive legislative and judicial functions. Because Congress had failed to pass the detailed type of legislation needed for complex regulation, the agencies wrote regulations in what might be regarded as a legislative function. Because the agencies resolved a huge volume of complex matters that the courts could not have handled without substantial change in their procedures, the agencies exercised judicial functions. This inevitable development raised the issue of how far the traditional procedures, particularly court procedures, should be followed, and to what extent they could be dispensed with, modified, or replaced with new procedures. Although this criticism often was expressed with exaggerated emphasis, it referred to a genuine problem.

The fifth problem, which arose constantly, was the combination of functions exercised by the administrative agencies that had judicial powers–that is, the combination in the same agency, such as the NLRB, of the investigating, prosecuting, and decision-making powers. This pattern, established in the Federal Trade Commission Act and expanded to a number of New Deal agencies, was criticized sharply as extremely unfair and in violation of basic principles of Anglo-American law. True, such a combination of functions could result in unfairness. On the other hand, effective government operation might require that the same agency rendering the ultimate decision should handle other aspects of the case.

Sixth, opponents contended that the administrative agencies were biased. A good deal of the Smith Committee investigation of the National Labor Relations Act had been focused on alleged bias and the same charges were leveled against other New Deal agencies, although not as strenuously.

Further, opponents attacked the process of agencies making what have been called "institutional decisions." That is, instead of a decision being made as a judge would make it, largely on his own study of the record and his own conclusions, the huge volume of work before the administrative agency had produced a method of decision making that was exemplified in the NLRB by the use of the Review Division: 105 attorneys in the Review Division in effect assisting three board members in making decisions. Obviously the process was quite different than if the three board members had done the work themselves, even with the help of one legal assistant. The decision-making process had become an institutional process performed with the aid of a large staff rather than the personal decisions that judges customarily made. This procedure was subjected to considerable attack by the Smith Committee and others.

Finally, critics cited inadequate judicial review of administrative agency decisions. Many of the statutes stipulated that the findings of fact of an agency, if supported by evidence, were binding on the courts. Opponents alleged that this compelled the courts to rubberstamp the findings of the agencies if *any* evidence existed to support the findings, even though the findings were contrary to the preponderance of the evidence. Also in some instances there was no judicial review of administrative action at all, as on the question of the awarding of government contracts. Consequently, a substantial part of the criticism was directed against deficient supervision by the courts.

The administration itself recognized the significance of these problems and made several attempts to deal with them. The first move was the appointment of the President's Committee on Administrative Management in March 1936. This committee duly issued a report, which contributed more to various reorganization plans than it did to solving the contemporary problems in administrative procedure. Although its criticism was significant and it was relied on to some extent, its impact was limited because it offered no practical solution to these problems.

Meanwhile, the ABA drafted legislation proposing an administrative court. This administrative court, with some forty judges, was to have jurisdiction over all administrative decisions of a quasi-judicial nature. In other words, administrative agencies were to relinquish all judicial functions. The separation was comparable to the French system of administrative law, which has a special system of administrative courts. The proposal struck me and most of those in the government as completely unworkable and contrary to the trend in American law at the time. It was taken seriously enough that the Senate Judiciary Committee held hearings on the bill in 1938, but in the face of notable opposition no further action developed.

**Counterattack**

At the end of 1938, as the attacks were growing more vociferous, the administration by way of counterattack appointed an investigating committee of its own. In December 1938, just after the abortive "purge" in the congressional elections, the attorney general suggested creation of a special committee to study administrative procedure in the government. The president gave his approval and the committee was appointed in February 1939.

When the committee issued its report a year later in early 1941, the majority of the committee concluded that the procedures of the agencies had gradually refined themselves to a point where no major legislation of a general nature was necessary. The committee believed that such a variety of functions were performed under such different sets of circumstances that generalized legislation was impractical and inadvisable. What was needed was a conscious effort to maintain general supervision over the various agencies, with a view to discerning particular problems that needed attention, recommending administrative changes if possible, or legislation if necessary, and handling problems on an issue by issue basis. The committee recommended the establishment of an office of administrative proceedings, which would continually monitor and supervise the various agencies and be able to deal with particular problems. The report also recommended certain improvements in the methods by which the agencies disseminated information concerning their actions, a procedure for obtaining declaratory judgments, and a strengthening of the trial examiner system. These last proposals would replace the trial examiner by hearing commissioners, establish them on a more independent basis, give them increased powers, and use them to facilitate the decisions of the board members by making their decisions of more weight and of better caliber. A similar proposal had been made with respect to NLRB procedures.

The four dissenting members of the committee were agreed with the majority report as far as it went, but believed it was necessary to go further. Their major proposal was an elaborate code of practice for the administrative agencies, which would have regulated all the major phases of agency operation, from the type of notice to be given to the manner of issuing the decision and the effective date of the decision.

Bills were introduced in Congress embodying both the majority and minority recommendations. Congress held hearings from April until July, 1941. The controversy over the issue was approaching a showdown when the attack on Pearl Harbor occurred. Once the United States became fully engaged in the war, more, not fewer, administrative controls were needed, particularly in regard to prices and production, and agency effectiveness became a high priority.

The New Deal administrative agencies had gradually refined and improved their procedures. The frequent investigations, court decisions, and American Bar Association criticisms created plenty of incentive to devise fair procedures, and so it was agreed on all sides that further action with respect to an administrative procedures act would be suspended. Consequently any effort at either codifying those improved procedures or carrying them further by legislative methods was suspended for the duration, and the issue was not reopened until World War II had come to a close.

## JOINING THE TALENTED OPACS STAFF
*Following my resignation from the NLRB, I move up to associate*
*general counsel of another new agency*

In June 1941 David Ginsburg, the general counsel of the Office of Price Administration and Civilian Supply (OPACS), asked me to become his chief assistant as associate general counsel. I joined the OPACS staff that same month. (The organization later became known as simply the Office of Price Administration.) Once again I was joining a new agency, about to tackle a whole new set of problems. No legislation had been passed, but it was contemplated and OPACS assumed that eventually enabling legislation would go through. The OPACS job precipitated me into an entirely different world from that of the Department of Justice or even the NLRB. The NLRB purview had been much narrower, even though a similar scale of human values and ability along certain administrative lines were involved. OPACS opened up much more vast vistas. It embraced the entire war operation and the entire economy. I entered a much broader domain and joined the remarkably talented and ambitious group of individuals Henderson had assembled for the task.

When I arrived, OPACS was an active, going concern. The main tasks that it was undertaking at this time were continuing the efforts of the National Defense Advisory Commission (NDAC) to hold down and stabilize prices and rents, planning for allocation of scarce materials and commodities for civilian purposes, and beginning a consumer rationing plan. To carry out these tasks OPACS was concerned with preparing and securing the passage of legislation that would give the agency statutory authority to conduct its operations and creating at least the nucleus of a trained organization, including regional or field offices, that could deal with the issues of stabilization, allocation, and rationing that the agency heads foresaw would become their responsibility.

142

Although I was familiar with the background, I did not participate in the beginning of many of the early activities. President Roosevelt had appointed the NDAC in May 1940, in the midst of the Nazi breakthrough into France. Composed of seven members, each of whom had been designated to deal with a particular aspect of the defense program, the NDAC began in a purely advisory role to study problems and make recommendations to the president. It was intended to function without any operational duties. But under the pressure of circumstances the Commission commenced to undertake actual operations in various fields.

Three sections of the NDAC dealt with price control. The major one was price stabilization under Leon Henderson. Second in importance was consumer protection under Harriet Elliott. The agricultural section, under Chester Davis, was also concerned with the problem, but at the time, agricultural prices were still relatively low and at the administrative level, persons dealing with agriculture were motivated to raise prices rather than to see them go lower.

In theory, the price stabilization section was intended to have jurisdiction primarily over prices of raw materials and manufactured products, whereas Elliott's consumer section was more concerned with retail and consumer prices. Actually, Henderson and his staff gradually assumed control over all aspects of the price problem, including retail. The consumer section tended to become steadily less important and gradually was merged, or practically submerged, into the Henderson organization. The agricultural section had an informal arrangement with Henderson by which he would not take any action involving agricultural prices or commodities processed from agricultural materials without consulting with Chester Davis. In effect that meant a veto, so at the beginning Henderson made no effort to deal with agricultural or food prices. Even at this early stage some of the basic conflicts that developed later appeared in incipient form, both between the Henderson price section and the consumer section, and between the Henderson price section and the agricultural section.

The price section's function soon passed from advising the president with respect to the course of prices into the area of directly trying to influence prices and hold them down. Little or no statutory basis existed for the operation of Henderson's section at this time. He attempted to accomplish results mainly through publicity, with some threat of vague statutory implementation in the background. Actually, he was working largely by public statements and through voluntary agreements with industry where he could make them.

## NDAC - OPM - WPB / WLB / OPACS - OPA

As the problems intensified, the original organization of the NDAC became outmoded. The need to establish agencies that could grapple more affirmatively with the problems was manifest. The NDAC was disbanded: each of the seven areas that had been assigned to the seven members was transferred to a separate and independent agency. The first of these was the creation of the Office of Production Management (OPM) on January 7, 1941. This agency later became the War Production Board (WPB). OPACS, established by executive order on April 1, 1941, encompassed Henderson's price stabilization section and Elliott's consumer section. Eventually, the War Labor Board (WLB) was created out of Sidney Hillman's group. The Office of Defense Advisory Transportation also derived from the nucleus of the NDAC.

The establishment of the OPM in January 1941 without simultaneously creating a special agency for price control was a setback for Henderson. OPM, established under Donald Nelson, was essentially dominated by business interests, which still maintained a "business as usual" attitude despite the increasing encroachment of the war. Interpreting the establishment of OPM and the failure to establish a price agency as a victory for the "business as usual" school, Henderson demonstrated his opposition by taking a vacation of several months. He simply departed from Washington and left his assistant, John Hamm, and David Ginsburg to conduct his section in the NDAC.

Under the influence of Bernard Baruch and others, the Department of War and the military had prepared elaborate blueprints of how all aspects of war or defense programs should be administered. Their plan had contemplated an immediate declaration of war, with a full scale administrative program to come into operation at once. Events turned out quite differently. Since the United States had not entered the war, the issues developed rather more slowly. Gradually personnel and vested interests were built up. The actual expansion had to follow lines that to some extent were already laid out. The blueprint simply did not fit into the actual situation, so the development of defense machinery completely ignored the carefully prepared plan.

When I arrived at OPACS, Henderson and his staff of about 85 were already functioning. Henderson was administrator, head of OPACS; the associate director was Harriet Elliott. The principal heads of the organization were unusually talented, ambitious, and possessed substantial know-how about the Washington scene. Henderson had set up three divisions. John Kenneth Galbraith directed one on price stabilization. Joseph Weiner directed a second on civilian allocation. (Civilian allocation was a euphemistic term for rationing of civilian supply. That part of the allocation and rationing program that directly affected consumers was under the jurisdiction of OPACS at this time. Weiner's division was to be concerned primarily with regulating that part of production and manufacture that went into consumer goods.) The third division, which existed only on paper, was to handle consumer rationing.

## Leon Henderson Takes Charge
*With Elliott, Hamm, Ginsburg, J.K. Galbraith...*

As 1940 opened, Leon Henderson was carrying the burden for the

Roosevelt administration of advocating and undertaking far-reaching controls in order to meet the situation that was developing. Henderson himself was an economist. He had worked for the Russell Sage Foundation for a while, but he had been in the government since the beginnings of the New Deal. On one occasion Henderson, representing some consumer interests, had testified vigorously with respect to a proposed NRA project. In response to Henderson's aggressive performance, General ("Iron Pants") Johnson had asked him to take charge of the Research and Planning Division of NRA. Later Henderson had worked for the Works Progress Administration, I believe, and then had become an economic adviser to the Democratic National Committee. He had gained quite a reputation early in 1937 by predicting the recession of 1937–38. He had stated forcefully the proposition that monopoly prices were taking the cream off the public's increased purchasing power and that the lack of sufficient support for purchasing power would bring about a depression or recession. When a severe recession confirmed his prediction, Henderson was credited with being quite an expert on economic matters. He then had served as one of the leading spirits in the TNEC study and subsequently had worked as one of the SEC commissioners. So he had considerable background in government operations.

Henderson was an unusual combination of theoretician, administrator, politician, and man of action. He was an able economist, not too scholarly or subtle, but with a clear eye for the main issue, and a clairvoyant ability to predict economic trends and problems of the near future. Always in the forefront, he advocated moves for some months before they took place, anticipating what was about to occur, urging action. He was the leader of the school opposed to the "business as usual" group, the chief proponent of the theory that the war situation would involve the United States fundamentally and that drastic measures would be indispensable to meet the situation. He was a person of broad views and considerable imagination. He was a tenacious individual, rather rough and tough in his manner, but underneath was not as tough as his appearance would indicate. As an administrator he rapidly appraised situations, was willing to delegate considerable power, did not get bogged down in details, and remained on top in the midst of the battle over the basic decisions. He had a tremendous amount of drive but not much inclination for detail work. His inclination was to participate in the broadest top-level decisions and use subordinates for much of the legwork. He managed an effective agency because he found people who were qualified to do the more routine work while he supplied the drive and liaison with the top level.

Henderson's chief assistant was John Hamm. A brother of Henderson's wife, he supplemented Henderson effectively. Hamm was a pleasant, quiet, attractive person who was able to pick up some of the pieces after Henderson had finished his blasting. Hardworking, he was a person who could handle the detail and turn out a rather good finished job, although he himself had his eye on the main developments, too. Although not nearly as imaginative or resourceful as Henderson, he had some of those same qualities. He was willing to experiment and take chances, and shared some of Henderson's daring on these issues. Hamm was completely loyal to Henderson and the pair worked together superbly.

The third most important member of the Henderson group was David Ginsburg. He was the son of parents who had come to this country from abroad; they lived in West Virginia and could hardly speak English. Ginsburg, obviously an extremely talented individual, had graduated from the University of West Virginia and Harvard Law School. He had been one of the bright stars of Washington whom I knew by reputation. He had been law clerk to Justice Douglas and then had served as legal assistant to Leon Henderson in the SEC. His career in Washington was meteoric. He must have finished law school in 1935 or 1936. When Leon Henderson formed OPACS, he made Dave Ginsburg his general counsel. Ginsburg at that time must have been thirty or under. He had the reputation of being one of the brightest boys in the New Deal. I had not met him until he came over to obtain the views of the Department of Justice on the draft of price legislation that we then worked on together.

Ginsburg was an excellent speaker with a remarkable command of language and an excellent writer with a pungent style. He was also a person of tremendous imagination and resourcefulness, and much like Henderson or perhaps even more endowed than Henderson with the ability to foresee the trend of events. Ginsburg was always three or six months ahead of everybody else in Washington as to what the next developments and problems were going to be. He had the capacity for planning in advance in considerable detail. He also kept his eye on the main developments, left practically all the day-to-day operations to subordinates, so he had the time, as well as the ingenuity, for participating in the framing of top-level decisions. Ginsburg was a personable individual, quite charming in many ways. Among his numerous enemies he had the reputation of being a megalomaniac and pathological liar. Both accusations had some substance. He was a self-centered person with a disconcerting inability to be straightforward in certain situations. For example, he was responsible for drafting the first price schedules in such a way as to give some readers the idea that the prices were legally enforceable and would be legally enforced. I think Ginsburg's underlying insecurity caused him to approach some problems by a devious route. But these defects were so overwhelmingly offset by his abilities that his contribution was extremely significant.

Another member of this group was J. Kenneth Galbraith, head of the Price Division under Henderson. Galbraith was an enormous man; when asked his height, he used to say he was five feet twenty inches. Working with Chester Davis and the group in the Agriculture Department had made him more acquainted with agricultural and food problems than Henderson was, who had concerned himself much more with the industrial aspect of prices and the economic structure. Galbraith was an extremely able individual, who undoubtedly had a higher I.Q. than anybody around there except Ginsburg. He was also a person who could recognize the broad trend of events. Resourceful, constantly coming up with ideas, somewhat unorthodox in his approach, he prided himself on being opposed to the general school of thought. On the whole, though, his unorthodoxies were not those that challenged the orthodox too far. He was a liberal, but certainly not a radical, in his views. He was somewhat a manipulator and tended to play a little politics around the organization.

The head of the other division, Joseph Weiner, was a New York lawyer who had headed the Public Utility Division of the SEC. The Public Utility Division, charged with the administration of the "death sentence" of the Public Utility Act, was one of the most controversial parts of the SEC and one that was most subject to attack. Weiner was also a lawyer of tremendous ability, very intelligent and quick. A tough guy like Henderson, his demeanor also was somewhat rough and uncouth. Lacking Henderson's charm, he readily made a great number of enemies. An indefatigable worker, Weiner would not hesitate to plunge into enterprises even though he might not necessarily know what the outcome would be. He had his feet on the ground, good judgment, and a bold spirit, willing to move ahead.

The other person of importance in this group was Richard Gilbert. He was head of the Research Division, not engaged in operating activities. Trained as an economist, Gilbert was another enormously able individual. Extremely persuasive in conversation and argument, he gave an impression of tremendous confidence. He seemed to be absolutely sure of his position even when making excursions into as unpredictable a field as future economic events. As was characteristic of this whole group, he had a broad view of the whole situation, focusing on the fundamental forces at work and attempting to anticipate what would happen.

These high-powered chiefs gathered around them a high-powered staff of subordinates. Harriet Elliott was quite outclassed. Although she was associate director, her influence was minimal. She had been dean of women at the North Carolina State College for Women. She was a pleasant, mild person, and she and her staff took a less compromising point of view than Henderson, less willing to accept reality. But neither she nor her staff were a match for the Henderson group. Her activities, except in the rent field where she continued the development of the rent committees, were mostly devoted to persuasion of a general nature. She never embarked upon the programs of action that the Henderson group adopted almost immediately. Miss Elliott was a lamb among wolves and succumbed fairly soon after OPACS was created.

### A Day That Will Live in Infamy

On December 7, 1941, I was sitting around reading the Sunday newspaper after lunch. Leon Keyserling called up to tell us that the radio had just reported that Japanese planes had attacked Pearl Harbor. That was all the news we had. With marked excitement we turned on the radio and listened to the news for the rest of the afternoon.

On Monday morning I went to the office as usual, only to find that Henderson, Ginsburg, and three or four of the staff had jumped in taxis as soon as the news came over the radio and rushed to the office. It had not occurred to me to connect that news from the distant Pacific to our OPACS work. Henderson and Ginsburg, however, had realized immediately that the event strengthened OPACS' position and enabled them to insist on changes. They had spent the rest of that Sunday afternoon in a long conference in which they had tentatively decided on what changes they could now ask Congress to make, to strengthen the House version of the price legislation that the House had passed only a few days before. By Monday morning, when the rest of the staff arrived in the office, not only had they already mapped out a line of action with respect to the legislation, they had also discussed rationing problems and were well along in their thinking of what changes the aftermath of Pearl Harbor would bring.

# 8

# GETTING OPA IN GEAR
# FOR WORLD WAR II

*Almost back on its feet, the economy must now be harnessed to fight a war.*

The second major period in OPACS history began with Pearl Harbor and lasted one year, until the Stabilization Act of 1942 was passed, permitting full control of inflation for the first time. Leon Henderson's resignation as administrator in December 1942 marked the end of the second phase.

## DRAFTING THE PRICE CONTROL BILL
*How to control prices?*

I had joined OPACS in June 1941, shortly after it had been created, under Leon Henderson, out of the old NDAC. The Japanese attacked Pearl Harbor in December 1941. Thus once again, barely had I joined a brand new agency when it was given a whole new mandate–in this case, coordinating the economy through the United States participation in World War II.

A major focus of my work in the early period was the drafting of legislation. Given Washington's focus on progress in the defense program, we worked in the context of the conflict between two forces: the New Dealers, who were anxiously insisting on a rapid advance, and the business groups, isolationists, and others who believed that the preparations of the defense program were leading toward a war contrary to our best interests, and who opposed the rapid pace and attempts at planning, preferring to rely on developments to take care of themselves without those tremendously novel interventions advocated by the New Dealers.

The Lend Lease Act had been passed in March 1941. President Roosevelt had declared an unlimited national emergency on May 27. The declaration of an unlimited national emergency was a somewhat novel device, of which the legal implications were not entirely clear. The pressures of the defense program reverberated strongly throughout the economy in this period. The Consumer Price Index (CPI) of the Bureau of Labor Statistics, 100.8 at the beginning of the year, barely above the levels of the late 1930s, rose rapidly in 1941, almost at the rate of one point a month. As prices skyrocketed, materials were growing scarce. It was clear that the effect of the defense program on the economy would necessitate substantial government controls if current trends continued.

Our office was convinced that price control was inevitable, but we could not present it publicly to Congress until the president was ready to back it. The first draft, prepared in February 1941, was circulated and discussed for almost six months, not by deliberate choice but because Roosevelt was unwilling until July to urge Congress to pass legislation. The president finally sent a special message to Congress on July 30, 1941. The bill was introduced on August 1st. I had been in OPACS for a little over one month.

The bill was quite unprecedented. The fact that the legislation incubated over a considerable period of time undoubtedly contributed to a remarkable product. The main influence from the past that guided our framing of the legislation was the United States experience in World War I, where price controls had been attempted on a much smaller scale and in a haphazard manner, without much success. Furthermore, to the extent that price controls had been buttressed by legislation, the statute had been declared unconstitutional by the Supreme Court as an invalid delegation of power. We also studied closely other countries' experience with price controls—all the industrial countries in World War II had some system of price controls.

### Price Controls

One of the first decisions, and the major decision, was to abandon any system like public utility regulation, based on the theory of fair return on investment, or on some theory of calculating cost and investment. It was clear to the economists that the economic and legal complexities generated by such rate regulations could not possibly work in widespread price control, and so the idea of assuring each individual producer a return based on a calculation of his investment or costs was rejected from the beginning. Instead, we substituted the basic standard that prices had to be generally fair and equitable, relying primarily on a technique of freezing prices in their present status, rather than attempting to devise a formula. As time went on the freeze became less applicable and it became necessary to evolve other formulas, some of which were based on cost calculations. But the economists were clear from the beginning that the project had to be conducted on the basis of regulations that were not premised on any principle of fair return and that gave the administrator as wide authority as possible to work out the details of the prices.

Considerable difference of opinion focused on the issue of whether price controls should be general across the board or selective—that is to say, whether only certain basic prices should be controlled or we should attempt to control all prices. The argument for controlling all prices by a freeze technique had been advanced primarily by Bernard Baruch, speaking on the basis of his experience in World War I. He had been advocating some such technique for many years. Leon Henderson and David Ginsburg were rather closely associated with Baruch, as was John Hamm, and they all frequently consulted him. The argument for selective price control was advanced primarily by J. K. Galbraith, who felt that at this point an effort should be made to control the basic prices as much as possible, since we had neither the public support nor the staff necessary to undertake blanket price controls. This debate was resolved by authorizing the administrator to implement either selective or blanket price controls. A provision was included authorizing a temporary freeze, either on selective prices or of a blanket nature, and the permanent regulation could have the same alternatives. So we evaded this issue by merely committing ourselves ultimately to one or the other solution.

The economists were also concerned about speed and delay in price regulations. The example of public utility regulation, which normally took many years for the rates to become fully effective, led them to insist on new devices, because such delays would completely undermine the effectiveness of price controls. This was to a large extent a legal problem and many of the other problems that bothered the economists were ones that the lawyers were called upon, in cooperation with the economists, to solve.

**Legal Issues**

Turning now to the legal issues, insofar as they can be separated from economic issues, we wrestled with a basic constitutional problem: under what provision of the Constitution could the system of price controls be established? Elaborate memoranda were prepared on this and other legal and economic issues. By far the safest and most likely source of authority for the legislation was the war powers. In addition, we thought that the commerce clause in the Constitution would justify a large part of the regulation, if not perhaps the whole of it. To justify the whole of the regulation under the commerce power would have carried it beyond what had been approved up until then, but there was an argument that could be made for that. Reliance was also placed on the power to coin money and to regulate the value of it–the monetary power. These bases for the constitutional power to control were incorporated in the preamble to the draft.

A second issue was the delegation of legislative power. The World War I statute had been declared unconstitutional as an overdelegation; we were determined to protect our draft from the same fate. Stating the basic standard for issuing price regulations–that the prices must be generally fair and equitable–contributed to resolving this issue. This extremely broad standard left numerous important decisions to the administrator. However, various devices tempered this broad standard and provided grounds for court approval despite its broad nature. Perhaps the most important device was that the whole system was to be administered under administrative procedures by an administrator who was to issue regulations fixing the actual prices. The World War I statute had merely stated that prices of certain articles should not be unjust or unreasonable and imposed on buyers and sellers the responsibility to determine what was a just and reasonable price. Our legislation established administrative machinery by which the administrator would make that determination; consequently, at least the issue of what the legal price was would be more certain.

The statute included not only a statement of the basic intention in the preamble, but a number of other devices that appeared to restrict the administrator. Provision that he take into consideration certain factors such as prices as of the base date and changes of costs since that date made the delegation seem more confined. Although these provisions were not mandatory, their mere statement in the act did to some extent restrict the administrator. One provision required the administrator to issue a statement of considerations in connection with the promulgation of any regulation. This meant that the administrator had to justify his regulation in public and to submit to industry and public scrutiny the basic facts and reasons upon which he had acted. Legally, these provisions were far removed from issues of delegation of power, but since they provided legislative guidelines for and curtailed the exercise of the administrator's power, they would have an effect upon the courts in considering the delegation point.

As it turned out, the source of authority and delegation issues were easily won by OPA in subsequent litigation. The basic authority of Congress was not challenged seriously in any case and the delegation point was argued half-heartedly. Courts had no difficulty deciding in our favor. By the time the issues arose in court the United States was immersed in war and it would have been unfeasible for the court to have declared the legislation unconstitutional on either ground.

Consequently, most subsequent litigation challenging the legislation related more to procedural issues, which were brought up in constitutional terms under the due process clause. The procedural issues were the most ingenious portions of the act. They arose out of certain problems anticipated by the economists and lawyers.

### Procedures and Appeals

First of all, I have mentioned the need for speed. Prices were changing extremely rapidly. Everyone realized from the beginning that an effort to reduce prices would be extremely difficult from an administrative point of view. Once prices rose, bringing them down would be a formidable task because a price increase on any item normally would be reflected in other prices, so we would never catch up with the chain of influence. The psychological problem of reducing the seller's price and enforcing that reduction was forbidding. So we had to take rapid action and make the prices stick.

Second, we realized that the problem was of such magnitude that it would be impossible to have on hand all the data necessary to prevent errors. We needed some method of testing a regulation and correcting mistakes caused by inadequate data or ignorance before the administrator was committed to court action. We also needed a process by which the administrator readily could obtain data on which to base a determination.

Third, it was important that the issues for judicial review be as narrow as possible. Almost from the beginning we decided that there must be court review of the administrator's action fixing the price. Despite some contrary arguments we generally agreed this was fair, and, perhaps more important, we judged it impossible politically to establish a system which did not permit review by the courts. It even might be declared unconstitutional. However, we wanted to narrow the court's consideration to particular issues on which both the administrator and our challengers could present data, avoiding a general challenge to the entire regulation with the risk of raising numerous issues not heretofore considered and on which the factual data could be supplied only through the trial process, which was not an effective way of presenting that kind of material.

Fourth, we decided that the regulations would have to be in effect during judicial review. A situation in which an appeal to the courts could result in a suspension of the regulation would have played havoc with the administration of the act.

Finally, based on prior New Deal experience, we searched for some way of avoiding the consequences of a declaration of invalidity by any one of the 85 or 90 federal district courts. A district court decision in any part of the country holding any aspect of the regulation invalid would probably make that regulation invalid throughout the country. If, for instance, the judge in the northern district of Illinois held the regulations dealing with the price of cattle or meat invalid insofar as Chicago was concerned, most cattle would be shipped to Chicago where regulations were not in force, and the markets in Kansas City, Omaha, Des Moines, St. Louis, and other midwestern centers would be stripped bare. We realized that under such pressure, with that kind of a diversion from the normal channels of commerce, continued enforcement of a regulation was not feasible; we probably would have had to withdraw the entire regulation throughout the country because of the decision in Chicago. Such consequences would arise in regard to numerous regulations. The experience of enforcing the National Labor Relations Act, the Public Utility Holding Company Act, and other legislation against injunction proceedings in various parts of the country must not be repeated.

These considerations led to the specifications about procedure embodied in the legislation. The legislation provided that a regulation could be issued immediately without a hearing, thus avoiding the delay necessary for a hearing, the accumulation of testimony and evidence, and the study of that record before a regulation could be issued. The only conditions were that the administrator had to issue a "statement of considerations," and a later provision added that the administrator had to consult with the industry if it were practicable to do so. After the regulation was issued anyone who wished to test the validity of any provision of the regulation would have to file a protest with the administrator. That protest would have to be directed to specific issues and give the basis for objection to that particular portion of the regulation. These arrangements gave the administrator a chance to correct any mistakes that he may have made, put the burden on the individual subject to the regulation to produce data supporting a resolution to his objection, and greatly narrowed both the issues that could be presented and the consideration the administrator would have to give to the particular point under protest. A hearing would then be held in response to the filed protest.

A hearing probably was not a constitutional requirement, but it was of great practical importance that the administrator hold a hearing, because otherwise the court was likely to conduct a hearing. By holding his own hearing, the administrator could control the admission of evidence and the development of fact, and make his own findings. Then those findings could be subject to review only on the limited basis that they were not supported by substantial evidence.

One of the most ingenious provisions limited the review to a single specially appointed court. The act provided for an Emergency Court of Appeals, consisting of judges from the regular federal courts, but designated to sit for this particular purpose. The original draft provided that the president make the designation of these judges, but when Chief Justice Hughes retired as chief justice and Stone became chief justice, we changed the draft to permit the appointments to be made by the chief justice. So the consideration of the validity of regulations was concentrated not in the district courts, or not even in the ten courts of appeal but in a single special court. If that court ruled against you, the matter could be appealed directly to the Supreme Court.

### Sanctions

Another aspect of the bill was a considerable arsenal of sanctions. The experience of prior agencies with criminal sanctions had led our draftsmen to include additional methods of enforcement. The act embraced not only a criminal penalty for willful violation, but also authorized an injunction to restrain violation. OPA persuaded Congress, perhaps without fully enlightening Congress on the legal consequences, to retain in the bill language that if a violation took place the court "shall" issue an injunction. The Supreme Court later interpreted this as "may" issue and I think the Court believed that Ginsburg had pulled a fast one in the drafting on that point. Some of the members of the Court were quite familiar with the actual progress of the legislation.

Provision was also made for triple damage suits–that is, enforcement through a civil suit for recovery of money. The suit could be brought for either three times the amount of the overcharge or fifty dollars, whichever was higher. This permitted a civil action that actually constituted a financial penalty on violators. The consumer could bring the suit on consumer purchases and the administrator on industrial purchases. These provisions later were modified in various respects. The legislation also provided for licensing and revocation of licenses of violators. The revocation was to be through court procedure rather than an administrative procedure.

So at least four methods of enforcement were provided. Elaborate provision also was made for investigation and obtaining of information. It was clear that the administrator would need substantial information on which to base his price regulations, as well as for enforcement. We searched prior statutes for various forms of subpoena powers, inspection of records, requirement of record-keeping, inspection of premises, and so forth. All of these were included in the statute, together with an additional one that had not been in any previous statute.

### Politics

The major political problem, of course, was whether the legislation would be accepted at all. Many forces opposed the bill when it was introduced in August 1941. Not much organized political support existed. The general public, unaware or apathetic on the issue of price control, did not express itself forcefully one way or another, and congressmen did not learn much from consulting their constituents.

Almost from the beginning we had to adopt the agreement that prices would not be fixed on agricultural commodities until those commodities had reached parity. This was a grave handicap because agricultural prices then were considerably below parity, which would mean that their prices could not be fixed until they had risen considerably. That would affect a great many other prices, upsetting the whole structure and any attempt at a freeze. Nevertheless, the opposition of the farm bloc was so formidable that we were convinced that unless this concession were made the bill would not pass. So the concession was embodied in the act as it was originally introduced.

The bill took about six months to get through Congress. The hearings were extremely elaborate. The hearings were quite prolonged, but eventually the bill was reported out by the House committee. After debate, the bill was approved on January 30, 1942, not long after Pearl Harbor.

Had the Japanese not attacked Pearl Harbor, it is not certain that the bill would have passed at all. The major debate occurred over the agricultural provisions. The provision respecting partity was amended to require that agricultural prices had to rise to 110 percent of parity before they could be fixed. These and other changes greatly weakened the act.

## RATIONING TIRES, SUGAR, AND GASOLINE

In addition to giving impetus to the passage of the price control legislation, the most immediate effect of Pearl Harbor on OPA was in connection with the rationing program, which occupied much of our attention for the next several months.

The most critical commodity for rationing was rubber *tires*. The United States precipitous entry into World War II was via the Pacific theater, which had the effect of abruptly cutting off our supply of natural rubber from the Far East. As we had no significant synthetic supplies, the country would have to manage with the stock on hand for the immediate future, and it would be the consumer of rubber tires who would be the first to feel the pinch. A good deal of our *sugar* supply was also cut off. Although some came from other sources, enough was stopped so that it was clear that there would also be a substantial shortage of sugar. *Gasoline* was the third commodity that clearly would be a problem. At the time, however, Henderson and the others at OPA were thinking of rationing gasoline for the purpose of conserving tires rather than conserving the supply of gasoline.

These were the major commodities that called for immediate action. Both tires and sugar were a problem of scarcity, and therefore a problem of fair distribution and distribution for the most essential needs. OPA had been thinking about using a rationing system for some time. We had been making some studies because of the significance of rationing as a means of price control. One of the most effective ways of handling price control might be by a system of easing the demand through a rationing or allocation method. OPA had done some work on consumer rationing problems with this in mind. Now the outbreak of the war presented the problem more immediately in terms of equitable distribution of a short supply rather than as an aid to price control.

The first question was which agency would be charged with tire and sugar rationing. Civilian Supply, which had been transferred to OPM (when OPACS became OPA), logically had jurisdiction over consumer rationing. However, OPM was not as far advanced from an administrative point of view as OPA. No one in OPM had thought about or fashioned a consumer rationing program, whereas a number of people, principally in OPA's Price Department, had given some thought and preliminary planning to such a program. Furthermore, the existence of Frank Bane's Division of Field Operations from the old NDAC and his relationship to the state and local defense councils permitted a rapid development of a field organization. I suppose, finally, OPA had the reputation of having a more energetic and innovative staff. David Ginsburg was concerned that taking on the enormous job of rationing would weaken the agency's capacity for handling price control; the agency might be overwhelmed by the required dispersal of resources and the onslaught of public opposition on rationing issues. In contrast to Ginsburg's reluctance, others in OPA were perfectly willing to tackle it.

In any event, within *one week* after Pearl Harbor the decision was made to turn the job over to OPA. On December 24, 1941, OPM issued a general delegation of authority to OPA to handle all consumer rationing.

The legal authority for rationing consumer goods at this time rested on several statutes that gave priority to use of commodities in short supply for military purposes. Our original actions were taken under these earlier statutes. The First War Powers Act, passed the week after Pearl Harbor, contained some provisions strengthening these military priority provisions. However, the major legislative source of authority for consumer rationing was the Second War Powers Act, which was signed by President Roosevelt on March 27, 1942. Both War Powers Acts were a potpourri of statutory authority needed in various disparate areas. The draftsman of the Second War Powers Act was Oscar Cox, who at that time was, I believe, in the Assistant Solicitor General's office. He simply pulled together either renewal or creation of a series of different types of governmental authority.

Title III of the Second War Powers Act related to priority and the precise source of authority was set forth in one sentence:

> Whenever the president is satisfied that the fulfillment of requirements for the defense of the United States will result in a shortage in the supply of any material, or of any facilities for defense, or for private account, or for export, the president may allocate such material or facilities in such manner, upon such conditions and to such extent as he shall deem necessary or appropriate in the public interest and to promote the national defense.

The remainder of Title III contained administrative provisions for obtaining information and the sanctions for violation of regulations, but the actual authority was contained in that single sentence, which simply said the president could allocate where there was a shortage "in such manner and upon such conditions as he shall deem necessary or appropriate in the public interest and to promote the national defense." This statute was in marked contrast with the Emergency Price Control Act, which had been worked out in exhaustive detail over a period of months. Under Title III all the allocation powers of the War Production Board–that is, industrial allocation-as well as OPA consumer rationing powers–derived from this single sentence expressed in the most general terms. There was simply not time to work out the details in the manner in which the price control statute had been worked out, and probably it would have been difficult for Congress to agree upon many of the details even if they had tried. In any event, it was statutory authority completely the opposite in nature from that under which OPA operated in the price control field.

The statutory authority was delegated by executive order to the OPM, except for particular commodities such as petroleum and petroleum products. In January 1942 the OPM was reorganized and became the War Production Board (WPB) with Donald Nelson as chairman. OPA's authority derived from an order issued by OPM, and later WPB, delegating its authority to OPA. We had to obtain a specific order from WPB dealing with each rationed commodity. Thus, OPA's authority derived in part from the general delegation and in part from the specific delegation on each commodity.

## Tires

Tire rationing was primarily an administrative task. Tires were sufficiently subject to control at the manufacturing, wholesale and retail levels, and the purchases of tires were sufficiently infrequent, that it was possible to work out a system whereby a person who needed a tire would be required to obtain a certificate from a governmental source in order to purchase it. Had purchases been more frequent, a coupon system would have been necessary. Certificates rather than a coupon system simplified the task, although the problem clearly was stupendous and one that no government agency in this country had ever tackled before.

Frank Bane started to work immediately. Perhaps three weeks after the decision was made to award OPA the job, he had in operation a tire rationing system. It was one of the most spectacular and effective, at least in short-range terms, of any accomplishment during the war, I think. His first step was to wire all the state governors asking them to appoint a state rationing director. The state rationing director was to appoint local tire rationing boards in the various localities. The state rationing director was usually the head of the State Defense Council. Thus Bane was able to utilize the defense councils that he had established (during his tenure with the NDAC), providing them with their first chance to tackle an operational task.

The commercial sale of tires was prohibited very soon after Pearl Harbor. By January 1, 1942, OPA issued a system of monthly quotas, and by January 5, 7000 Tire Rationing Boards were ready for business. Quotas had been assigned to them, they had instructions as to under what circumstances individuals were to receive new tires, and they were beginning to process applications. On January 7, the Tire Rationing Boards opened for business and started issuing certificates. In approximately three weeks the whole system was set up on a nationwide basis with instructions issued, forms distributed, and boards organized and in operation.

(I should note that the state rationing director appointed for Connecticut was Chester Bowles. As we will see, this was to be the beginning of his career in OPA.)

Most policy decisions on the rationing of tires were made by the section of J. K. Galbraith's Price Department that dealt with rubber products. Ben Lewis (a professor of economics from Oberlin) was the section head. He had conducted studies on rationing during 1941. The major detailed decisions that went into the initial regulation, such as who would be eligible to receive a tire, were made in Lewis' office. I do not recall now who from the Legal Department did the initial drafting. I think Harold Leventhal was assigned to that. The job was easier than drafting a price regulation, but many contingencies had to be anticipated and difficult procedural problems had to be worked out. The Price Department, Legal Department, and Bane's Division of Field Operations all cooperated on the tire rationing job. Tire rationing proceeded fairly smoothly and was rightly considered an excellent accomplishment from the beginning.

The issue immediately arose of whether rationing should be handled by the Price Department or whether a separate department should be established for rationing. Some weeks later we decided that a special department, coordinated with the Price Department, would handle rationing problems, even though this separate department dealt with the same commodities to which prices were being fixed. (Leon Henderson's theory was that if you had a big new job to do, the best approach was to call in some new talent that would be able to specialize on that job and push it.) The Price Department was overwhelmed with work preparing for the passage of legislation and shortly after that with handling price problems under the Price Control Act.

### Sugar

The next commodity that OPA was called upon to manage was sugar. Henderson had announced in January 1942 that sugar would be rationed and had requested both institutional users and private consumers not to hoard. His request probably had no substantial effect. Rationing sugar was considerably more difficult than tires, because everybody used sugar and bought it weekly. Consequently, a coupon system was necessary; every consumer would have a coupon book for the purchase of sugar. The institutional users, such as restaurants, hotels, and candy manufacturers, could be handled on a certificate basis because the limited size of this group made it feasible and they bought in quantities that made the use of stamps impracticable. So we had to establish both a certificate system for institutional users and a coupon system for ordinary consumers.

The coupon system entailed the practical challenge of printing and distributing millions of ration books. Virtually every member of the population would have one. To correct distribution errors additional copies would have to be available. As I recall they ordered 190,000,000 books printed. At that time we had visualized the possibility of counterfeiting books, but we were not particularly concerned with that issue. The impact on defense would not have been overwhelming in sugar rationing, anyway. So no special paper or ink was used. The printing job was relatively simple, but designing and printing the books, distributing them to state offices and local boards, and then handing them to consumers obviously would take a while.

Consequently, it was not until April 1942 that the system was ready. OPA then issued an order prohibiting the sale of sugar except under the new system and establishing registration for institutional users. Our aim was to obtain control over the institutional users, to make them report their inventories on hand, so that those who had hoarded during the interval would not be in a favored position, and to establish their quotas for purposes of issuing certificates. Establishing these quotas alone was quite a job. The enforcement staff of OPA swung into action for the first time on a large scale to check the honesty of the inventory figures required by registration.

The high percentage of institutional users who failed to report the extent of their sugar inventories shocked us. OPA compared the report with the actual inventory at the hotel, restaurant, or manufacturer in as many cities as possible. Less sugar was reported than the business had on hand in 85 percent of the establishments checked in some cities, and no city had fewer than 35 or 50 percent underreporting. These figures are a fair sample of what happened because the investigators included the major hotels and restaurants, as well as some of the leading manufacturers, in a cross section of restaurants, hotels, bakeries, grocery stores, and small candy manufacturers. We were not simply attempting to select those that would be most likely to misrepresent. We made the check practically all in one day because by the next day businesses might have disposed of or concealed the sugar.

This misrepresentation of the amount of sugar on hand was a criminal offense, because a provision of the criminal code already existed that made it a criminal offense to misrepresent to the government information that could be required from a person. As a violation of the rationing regulations, it also would have been subject to criminal penalty. I was not in immediate charge of enforcement, though it was under me generally, but my recollection is that no criminal proceedings were brought; our only response was to deduct the excess sugar found from the amount allowable. We were far from prepared to follow through with criminal prosecutions. As a matter of public relations that would have been a dubious move. A rationing program had to have strong public support in order to work. We believed that an educational process was far more advisable than an immediate crackdown at the beginning. Apart from that we were not prepared at that time to bring criminal cases. Any case brought against a little restaurant in Oshkosh would have to go through the Department of Justice's Criminal Division in Washington at that time, and we had not worked out our relations with the Department of Justice. Even if we had decided to choose a couple of good test cases and publicize them, we were not prepared to follow through at that time in terms of investigators, attorneys, or the Department of Justice.

Happening a few months after Pearl Harbor in the midst of the war excitement, these misrepresentations foreboded some of the difficulties that would arise in connection with enforcement of rationing regulations. We realized, and later this assumption was fully confirmed, that widespread violation by a high percentage of business groups would occur.

Ration Book No. 1 had to reach the hands of every individual in the country who wanted a ration book, and only one per person. Consumers also were required to report any sugar they had on hand. If they had more than a certain amount, the ration books issued to them were to be "tailored" by having some of the stamps torn out. Then we had to plan what to do with the loose stamps so that they did not fall into the hands of people who would use them illegitimately. We decided to use the school system. Through the cooperation of the U.S. Office of Education and various state school officials, registration took place in public schools. School teachers volunteered their services to register individuals and issue ration books. During a four-day period, May 4 – 7, the teachers performed excellently and the distribution was amazingly successful.

OPA worried that people would visit more than one school and collect extra books. But the number of books issued tallied closely with the figures on the population, so we assumed not many people received extra books. Whether or not people accurately reported the amount of sugar on hand was another question. OPA made no effort to check that. It obviously would have been unwise and impractical to attempt to enter people's homes and check how much sugar they had on their kitchen shelves or stacked in their cellars.

### Gasoline

Gasoline was the third commodity that required rationing fairly early. Gasoline shortages appeared on the East Coast in early 1942 but not in the rest of the country. The East Coast had received most of its supplies by shipping on coastal vessels or other water transportation. Many of these shipments were cut off, mostly because tankers were diverted to supply army needs. Consequently, the East Coast had to depend on railroads to transport gasoline. Since rail transport was more expensive and less effective, gasoline prices tended to increase and a shortage developed. Another reason for the shortage was that much of the oil used by the armed forces was shipped from eastern ports. In this period if any stocks accumulated in the East, the army requisitioned them. So the gasoline shortage was confined to the East Coast in the beginning. And contrary to the initial sentiments of Henderson et al., we implemented rationing primarily because of an actual shortage of gasoline rather than to curtail wear on tires.

The first gasoline rationing was a punch card system, which was instituted in the middle of May 1942. We issued cards to automobile owners; each time gasoline was purchased, the dealer was supposed to punch a hole in the card, and in that way to confine the individual to the amount on the card. Drivers were classified as A, B, or C drivers; stickers were pasted on the cars to indicate what kind of punch card the individual was authorized to have. Even this lax system reduced the consumption of gasoline, but it was not destined to last long as it was subject to so many loopholes that it was almost a voluntary system.

The punch card was superseded in July by a coupon system. From that point on, gasoline rationing was conducted by this notably stricter system. Rationing was still confined to the East Coast, although as oil and petroleum supplies dwindled we realized that eventually we would have to extend it to other parts of the country. In December 1942, gasoline rationing became nationwide, although the East Coast remained one of our most difficult problems.

We instituted a few other comparatively simple rationing systems such as on automobiles, bicycles, and typewriters. We began a complicated program for rationing fuel oil in October 1942, barely in time for the winter season. The troublesome meat and food rationing did not start until 1943.

The transportation system, which was under tremendous strain due to the pressing needs of the armed services, affected both rationing and price control because those areas at the end of the transportation line were least likely to receive supplies and the supplies that did arrive had higher freight charges, which meant higher prices. New England, for instance, had difficulty in receiving supplies and that affected both the rationing and the price program.

## Coupons

The rationing system was refined continually during this period. As rationing was totally new, many of the problems could not be foreseen; in resolving the issues that arose the Rationing Department modified and improved the system. I am surprised as I look back how rapidly some of these changes were made. One of the most effective changes was the introduction of the ration banking system in October 1942. The coupon rationing system was based on ration coupons issued to the consumer. When he made purchases the consumer gave the retailer coupons. In order to replenish his supply from the wholesaler, the retailer would have to pass coupons to the wholesaler; wholesalers could deliver to retailers only in return for coupons. In the same way the wholesaler could receive supplies from the manufacturer only with coupons. So coupons flowed from the ration board to the consumer and returned through the chain of distribution. Thus, ration currency was used very much like money.

Personnel in the field asked us in Washington what to do with these used coupons. The first plan was to paste them on sheets so they would be easy to count. If you had sheets of a hundred, you could count the sheets instead of counting each coupon. But as the system grew more complicated, particularly as food rationing introduced tokens of various colors and the point system, handling the coupons became more difficult. Wholesalers were permitted to collect the stamps in envelopes; gradually retailers were allowed to do so. Transferring coupons from a retailer to a wholesaler as purchases were made became cumbersome. So an ingenious system was devised to use the banks for a ration banking system. An experiment in three cities produced favorable results, so the plan was instituted at the end of 1942. Under this system a retailer would deposit his coupons with the bank. They would be entered on his ration banking account and then he would write a check, similar to an ordinary check, which the bank would deduct from the retailer's account. The banks were compensated based on an estimation of what their services cost. Treating ration coupons like money eliminated a tremendous amount of paperwork and the system operated effectively.

Other improvements frequently occurred. A good many of these I will explain in the chapters on enforcement, because problems of counterfeiting coupons, stealing coupons, and buying without coupons, were major enforcement problems. Solutions often did not rely on prosecuting after the violations had taken place, but on instituting a system which would be proof against violations. The enforcement staff spent substantial time working with the Rationing Department on methods of refining the system.

Another aspect of rationing in which the Legal Department was particularly interested was the procedure for appeal. Originally, the local board had the final word. If they decided that you did not deserve a tire, you just did not get a tire, at least legitimately. By the middle of 1942 the Legal Department had worked out a system of appeal, whereby you could appeal the decision of the ration board to an OPA district office. Thus the decision of the ration board became subject to administrative review. At this time no question of court review arose.

The legal aspect of rationing involved the issuance of interpretations, amendments, consultation on improving methods, formulation of the procedural devices and methods of appeal, plus the enforcement problem. The technical legal work was less challenging than in the price control field because rationing regulations were simple compared to price regulations. On the other hand, since rationing seemed to affect the public more, we had to consider more carefully the potential public outcry. The public indignation that could be aroused over the failure to obtain sugar for canning or cooking, and particularly the failure to obtain gasoline for driving, reached emotional heights far beyond the reaction to price overcharges. The public seemed much more aware of the rationing program and much readier to complain about it.

### Public Opinion

At least at the beginning the public misunderstood rationing. Rationing was regarded as a sign that the economy was not strong enough to support a high scale of civilian living. When Germany had instituted a rationing system, the American public assumed that the German economy was weak. That general attitude toward rationing had persisted in this country.

We quickly discovered that many people were willing to comply with rationing regulations if other people did, but as soon as any substantial number of others violated the regulations, the whole system tended to break down. Apparently, people would sacrifice if they were convinced everyone else was sacrificing equally, but they would not become suckers by honoring regulations that they were aware others were violating.

OPA did not undertake much public relations in these early days. Not until the end of the year was there a major effort at public education on the reasons for rationing, how the program worked, why it was necessary, and what relation it had to the war effort. We took polls to discover what people were thinking and tailored our public relations accordingly.

Tire rationing had proceeded very smoothly. Sugar rationing went quite smoothly too, but great confusion surrounded gasoline rationing because various agencies and different people in the same agency repeatedly issued conflicting statements on the size of the supply and whether rationing was necessary. Gasoline rationing seemed to hit more people in a more sensitive spot than any other rationing. Although early rationing was conducted amazingly well under the circumstances, OPA never had notable public support for its rationing program. As time went on public support tended to deteriorate.

The OPA staff, the ration boards, and their staffs took public criticism seriously and worked extremely hard. Their morale was not affected substantially by the lack of public support, with the exception of the pleasure driving ban. In 1943, OPA tried to prohibit the use of automobiles for pleasure driving. Obviously unenforceable from the beginning, the collapse of this regulation was a demoralizing factor in the whole ration program. But, on the whole, I would say that the staff maintained a high morale.

Congress did not offer much support for rationing. At the onset of the tire and sugar rationing, some support probably was manifest. By the time gasoline rationing arrived, everything coming out of Congress was critical. Considerable controversy erupted in Congress over the need for gasoline rationing. By the end of 1942 congressional committees were beginning to hold hearings on defects in the rationing program and generally criticized OPA's handling of it.

Another difficulty that OPA had concerned the supply agencies. OPA had no control over supplies. The supply agency (usually WPB, but for gasoline it was the Petroleum Administrative Board, PAB) would require OPA to ration a certain commodity, indicating from month to month how much was available to distribute. OPA would devise the scheme, operate and administer it, without having had any input on whether to ration, or the amount allocated. That division of labor caused constant friction between OPA and the supply agencies for several reasons. One reason was that the supply agencies would not indicate to OPA soon enough how much would be available; they could not know the total amount nor how much the armed forces would require, so they disliked making advance estimates. Therefore, OPA did not have sufficient time to establish a plan based on how much would be available that month.

A second cause of friction derived from the different purposes of the agencies. The primary job of the supply agencies was increasing supplies; they wanted to give the public the impression that they were doing a good job and that supplies were increasing. Their publicity completely undermined any effort to convey that supply was really scarce and therefore had to be rationed. Publicity from the supply agencies tended to be optimistic in contrast to the pessimism of OPA publicity, which tended to be along the lines of: "The situation is terrible and it is absolutely essential that this be done." Conflicting publicity was the basis for the controversy and subsequent enforcement struggles over gasoline.

A third reason was that the supply agencies were almost invariably run by the industry representatives, whereas the OPA staff held a different point of view. The oilmen who ran the PAB were unwilling to concede that they could not produce a sufficient supply, and were unwilling to shift from a peacetime to a wartime structure. For instance, one of the major troubles that developed later was that the industries that controlled the PAB did not want to disrupt the division of the gasoline market that had prevailed prior to the war, even though the market already had been seriously disrupted by the transfer of transportation from water to rail. Under a rationing system the distribution of supply would be determined by the flow of ration coupons. However, the companies did not want the percentage distributed by each company in any particular territory changed. They insisted on maintaining the prewar system of supplies to the East Coast, resulting in a greater shortage on the East Coast than would otherwise have been necessary and making OPA's job more difficult.

In general, OPA advocated quite a different point of view than other agencies. As a result, we constantly found ourselves in conflict with other agencies. Strangely enough, Ickes backed the oil companies. He and Henderson and Chester Bowles engaged in virulent controversies over the gasoline situation, with Ickes taking the oil companies' point of view, and Bowles and Henderson arguing for what they considered the public interest.

## RENT CONTROL

As rent control had unique features differentiating it from other types of price control, a separate department was created for rent control. Originally it had been part of the Consumer Division and later a rent section was included in the Price Department. But with the passage of the Price Control Act and the mounting of rent control problems, Henderson wisely decided to create a new department with authority over the rent picture. The task required the special responsibility of a person in a sufficiently high position to carry weight and report directly to the administrator. By creating a new department it was possible to attract additional talent interested in the direct responsibility of the position.

Karl Borders, who previously had done the main work on rent, was fully committed to the principles of rent control, a nice and decent person, but rather weak in his handling of people and not sufficiently forceful. As head of the Rent Department, Henderson brought in Paul Porter, who had the stronger and more aggressive talent needed to fill this job. A tall, handsome fellow from Kentucky, Paul was a lawyer, although recently he had not been practicing law. I believe he had been in some form of public relations for the Columbia Broadcasting System. Hence, he was a combination of lawyer and public relations man. A very able person, he was not profound, but extremely quick and perhaps somewhat flashy. Simultaneously aggressive and charming, jovial and companionable, he amused us with stories about Kentucky.

Paul did his job very effectively. In fact, he once succeeded in stealing the funds allocated to my Legal Department for 250 investigators for enforcement purposes. That was rather typical of Paul's operations. I forget exactly how it happened, but I had a commitment from Henderson for additional funds for my legal division for investigators to enforce the rent control provisions. I went to Paul Porter to arrange the details of how these people should operate in connection with his program. Before I knew it, he had all the money in his budget and I was completely out in the cold. He cut my throat so pleasantly, however, that I could not take much offense.

We could see at an early point that the voluntary control of rents under the system of fair rent committees would not operate successfully. Despite the fair rent committees, rents were rising rapidly in many sections of the country. Consequently, we needed to take measures under the Price Control Act when it passed in January 1942 with special provisions establishing a system for rent control. The act incorporated the possibility that rent control could be secured through voluntary action, or through state and local action. The law provided that the administrator must first designate a particular area as one to be subject to rent control and then allow 60 days to elapse before issuing any federal regulation for rent control. Those 60 days allowed time for the establishment of either a system of voluntary control–which was considered unlikely–or more important, a system of state or local control. If such voluntary or state or local controls were put into effect, and did stabilize rents, then the administrator was not authorized to establish federal rent control.

Consequently, our first job was to designate areas where rents had risen to a degree that indicated control was necessary. OPA moved fairly rapidly on that. By March 1 or 2, 1942, we had designated twenty areas in which rent controls should be instituted first. Eventually, some 450 or 500 areas were designated. Only in Flint, Michigan, was effective local action taken. In most cases no local or state action occurred. In a few cases the state or local action was obviously ineffective, so that, except in Flint, the federal agency proceeded with rent control.

Paul Porter brought a great deal of energy and competence to the rent control program. After the original 20 areas were designated, consistent progress occurred in the designation of areas and the issuance of regulations, so that by the end of 1942, 313 areas, including all the major population centers of the country, had rent regulations covering a population of 75 million people.

The regulations were much simpler than most of the price regulations. The basic principle was the freeze: the rent was frozen as of a certain date. Frequently, this base date was pushed back a year: April 1941 was commonly used for regulations issued in 1942. Reducing rents was possible because usually a record existed of what the rental fee had been at that time and because it was a single transaction that did not enter into the prices of other commodities.

Of course, almost immediately complications began to arise. The obvious one was that some housing accommodations were not rented at all on the base date. Some were not even in existence. So we needed a method for fixing rents of accommodations that had not been rented as of the base date. We accomplished this relatively simply by allowing the landlord and tenant to agree on a rent. The rent was reported to OPA, and if OPA judged it out of line with other rents of comparable accommodations in that neighborhood, then we could reduce the rent retroactively. Although a number of such cases arose, there were not so many but what OPA could handle each as an individual case. Some landlords alleged that the rent on the base date was not a normal rent. For instance, the landlord would claim that he had been renting to his grandmother at a reduced rate; now that his grandmother was dead, he wanted to raise the rent. That landlord was entitled to a higher rent. We made individual adjustments in a variety of situations. Another complication was: what was to be done in the case of a major improvement on the property? When did you have a major improvement rather than simply a repair job? If it was really a major improvement, a rent increase should be allowed, but keeping the accommodations in a state of repair warranted no increase. That distinction was difficult to determine at times. Altogether, though, administering rent control was much easier than price control because fewer transactions were involved, the time element was less important, and we could take the time necessary to examine each particular case and attempt to settle it in accordance with principles that were rapidly evolving.

One aspect of special interest to the enforcement lawyers was the problem of eviction. Assessment of rent control in World War I and other programs had alerted OPA to the significance of control over eviction. If restrictions curtail a landlord's power to evict a tenant, the bargaining balance is retained to a sufficient degree that the tenant can defend himself against efforts by the landlord to get him out. The more turnover of tenants, the more likelihood that rents would increase. An old tenant immediately would squawk and refuse to pay a rent increase, but a new tenant might not know what the previous rent was. Furthermore, if a landlord could freely evict a tenant, the landlord could use the threat of eviction to extract extra rent and change other arrangements to the landlord's advantage. Control of evictions became a key part of rent regulations. Rather strict provisions prevented evictions except under certain designated circumstances. Failure to pay the rent was the only surefire grounds for eviction, but other grounds, such as creating a nuisance, also were recognized. OPA did not attempt to substitute its own eviction procedures for the established local procedures. We merely required that before the landlord could begin local procedures for eviction, he had to secure a certificate from OPA authorizing him to start eviction action. In this way OPA kept control over evictions without actually running the legal system of evictions itself.

We devised procedures that substantially contributed towards creating a state of almost automatic compliance. All landlords were required to register, so that it was a violation of the regulations to rent any property without having registered the property with OPA. One copy of the registration was sent to the tenant, one copy was retained by the landlord, and one retained by OPA. The landlord had to show proof that the tenant had received his copy. Therefore, the tenant could check on the landlord's statement as to what the rent on the base date had been. In this way, it was virtually impossible for the landlord to misrepresent the rent as of the base date, so that OPA had on file a report that normally was an accurate statement of what the rent should be. Whenever a new tenant came in, a copy of this registration was served on him so that he also knew what the rent on the base date had been. The eviction controls protected a tenant should he need to protest.

As these provisions resulted in a high degree of automatic compliance, the rent program from the beginning was the most successful of any of the OPA price programs. The easily determined rent ceiling on each unit was known by all the parties involved. Sufficient time was available so adjustments could be handled properly. As a general proposition, court proceedings over evictions favored the tenant either indirectly, through delay, or deliberately, through a general prejudice on the part of courts and juries to favor tenants over landlords. The balance of forces in rent control was fairly even among landlord, tenant, and OPA. Subject to rather tight administration, the program worked so well that it was a trifle unfair in the sense that landlords should be so tightly controlled when other entrepreneurs were not as successfully controlled.

The Legal Department functioned in rent control similarly as it did in price control, except that drafting regulations was simpler. Although hundreds of rent areas existed, the problems in most of them were exactly the same, the only differences being what the rent of each unit should be or what the base date should be. So, very soon two basic regulations were drafted that were generally applicable, one dealing with privately rented housing accommodations and the other with hotels. Issues of interpretation arose, but as those were ironed out, their significance receded. The most challenging issues for the rent attorneys concerned individual adjustments such as new rentals, grandmother cases, and other petitions for rent increases.

In conclusion, the rent program from the beginning was a tight, well-organized, successful operation. It was better in some areas than in others, and plenty of problems developed; particularly at the beginning a multitude of cases piled up for decision and individual adjustments. But compared to other OPA programs it was an easier, and consequently more effective, operation.

# 9

# THE LEGAL DEPARTMENT OF OPA

*Taking on lawyers for the New Deal, among them a young Richard Nixon.*

As associate general counsel, I oversaw most of the operating aspects of the Legal Department. David Ginsburg was the general counsel, and as Leon Henderson's assistant, his time was spent mostly in top policy conferences and decisions. As the months passed, I began to do less work in the Price Department and gradually that function was taken over by a group of attorneys who ran the price section of the Legal Department.

Officially, the functions of the Legal Department were to draft and interpret documents and amendments, and to resolve problems of particular cases. At the top level we conducted relations with Congress and high governmental officials, and wrote legislation and statutory amendments. Actually, as head of OPA, Henderson visualized the Legal Department partly as a check and partly as an energizer of the Price Department. He believed that decisions with respect to both major and minor policies should be made by a small group. He would have liked a representative of industry or business and a young lawyer to combine their talents as a team. Henderson let it be known that the lawyers had what amounted to a veto power over price, rationing, and rent executives. No written order gave the Legal Department veto power, but Henderson required the lawyers to approve any document that was issued. Since practically all decisions were issued in written form, that requirement constituted a formal veto. It was also generally understood that the Legal Department could block anything and transfer it to a higher level for decision. Because of Ginsburg's personal relationship with Henderson, and because of Henderson's excellent experience with Ginsburg, because of the ability of the legal staff, and because of their broad perspective on what was happening (which made it natural for them to coordinate policy), the Legal Department played an extremely important role in the program under Henderson.

Inevitably, the Legal Department's informal role aroused friction. Friction was inherent in the divided responsibility and it also arose from different approaches. The Legal Department was inclined to be tougher than the price, rent, or rationing executives, partly because the Legal Department was more committed to tougher price control than were some in the other divisions and partly because they did not have to deal as frequently with businessmen and others subject to the regulation.  The lawyers also had a more legal approach, naturally, as on the question of adjustments, and approached problems from the point of view of general principles rather than as individual problems.

Although the lawyers' influential position gave rise to controversy, the situation worked remarkably smoothly most of the time.  Tensions exploded occasionally, but discord was generally smoothed over.  However, the other departments resented the arrangement and when Henderson left, there was a strong move to curtail the functions of the Legal Department. That was  done, at least in theory.  We continued to play an important role, but it was most marked under Henderson.

## TOP PERSONNEL

Toward the end of the fall of 1942, Henry Hart was designated as another associate general counsel to head the price aspect of the Legal Department's operations.  From then on I did not participate much in the price, rationing, or rent areas, each of which had their own chiefs, except to deal with organizational, enforcement, or very general problems.

Henry Hart was a professor of law at the Harvard Law School, from which he had graduated about the same time as I had graduated from Yale.  He had been editor-in-chief of the *Harvard Law Review*, a top academic honor.  I believe he had been secretary to Justice Brandeis for several years.  He was one of the ablest lawyers in Washington.  Very resourceful, he would generate more fruitful suggestions for compromises of various situations than almost any lawyer I have seen.  He was constantly taking a middle way that would reconcile various points of view. He was an excellent draftsman, meticulous in his use of language, and eminently suitable for the job.   Hart's chief weakness was his lack of a broad view.  Not in Ginsburg's class in terms of understanding the context in which price control was taking place and the basic forces operating on the scene, Hart tended to confine himself to rather narrow legal issues. His other limitation was that he was not entirely in touch with the practical aspects of what was happening.  This was particularly true of the labor situation, where price involved a wage problem, and at times interfered with his work.  On the whole, however, Hart performed excellently as head of the price section of the Legal Department.

Hart had four major assistants.  One was Harold Leventhal, whom I have already mentioned.  The second was David Cobb, who took most of the responsibility for drafting the Maximum Price Regulation.  Cobb had graduated from Harvard Law School about 1936.  He did not have the innate ability that Hart and Leventhal had, but his high level of practical ability complemented the others' talents.  Undoubtedly the toughest-minded of the group of price lawyers, Cobb stood firm on price control, outspoken for his position without demonstrating disrespect for others, impressing people as completely honest. David Cavers, the third assistant, came in somewhat later. Cavers had been teaching at Duke Law School up to this time. After he left OPA he joined the Harvard faculty. Cavers was much more the academic, similar in many respects to Hart, although not as able, and surpassing Hart in the same defects. But Cavers also was a resourceful negotiator and an excellent draftsman. Although more retiring than Cobb, Leventhal, or Hart, Cavers performed well. The fourth assistant, Henry Reuss, was the weakest of the group, despite considerable ability and toughmindedness. After he left OPA, he entered Wisconsin politics, running for mayor of Milwaukee and for Congress. Originally, Leventhal and Cobb did most of the price work, with Hart acting as consultant. Later Reuss came in, and Cavers joined last of all. Eventually, Hart became head of the group as associate general counsel and the others became assistant general counsels. It was a very high-powered outfit.

Thomas E. Harris headed the rationing section of the Legal Department. He had graduated from Columbia Law School about 1933, served as law clerk to Justice Stone, and worked in the solicitor general's office of the Department of Justice. There were two schools of thought about Harris. My own view was that he was one of the half-dozen most brilliant lawyers in Washington. He assimilated material rapidly, conceived solutions to problems quickly, and pressed for resolutions. His rapid-fire mind was connected to a sharp tongue. He was a very biting individual, who was somewhat unrestrained in his dealings with people. As a person of intense likes and dislikes, with far more *bêtes noires* than angels, he was not reluctant to express his views. Ginsburg and I had to go around cleaning up after him. When he had finished with a conference, tempers would be high and we would need to smooth things over. But he was such an able person that we found it worthwhile to put up with his arousal of antagonisms.

Harris had a witty tongue as well. Toward the end of 1942 we had called a conference in New Orleans of about one hundred attorneys from the Atlanta and New Orleans regional offices. I digress for a moment to mention that as Ginsburg rose to open the conference on a Sunday morning, one of the southern attorneys stood up and said, "Mr. Ginsburg, since we are meeting on Sunday morning, I think it would be a good thing if we opened with a prayer." At this, I nearly fell off my chair, because usually in that kind of a crisis Ginsburg would turn to me and I was expecting him to say, "Well, that's a good idea. Mr. Emerson, will you lead us in a prayer?" After rejecting the choir robe of my childhood for a lifelong commitment to atheism, the only thing which came to mind was the final prayer of the Episcopal service, which starts out, "May the peace of God which passeth all understanding. . . ." I was in a sweat, but Ginsburg paused only a second or two before replying to the southern gentleman, "That's an excellent idea. Will you lead us in prayer?" and so I was off the hook.

After Ginsburg gave excellent summaries of the whole situation, we turned to the ration picture. Harris started off with a discussion of the future prospects of rationing. He then began to elaborate an idea he had heard batted around the Department of Agriculture a few days earlier: the meat shortage could be solved by taking all meat–steaks, chops, everything–grinding it up, and mixing it with a lot of soybeans to produce "victory sausage." He developed this theme with great gusto, insisting that all meat, no matter of how choice quality, would be chopped up together and adulterated with soybeans, so that the only form of meat that would be available would be the victory sausage. Harris' humorous exaggeration was intended to illustrate the possibilities of this suggestion. As Harris reached the heights of eloquence in describing this solution, somebody in the audience fell off his chair onto the floor with a great crash. With the timing of a standup comedian Harris shouted, "Carry that weakling out of here and hire a new lawyer!" He brought down the house. (The rate at which OPA was hiring lawyers made the remark particularly amusing to those present.) That gives you a hint of how lively and entertaining Harris was.

Robert Wales headed the legal work in the rent field. A lawyer from Chicago, a few years older than the rest of us, Wales had been at the top of his Harvard law class, chief editor of the *Harvard Law Review*, and law clerk to Justice Holmes. An able lawyer with a somewhat stiff demeanor, quiet and colorless compared to the others, he did a first-class job on rent control.

The head of the research section of the Legal Department, Nathaniel L. Nathanson, had been there almost from the beginning, and had worked with Leventhal in the drafting of the statute. He had been my successor as editor-in-chief of the *Yale Law Journal*. Since that time, he had been teaching, I think, and was then teaching at Northwestern Law School. Nathanson was an excellent legal theoretician, careful and conscientious, and we used him for research and emergency court work. Shy and retiring, he would be rather lost in the hurly-burly of a price conference with economists, representatives of industry, and so forth.

The other major lawyer in the Legal Department was Brunson MacChesney. MacChesney had graduated from the University of Michigan Law School about 1933, had been in practice for a while, and then was teaching administrative and public law at Northwestern. Shortly after I arrived he was brought in to head the enforcement work of the Legal Department. MacChesney was by far the weakest link among the top personnel of the Legal Department. An intelligent lawyer with considerable ability, he seemed to lack a sense of priorities. In a situation where a million tasks clamored for attention and only a fraction of them could be accomplished because of the time and staff available, he could not seize on the most important tasks and disregard the others. He was inclined to become sidetracked and bogged down in details that should have been handled by others or let go. A poor administrator, he was almost incapable of delegating authority–in this situation, a fatal flaw. MacChesney tried to keep everything in his own hands and have everybody reporting directly to him. Or suddenly realizing this was not working, he would shift to the opposite position and set up a single individual between him and everybody else. Difficulties developed when he could not come to terms with a large staff where it was feasible that only a limited number of persons report directly to the top.

## Recruitment

Before I concentrated on enforcement, one of the more important aspects of my job was building up the legal staff. The recruitment of personnel occupied a good deal of my time. An enormous number of lawyers eagerly flocked to Washington looking for jobs in this period. I could almost have sat around my office and waited for people to drop in, and I would have assembled a pretty good staff for the Washington office. For a period of months I spent a large part of my time interviewing applicants. I would see perhaps eight or ten a day and try to crowd them into 10-minute interviews. There were so many that on one occasion it turned out that I had two interviews scheduled at the same time with two persons both named Ed Friedman. A fellow named Ed Friedman had called up while my secretary was out; I talked with him, made the appointment with him, and put it down on the calendar. Then another lawyer with the same name telephoned. My secretary, thinking it was the same man, made the appointment for the same time.

Many young lawyers were interested in contributing to the war effort right after Pearl Harbor. Consequently, perhaps two or three lawyers a day might contact our office. These applicants often held what were considered the best legal jobs available to young lawyers, with the leading firms of the major cities. They were mostly younger lawyers who had graduated in the 1930s. By and large the older lawyers who had graduated in the 1920s or earlier were sufficiently established that they were not as motivated or free to walk away from commitments. Consequently, if a lawyer of that generation applied, chances were that he was a misfit. To obtain lawyers of good caliber from that age level, we had to discover who they were and persuade them to enter government work.

Among those who came into the office and whom I hired immediately was Richard Nixon. I gave him his first government job. Perhaps I bungled the paramount opportunity of my lifetime to make the world a better place, but I had no hesitation in offering Nixon a job at the time. He had graduated second or third in his class at Duke Law School, practiced law in a small town in California, and after only a few years of practice was making an income of $5000 or $6000 net. He was willing to work for $3200 or $3800. He was good-looking and clearly a reasonably able person. I spoke with him for about five minutes. All I had to do was persuade him that he should take a job with OPA. Actually, he did not work out too well. He was assigned to our hottest spot at the time–the rationing program, under Tom Harris, who immediately took one of his notorious dislikes to Nixon (as I said, Harris was one of the most brilliant lawyers in Washington). I had no direct dealings with Nixon, since he worked under Harris, but his general reputation was that he did not know, at least in the legal sense, too well what was going on, that he was not very smart. He did not stay more than five or six months, and then he obtained a commission in the navy. It is noteworthy that during the campaign for the vice-presidency he never once mentioned his connection with OPA. All his official biographies completely omitted any reference to his employment with OPA. Even in his radio and television program in which he recounted in some detail his income since his graduation from law school, he left out any income paid to him by OPA. Apparently, he considered this a political liability.

## ENFORCEMENT

The demanding task that was obviously mounting, and had not, up to then, been satisfactorily solved, was enforcement of the various OPA regulations. Since price and rent control, rationing, legal research, and emergency court work were being handled effectively by others, I turned my attention to enforcement. I had felt all along that MacChesney was not functioning well in this post, and when I looked into the matter further I decided that it would be impossible for me to take over that area with MacChesney there. I thought that it would not be feasible to work through him. The basic reorganization and re-orientation to the whole issue that was necessary could not be accomplished with MacChesney in charge of the enforcement section. Therefore, somewhat reluctantly, because we were always on the best of terms, I decided that MacChesney would have to be replaced. This decision thrust me into an embarrassing position because, as I was to take over the job, I was hardly in an unbiased position. However, I discussed the matter at some length with Ginsburg and he agreed that the enforcement job needed a great deal more push and administrative ability than MacChesney was demonstrating. Unless drastic measures were taken, Ginsburg foresaw that we would soon be in difficult straits as far as enforcement was concerned. He agreed that MacChesney should be let go.

Almost a month of agonizing relations with MacChesney followed my conversation with Ginsburg. MacChesney himself recognized that things were not going well in the enforcement section, and about this time he submitted to me a proposal for reorganization and expansion. Normally, I would have acted on his proposal and put it through, or done whatever was necessary. But since we had decided to let MacChesney go, that placed me in an impossible position of stalling MacChesney. It was not my responsibility to fire him; particularly since I was to take his place, my involvement would only add to his embarrassment. That move was up to Ginsburg. So I kept stalling him on the reorganization plans. Not being open with him became extremely painful.

Finally Ginsburg did call him in and told him he was replacing him as head of enforcement, and the matter was settled. MacChesney could have transferred within the organization; we did not intend to throw him out entirely. He preferred to leave, and moved to the Board of Economic Warfare. So I took over direct charge of the enforcement section. From the end of 1942, most of my work involved the enforcement aspect.

In general, the staff of the Legal Department was hard-working and extremely competent. How hard we worked is indicated by the following incident. One of our attorneys obtained a commission in the navy. He successfully passed all the physical tests for this commission and announced his departure. We gave him a farewell party. Farewell parties were one of the principal occasions for staff socializing. Then, as the navy did not assign him anywhere for a period of time, he stayed with OPA and continued to work. Meanwhile, he attended a number of other farewell parties for other people. At the end of about six months, the navy called him up. He reported for duty, underwent another physical examination, and was rejected on the ground that his blood pressure was too high. Six months of taxing work in OPA had escalated his blood pressure beyond navy requirements! This attorney had to take several months' vacation to lower his blood pressure before he could be accepted by the navy.

That is some indication of the pace of the work throughout this period. It was not the enormous, strenuous pace of NRA, but we worked under difficult circumstances. The experience of NRA was quite important in connection with OPA's work, which was not a rough-and-ready breaking of new ground as NRA had been. OPA operated on a much higher level of workmanship. At times we were forced to allocate responsibility to people with little background, but not on anything like the scale on which it happened in NRA.

There was considerable turnover in the top level. Of course, Ginsburg resigned shortly after Henderson did. Henry Hart and Dave Cavers stayed throughout the whole era. Leventhal resigned to take a commission in the middle of 1943. Cobb was drafted at about the same time. Harris resigned to go with the Board of Economic Warfare sometime in 1943, after about a year and a half. Nathanson stayed throughout. I stayed for almost four years, through April 1945. Wales stayed most of the time; after the height of the activity he took a job in the Treasury Department.

The top level of the Legal Department, with the exception of Ginsburg and the general counsel position thereafter, provided a reasonable amount of continuity. The top and secondary levels always remained long enough and overlapped enough to provide continuity. After Ginsburg, the general counsel became of much less significance and to some extent was a figurehead. But the approach and procedures established in 1942 continued throughout the war period.

## LOYALTY ISSUES

The loyalty issue had been in the picture pretty much from the beginning, raised by Rep. Martin Dies (Democrat, Texas). He had attacked Henderson strongly throughout 1941, claiming Henderson was engaged in subversive activity. He pointed particularly to Henderson's activities with an organization supporting loyalist Spain. Henderson answered these attacks forthrightly and nobody paid much attention to them at the time–at least, nobody in the administration did. Congress paid more attention, but Henderson's work with congressional committees on the price control legislation had brought him into touch with numerous congressmen, and he had little trouble convincing them that the charges were unfounded, so he remained unscathed.

Dies also attacked at least one other member of Henderson's staff in the pre-statutory days: Tom Tippett, who was working in the consumer division on rent matters. Tippett had a background in the radical movement, most likely a non-communist affiliation, of which he had left some traces in the form of books. *When Southern Labor Stirs* was an account of efforts to organize labor in the South, particularly the textile mills, in the early 1920s. In 1953 Tippett would not have lasted five seconds in any agency in Washington. However, Henderson took the view that Tippett's background was a question for the Civil Service Commission: "If their investigation finds him qualified, I'll accept that. It is perfectly all right with me." The Civil Service Commission apparently cleared Tippett, because he continued with the agency for some years.

I think Henderson and Tippett were the only two public targets at this time. Later, as the attacks on OPA accumulated, more charges of this nature flew around. I personally became embroiled in a loyalty problem at this time, which I think is worth examining in detail.

### I Am Investigated

As I already have mentioned, I had been investigated by the FBI when I was in the Assistant Solicitor General's Office. From what Charles Fahy had told me, I had gathered that the report was unfavorable, but as Fahy knew me personally, and Biddle, the attorney general, knew me, they had paid no attention and nothing further was said or done about the report. When I went to OPA I was investigated again as a routine matter by the Treasury intelligence unit. The intelligence unit included all of their investigative agencies: Secret Service, alcohol tax investigating staff, and probably the Bureau of Internal Revenue [later the Internal Revenue Service] investigators. Their investigative facilities handled the numerous checks needed on people at OPA and other war agencies. To what extent these investigations at this time specifically focused on the loyalty aspect, I do not know. Basically, they were investigations of general character and qualifications, but at times loyalty issues showed up, and apparently the FBI already was attuned to that area, as indicated by the FBI investigation of me. The results of the Treasury investigation were submitted to Dallas Dort, the director of the Central Administrative Services in the Office for Emergency Management. The Office for Emergency Management at this time was acting as a housekeeping agency for OPA and other agencies. Dort wrote a letter to Henderson summarizing the Treasury report. It turned out that the Treasury report was based almost entirely on the earlier FBI report. In other words, in the press of work they had apparently checked with the FBI, learned a report on me existed, and had copied most of that report. Hence, what the Treasury turned up was really the FBI report.

The charges made in the report were these: The FBI had information in its files that I was either a member or former member of the Communist Party. The informant had stated that several persons in Seattle, Washington, had told him I was a member of a Communist unit with them. It was also alleged that I was active in the National Lawyers Guild and a leader of the extreme pro-Communist faction. The report noted that Earl Browder, in his testimony before the Dies Committee, had said the Guild was a transmission belt for the Communist cause. The report also alleged that I was a member of the International Juridical Association, which was said to be affiliated with the International Labor Defense, a Communist organization alleged to be affiliated in turn with an organization in Moscow. Seven members of the Board of the International Juridical Association were listed and the report implied they were Communists. It was also alleged that when I was employed as assistant general counsel of the NLRB, certain employees were not promoted to supervisory positions because they were not considered leftist enough, and that these persons had been promoted after I and Nat Witt had left the board:

> Employees of the National Labor Relations Board referred to above alleged in their statements that Mr. Emerson would attempt to control personnel appointments in his new office and proceed to fill them with communists.

An interview with Charles Fahy apparently probed only my legal ability. Fahy also said that there had been an unfavorable report by the FBI, but that he, Solicitor General Biddle, and Justice Douglas were "instrumental in having the appointment pushed through." The report also alleged that my wife, "better known as Bertha Paret" (that was her maiden name, although she had not used it in Washington at all) was a leading member of the League of Women Shoppers, as well as a "fellow traveler" [i.e., Communist].

I was permitted to see the full text of the Treasury report, which quoted in great detail from the FBI report. The FBI report contained other incidental material. For example, the landlady from whom we rented our house told the FBI investigator that I had a lot of books on Russia right next to my easy chair. This was untrue, in the sense that there were no books next to the easy chair—if any of the chairs that she had rented to us could have been called easy chairs. It was true that my library contained half a dozen books on Russia, the one most likely to strike the eye being Trotsky's *History of the Russian Revolution*. The FBI had taken this statement and inserted it in the report without further comment. The FBI report also stated that our pediatrician had stated that we had socialist views and believed in socialized medicine. This was a result of a conversation we had had with him of a rather casual nature on the health insurance problem. There was other material of a similar nature. The material concerning my wife, and much of the material concerning me, was taken from an article published in the *New Leader* about a year earlier, in which I had been attacked as a leader of the Stalinist wing in the Lawyers Guild, and as forming with Edwin Smith and Nat Witt a triumvirate to dictate the policies of the NLRB. This article had also attacked my wife as a Stalinist leader of the League of Women Shoppers. The FBI report had simply quoted this article at great length, with no further effort to check the material or to inquire about the source.

I wrote a memorandum, dated December 1941, for Leon Henderson in reply to Dallas Dort's letter. In that memorandum I pointed out that I had never been in Seattle, or in the state of Washington, that I knew only one person there, so far as I could remember, and he was a college classmate who was a member of the Washington state legislature, and that therefore the statement with respect to my Communist Party membership must have been a mistake in identity. I reviewed the activities, policies, and positions of the National Lawyers Guild and appended a long list of well-known persons who were still members. I reviewed the history of the International Juridical Association and listed well-known persons who were members of its executive board but had not been mentioned in the Treasury report. With respect to appointments at the NLRB, I pointed out that my job had been simply to recommend appointments, and that all appointments had actually been made by Charles Fahy and by the board itself; further, that the board actually knew the qualifications and point of view of each one of the individuals involved, because these individuals had constantly appeared before the board in reporting cases in the course of their work. I also pointed out that my chief assistant at the NLRB took my place when I left, and was appointed to the position by the new board, of which William M. Leiserson and H.A. Millis were members, and that others of my supervisory staff were either working there or in defense agencies, where they presumably had been investigated. I then gave a list of the famous people who were members of the League of Women Shoppers, including Mrs. William O. Douglas and Mrs. Leon Henderson.

I also pointed out the failure of the report to check with those persons who really knew my position, stating that of all those for whom I had worked, and been in close contact with, only Charles Fahy had been consulted in this, and apparently he had not actually been asked his opinion on the loyalty issue. I gave a list of people whom I knew and had worked closely with, and suggested that the investigators contact them. This list included Lloyd Garrison, Calvert Magruder, John Winant, J. Warren Madden, Charles Fahy, Thomas H. Eliot, David Ginsburg, Abe Fortas, Murray W. Latimer, David K. Niles, Thomas Copeland (who was my roommate at college), Mortimer Kollender (who was my assistant at the NLRB), and Blackwell Smith (who was with the OPM). I also suggested as people who knew me and would testify with respect to my views Justice William O. Douglas, Robert H. Jackson, Charles E. Clark, Francis Biddle, Francis Shea, John Carmody, Arthur Altmeyer, and Leon Henderson. I then asked for a re-opening of the investigation.

Henderson sent my memorandum with a letter to Morgenthau at Treasury, saying that on the basis of the documents, his knowledge of me, and assurances from Dave Ginsburg, a serious injustice had been done to Mr. Emerson, and that the investigation seemed to fall seriously short of "that standard of competence, of impartiality, which should be required by responsible agencies to govern in matters of this sort." He then joined with me in requesting that the matter be re-opened and a full investigation made.

Morgenthau–I learned from other sources later–was considerably disturbed on receiving these documents and noting what kind of an investigation had been made. In fact, shortly thereafter he insisted on Treasury's withdrawing from any investigations of this nature. He turned the matter over to Herbert Gaston, the assistant secretary in charge of the units that included the intelligence unit. Gaston read the material and wrote to Henderson that the matter had been referred to him. He said that he had reviewed the problem with Elmer Irey, who was then chief of the intelligence unit and:

> We agree that it contains irrelevant material, that it is deficient
> in other respects, and that it should not have been submitted.

He accordingly requested that the report be withdrawn and a further investigation be made. A secret service agent was assigned to the new investigation. He came over and snapped a photograph, which he took out to Seattle, talked to one of the people I had mentioned as being familiar with me, and ran down other leads. He then submitted a report to Elmer Irey, and Irey sent it over to Dallas Dort, with the statement that it would certainly completely exonerate me.

Dallas Dort then summarized the second report for Henderson in a letter dated January 1942. Taking up first the alleged leftist tendencies of the NLRB, Dort summarized the Treasury investigation as revealing this:

> Testimony obtained from members of the board, its former and
> present general counsel, an appellate judge who reviewed some
> of its cases, and others, disclosed that all but three of these
> persons contradicted the intimation of communism. Of those
> three, one said that Mr. Emerson consistently followed the
> Communist Party line; another attributed his failure to win
> promotion to Mr. Emerson's dislike of his anti-communist views.
> It should be noted that this man was employed under Mr.
> Emerson for only two months during his entire employment with
> the board. The third person asserted his belief that the attorney
> was denied promotion because of his not being "a leftist."

He then went on to discuss the Lawyers Guild:

> Various past and present members of the Guild, together with
> non-member observers of its activities, were interviewed. All but
> three of these persons, including Justice Jackson, Judges

181

Rutledge and Edgerton of the Court of Appeals, and general counsels and solicitors of the Departments of Interior and Labor, and of the Railroad Retirement Board, said that they did not regard the Guild as being communist-dominated, or believe that Emerson was "leftist" or subversive in his Guild activities. However, three representative persons said that, while they did not regard Mr. Emerson as a communist, he consistently voted the party line.

The new investigation contained little information on the International Juridical Association:

Only one witness expressed an opinion of this organization. He said its primary function was to issue a law journal, which was the best in its field, and that he did not regard it as subversive.

Then, with respect to the Seattle incident, the Treasury reported that:

Upon being shown a photograph one of the three persons in Seattle said that he had referred to another man named Emerson, and didn't know anything whatever about the subject of this investigation. The other two, who are attorneys, husband and wife, denied having any personal knowledge as to whether Mr. Emerson is or is not a member of the Communist Party.

Then it went on:

Expressions of opinion were obtained from a total of twenty-six persons in Washington, D.C., concerning Mr. Emerson's character, reputation, and loyalty to the United States. Twenty of these persons regarded him as a liberal, but not Communistically inclined, and as a loyal American. Four of them assert that he had consistently followed the Communist Party line. One described him as "parlor pink" but not a party member [I think that was Thurman Arnold], and one said he would not trust Mr. Emerson on matters of policy because of his association with dangerous radicals. None of them asserted a belief that he is a member of the Communist Party.

It concluded:

Attorney General Biddle was ill at the time the investigation was made and was not available for interviews. Mr. Elmer R. Irey, chief, intelligence unit, Bureau of Internal Revenue, later personally talked to the attorney general, who said that in his opinion, Mr. Emerson is "a very fine man, by no means a red, and that he regards him as a loyal American citizen." Mr. Irey, in commenting on the case, stated that "in my opinion, there is no question of his good character and his loyalty to the United States."

On the basis of that new investigation, the Civil Service Commissioner and OPA sent me notices that I was cleared and the case was closed. I realized that the files still remained with the FBI, unanswered, and although I could not foresee all the future developments, I had enough sense to realize that it was probably not advisable to leave matters in that state. I then went to see Attorney General Francis Biddle, explained the situation to him, and asked if he would see that the second Treasurey report was secured by the FBI and placed in the FBI files. He said he would do that, but whether he did or not I do not know. In any event, in April 1942, the FBI was given a tentative appropriation of $100,000 for investigation of subversives in the government, called me in, and asked me some formal questions about my activities. I took the opportunity to put into the record of that investigation the full letter from Dort with documents of the Treasury investigation, in that way hoping to get the material into the FBI files.

I think those details significant as an indication of the kind of investigations the FBI, at least at that time, was making of individuals. It certainly foreshadowed some of the problems that would arise later.

That was the last I heard of any personal loyalty problem from governmental agencies where I was employed. Later I experienced congressional and other attacks, but they too were straightened out.

Another incident in connection with the loyalty problem illustrates the atmosphere of the period. An attorney, Abraham Glasser, who had worked in the Department of Justice, applied for a position on our legal staff and told the following story at his interview. He had been discharged from the Department of Justice for revealing information to foreign agents. His side of the story was that he had not known the individuals involved were agents of a foreign government. He had been working on some files in the Department of Justice, had talked with his roommate and other people about the contents of the files, had become interested in various issues that he was not particularly concerned with in his work, had checked those in the files, and had talked to others about these matters. This was, he said, all innocent on his part, and he had no knowledge or reason to believe that the information was being conveyed to foreign agents. Who the foreign agents were was not clear, except that it was a group working out of Canada. (They were the Russian spy ring that was later uncovered in Canada.) As a result of a report on his activities by the FBI, he was suspended. Hearings were then held, and eventually the board that heard his case—consisting of Charles Fahy, Ugo Carusi, and Edwin Dickinson—had come to the conclusion that Glasser had not intentionally disclosed any information, but that he had been negligent and careless in his handling of Department of Justice files. They therefore recommended that he be dismissed or refused to recommend that he be reinstated.

At the time OPA seriously needed lawyers with Glasser's talent. He was a research man, an idea man with imagination in legal analysis, and willing to work solely on research projects. It was not easy to find anyone with ability willing to confine himself to research when so many active areas of legal work were available. Glasser, temperamentally inclined to research, was willing because he was caught in this unfortunate situation. He wanted another government job to vindicate himself rather than leaving the government under a cloud. We could use him. He brought letters from perhaps ten or a dozen of the chief officials of the Justice Department, including Thurman Arnold, Holmes Baldridge, Gerry Gesell, and a number of other people he had worked with, all of whom vouched in unequivocal terms for his loyalty and ability.

I put the whole matter to Ginsburg in full detail. Ginsburg talked with Henderson. We then decided to offer Glasser a job. The record at Justice had shown no improper motivation. The work he would do, legal research on case histories pending in the courts, was not in any sense secret work or of any possible use to any enemy agent. Of course, it would be unthinkable at the present day [1953] that anyone who had been involved in such circumstances could ever get another job anywhere in the government.

In 1949 Glasser was called before the House Committee on Un-American Activities. He told his story to various government agents under oath. He retained as counsel Thurman Arnold, then in private practice, and Arnold persuaded the committee not to hear the matter publicly. In 1953 Glasser was again called before the Committee on Un-American Activities and he pleaded the privilege against self-incrimination in answering questions regarding this incident. He explained to me that he did not want to give the committee the possibility of an alleged espionage case directed against the New Deal. I remain convinced, in spite of his plea under the Fifth Amendment, that there was no improper motivation in what he did, and no criminal intent. I mention the incident as indicating the attitude of the time towards loyalty problems. It was reasonable to believe that an individual caught in such a situation should be given another chance. OPA was, of course, running a serious risk of congressional attack, even at that time, from such an incident, but we were willing to take that risk.


## WASHINGTON ATMOSPHERE IN WARTIME

During the period that I worked at OPA I had little time for outside interests. Virtually my only outside activity was the National Lawyers Guild. For exercise I played tennis and touch football on weekends. I did not do much reading—I simply did not have time. I worked during the entire day and usually in the evenings. Most of my evening work I did at home. I would take home reports or papers to read, or sometimes particular tasks that required concentration. We worked also at lunchtime.

Practically every lunch was a conference of some sort. In addition to that, I was out of town a fair proportion of the time on trips to the field offices. Vacations were rather short and sometimes cancelled if a crisis developed. I usually arranged for my family to leave Washington during the heat of the summer. We would rent a cottage for the summer months, either at Blue Ridge Summit in the mountains or at Bethany Beach by the seashore, planning for me to join the family over weekends. Sometimes I was able to do that, sometimes not. I usually planned a two-week vacation but that did not always materialize. OPA work, then, took my constant attention and occupied by far the greater part of my time. It was, of course, a tremendous strain. The responsibilities were heavy, the problems were difficult, the solutions were not clear, and most of us in the organization were operating under considerable pressure.

We lived in the Cleveland Park area of Washington, a middle-class neighborhood with a modified southern atmosphere where many people were connected with the army. Our eldest child, Joan, was starting school; conflicts between ideas that she had picked up at home and ideas that circulated in the neighborhood caused difficulty, particularly in regard to discrimination against Negroes. The neighborhood had little of the intellectual ferment that prevailed in our house, so our children held different views and interests than the other children in the neighborhood. Our social life was largely with people who shared our interests, and to some extent our children played with the children of our friends. Our limited social life consisted mainly of numerous cocktail parties, dinners at other people's homes, and asking friends to dine at our house. It was largely confined to a narrow circle of friends, mostly lawyers, some economists–generally people that I or my wife associated with at work. We engaged in shop talk and gossip, but mainly we discussed general trends in terms of political and economic events.

The atmosphere of Washington was still very interesting to me. I found the same excitement as before, the same efforts in new fields, the same significance of my work, the same feeling that I was having some influence on what was happening. I continued to enjoy meeting people who were doing very important or unusual things. More through work than our social life we met quite a number of interesting and unusual people at lunches and conferences. The young New Deal crowd was beginning to grow up and settle down. The ones with more permanent kinds of ability were moving into the more important posts. A few were leaving the government, but most of the New Deal group stayed in Washington through the war.

The atmosphere with respect to loyalty and security remained fairly relaxed during the war. The House Committee on Un-American Activities continued its activities, perhaps slightly toned down during the war period, and received increasing support from Congress. Every year or two when the appropriations for the committee came up, some opposition would develop, but the number who voted against the committee in the House consistently declined. However, we were not much concerned with this at the time, failing to realize its longer-term implications. The Roosevelt administration continued to oppose the Committee on Un-American Activities, and in general it was not taken seriously by most of the people in the administration with whom I was in contact. We had a foretaste of where this attitude might lead, but generally those people in the administration with whom I was in touch either opposed the committee or did not take it seriously and tended to make fun of it. A person could be confident that if he were attacked by the committee on Un-American Activities, he would receive sympathetic support from his colleagues and superiors in the administration. However, in the light of the decline of the Washington chapter of the National Lawyers Guild during this period, people may have been more concerned than appeared on the surface.

Nor was there any concern with security problems in Washington at this period. Very few restrictions of a security nature were in place. Of all the thousands and thousands of documents I saw in connection with OPA work, as well as OES and OWMR (discussed later), I cannot recall ever seeing one that was classified as secret, much less top secret. A few were stamped "confidential," but in the agencies where I worked no attention was paid to security problems at all. Certainly, the armed forces were concerned with security problems, but the issue did not permeate the thinking of Washington to any extent. We took papers home, or left them around on office desks, without a thought about espionage or the possibility of information leaking. The atmosphere was relaxed in regard to security.

We also did not hesitate to criticize the policies of the government as a whole or the agency where we worked. Certain standards of loyalty to the agency existed, and perhaps rather looser standards of loyalty to the individuals we were working for. However, loyalty did not entail an absence of criticism. On the contrary, criticism was free, vigorous, and continuous. No penalties or sanctions whatsoever seemed to be attached to criticism. Occasionally someone would go too far. Joseph Rauh, one of the leading young New Dealers, a member of the second generation growing up in that period, was discovered to have given information to the newspapers, contrary to instructions, for the purpose of attempting to build up a backfire against something that his boss, Stettinius, was doing. As he had clearly carried the matter too far, he was discharged, or rather forced out of his work with Stettinius. He obtained a commission in the navy. Things of that sort happened. In that case, it was probably entirely justified. But we had no fear of expressing ourselves, criticizing, or experimenting.

By this time the atmosphere from the early days of the New Deal no longer existed. The free-swinging period was over. The basic forces were pressing in the other direction. The president had openly admitted that he was running the war through a coalition and was holding things together at a much less advanced position than he had previously. Although events were not moving in the reactionary path that they did from V-J Day on, forward motion had definitely come to a halt and was perhaps gradually receding. The atmosphere focused less on creating the ideal society, and liberals did not occupy as prominent positions. Political careers could no longer be based on an advanced liberal position after 1938.

War restrictions and the need for unified effort might have suppressed conflicting views and independent ideas. My own experience was that this did not happen during World War II. The war spirit was one of tremendous energy and devotion to the goal of winning, but it did not lead to conformity. Pressure for conformity followed the war. The bipartisan foreign policy and the total decline of intelligent criticism of our foreign policy was a product of the post-war period. I suppose that there was much less opportunity during the war for disagreement on fundamentals anyway. Practically all groups were united on basic objectives or, as some pro-fascist or neo-fascist groups, not powerful enough to have any effect on the result. Disagreement would have emerged on post-war planing, but President Roosevelt deliberately postponed discussion of postwar problems–unfortunately, from my point of view. It may well be that the insistence on uniformity in the post-war period was partially a product of the war period, when the right of dissent on basic objectives was not tested.

**Trying To Join the Navy**
The possibility of my being drafted arose during this period. It would have been possible for me to obtain a deferment from the draft, at least for six months or a year. However, I strenuously insisted that OPA not ask for a deferment for me. Although I was not ambitious for election to political office, I somewhat shared the general feeling in Washington that any political career would be obstructed beyond repair by failure to serve in the army through obtaining a draft deferment. Also I judged that a career in public service would become difficult if one accepted a deferment. I was perfectly willing to try army life. With millions of other people undergoing that experience I was eager to understand what the experience was like.

The army sent me and a number of others invitations to apply for commissions in military government. We were to go through their training school at the University of Virginia and be trained for military government. One or two in the OPA legal staff accepted these commissions. I do not know whether I would have been able to obtain one, but I did not apply, nor did I make any effort to obtain a commission otherwise. I chose to enter as a private in the ranks because I abhorred the military governing caste and preferred to experience the war from the rank and file point of view. In any event, that was my fixed intention. I was planning to join the navy; I cannot recall now what influenced me to plan that, except that I had heard some rumor that the navy was more rigid than the army. My approach was considered quixotic and crazy by all my friends.

I was called up in the winter of 1943 at the age of thirty-six. I successfully passed the preliminary physical examination and reported for the final physical examination at Fort Meyer. As I have said, as a child I suffered a brief attack of infantile paralysis. I had resolved to attempt to conceal the effects of the disease that still affected my right foot. During the preliminary examination no one had mentioned any difficulty. At Fort Meyer I made it almost all the way through the physical examination until just about the end, when one of the doctors noticed that I was favoring my right foot—or rather he asked me, "Why aren't you standing on your right heel?" I had never noticed that in a normal standing position my right heel is slightly off the floor because my right leg is slightly shorter than my left. I did not have the presence of mind to tell him that I had hurt my heel or some such reason, so I replied that it was an effect of polio but that it did not bother me. Well, from that they finally discovered I had had polio, that there was a slight difference in length of my legs, and that one of the muscles in the instep of my foot was partly paralyzed. Noting this on my forms, the doctor wrote that there was no impairment of locomotion. However, this put me into a special class to be considered by a reviewing officer. I went before a reviewing officer and he turned me down. I was keenly disappointed and argued with the officer for some time, but he reiterated that at my age the army did not want a person with as much of a handicap as that.

I was extremely dejected at being turned down. I had looked forward to the adventure. I guess I must have been unconsciously tired of OPA and the strain of working at impossible problems, and longed for the change of army life. I recovered my spirits shortly afterward and returned to work at OPA.

# 10

# OPA IN ITS PRIME

*The "hold the line" order.*

As the United States entry into World War II swung into high gear, the pressures from war preparations were steadily increasing. As a result of all this, prices at home were steadily rising and the economic situation deteriorated through the fall of 1942. The Price Control Act was incapable of controlling the inflationary process. Many other types of controls that would have been necessary to supplement price controls were not being put into effect. The seven point program announced by President Roosevelt in April had not been implemented.

## THE STABILIZATION ACT OF 1942

By the fall of 1942, after almost a year of trying, Roosevelt was convinced that drastic measures had to be taken immediately if the situation was not to deteriorate beyond repair. Since Congress had not acted, and in order to put sufficient pressure on Congress to provoke action, the president issued his famous statement of September 7, 1942. He stressed that legislation to provide for effective controls on agricultural prices and wages was essential, and essential immediately. He then went on to say:

I ask the Congress to take this action by the first of October.
. . . In the event that the Congress should fail to act, and act adequately, I accept the responsibility, and I will act.

This statement has been generally interpreted as an indication that Roosevelt was prepared to assume dictatorial powers. It came as a shock to many of us in OPA. I assume Henderson must have known about it, and apparently Ginsburg knew about it in advance. I talked with him, expressing my sense of shock that the president was taking matters so far into his own hands. Ginsburg only smiled and said, "Well, probably it will never get to an issue."

That, of course, was how it turned out. Congress did pass the legislation, not by October 1, but by October 3. The president gave them the two days grace. He apparently was confident that this would be the outcome all along, and was using the threat of executive action primarily as a method of pressure and to impart a sense of urgency. No preparations were made to carry into operation Roosevelt's statement that he would take over price control if there were no legislation. I asked Ginsburg what the president intended to do and what he would use to justify the assumption of power. Ginsburg said that there was nothing specific in mind. Nobody in OPA made any study or preparations for action along executive lines in the event that Congress failed to act. Since Ginsburg and OPA usually prepared things well in advance, it was clear that the president's statement was taken purely as a bluff by those in the price control program. Top leadership rather confidently expected that the threat would work, and although many of us were concerned about the principle involved, there apparently was little expectation that the president would ever have his bluff called. Later the statement became one of the major pieces of evidence that the president was ready to become a dictator. I do not think it had any such significance.

The Stabilization Act carried out, in general, the president's demand that there be legislation authorizing the stabilization of agricultural prices and of wages. The major provision of the legislation authorized the president to issue an order stabilizing prices, wages, and salaries affecting the cost of living. It went on to say that, so far as practicable, this stabilization should be on the basis of levels that existed on September 15, 1942.

The act contained further provisions with respect to wage stabilization, providing specifically that no employer could pay, or employee receive, wages or salaries contrary to the regulations promulgated by the president. The act implemented the wage provisions by providing that the president could determine the extent to which any wage payment that was made in violation of the regulation would have to be disregarded by government agencies in determining costs or expense of any employer for the purposes of any other law or regulation. In other words, this authorized the government to enforce the wage regulation by refusing to permit wages above the permitted ceiling to be counted as expenses for income tax purposes, or for making calculations of prices or of costs in government contracts and matters of that sort—an action of considerable importance.

A third important provision authorized the use of the subsidy and loan powers of the Commodity Credit Corporation for the purposes of preventing price increases in agricultural commodities. The remaining provisions of the act were largely technical in nature.

The act contemplated that the president would issue a general order setting forth this stabilization program, including farm prices and wages. The president issued that order the same day he signed the statute. Executive Order 9250 established the Office of Economic Stabilization (OES). The OES was to take general charge of the entire stabilization program, and beyond that, general economic policy. The OES was to have the power of determining basic policies with respect to civilian purchasing power, prices, rents, wages, salaries, profits, rationing, subsidies, and all related matters. The OES was also to adjudicate any disputes arising among the various agencies dealing with different aspects of economic policy.

In addition to setting up the OES, Executive Order 9250 specifically provided that there should be no increases in wage rates or salaries except with the approval of the War Labor Board (WLB). This put a complete freeze on wages, except insofar as the regulations of the WLB authorized increases. The order provided that the board should not approve any increase above the rates prevailing on September 15, 1942, unless such increase was necessary to correct maladjustments or inequalities, or to aid in the effective prosecution of the war. That last phrase left a loophole should the board decide to grant wage increases. It was further provided that no wage increase could be granted under any circumstances that would require a change in the price ceiling, unless the increase were approved by the director of the OES. The administration of these wage provisions was put in the hands of the WLB, subject to the supervision of the OES.

The order provided that prices of agricultural commodities and of commodities manufactured or processed from agricultural commodities should be stabilized so far as practicable on the basis of levels that existed on September 15, 1942.

The act, plus the order, established for the first time the possibility of a stabilization program dealing with all the immediate aspects of economic stabilization and carrying sufficient power to control those aspects, particularly the agriculture and wage matters. In addition, it provided measures for a subsidy program. Of great importance was the establishment of a coordinating agency that could effectively adjust disputes between OPA, the Department of Agriculture, WPB, and other agencies whose operations affected stabilization. The importance attached to the OES appeared from the fact that Justice James F. Byrnes resigned from the Supreme Court to take the post of director. The creation of OES marked a significant advance in the administration of the whole stabilization program during the war. It was to prove effective not only in settling disputes between the various agencies concerned with economic stabilization, a matter of extreme urgency and importance, but also served an important function in backing up the efforts of OPA to hold prices and not grant increases. Under certain circumstances, actions that would have involved price increases could have been put into effect only with the approval of the director of OES. This meant that it was much easier to resist pressures from industry and Congress because the responsibility now was moved beyond OPA. Hence OPA could say, "We can't grant this because a directive from the Office of Economic Stabilization prevents us from doing so." The possibility of pressuring Byrnes to change the directive obviously was much more remote than the possibility of putting pressure on OPA, always in a more vulnerable position, or upon some subordinate in OPA. So the device divided responsibility and also, from the political point of view, divided the vulnerability of OPA to industry and political pressure.

## STAFF CHANGES
*Leon Henderson resigns, followed by Ginsberg*

The next major event in OPA was the resignation of Leon Henderson in December of 1942. The reasons for Henderson's resignation were varied. First, and most important, there was extreme congressional opposition to Henderson at this time. Henderson's support in Congress at the time of the hearing on the Price Control Act had almost completely dissipated. In addition, Henderson had antagonized one of the most powerful industrial groups in the country, the oil industry, in connection with his struggles over gasoline rationing. Big business generally was strongly opposed to Henderson. They had felt unduly controlled by OPA legislation in contrast to other groups in the economy, particularly labor and farmers, who were relatively uncontrolled. In addition, Henderson had antagonized a number of congressmen who were New Deal in their outlook and might otherwise have supported him, because of the policies of his assistant, Frank Bane, in creating the district ration offices. (Bane had worked almost entirely through the state governments, thus mitigating the "right" of national political figures to dole out what were in effect patronage jobs.)

There was also in Congress an anti-intellectual attitude, contending that the OPA was dominated by the academic profession and that it ought to be reorganized to bring in more businessmen and men with business experience. This attitude persisted after Henderson resigned.

Finally, the congressional elections of 1942 had resulted in a rather severe defeat for the Democratic party, insofar as they lost several important senators and a number of members of the House. Substantial responsibility for the political defeat was attributed to OPA at the time. Looking forward to the 1944 presidential election, the Democrats were concerned that OPA under Henderson might become a serious political liability.

Could any person who had been responsible for the institution of the system of price control, rationing, and rent control have survived? Henderson himself was always pessimistic about his chances of remaining at the head of OPA. Throughout his speeches and private conversations he emphasized that anybody was expendable; that it was impossible to accomplish what was necessary without antagonizing so many people that one simply could not last. In the other major wartime agency, WPB, substantial turnover and other reorganizations had occurred. A high rate of mortality for those in charge of crucial programs was typical of governmental agencies in the war period, due to incompetence, mistakes, or the inevitable accumulation of antagonisms. Perhaps no one could have survived the effective job of price control that Henderson rendered. But they might have. Henderson tended to define himself as the most hated man in America. Later, when he was working for the O'Sullivan Rubber Heel Company, he was proud of advertising on his radio program, "Hear Leon Henderson, America's Number One Heel!" He took a certain pride in his toughness and unwillingness to placate people. Actually, as I have said, he was not anywhere near as tough as he posed. He may have unnecessarily set himself up as an easy mark by his own expectation that he could not last.

Henderson's position, insofar as I discussed it with him, was that now the agency was in a situation where it could effectively perform its function. It had the legislation that now permitted the control of agriculture prices and wages. The legislative foundations were secure. The staff was built up and trained, experienced, and able to carry on. The major policies had been worked out. He personally had become a liability, and the program could proceed more effectively if someone else who would be able to handle Congress and public relations took charge. I think that was an accurate appraisal.

As a matter of fact, OPA was about the only agency in Washington that did not undergo a major reorganization such as Agriculture, or OPM or WPB, did almost constantly. From the beginning OPA had steered a firm course that was virtually unvaried. The departure of Henderson actually was not a reorganization. The organization survived eight or ten months of virtual leaderlessness under Prentiss Brown and then continued under Chester Bowles in the Henderson style, subject to refinements and superficial changes that Bowles made.

Dave Ginsburg resigned shortly after Henderson. As a youngster who had the complete confidence of Henderson, his fortunes were almost inevitably tied to Henderson's, and his position became untenable following Henderson's departure. Other top Henderson aides stayed on through most of the Prentiss Brown period. Galbraith stayed on as head of the Price Department until June 1943. John Hamm resigned as senior deputy administrator in September. Paul Porter left as head of the Rent Department and Paul O'Leary left as head of the Rationing Department in October, so that all the major division heads had left by the time Chester Bowles appeared to head OPA at the end of 1943. Dick Gilbert as head of the Research Department and I as head of the Enforcement Department were the only top staff to continue into the Bowles regime. However, a very large proportion of the rest of the staff continued. The usual high rate of turnover experienced by any government agency occurred, but no purge or mass resignation, so that the influence of the original regular staff continued throughout most of the life of the organization.

**The Prentiss Brown Interregnum**
The next major phase was the regime of Prentiss Brown, who was appointed administrator in January 1943 and resigned at the end of October. In July Brown appointed Chester Bowles as general manager of OPA, and from that time on it was Bowles who ran the organization,

pretty much without interference from Brown.

Brown had not been at OPA more than two months when it began to be clear that the job was beyond his capacity. It was generally known that he was looking for someone who could take over as executive vice president. He finally settled on Bowles, who came in as general manager. Bowles made all the basic decisions, and Brown was almost entirely a figurehead. It was not until November, however, that Bowles became administrator with full control.

## DEVELOPMENTS IN PRICE POLICIES
*The "hold the line" order*

From what I have indicated, one might expect that the entire organization would have fallen to pieces and price control would have suffered a serious setback. Ironically, the Brown administration marked the point at which price controls first became effective, so that, from April 1943 until V-E Day, prices hardly rose at all.

For the first few months of the Brown regime, however, prices continued to spiral upward. The Bureau of Labor Statistics' Consumer Price Index was at 120.7 in January 1943 when Brown was appointed, and by the end of April it had gone up to 125.1, still rising at approximately the rate of almost one point a month as it had for the past several years. At the end of March, another strenuous effort was made to establish a hold on prices. This effort eventually took the form of an executive order that the president issued on April 8. It came to be known as the "Hold the Line" order.

The Hold the Line order incorporated input from men in Byrnes' office in OES, OPA staff members Henry Hart and J. K. Galbraith, and White House consultants, particularly Ben Cohen. The order directed the price administrator and the food administrator to place ceilings on all commodities affecting the cost of living and to authorize no further increases in ceiling prices except to the minimum extent required by law. The order also enjoined the price administrator and the food administrator to use all discretionary powers vested in them to prevent further price increases and to reduce prices that were deemed excessively high, unfair, or inequitable. The authority of the director of the OES to coordinate and establish general policies was reaffirmed. In fact, the order contemplated that the director of stabilization would be the principal agent in carrying out the terms of the Hold the Line order by preventing further increases and settling disputes between stabilization agencies. The WLB was directed to authorize no further increases in wages, except such as were necessary to correct sub-standards of living, with a proviso that the "Little Steel Formula" could continue to be applied. The purpose of the Little Steel Formula was to bring wages up to the rise in the cost of living as of May 1, 1942. Directions were included for the War Manpower Commission and other agencies that dealt with public utility rates, railroad transportation, freight rates, and so on.

Actually, the order contained little that was new, either in terms of policy or in terms of authority granted. OPA, the Department of Agriculture, and the WLB already were directed to hold the price level steady, and if possible to roll back the cost of living. The order emphasized the rollback because the provisions for wage stabilization contemplated bringing wage levels up to the May 1942 level, but the cost of living had increased substantially since that date. Rather than allow wages to rise to meet the new cost of living, and thereby start a new spiral, the objective was to bring the cost of living down, and thus put labor in a position of equality. But the order was simply a forceful statement of an overall administration policy, an indication of the serious intention of the administration to prevent any further price increases from that point on. It enabled the price agencies to resist pressures from industry and Congress. It gave a psychological lift to the price agencies in their efforts to do this, and it reaffirmed and somewhat increased the authority of OES to sit on the lid and prevent further increases. OES was to do this both by a sort of veto power over price increases that were not required by law, as well as by an affirmative power to direct action on the part of all the agencies to facilitate the price program. OES was to require the use of WPB allocation power in such a way as to aid the price picture. This was of particular importance in an area such as clothing, where the price controls were particularly difficult because of the constant change in styles and hence in the product. The order, then, was intended to give OES the authority to tell WPB to adopt policies that would aid OPA. The Stabilization Act policy of using other governmental powers for the purpose of assisting and complementing OPA powers was reaffirmed.

In any event, the Hold the Line order proved to be the turning point. The Consumer Price Index (CPI) two years later was only 127.1, a rise of two points for the entire two years. Actually, in the summer after the Hold the Line order was issued, the CPI declined somewhat. OPA's record in holding the CPI steady was perhaps the major evidence of its successful operations during that period, even though the CPI was a little misleading. Our job was not accomplished quite as well as the statistics would indicate, because the Index measured black market prices only slightly. Also, it did not measure completely the cost of living, because as patterns of production shifted, the actual cost-of-living change depended on somewhat different prices, which were not represented in the index, or whose significance was not fully represented. Nevertheless, we managed a very effective operation for those two years.

The developments in price policy that continued through the Prentiss Brown interregnum included an expansion of subsidy programs. This was one of the major factors in the ability of OPA actually to reduce prices for a period. Subsidies had been used previously in connection with such areas as copper to prevent a drop in copper production. We now used them for a different purpose: holding or even reducing consumer prices. The concept of their use in this respect was worked out largely by Dick Gilbert, one of the first and most powerful advocates of subsidy programs from the very beginning. An ingenious and rather daring operation, it is a good illustration of the bold moves that OPA was willing to undertake.

We paid subsidies to certain producers rather than granting price increases, or, in some cases, with an agreement that the producer would reduce prices. For some commodities, mostly in the food field, such as processed foods, meat, butter, coffee, and to some extent milk, we paid subsidies in an amount necessary to permit producers to absorb increased labor or material costs without increasing their prices. Actually, it was a system for redistributing income because general tax funds were used to save money for consumers. The amount saved by consumers was equivalent to the amount paid to the producers, plus the amount consumers would have had to pay as a result of percentage mark-ups by the wholesaler, retailer, and other middlemen. The consumer subsidy programs had an extremely important effect, one far beyond the actual amount saved by consumers. By this method, OPA was able to keep down, and to some extent roll back, the cost of living. That, in turn, prevented pressures for increases in wage rates. By the expenditure of this relatively small sum at key points in the economy, it was possible to maintain a stable structure that otherwise would have affected other prices and wages, so that the spiral would have continued. The consumer subsidy programs were designed to, and did, stop the spiral by allowing adjustments and stopping price increases at the source.

OPA's Enforcement Department was interested in consumer subsidy programs because they provided another means of enforcing price regulations. The possibility of withdrawing subsidies for violations of price regulations could become a fairly effective sanction, and was so used. We could immediately deprive businesses of cash as an administrative decision, without court action except insofar as there was limited judicial review later. This sanction was readily applicable and quite persuasive.

In general, OPA's Price Department operated through these months in accordance with previous policies. Refinements and improvements in technique continued. There were constant revisions, as well as experimentation with different methods of price control. Of these, the most important was the expansion of dollars-and-cents prices into a number of fields. We had always believed that by far the most effective method of price control was a dollars-and-cents form of control. The Enforcement Department was constantly hammering at the Price Department to establish dollars-and-cents ceilings wherever possible, and the Price Department itself was interested in doing that. During this period we formulated dollars-and-cents ceilings for many new areas. They were applied with particular effectiveness in the food area and, together with subsidies, perhaps were the major cause for the stable price index throughout this and the later period.

In the food field, we delegated authority to the district offices to fix dollars-and-cents prices on major food items at retail, with prices adjusted to the needs of the particular community. Furthermore, the Enforcement Department finally convinced the Price Department of the necessity for posting prices. So we fixed specific dollars-and-cents prices for major cost-of-living items of food and had those prices posted in the stores for consumers to see. This complicated operation entailed changing the prices every month as the wholesale prices rose or fell and as local supplies varied. In the case of fresh fruits and vegetables we had to fix prices every week, in relation to the supplies of the particular product, many of which were, of course, local in origin. (This area was not under control until 1944.)

OPA undertook to negotiate with WPB for provisions that would require suppliers of raw materials to make available to manufacturers the kind of materials that would be needed for the low-cost items, for instance, to require the textile industry to supply the kind of cloth that would be needed. Also we undertook negotiations with WPB about certain standardizations in the clothing industry and in other industries. In Britain, for instance, price control had become effective primarily because the government had controlled the types of commodities that could be produced. The British had a system of utility clothing and utility consumer durables that required that manufacturers make their products in accordance with certain specifications. In this way the price controllers were able to describe a product and attach a price to it. We became increasingly convinced that successful pricing in the clothing industry, and to some extent in consumer durables, could only be accomplished if such specifications were imposed on manufacturers. OPA had no power to do this. WPB had to do it. They did so in certain respects, insofar as they issued orders providing that cuffs could not be put on trousers or frills on the sleeves of ladies' blouses, and so on, conserving material in that way. But WPB was unwilling to establish any form of utility product as the British had done. We constantly struggled with WPB on this topic. Toward the end of the year, OES issued a directive to WPB, requiring them to work out a program of control, both in terms of allocation of supplies and in terms of standardization, which would permit effective OPA price control in clothing and other areas. This directive was largely the work of Edward F. Prichard, assistant to Fred M. Vinson, the head of OES at that time. It was a bold and beautiful order on paper, but there was no way by which Vinson or Prichard could actually force WPB to carry it into execution, and hence the problem continued to plague OPA.

During this period OPA began to institute some forms of grade labeling in connection with processed foods such as canned goods. The Department of Agriculture had certain standards for the nature and thickness of the syrup in canned fruits and the quality of the fruit. These standards were fairly vague, but were generally accepted in the trade and used as the basis for commercial transactions. However, they usually did not appear on the can so that consumers could tell what they were buying. Government grading also occurred in the area of meat. OPA began moving toward a system of requiring labels on products in accordance with the established standards for the trade, hoping to facilitate price control by preventing down-grading and enabling the consumer to exercise more power in policing prices. This policy aroused terrific antagonism from industry, particularly the canning industry, and later resulted in congressional action.

## DEVELOPMENTS IN RENT CONTROL AND RATIONING

The rent program was proceeding reasonably well. Landlords were prospering because of the increased occupancy rates and despite the higher costs of repairs, since they decreased the amount of repairs and redecoration that they did. The level of rents was held almost steady with virtually no serious repercussions to anyone.

However, problems constantly arose in the rent field. One attempted evasion was the device of ostensible sales instead of rents. Instead of renting housing accommodations, some landlords would enter into a contract for a "sale," with monthly payments that were in effect rents and a provision for a reversion to the landlord if payments were not made. These landlords intended to avoid the rent regulations rather than actually sell. OPA's answer to false purchase contracts was to issue a regulation requiring a substantial down payment (originally, one-third of the purchase price) on the sale of any housing accommodations. The regulation also provided that a person who bought housing accommodations could not evict the present tenant unless he wished to move in himself and even then could not take occupancy for a period of six months, all of which was designed to discourage phony sales for the purpose of evading rent control. These requirements were fairly effective in doing that.

Another device was misuse of security deposits. The landlords required deposits from tenants at the time of renting, ostensibly to cover possible damage to the premises. Actually, the security deposits often operated as a fee the tenant was required to pay to obtain a rental, and the landlord pocketed it without ever intending to repay it. However, the landlord was protected against violation, as there remained a legal obligation on his part to return the deposit to the tenant. Misused security deposits were difficult to handle because under some circumstances the practice of making security deposits had been accepted in some areas, and on its face, if not misused, it was not improper. Only later did OPA take strong measures against this evasion by prohibiting security deposits except under certain circumstances.

Another major loophole in the rent regulations was that they did not apply to commercial rents. The Price Control Act did not extend powers to control rents paid by business. Business rents increased considerably in some areas, particularly in New York City. Businessmen responded by clamoring for price control. Sufficient pressure was generated that Congress was induced to study the problem through committee hearings. Sen. Robert Wagner introduced a bill for control of commercial rents. Nothing came of it, but throughout the existence of OPA, commercial rents remained a problem. New York City eventually adopted a program of its own to control commercial rents.

In the rationing field more headaches developed than before and some things did not go very well. At the beginning of 1943, shoes were rationed. A shortage existed because the army used up shoes at a fantastic rate. Every soldier required a new pair of shoes every three months, I believe. They also required shoes of particularly high quality, and the efforts of the shoe manufacturers to supply this tremendous increase meant both fewer shoes and poorer quality for civilians. This was one of the most effective programs, partly because impending shoe rationing was one of the best kept secrets. It was more important than almost any other program that word not get out that shoes were to be rationed, as there would have been an immediate run on all the stores. As shoes lasted adults for a year or more and children for some months, people would have bought what they could, which would have seriously interfered with the fair distribution of the available supply. Strangely enough, the secret that shoes were to be rationed was actually kept. There were no rumors, and no word got out. The process was fairly simple; we put a freeze on sales and designated one of the coupons in the back of the first ration book as the one needed to buy a pair of shoes. We did not need to print or distribute coupon books.

## Gasoline Rationing
*Only if everybody else does too. . .*

OPA's major difficulty in this period was gasoline rationing. Gasoline rationing had been extended throughout the country in December 1942, partly as a measure to preserve tires (Henderson's brainchild, as mentioned before). But the real problems continued to be on the East Coast. Supplies were dwindling. It was necessary to reduce the number of gallons that could be obtained with each stamp. Yet the amount consumed still exceeded the quotas allocated, and spot shortages were occurring. Supplies on the East Coast did not arrive regularly because the industry, still attempting to maintain the competitive situation as it had previously existed, was unwilling to ship supplies in accordance with the ration program—and the Petroleum Administrative board was unwilling to force industry to change its practices in these respects. Consequently, the situation on the East Coast became rather critical.

In desperation, on January 7, 1943, OPA announced a ban on pleasure driving, applicable only to the East Coast. Even if an individual had gasoline obtained legitimately with his ration stamps, he was prohibited by this order from driving except for an essential purpose. The penalty for driving for unessential purposes was that the local board would refuse to issue the offender any more ration stamps for gasoline. The ban on pleasure driving was decided on before Prentiss Brown actually took over, but he inherited the burden of carrying it out.

The ban on pleasure driving created a nightmare for us. In the first place, the regulation made no effort to define what was essential, and probably it was impossible to define, at least until courts had decided a huge number of cases. Certainly, driving to the doctor was essential and driving to a baseball game would be considered nonessential. But hundreds of thousands of situations in between resisted classification. In addition, the enforcement problem was obviously insuperable. The Enforcement Department adamantly opposed the ban, pointing out that it was absolutely impossible to enforce; we could not stop every automobile and ask where the driver was going. Some people would drive for nonessential purposes without adverse consequences, this would become known, and the whole system would break down quickly. The Rationing Department realized this, but believed that the need for conserving gasoline was so critical that the experiment had to be undertaken. In January, for the first time in some time, the consumption of gasoline decreased. It was the only month in which the consumption came within the allocated quota. However, after January consumption rose again and the experiment quickly was proved ineffective.

Police in various cities were asked to enforce the ban. In some localities police did stop cars and reported drivers to ration boards if they did not offer a suitable purpose for their trip. The OPA Enforcement Department made some token efforts at enforcement. We sent investigators to race tracks to write down the license numbers of the automobiles there and reported car owners to the ration boards. Later the investigators were sent to check on Michigan deer hunters. The deer hunters would cross over into the upper peninsula at some ferry point, which provided us with a bottle neck; by posting an investigator at the ferry we could record the license numbers of those who were using their gasoline for deer hunting. Tracking down the deer hunters turned out to be a hazardous task. The investigators were stationed out in the wilds and the deer hunters were a rather tough lot, and armed, so it was somewhat dangerous for an investigator to inquire too closely. Actually, now that I think about it again, the check on the deer hunters came not in connection with pleasure driving, but with the general enforcement of gasoline rationing. That is, the issue was not that they were using gasoline to go deer hunting, but whether they were using gasoline obtained from their coupons or from the black market. Obviously, this was a much more difficult point to ascertain, and the inquiries, fraught with danger to the lives of the OPA investigators, were not notably successful.

The Enforcement Department from the beginning had told the Rationing Department that the ban was impossible to enforce, and we would not deploy any substantial portion of our manpower to do so. We did attempt to get the police departments to cooperate and we made a dramatic move here or there, as when we checked the cars at some sporting event or people entering a night club. But even when we found violations, the follow-up procedure was not workable. Many local boards refused to revoke coupons. Others were rather arbitrary. Revoking a person's gasoline coupons required an informal hearing where the person could tell his story. Bogged down with other work, local boards did not have time for these hearings, so that aspect of the enforcement failed too.

Obviously, as head of OPA's Enforcement Department, I could not be caught pleasure driving. I could anticipate what the headlines would be. However, one evening in summer when my family was away in the mountains and a couple of fellows were living with me temporarily, one of them gave a party. He worked in the monitoring division of the FCC. His office workers, whom he invited to the party, were translators who listened to foreign broadcasts and translated them. Consequently, they were all different nationalities and spoke different languages. The party became rather intensive towards the end; about two o'clock in the morning people were under the table and in all the beds dead drunk and asleep. But there remained three or four girls who wanted to go home. No taxis could be summoned. I had the only car that was available. So we haggled for half an hour, I maintaining that I would not drive them home, that they would have to sleep on the floor. They persisted, and finally I got the car out and drove them home, with great trepidation as to whether a policeman would stop me and ask where I was going and what the purpose was. I was not at all sure I could defend myself. I finally got them all home without being stopped by a policemen, but I was considerably worried for a period.

The pleasure driving ban provoked a tremendous protest from the public. As soon as a substantial number of people started violating, others became outraged and either violated the law themselves or criticized the whole scheme. The situation quickly became a farce. By March 3, Brown announced that from then on the pleasure driving ban would be voluntary. On March 22, he withdrew the entire provision. When the gasoline shortage became even more desperate in May, he announced that the pleasure driving ban would be reinstated. Reinstituted on May 20, 1943, this time it was completely unsuccessful in limiting the consumption of gasoline. In fact, the consumption in June was higher than any preceding month and exceeded the quota by more than any previous month. People objected vociferously, particularly those who had saved up their gasoline rations for vacations. Finally, the program was relaxed on July 15 to allow persons to make one trip in their automobiles to summer homes, a concession that demoralized the picture further. However, the ban continued with less and less effect until it was finally revoked in September.

We learned several lessons from the pleasure driving ban. One was that regulations, at least those relating to consumption of this nature–driving automobiles, in any event–would not be complied with in the absence of a reasonable certainty of enforcement. People were not sufficiently committed to rationing programs affecting the use of automobiles that they would voluntarily comply. It was clear that the system would quickly break down. It illustrated what I think was true throughout the war: that some consumers were willing to flagrantly disregard price and rationing regulations, and that as soon as any substantial number violated the laws, public pressure, instead of ostracizing this group as unpatriotic, simply took these unscrupulous violators as an excuse for violating themselves, refusing to be suckers and comply when others did not comply. The result was a rapid and progressive breakdown, started by a few, but eventually participated in by a substantial majority. Only a system with some degree of enforcement to prevent the start of this process of deterioration would work. At least, this was true in the areas where people felt as strongly as they did about automobile driving.

The other lesson was that the notion that regulations could be made simple was not as simple as it seemed on its face. This was an effort to promulgate a simple regulation. It simply said that gasoline could not be used for unessential driving, with no explanation attempted as to what was or was not essential. It was simple, but it was confusing and demoralizing to everyone because it was not at all clear. The moral was brought home that even though the attempt to state the rules with precision resulted in complications, nevertheless this alternative was preferable to great simplicity that left everything vague and uncertain. The basic OPA policy of using great precision in draftsmanship seemed to be confirmed by the "pleasure driving" debacle.

The pleasure driving ban probably compounded the difficulties of the whole ration program, and to some extent the price program, as much as any single thing that happened. It tended to discredit OPA regulations and to propel people into the habit of not complying with them, in a way that seriously undermined the whole program. The actual savings in gasoline must have been minuscule or nonexistent after the first month or so. In my judgment, however, the harmful effects were overwhelming.

### Ration Books Nos. 2, 3, 4

By the time we were faced with rationing meats, butter, fats, and canned food, we had learned something about ration programs. We issued a new ration book, Ration Book No. 2, which was distributed in February 1943. The Enforcement Department had persuaded the Rationing Department to make a careful study of the choice of paper; we discovered it was possible to devise a kind of paper that would be fairly cheap and at the same time difficult to counterfeit. This precaution was taken with respect to Ration Book No. 2. Instead of printing 190 million copies, we relied on our experience and the established system of distribution to cut back to 150 million. This not only saved on paper and expense, but also reduced the possibility of large quantities being stolen. The distribution was again effected through the schools, this time even more effectively than before because of the prior experience. A certain amount of "tailoring" was necessary. Instead of filling out an application form, individuals were required to bring in Ration Book No. 1, which had their name and address on it, and receive Ration Book No. 2 on the basis of that. One of the coupons in Ration Book No. 1 was for coffee, and since coffee was not supposed to be available to persons under sixteen, OPA took this opportunity to tear out the coffee coupons from books that were presented for children under sixteen. This caused some difficulty, but was successfully maneuvered. In addition, people were required to declare their supplies of rationed canned foods and stamps were torn out in proportion. That was a complication that was fairly successfully surmounted. We had no idea how honest the declarations were. We made no effort to tear out meat coupons. Freezing facilities were not sufficiently available to consumers at that time to make the bother of attempting to tailor the coupons to meat supplies worthwhile.

Ration Book No. 2 introduced a further complication in the rationing program. It required the use of a point system. With sugar, typewriters, shoes, bicycles, or automobiles, there was only one commodity and one stamp. In canned foods and meat, however, a variety of the commodities were sold, and the supply available of each commodity also varied greatly. At different times a greater supply of beef existed than of pork, and different cuts of meat existed, some of which were in greater demand than others. The supply of certain canned vegetables waxed and waned. Altogether, the supply of the different kinds of food commodities constantly shifted under the ration system. The fair way to deal with this was to allow each person a certain number of points, and then to assign each classification of a commodity or each cut of meat a specific number of points. In this way, the less coveted cuts could be given a lower number of points, and steak or roast beef a higher number, and supplies could be graded to the demand.

The point system introduced complications because it meant there had to be many more coupons, and coupons of different value, as well as coupons distinguishing between processed foods and meats. Coupons for processed food were blue; meat and butter coupons were red. Point values of 10, 8, 5, 2 and 1, as I recall, were assigned to coupons. The stores became swamped with coupons. Counting coupons, separating red and blue coupons, and related tasks placed extra demands on store personnel. At this time we instituted the system of putting the coupons in envelopes instead of pasting them on sheets for the ration banking system. But even with depositing coupons in bank accounts, difficulties arose. So many coupons had to be processed that it became impossible to verify the coupons and check the amount. Sometimes we would open sealed envelopes which stated on the outside that they contained a thousand coupons and find blank sheets of paper. In June 1943 the banks engaged in the ration banking project were required to check three percent of the envelopes on a sample basis, counting the stamps and looking for counterfeit forms. This plan was not the solution, however. Some banks refused to do it as it imposed a strain on their staff and they did not have the personnel who could spot the counterfeits. Later OPA verification centers were established. But at this time the problem was mounting without a satisfactory resolution.

Ration Book No. 3 was issued in July and August 1943. This time the schools were closed for summer vacation, so the book was distributed by mail. The postman left application blanks in each mailbox; people sent them to the local ration board, whereupon the board mailed the books. The operation was reasonably successful, but not as effective as use of the schools, so when Ration Book No. 4 was issued, we used the schools again.

I cannot recall now what Ration Book No. 3 covered. The first half was for some program that was necessary; some were for shoes. The second half of the book just had pictures of tanks and planes and guns; we called them "blind stamps" because they were not designated for any rationing purpose. The public was mystified. We had thought that a clothing ration might become necessary; negotiations and discussions were underway with WPB. These stamps were designed to be used for a clothing rationing program, if one were put into operation, but we could not explain or there would immediately be a rush on the stores. Just before the books were issued, but after they had been printed, WPB decided finally it would not be necessary to ration clothes, so the stamps were not necessary for that purpose. Some were used later for other purposes, some for shoe rationing, but most were never used. Even then, OPA did not want to announce the reason for the blind stamps. I suppose the public eventually found out, but I do not know whether it was ever generally known or not. The explanation was that they could be used later for shoe stamps, or something of that sort, but obviously there were many more than were necessary for any existing program.

## Legal Problems

So far as the legal developments were concerned, there was beginning to be a series of decisions by the Emergency Court of Appeals dealing with the validity of price regulations. The validity of the rent regulations was upheld in a case involving a Bridgeport rental area in May 1943. Some aspects of the price regulations were sustained in this period. A sort of common law of price controls was gradually beginning to build up; policies not spelled out in the legislation but that had been adopted by OPA were beginning to come before the emergency court and decisions were beginning to come down. Perhaps the major ones did not happen until 1944, but certain decisions in 1943 put the stamp of judicial approval on OPA's operations. Only one setback occurred, in connection with the meat regulations, which were among the most difficult and under constant attack. A challenge by Armour and Company and the other packers had come before the Emergency Court of Appeals. The emergency court had sent it back for further factual material relating to one of the major issues. That was only a temporary setback, a request for further information rather than a decision against OPA's policies. Otherwise, the decisions, with some insignificant exceptions supported the OPA position.

We won a major victory over the Mars candy bar company. The Mars company had reduced the size of its candy bars while retaining the same price. From the beginning we were aware that enforcement would be tricky when the price remained the same, yet the quality or quantity was reduced, resulting in a hidden price increase in effect. The Mars company claimed that, as a technical matter, it was impossible to produce candy bars all weighing exactly the same. We were able to demonstrate that the average weight of current bars varied sufficiently from the previous average weight so that there was an overcharge. We brought a suit for damages, I believe for $1.5 million. The company defended themselves vigorously and bitterly. In the spring of 1943 we obtained a victory over the company in the circuit court. A petition for *certiorari* to the Supreme Court was later denied, so that OPA was successful here. The Mars candy company had also become a rather well-known case and was a strategic one in the whole enforcement program.

I was continually surprised at how boldly pressure groups and congressmen were willing to advocate changes that benefited only a special interest, changes that almost any objective person, looking at the price control picture from the point of view of the country and the war effort as a whole, would have to judge as undermining the effort and dangerous to the public interest. Why, then, were special interests not regarded as "unpatriotic" when they revealed their desire for more and more profits, at the expense of the war effort? Of course, they did not state it in those terms. Instead they complained about being beaten over the head and driven into bankruptcy by OPA. Despite these unsubstantiated accusations, however, what they were really asking for was special consideration, while overlooking the detrimental effect on the public interest of what they were demanding. As I was to learn, this attitude continued throughout the war.

# 11

## CHESTER BOWLES AS BOSS

*From lawyers, leadership in America turns to public relations.*

It was well known that Prentiss Brown, the new administrator who assumed control of OPA following Leon Henderson's resignation in 1942, did not like his job and was attempting to withdraw, so when he appointed Chester Bowles to the post of general manager it was rather clearly understood that it was going to be Bowles who would run OPA. John Hamm was replaced by James Rogers, who became Bowles' chief deputy. John K. Galbraith was replaced by James F. Brownlee. Ivan Carson, one of the division heads in the Rent Department, replaced Paul Porter. Paul O'Leary, Henderson's head of rationing, was replaced by Bryan Houston. Thus when Brown left and Bowles was promoted to administrator on November 8, 1943, he had practically a new staff of top officials working with him. A week or two later George Burke resigned as general counsel. Bowles then continued as administrator of OPA until approximately the end of 1945.

### THE NEW STAFF AND POLICIES

Chester Bowles came from an old New England family. His grandfather had founded the *Springfield Republican*, a well-known Massachusetts newspaper, and his father had run it afterward. After Bowles had graduated from Yale in 1924, he had entered the advertising business with William Benton. Within a few years the firm of Benton and Bowles became one of the leading advertising firms in New York City. By 1941 Bowles had retired from business, having made a considerable amount of money. Thus, at the age of about forty, he was becoming interested in other things. When the war broke out, he was appointed head of OPA's Connecticut rationing office.

As a lively critic of the Washington office, Bowles was fairly well-known within OPA during the Henderson and Brown regimes. When we held a meeting of the heads of the field offices, we could count on Bowles to make a vigorous speech criticizing a number of aspects of the operations. His position always was a reasonably friendly one, but it was rather sharp in its criticisms. His ideas were accorded considerable attention and many were put into operation. Bowles was an extremely able person with imagination and resourcefulness. Confident of his own ability, he was a smooth-talking individual and intensely ambitious, not to succeed in the business world, but outside the business world in public or intellectual life. Strongly committed to price control, he was firm in his position at all times, although he preferred to handle matters with a velvet glove. Bowles was not a hail-fellow-well-met and had no great rapport with the ordinary congressman, but he was respected by congressmen, in large part because he had been a successful businessman. His background of public relations and manipulation of public opinion carried over into his OPA work. In other words, he brought to the organization a point of view influenced by the perspective of a public relations man.

Bowles' second wife had been a classmate of my wife at Vassar; my wife reports that she was one of the leading spirits in the class. She had been president of the class and a recognized campus leader. In some ways Mrs. Bowles had even more character than her husband. She had a lot of drive and knew where she wanted to go. She was very intelligent and probably exerted a marked influence on Bowles himself.

Bowles's chief associate was James Rogers. Rogers had a background similar to Bowles in that he was a Yale graduate. His father was James Gamble Rogers, the architect who designed many of the Yale buildings. Jim Rogers had rowed on the Yale crew. He was tall and handsome, without the ability or depth of Bowles, but certainly an intelligent person in his own right. He was rather quiet, not a man for public appearances as Bowles was. He was extremely loyal to Bowles and worked with him closely. He was a younger man and had been trained by Bowles in his advertising agency. The pair worked very well together. Rogers was able to take a good deal of the burden off Bowles' shoulders. They understood each other and were able to work as a team.

The other close associate that Bowles brought in as a personal assistant was Douglas J. Bennett. Bennett also had worked in Bowles's advertising agency. He did not have the judgment or stature of Rogers but, used primarily in OPA's Information Department, played a fairly important role as a personal assistant to Bowles in many of his public relations ventures.

The head of OPA's Price Department was James Brownlee, a businessman who had been vice president of General Foods. Firmly committed to price control, Brownlee was very intelligent and honest, but not particularly experienced outside the business field. As his knowledge of political matters was rather limited, he was constantly surprised at various congressional activities. Brownlee looked at the issues from a public point of view; he was by no means narrow in his approach to price control. He was not strong or vigorous, but reasonably firm, and on the whole he did an excellent job. He was not a theoretical economist as Galbraith was, nor did he have Galbraith's brilliance, but he had a good deal of business experience, a pretty sound business judgment, was ready to listen to the men around him who had more ideas, and under the circumstances carried on quite effectively. Since the appropriation rider dictated the appointment of a businessman, OPA was lucky to find a man of as stout a heart and as decent a person as James Brownlee.

The head of OPA's Rationing Department was Bryan Houston. He had an army background (he was called "Colonel Houston") and was pretty much at a loss as head of the Rationing Department. He was headstrong and aggressive, without much judgment or understanding of other people, nor did he know much about rationing. A bull in a china shop, he did not last long. At an early date, he had to be supported by a deputy named Patterson French, who was a university man with his feet much more on the ground. After about six months, the job was taken over by Charles F. Phillips, who was also a university man.

The head of OPA's Rent Department was Ivan Carson. He also was a weak sister, primarily because, although he meant well, he lacked intellectual ability. He was overly cautious and tended to run away from things. However, the Rent Department had become pretty well stabilized, so it did not require either a vigorous or imaginative person to operate it. To some extent it required a plugger, which Carson was, and that is why he was not entirely out of place.

All three of these men were entirely different from their predecessors, and Houston and Carson were on an entirely different level than their predecessors.

Dick Gilbert remained as economic advisor, and became quite influential with Bowles. Bowles relied on him a good deal.

After Burke resigned as general counsel, Bowles appointed Richard Field. Field had been regional attorney for New England and had worked with Bowles in that connection. Although not a brilliant lawyer, Field was very able, with a good point of view on price control. By this time the job of general counsel had become considerably less important than previously. The attorneys working in the Price, Rationing, and Rent Departments had been assigned to these departments and were no longer subject to the general counsel. The Enforcement attorneys also had become a separate department, so they were not part of the General Counsel's Office. The general counsel's staff consisted of the attorneys in the research and court review sections, that is, the general research attorneys and those who handled the appeals to the Emergency Court of Appeals, and a scattering of other attorneys, who performed general legal advisory functions. Field worked well with all the other attorneys so an informal relationship continued; he also brought together all the Washington OPA attorneys in formal staff meetings from time to time. Despite the formal reorganization, control of the Legal Department over attorneys in the national office did not change markedly from what it had been before. As Bowles relied quite heavily on Field, and his work included relationships with Congress and renewal of the legislation, Field played quite an influential role.

During Bowles' tenure directors of information came and went, about every four to six months. Perhaps half a dozen occupants filled the post in this period. It was surprising, since Bowles placed so much emphasis on public relations, that he was never able to obtain someone who functioned satisfactorily as head of the Information Department. Perhaps his own expertise in the area made him finicky.

## The Enforcement Department

When Prentiss Brown began as administrator, I was associate general counsel and already had taken over the enforcement work. Enforcement at that time was a separate division of the Legal Department. When Bowles joined Brown as general manager, his first impulse, I learned later, was to reorganize the entire Enforcement Division. Bowles toyed with the idea of turning enforcement over to the FBI, or at least transferring our investigative work to them. J. Edgar Hoover refused to touch it with a ten-foot pole. Why Hoover declined OPA investigative work at this and other times I do not know exactly. Probably Hoover realized that OPA enforcement was a splitting headache and the responsibility would risk undermining and discrediting the FBI rather than capping their empire with glory. In any event, he kept his hands completely off, not even agreeing to investigate criminal gangs for us; the only investigations he would accept were investigations of dishonesty or corruption on the part of OPA employees.

Bowles envisioned the Enforcement Division operating like the police department of a city. Consequently, he was looking around for someone to take it over. I understand he attempted to persuade William O'Dwyer, who had been prosecuting attorney in Brooklyn, to take the job. He also attempted to recruit the head of the state police in Michigan, a man by the name of Bennett. Neither would accept the position. Bowles hardly knew me at this time. I did not know all this was happening. I felt, however, that something should be done, and when Bowles came in as general manager under Brown, I started to prepare a report on the activities of the Enforcement Division, an estimate of what it had accomplished, what the problems were, and some indication of the amount of personnel needed to do a more effective job. This elaborate report summarized the work of the division up to then, the issues before it, and recommended solutions. I was rather dubious that Bowles, as a busy general manager, would take the time to read a 50-page document. However, Bowles was one of those people who took reports home, actually read them, and was able to absorb material quickly. He read my report and was impressed with my analysis of the issues. Although he had barely talked to me before and apparently had not considered keeping me as head of enforcement, he decided that I should stay on as head of the Enforcement Division. He also felt that enforcement work was of sufficient importance that a new department should be created. The new Enforcement Department that he created was one of the major groupings of OPA, on a level with the Price, Rationing, and Rent Departments. I became head of this new department in the post of deputy administrator for enforcement.

Bowles was eager to hire a chief of police as head of the investigative branch of the Enforcement Department. He and I talked to a number of professional police chiefs around the country. However, none who were willing seemed to have the capacity and none of those who might have had the capacity were willing, so the plan fell through. From then on, Bowles let me run the Enforcement Department with my own personnel.

The rest of the OPA staff continued pretty much as before. Again, the changes were more on the top than throughout the organization. There was a continual turnover of personnel, but no purges, reorganizations, or mass resignations. A high rate of turnover was due to the military draft and the general shortage of manpower. Turnover averaged at least 50 percent a year and it sometimes was higher. In the national office from June 1943 to January 1944, a period of seven months, turnover reached 74 percent. At the same time, enough of the staff remained and the development of training programs indoctrinated new staff so that an amazing continuity of policy characterized the agency despite this extremely high turnover in personnel.

Bowles struck me as a person who often misjudged people initially, but eventually discovered his error. He tended to be beguiled by people who made a good first impression. When he discovered their actual capacities, he took action to amend the situation. Thus, he was constantly correcting his mistakes; he didn't just let it ride. It did not take him long to re-evaluate Bryan Houston and ease him out. Bowles realized that his directors of information were not performing well and consistently replaced them. He knew the limitations of Ivan Carson as head of rent, but that was the kind of a job that was possible for Carson to do with a little extra supervision, so he left him there.

Bowles was better on ideas than on people. Generally, his initial reaction and his initial ideas were pretty good; they certainly did not need as much correction by a second judgment as his selection of personnel did. He was never a person who fell asleep, however, in any situation. Bowles was constantly reevaluating and looking at things from different angles. He shifted and developed as time went on. His subsequent judgments usually surpassed his initial ones.

Bowles was not a pioneer in the same class as Henderson, Ginsburg, Galbraith, O'Leary, and the others were. Although he played an innovative role in terms of public relations and congressional relations, he was not a trained economist and hence it would have been difficult for him to take the initiative in that area as Henderson could. Of course, Ginsburg was not a trained economist either, but his rapid mind assimilated things so fast that he was able to master economic issues pretty well, at least with the help of technical advisers. But Bowles was not outstanding in that field. Although his overall perspective was somewhat pedestrian, he was interested, he worked hard, and eventually he accomplished results. He learned a lot as time went on. In the end he was learning to play more with basic economic forces, such as labor support, than at the beginning. As he continued in OPA, he began to absorb a good understanding of the economic structure, and toward the end his expertise was such that if the original challenges had still existed, he might have been able to make a pioneering contribution. But he never would have accomplished the superb job that Henderson did because he would not have departed so drastically from precedent. He would not have made the daring innovations or visualized the major shifts. He was more conservative in the sense that he honored more the necessity of bringing the public and Congress along with him before things were done.

## Public Relations

Bowles' major contribution probably was in the field of public relations. This was a natural result of his training and what he had been thinking about for years. He placed major emphasis on public relations policy and devising methods for implementing it. Thus, as soon as he was appointed general manager, he instituted a series of nationwide broadcasts. Once a week he would give a sort of fireside chat to the people on problems of OPA and what was being done to solve them. He encouraged people to write him with questions and suggestions, which he would then discuss on his program. He did an excellent job in his broadcasts, developed quite an audience, and undoubtedly made a notable difference in public education.

Bowles instructed all the field office heads to make similar weekly broadcasts, so that the regional administrators and the heads of the district offices soon had arranged for radio time and they gave weekly broadcasts on a different day from Bowles. These broadcasts combined a script on national problems prepared by Bowles' men in Washington with a certain amount of local color, depending upon the capacity of the district director.

Bowles started his people making movies. Six or eight short films dealing with OPA problems were made. The Information Department produced pamphlets explaining certain aspects of price control. They arranged for the publication of articles in magazines. They kept a sharp watch on newspapers. Every time an unfavorable editorial appeared in any newspaper, Bowles had given instructions that it should be answered immediately by the head of the office in that territory. A letter would be written, signed by the head of the office and sent to the newspaper, which frequently printed it. The letters might not have had much effect on the particular issues they concerned, but they made editors think twice about printing unfriendly editorials. Editors realized that they had better be careful what they were saying because there would be an answer to it. The OPA staff was instructed to write letters of appreciation for friendly editorials. All this was a deliberate attempt to improve public relations.

Bowles was an early advocate of public opinion polls. In his advertising business he had used market research extensively. He instituted polls of public opinion on various aspects of OPA operations, particularly dealing with consumer reaction to rationing, first and foremost gasoline rationing.

Bowles' expansive public relations policy was a drastic departure from that of Henderson. The Henderson public relations had been run largely by Robert Horton, who had been a reporter for the Scripps-Howard paper, the *Washington News*. The Scripps-Howard papers at that time were very liberal and Horton was a liberal reporter in the New Deal-Henderson tradition. His approach toward public relations was to give the straight facts. He conceived his function as making available the factual material the media required. Bowles conducted much more of a propaganda campaign. In an effort to mold public opinion he was quite ready to slant material in a certain direction. Bowles' more successful operation raises a basic issue about the implications of government manipulation of public opinion which deserved serious consideration at that time and in the present.

Bowles' second major contribution concerned congressional relations. Recognizing how imperative it was that OPA get along better with Congress, he made every effort to improve relations. He lacked Prentiss Brown's advantage of having been a senator, but by exerting much more initiative and energy than Brown had, he managed to take measures that had the effect of considerably improving relations with Congress. For one thing, he carried much further than Henderson had the practice of the supplying congressional committees with economic material in connection with hearings on appropriations and hearings on amendments, or special investigations inquiring into particular aspects of OPA operations. He jazzed up and simplified the material by developing pie charts and other graphic presentations. He would put on a tremendous show as he presented his case illustrated by the charts. This advertising technique of presenting material was new to most congressmen and made quite an impression, particularly at the beginning.

Bowles also appointed a special official as liaison with Congress, Zenus Potter. I do not recall that Potter had any special qualifications for the job–he was not a former congressman or anything–but he was quite effective. Potter established an office on Capitol Hill to answer congressional questions. congressmen were flooded with all sorts of requests for information about OPA, as well as complaints and requests for action. Their offices had great difficulty at times finding out who in OPA knew anything about the matter. They sometimes would call all around the agency, trying to find someone who could explain. Now they could simply call the OPA office on Capitol Hill and the office would put them in touch with the proper person immediately or search out the information itself. The convenience of this office reduced the hassles and frustrations that had clouded OPA contacts with Congress behind the scenes.

In addition, Potter and his office supplied information to friendly congressmen. Whenever any congressman made any remark about OPA, it was noted. Unfriendly remarks were answered by a private letter or by a letter to be published in the *Congressional Record* by a friendly congressman. Knowing an answer would be forthcoming immediately from OPA, congressmen inclined to attack OPA became more cautious in what they said and sometimes chose to remain silent. Congressmen who made friendly remarks about OPA received a personal letter from Bowles thanking them for their understanding of OPA problems.

These techniques did not produce a major change in the

congressional attitude toward OPA, but particularly in the latter part of 1943 and the the beginning of 1944–the crucial period–they had some effect. Later on the tentative rapprochement tended to dissipate.

The major factor in agency morale was the top leadership. At times OPA morale declined because of concessions by the top leadership. The organization was sufficiently dedicated and committed that it could accept criticism from Congress, newspapers, or the public and use it to correct deficiencies. But when the top leadership yielded too much, that really interfered with morale. This rapprochement with Congress tended to do just that because it necessarily was accompanied by a somewhat softer policy. But on the whole Bowles maintained morale at a very high level. He backed his people up. He did not yield too much, or if he did, his second thoughts tended to correct it. Particularly coming after the chaos of the Prentiss Brown regime, the effect of Bowles was to strengthen morale. The public relations approach was a great lift for the organization. With Bowles as firm as he was, it put the organization back on the track quickly.

This advertising-campaign style did not dilute the aims of OPA to any great extent. Bowles had tremendous confidence in his public relations approach in the beginning. Not being politically sophisticated, he assumed that "if we only can explain to these congressmen what the issues are and show them why this has to be done, they will go along." It was the same with the public: "If we can only get it across to them, they will take it." As to the public, I think he was probably right; as to Congress, he was definitely wrong. But it took a while before the issue was joined. Congress in the beginning tended to be impressed by Bowles' approach and he had some effect on them. As the iron law of economics and politics closed in, however, Bowles was constantly shocked at this or that congressman, responding to some economic pressure back home, reneging and attacking OPA. Eventually he became much more sophisticated about the matter and tended to modify his public relations approach. He never changed drastically, but he learned to count less on the tinsel and the advertising stuff.

Bowles' third major contribution was in his relations with business. As I have already indicated, he was eager to bring in business people as officials in the organization. In fact, he was compelled to do so because of the rider to the appropriation, but he would have done so anyway. He also pressed the Industry Advisory Committee program strongly, and made many public statements about the business people he had brought into the OPA and the creation of the Industry Advisory Committees. Business influence did increase appreciably, although it never reached the level that it did in NRA or WPB.

Bowles had the same attitude to business that he had toward Congress: that he could *sell* this program, that he would get substantial cooperation from them if he could only have the opportunity to explain it to them and convince them. He was surprised, as time passed, that business did not react with more cooperation. Whenever they were in any sense pinched, or often when they were not pinched at all, they would attack Bowles bitterly. Experience constantly opened his eyes. He ultimately came to lean less heavily on his business relations as a basic method of price control. Particularly at the beginning, however, he thought this approach was promising and took significant steps to bring businessmen into the organization.

On a fourth level, it must be said that Bowles did not share the anti-intellectual feelings that were seldom far below the surface in Washington. Quite the contrary, he was attuned to the person who had more than a narrow political or business view. A nonconformist, intellectual flair intrigued Bowles. He always had a basic sympathy for unconventional thinking, and for thinking on the frontiers of a problem, for thinking in broad, social terms. He was, therefore, very sympathetic with the university people, and would have used them more than he did except that he believed it was bad public relations. At the same time, he thought some of the university people were going too far. He would have liked a combination that included a higher proportion of business influence, not to replace the university people, but to add a new element. Recognizing the congressional and public opposition to professors, at times he attempted to avoid adverse criticism by hiding his professors behind the scenes so far as possible.

Concerning labor, Bowles probably had an intellectual appreciation of the labor movement in the beginning, but he certainly had had no practical experience with it and knew nothing about it. He did appoint a labor adviser, Robert R. R. Brooks. Later he learned that, as a political matter, he had to have some labor support, and that usually labor support was a good bet for what he was interested in.

Finally, concerning Bowles' contribution to OPA, the consumer groups had somewhat of a revival. Bowles–influenced, I suspect, by Mrs. Bowles–had a greater interest in consumer groups than Prentiss Brown had had. He built them up in an advisory capacity and listened to them considerably more than Henderson or Brown had. The consumer groups, from then on at least, increased in prestige, as well as in numbers, and participated more in policy discussions, although they never reached the point where they were really influential.

**Decentralization**

Another of Bowles' major policies related to decentralization. Started under Prentiss Brown, Bowles extended it further. He revived a Division of Field Operations, although it never regained the power that Frank Bane had had originally (and which had led to the conflict that had eventually resulted in Bane's resignation and the elimination of the Division of Field Operations). Bowles delegated substantially more power to the regional and district offices. By this time a good deal of the administration of the rent controls was decentralized and rationing controls had always been rather completely decentralized. Bowles, however, inaugurated further decentralization of price control, deliberately urging and conferring upon local offices the power to fix local prices in certain situations. Bowles also strengthened the control of regional and district directors over their offices. Price personnel in the field always had been subject to the conflicting authority of the regional director on the one hand and the price officials in Washington on the other. The same type of conflict in the district offices affected the price staff in relation to the regional price official on the one hand and the district director on the other. This dual authority and the resulting conflict were inherent in the organizational structure. But Bowles shifted the emphasis decidedly in the direction of greater local authority. Bowles rather quickly reached a national point of view, but nevertheless he had seen the operation from the Connecticut office and that experience caused him to emphasize further delegation and decentralization, building up the field offices. On the whole, I think he was quite correct in this move. The Washington office tended to hold on to power longer than was necessary; a more effective performance would result from a supervised delegation than from attempting to perform too much from the Washington office.

Richard Field advised Bowles to increase decentralization, although he was more skeptical of what the field offices might do and the trouble they might get the agency into than was Bowles. However, Field did not have to decide how much to decentralize his own unit as his control did not extend to any of the lawyers in the field offices. The problem was with the price, rent, rationing, and enforcement lawyers, who had a counterpart in the field offices. The lawyers in the Washington general counsel's office did not have their counterpart in the field offices. There was no research staff in the field because that task clearly had to be centralized. There was no point in having eight regional offices do research on the same legal problems. Similarly, the emergency court work and legislative work had to be centralized.

Bowles' major policies did not change the fundamental direction of OPA. They refined our operations rather than changing our basic price, rationing, and rent policies.

The organization under Bowles functioned pretty much along the same lines during the entire period of his administration. The budget for the fiscal year beginning July 1, 1944, was $178 million. There was a deficiency appropriation that year of an additional $6.7 million. That was about the peak of the OPA operations. Incidentally, the OPA staff had originally estimated it would need $209 million for the year. Bowles himself had cut the request down to $192 million, and the Department of the Budget had cut that to $182 million. So the appropriation of $178 million was almost what the Department of the Budget had recommended, and with the deficiency appropriation was more. This was in the spring of 1944, at the time when Bowles' relations with Congress were at their best.

As the price program moved into 1945, the strains were becoming more apparent. Legitimate as well as illegitimate pressures for price increases were continuing. We were experiencing the difficulties of maintaining a freeze over a long period of time and problems were multiplying. Early in 1945, for instance, OPA was forced to grant a price increase of $2–$5 a ton on most steel products. This was necessary under the product standard because the steel producers could show that on many of these products they were not meeting "out-of-pocket" expenses. Steel prices, of course, were basic to the whole economy; higher prices eventually would create pressure in many other sectors of the economy.

There was strong pressure on textile prices, too, in the beginning of 1945. This was due in part to an amendment passed in the 1944 extension of the Price Control Act, called the Bankhead Amendment, which required the price of every textile product to reflect parity for cotton. This meant that low prices would have to be raised, even though the overall profit of the textile companies might be adequate, because each textile price had to be high enough to reflect parity prices for cotton. This and other factors caused considerable pressure for increases in textile prices, and OPA was forced to grant some textile increases.

The rent program continued to operate most effectively. Although real estate interests mounted substantial pressure, counterpressures from the public were also fairly strong. As the single largest item in the household budget, people felt strongly about rent, so considerable political pressure against rent increases was generated. The result was that rents were held very firm, much more firmly than other sectors of the economy.

No doubt as a result, rent regulations did not change much. A few problems came up. One was the tie-in sales of furniture. It had become increasingly frequent for a landlord to rent at the ceiling level, but only on condition that the tenant buy some piece of furniture at an exorbitant price. Clearly a violation of the rent regulations, this was a tricky matter to deal with, but steps were taken to prevent this evasion.

There were various challenges to the rent ceilings in some areas, particularly in New York City, but on the whole OPA held firm. Some of these cases went to the Emergency Court of Appeals, where OPA was sustained. By the beginning of 1945, OPA had rent control in 414 areas, covering 91 million people.

Bowles' attitude toward rationing showed the greatest signs of softness of any of the programs. Bowles' theory was that it was more important to hold the price line, that this required substantial public support, and that concessions might be necessary in rationing to obtain public support. Consequently, he was inclined to ease off on the rationing program in the hopes of winning popular support for the price and rent programs. In the latter part of 1943 and the early part of 1944 he relaxed some of the rationing program. However, as shortages grew more acute in the latter part of 1944, it was necessary to tighten up on rationing again. After the relaxation this was difficult and this reversal probably created more demoralization than Bowles' policies in the other fields. After V-J Day Bowles took the same point of view and advocated a rapid abandonment of all rationing, hoping to gain public support for continued price control programs.

Thus, as V-E Day approached, pressures were accumulating that were straining the whole structure of OPA's control over the economy. Had the larger issues of World War II not intervened, it is hard to say what the outcome would have been. Prices increased after V-E Day, but stabilized again towards the summer, and then following V-J Day the whole picture changed completely. Whether or not OPA could have retained a firm grip on prices in a postwar world is uncertain; in any event, despite our growing experience and established practices, our task became more difficult as time went on because of pressures in the economy.

## ATTACKS FROM CONGRESS

Bowles' efforts to obtain congressional support were by no means uniformly successful. While he did temporarily achieve a better relationship in late 1943 and the first part of 1944, it was not smooth sailing. The congressional committees that had become active in the Brown regime continued even more vigorously, and other committees joined in. The amount of time that Bowles and his top officials devoted to congressional inquiries was enormous. I do not know of any figure kept over a long period of time, but Bowles occasionally kept records of his own time for a period of a few weeks. Some weeks he would be spending a third to a half of his time before congressional committees. The same was true of many other top staff members. At one time nine or ten congressional committees were simultaneously inquiring into various aspects of OPA operations. Congressional investigations constituted a tremendous drain on the energies and time of many of the most important OPA officials.

### Another Smith Committee
It was the second Smith Committee that investigated us the most systematically and ruthlessly. [The first Smith Committee under the leadership of the same chairman had investigated the NLRB in 1940.] Appointed in February 1943, the Smith Committee consisted of Chairman Howard W. Smith and three other Democrats: Reps. Hugh Peterson (Georgia), John J. Delaney (New York), and Jerry Voorhis (California). Delaney and Voorhis were considered New Dealers; Peterson and Smith were southern Democrats. The Republicans on the committee were Fred Hartley, one of the most vociferous critics of OPA, John Jennings, Jr. (Tennessee) and Clare E. Hoffman (Michigan), who was generally considered an eccentric. Their ostensible purpose was to investigate and check abuses of authority by executive agencies during the war period. Actually, the committee was used to campaign against policies of the war agencies opposed by conservative groups in Congress and the country. They also became a forum by which anyone who had a protest against OPA could receive a sympathetic hearing. That in itself was not objectionable, but the methods by which it was carried out seemed outrageous to us. The Smith Committee functioned in somewhat the same way that the Smith Committee investigating the NLRB had done. They seized upon minor and insignificant incidents that presented dramatic possibilities for newspaper publicity, and tended to distort and misrepresent in much the same way the the prior Smith Committee had.

A typical incident was the treatment of David Ginsburg's files. Sometime during the course of the committee's investigation, it occurred to them that by searching through the files of David Ginsburg they might find some very juicy material. Two investigators of the committee went to George Burke, OPA general counsel at the time, and asked him for Ginsburg's files. Burke told them they were not in his office; that when he had moved into the office, he had ordered all files sent to the main filing room. The investigators went to the main filing room and were told the Ginsburg files were not there, either. They were told to check the Legal Department files. They went to the Legal Department files and were told by the file clerk that there were no Ginsburg files. At this point, the investigators had a good story. They returned to their office and secured a subpoena to be served on Burke as general counsel, ordering him to produce the files, lustily publicizing the assertion that the files of David Ginsburg were mysteriously missing and insinuating that they contained much material that would throw light upon the nefarious activities of OPA.

Burke and I went down to testify. The subpoena was the first I had known that they were looking for Ginsburg's files. Had they asked me, I would have been able to tell them immediately where they were. We explained that the files had been dispersed among the various sections of the Legal Department when Ginsburg left, that those relating to enforcement had gone into my office, those relating to rent had gone into the rent office or to the assistant general counsel in charge of rent, and so on with price, rationing, research, and the other areas. We could not tell exactly what material in our files had once been in the Ginsburg files, and therefore it would be difficult to reconstruct them. We also told them that Ginsburg had taken to his house in Huntington, West Virginia, several packing-boxes of duplicate files. It was customary for government officials to place in personal files duplicate copies of significant documents and notes.

This precipitated a great outcry about Ginsburg taking government files to West Virginia. So we had his family send them back again and made them available to the committee. The committee searched all through them and discovered nothing. Ginsburg had learned a lesson from the Smith Committee investigation of the NLRB and had anticipated a similar investigation of himself or OPA. However, in their report, the committee continued to play up the strange disappearance of the Ginsburg files and referred to them as being unaccountably missing.

They also used the files to draw an insinuation that an undercover subversive plan existed in OPA for the control of profits. They found in the files a memorandum dealing with price policies, which discussed the question of the standard for fixing prices in terms of profit and formulating an industry earning standard. The memo said that if profits during the base period of 1936–39 were equalled by present profits, a price increase should not be granted. This document, not written by Ginsburg, had been distributed widely through OPA and represented a well-known OPA policy. The committee, however, treated it as evidence that the OPA was attempting to exercise control over profits in American industry, which they were not authorized to do under the act. They put it this way: "Our committee has found, in examining the files of the former general counsel of the Office of Price Administration, a well-devised and planned scheme to control the profits of American industry." This language implied that Ginsburg and OPA were plotting a system of profit control.

The Smith Committee had access to all our files. They never conducted the kind of inquiry the Smith Committee had in NLRB, in which they extracted from the files all the indiscretions and colorful language they could find. They dealt much more with the merits of situations than the earlier Smith Committee had, and less with personalities, although to some extent with personalities, too. They searched through my files. Nowadays, I think the executive, in view of the point to which congressional investigations have gone, would withhold the files more, and certainly not permit a general search through the files. But, at that time, it was considered the better part of good politics not to protest the committee's access to the files. There was much less to uncover in the OPA files, though, than in the NLRB files. I guess OPA's staff had less time to write memoranda, or wrote less colorful ones. The committee did extract one or two items. One, I remember, was found in the files of Henry Hart, who was one of the most respected persons that one could ever find, although he was firm. He had written a memorandum on the rider in the 1943 Appropriations Act that restricted grade labelling and standardization. After an elaborate analysis of the language and the committee debates preceding adoption, Hart concluded, "The discussion [referring to the congressional debate] shows conclusively that neither the Senate nor the House understood with any exactness what the effect of the provision was." The Smith Committee highlighted this statement as showing disrespect for Congress, charging that "if the Associate General Counsel can't understand what Congress means, it is obvious OPA must be operating entirely outside of its statutory authority." The reports that the committee issued were full of things of that nature.

Occasionally the Smith Committee, which functioned throughout all this period and long after V-J Day, was used simply as a forum by which a disgruntled attorney objecting to an enforcement proceeding of OPA could come down and make public his complaints. In one case we were called by the committee in reference to a suit we had filed in New York. The chief investigator of the committee asked us to come over and testify on this. I asked Fleming James, who was the head of the Litigation Division of the Enforcement Department, to go over. He wrote me a memorandum describing what had happened. He said that Representatives Delaney, Peterson, and Hartley were present, Peterson for only a few minutes. The defendant in the proceedings and his attorney were present. We were told by our field office that the attorney was also the attorney for Representative Hartley. The proceedings consisted of the defendant and his attorney objecting to the bringing of the case by OPA. Fortunately Delaney, who was the presiding officer, realized that this was simply a run-of-the-mill enforcement proceeding that the court would have to decide, and passed it off on that basis. Representative Hartley objected strenuously, but nothing further came of it. That was simply an example of the use of the committee for bringing judicial proceedings into a political arena.

The Smith Committee filed its second report on November 15, 1943, a week or so after Bowles had been appointed administrator. This report was devoted to the price and rationing programs of OPA. Again they paid lip service to the need for price control but attacked very strongly many of the administrative practices of OPA. The report was unfair in its misrepresentations and one-sidedness. For instance, they attacked the whole scheme for judicial review and the exclusive jurisdiction provisions of the statute, failing to mention that the issue had been brought up in the courts as to whether it was a violation of due process, and not referring to these court decisions. A footnote mentioned the *Lockerty v. Phillips* case, in which the Supreme Court upheld an important aspect of this, namely that you could not bring an injunction to stay the operation of the price regulation in a federal district court, in such a way that no one could tell what the decision had held. Other decisions supporting the OPA position, including the favorable decision of the Court of Appeals for the First Circuit in the Yakus case, were not even mentioned. The report neglected this whole line of court decisions saying the judicial review procedure was not a violation of due process.

The report attacked the proliferation of OPA regulations. They pointed out that the office had issued 3119 regulations, orders, and amendments between February 11, 1942 and September 1, 1943, somewhat less than two years. However, they did not point out that of these there were 454 price regulations, 24 ration regulations, and 67 rent regulations, that the rest were amendments, and dealt with 700 trades and industries, including 3,000,000 sellers. Admittedly, we issued a large number of regulations and amendments, but the number reflected the complexity of our mandated task.

As an example of the complexity of OPA regulations, they quoted with evident relish, as a typical example of the legalistic language employed by OPA, this provision:

> All commodities listed in Appendix A are those known to the trade as such excepting therefrom such thereof, if any, while subject to another regulation.

Well, that particular provision was one of the more unfortunate products of OPA drafting, and had appeared in *The New Yorker* with a note, probably sent in by some OPA attorney. It was an extreme and horrible example, but certainly not typical as the committee said.

The committee attacked OPA for forcing people into bankruptcy, under the generally fair and equitable rule, relying upon the testimony of a former OPA employee, who had said that there had been many cases in which relief had been refused in the canning industry that might have been granted and that had caused financial hardships. The report generalized from this that there had been hundreds of bankruptcies and business failures, ignoring current statistics showing that the number of business failures in the country had declined to the lowest level in the past fifty years and that profits were 4.5 times their 1936–1939 levels. They played up as a political slogan that OPA was controlling the profits of American industry, a demagogic play on words, since it was impossible to control prices without controlling profits.

Bowles made a vigorous statement in answer to the Smith Committee report. His statement pointed out that most of the things had happened before his arrival, but he included a fairly strong attack upon the committee. OPA prepared a detailed answer of some twenty thousand words or so which analyzed every portion of the report. However, our rebuttal received little publicity and probably had little effect in offsetting the impact of the original report.

The Smith Committee could have served a valuable purpose; some congressional check on OPA actions and procedures certainly would have been justified. But the kind of investigation that the Smith Committee held made no contribution to the problem. Its methods were demagogic, it distorted the evidence, it failed to state the full facts, and it was completely one-sided. At times, it dealt with genuine problems with which we also were concerned, but it offered us no help with their solution. The effect on the public is hard to say. While it did not receive the publicity or have the impact of the Smith Committee report on the National Labor Relations Board, it certainly contributed to public and congressional opposition to OPA.

The Smith Committee filed continuous reports from that time on, some of them dealing with OPA and some with other agencies. The third report, also filed in November 1943, dealt with the meat and livestock programs. They filed a report in January 1944, attacking the National War Labor Board; Reps. Delaney and Voorhis dissented. I could not understand why they went along with the majority in the earlier reports on OPA. In April 1944 the committee filed a report designed to support the campaign for significant amendment to the legislation that was about to come before Congress. Throughout the period of OPA's existence, they continued investigations and reports, and were a constant thorn in our side, occupying not only our time, but undoubtedly having a substantial effect on public opinion.

This continuing harassment occupied OPA's time and demanded answers. It affected our public relations, but had a negligible effect on our procedures. I do not think OPA tried more carefully to be fair in its procedures because of the Smith Committee than it would have done otherwise. The Smith Committee was so far off the beam that it obviously would not have been possible ever to satisfy such a committee. We had plenty of other pressures and reasons for acting carefully and cautiously. Perhaps the combination of all the committees kept OPA watching its actions to avoid criticism. To some extent that is good and to some extent it made OPA too cautious. But OPA viewed the Smith Committee as so extreme that we judged nothing could be done to avoid their criticism, so we had no motivation to try. I suppose the committee did have some effect, but it did not strike me at the time as having as substantial an effect as the earlier Smith Committee had had on the NLRB. For one thing,

OPA was such a vast organization that one could not predict where the committee lightning would strike on any particular occasion.

## ATTACKS ON OPA EMPLOYEES

The stab-in-the-back nature of the Pearl Harbor attack was an important factor in uniting many people. I suppose the country was more united in World War II than in any other war, previously or since. Because of the war and our alliance with the Soviet Union, attacks on government officials by the House Committee on Un-American Activities and other sources had decreased. The fact that the Communist Party was following a policy of strenuous collaboration rather than criticism of the Roosevelt administration, and the lessening of tensions both domestically and abroad, also meant that the strong, violent anti-Communist attitude and tactics received much less public support. The trends that had started, and that were to flourish later, temporarily were submerged and postponed.

However, the attack against the Communists and alleged pro-Communists had not let up completely, nor had the tactics of the Committee on Un-American Activities changed. Severe attacks occurred. The more extreme members of Congress, such as Reps. Fred E. Busbey (Illinois), Clare Hoffman, E. E. Cox (Georgia), John Rankin (Mississippi), and others, continued this line of action, which was consistent with the efforts of the committee's forerunner, the Dies Committee. The movement in the government for protection against possible subversive activities on the part of its employees continued to some extent during this period. Even at the height of the war, preparations moved toward the ultimate comprehensive loyalty program that came out in 1947. The Department of Justice, in connection with the administration of the Hatch Act, prepared a list of alleged subversive organizations. This was not made public, but was circulated for the benefit of other government agencies. FBI activities were continuing and receiving greater appropriations. There were increasing investigations made in connection with alleged subversive organizations. It simply was that the activity was by no means as intensive.

The problem of subversive activities and attacks on OPA employees because of alleged subversive activities continued to some extent during this period under Bowles. Two attacks that involved me personally were perhaps typical.

In June 1944, in the course of the debate on the extension of the Price Control Act in the House, Representative Morrison had made an impassioned speech in favor of removing strawberries from price control. Immediately afterward Rep. Fred E. Busbey of Illinois arose and made an attack on three OPA employees. Representative Busbey was a product of, or at least was supported by, the *Chicago Tribune*, and was one of the more reactionary members of Congress. The point of his speech was that the difficulty with OPA was primarily the personnel. He declared:

> There will always be trouble as long as you have men in key
> positions administering these laws who oppose our republican
> form of government.  I refer to three individuals particularly;
> Tom Tippett, Shad Polier, and Thomas I. Emerson, who, in my
> judgment, are not qualified to be on the federal payroll.

Busbey then enlarged on each of us, giving a sketch of our alleged
subversive activities.  Where he had obtained this material I do not know.
He said he had examined my personnel file in the OPA office.  He may
have.  He claimed to have examined the files of all three of us.  Why the
OPA would let congressmen come in and examine personnel files I do not
know, but that is apparently what happened.  He also had some additional
material I suppose someone had supplied him with.  Tom Tippett was in
the Rent Department, and had been under fire before, actually at the time
the law was passed.  Shad Polier was a close friend of mine, and was head
of the section of the Enforcement Department that dealt with gasoline
rationing.

With respect to me, the speech listed all my prior positions in the
government with their salaries, and then went on to say that I had been:

> extraordinarily active in three of the most influential communist
> front organizations in Washington, D.C.  These three are the
> International Juridical Association, the National Lawyers Guild,
> and the Washington Committee for Democratic Action.  His
> position in these organizations for the past few years has not
> been simply that of a rank-and-file member, but of a leader.

He then went on to detail the charges that had been made against these
three organizations, and to list some of the alleged Communists who were
members of the International Juridical Association.  He then attacked me
for being associated with Nathan Witt, the secretary of the NLRB, saying:

> It is quite significant that Emerson and Witt tendered their
> resignations to the NLRB at the same time.

He continued:

> Non-communist associates of Emerson in the National Labor
> Relations Board have informed the various intelligence agencies
> in Washington of his open and aggressive communist activities
> while he served with the board.  When Emerson first went with
> the Office of Price Administration, the Civil Service Commission
> sent Leon Henderson an adverse report on him.  This adverse
> report was based on the testimony of numerous witnesses who
> told the Commission investigators of Emerson's devotion to the
> ideology of communism.  It has been reported that the file of
> Thomas I. Emerson, containing many adverse reports on him, is
> now missing from the files of the Civil Service Commission, and

is a real mystery of underground sabotage.

He then concluded:

> In view of the record of these three men, there is only one
> logical conclusion to which we can arrive. That is, the New Deal
> administration not only condones men of their type in
> government positions of responsibility, but insists on their being
> there. I was amazed to find, when I examined the personnel
> files of these three men in the Office of Price Administration
> today that there was not a single record in the files of an
> investigation having been made regarding their qualifications for
> office.

He went on with a reference to the boys fighting in the armed services,
and ended up:

> I insist that the battle on the home front can not be won unless
> men who understand and appreciate our form of government are
> put in positions of trust and responsibility.

This attack received publicity in the *Washington News*, the Scripps-Howard
paper, which by then had turned anti-New Deal. It was also given
publicity in the *Washington Times-Herald*. Beyond that, it received
practically no notice in the newspapers. The *New York Times*, I am almost
certain, carried no reference to it.

Today [1953], of course, an attack of that kind would mean immediate
suspension of an individual from government service and probably the end
of his career. The atmosphere of that time, however, was different, and
all that was done was that Bowles wrote a letter to House Speaker Sam
Rayburn, denying the charges and asking him to put it into the
*Congressional Record*, together with a brief summary of the facts with
respect to each of the three individuals involved. The facts, he pointed
out, would show that Busbey was incorrect in saying I had been a member
of the Washington Committee for Democratic Action. I had never been
a member or associated in any way with that organization. Where he had
gotten that information I have no idea. The statement defended the
Lawyers Guild and the International Juridical Association. By this time we
had almost a form letter on that. It also pointed out that Busbey was
wrong in saying the Civil Service Commission had sent an adverse report.
It was simply a summary of the first Treasury report, without itself coming
to any conclusions. Busbey, of course, did not mention the re-opening of
the investigation and the subsequent exoneration. Busbey's statement that
my files were missing from the Civil Service Commission was simply
untrue. The Civil Service Commission reported that my file never had
been out of the office.

That ended that incident. As far as appears, it had no serious
repercussions. General opposition to much of the OPA personnel existed,

not on the grounds that they were Communist subversives, but because they were carrying out policies with which many congressmen disagreed. Attacks on personnel were fairly frequent in connection with the extension of the National Labor Relations Act and also in connection with the appropriations. However, there was no indication that this particular attack with the charges of subversion had any significant impact.

Subsequently, during the 1948 presidential campaign, Ohio Governor John W. Bricker, who had been the Republican candidate for vice president in 1944, made a speech in which he attacked me and half-a-dozen others as examples of Communists in government. There were no details given; it was just a charge that the government was full of Communists, giving as examples me, Walter Gellhorn, and some others I have forgotten.

I could have won a suit against Bricker for libel, I suppose, but I was not inclined to pursue it. Nothing was done except that Bowles wrote a private letter to Bricker in which he defended me. Bowles' letter said:

> I was deeply disturbed to read a newspaper account of one of your recent speeches in which you stated that Tom Emerson, Deputy Administrator for Enforcement, was a communist. I know you could not have checked that statement, because if you had, you could not, in all honesty have made it.

Bowles described the investigation that had cleared me. Then he added:

> I did not know Mr. Emerson before I came to Washington a year and a half ago. However, I was sufficiently impressed with his ability to select him for the important position of deputy administrator in charge of enforcement. In this difficult capacity, he has done an outstanding job. He has demonstrated unusual executive ability, good judgment, and courage. Perhaps I am old-fashioned, but I do not believe that anyone has the right, even in the heat of a political campaign, to level unchecked charges against an individual who is in a position where he can neither reply nor retaliate. Your indictment of Mr. Emerson, was in effect, a charge of bad faith leveled both at the Civil Service Commission and at me personally, as Administrator of the Office of Price Administration. I cannot believe that you could thoughtfully make such a charge.

Bricker did not respond to this, as far as I know.

The attacks made by Busbey and Bricker were not untypical of the kinds of charges that were made. They assumed, of course, an atmosphere of at least the beginnings of the hysteria on this. It simply did not receive so much attention at that time.

Other OPA employees were under attack in addition to myself, but I would not say that these attacks were a serious influence in the OPA picture. They were devised as a means of opposing OPA policy, but they were too extreme in their distortions to receive general congressional acceptance. The way the newspapers treated them, for instance, indicated that they were not of the news value that similar attacks are today [1953].

The charges made against OPA employees on the grounds of subversive activities did not have much effect on OPA's public position. Occasionally, a regional office would write me and say, "The Landlords Association in San Francisco has attacked you as being a member of a communist organization," and I would write back, giving them some information they could use in answering. That was quite rare, though.

In contrast to this outcry about communism, little investigation and hounding of pro-Nazis occurred during the war period. The Department of Justice prosecuted 28 pro-Nazis for conspiracy to interfere with the operation of the war, as well as under the Smith Act. In its early days the House Committee on Un-American Activities made routine investigations of some fascist organizations, but never probed deeply. As I recall, by this period the topic had been abandoned. With the exception of the Department of Justice case, I cannot recall anything of significance occurring. Once in a while a labor union or political group would allege that the army had appointed a pro-Nazi to some position or had awarded him a contract. But the bloodhounds were not set loose to run down these people and expose them publicly in the manner in which this has happened with respect to people alleged to hold Communist views in the early 1950s. It is surprising that pro-fascist and pro-Nazi individuals were attacked as little as they were. I suppose that most persons opposed to those views were not in any extreme group, and not having an extreme emotional reaction to the issue, kept their discussions on a more rational level.

# 12

# TROUBLESOME PRODUCTS

*Americans will forgo, but only if everyone else does too.*

Under Chester Bowles as administrator of the Office of Price Administration I was now the attorney in charge of the Enforcement Department. It was our job to see to it that the price and rent policies established by OPA were being adhered to by American businesses and the citizenry at large. I will now detail some of the problems we faced as well as our general contribution to the administration of OPA.

## MAJOR HEADACHE I: MEAT

Two major headaches faced the Enforcement Department throughout most of the period of our operations: enforcement of the meat and the gasoline regulations. The meat regulations probably were our worst headache. Our trials and tribulations with meat began during the first days of OPA and continued right through to the end. The enforcement of meat regulations was particularly important for several reasons. One was that meat was such a large component in the cost of living. Food was rated in the Bureau of Labor Statistics' Cost of Living Index as 40 percent, I believe, of the total index, and meat was the most important food item. Keeping down the Cost of Living Index, which was the goal of much of OPA's enforcement, depended greatly on control of meat. In addition, the public became tremendously excited over the meat question. People wanted better grades and cuts of meat; they became extremely upset over meat shortages. So the meat situation affected public morale during the war. Public attention was focused more on meat regulations than on most other aspects of OPA operations.

Meat prices and the distribution of meat were subject to terrific pressures. In the first place, individual income, particularly in the lower income brackets, increased tremendously during the war. One of the first outlets for this vastly increased purchasing power turned out to be meat, especially beef. The potential per capita consumption of meat rose to a markedly high point during the war as a result of this increase in income.

Second, the armed forces consumed a tremendous amount of meat. There were 11 million men in the armed forces and they were eating substantially more than they had ever eaten before. As the armed forces usually received the better grades and cuts of meat, the supply available for the civilian population was drained. In spite of the vast amounts taken by the armed forces, however, civilian demand—and consumption—increased throughout the war. Meat production also increased considerably during the war years. Nevertheless, demand far surpassed the available meat supplies, resulting in formidable pressures on meat prices.

OPA was concerned with price and rationing regulations, but in developing these controls OPA—and particularly other agencies sharing the same responsibility—had to work out additional regulations to control slaughtering operations and other aspects of distribution. Almost from the very beginning widespread violation of the meat regulations occurred. In 1942 packers, wholesalers, and retailers had all begun violating the meat regulations. In 1943 the rate of violation increased, and by 1944 violations had increased still further. The entire meat industry was disrupted by the pervasive pattern of violations and the shift into black market operations. This disruption persisted through 1945 and later.

We were well aware that these violations were taking place, but to obtain an accurate estimate of the amount of violation was impossible. The Senate Agricultural Committee called a hearing on enforcement of meat regulations in the spring of 1945. During my testimony, Sen. Kenneth Wherry of Nebraska charged that 95 percent of the meat was being sold at prices above the ceiling. I told him that was ridiculous, challenged his figures, and suggested a much lower estimate. I said I thought perhaps 30 or 40 percent was the figure. Neither of us really knew. Whatever the figure, there was no doubt that overpricing was exceedingly widespread. Since the large chain stores controlled about a third of the retail distribution, and most of them were not openly violating, in the sense of selling without coupons or selling at increased prices clearly above ceiling, a substantial portion of the meat must have been sold within the regulations. Large chain stores committed some violations in terms of upgrading. On the other hand, probably a lot of the meat sold by independent stores was sold in violation.

Substantial violation of the rationing regulations also occurred. About this time, a reporter for the *Pittsburgh Post-Gazette* was sent by his newspaper to buy on the black market. Posing as a meat dealer, accompanied by someone who knew the industry, he had no trouble in buying, within the course of a week, a ton of meat from wholesale distributors without using any ration coupons at all. This foray cost his newspaper about $2,000 and the meat was donated to charitable organizations, but he had his newspaper story. The situation was worse in Pittsburgh than elsewhere because the United States attorney there had not brought a single criminal case involving the meat market. However it would have been possible in many areas of the country to buy substantial quantities of meat without coupons and very likely escape prosecution.

Large-scale violation persisted through 1946, and indeed (as I will discuss later), it was the meat regulations that precipitated the final blow to OPA in October 1946. Before the congressional elections of 1946 President Truman suddenly announced that all controls could be lifted from meat. That marked the end of OPA price control, in effect. The meat problem proved a critical one right up to the end and was the major factor in the de facto liquidation of OPA controls.

Large packers violated mainly in terms of grading and quality. I have already alluded to the first difficulty we ran into: the big-four meat packers (Armour, Cudahy, Swift, and Wilson) were trimming pork cuts so as to leave substantially more fat on the cut than was normal practice. OPA regulations allowed a maximum of half-an-inch and the average cut contained about an inch or more of fat. This meant that the housewife was paying regular pork prices for fat. The government was urging housewives to sell back their fat to butchers or to the rendering-houses at 2 cents a pound, plus one or two ration points. The trimming was exceedingly unfair and a clear violation of the regulations. We brought injunction proceedings. Our first request for an injunction was denied, but subsequent petitions were successful and more or less corrected that situation.

The larger packers also engaged in a certain amount of tie-in sales. They would sell the fresh cuts of meat, which were the ones in real demand, only if the retailers would buy sausages or other by-products, items that were in excess supply. This also was equivalent to a price increase. It forced the retailers to sell above their ceilings if they were to maintain their rate of profit and stay in business.

Some large packers asked for cash on the side, but the tie-in sales and cash on the side violations were attributable primarily to agents of the wholesale distributing branches of the packers. It was difficult to trace these violations back to headquarters, except insofar as headquarters would insist a branch distributing house dispose of a certain amount of sausages and other by-products in a certain period or would press to have them disposed of through tie-in sales. It was hard to prove that the packing-houses were responsible for the cash on the side that delivery men of the branch houses might exact. In fact, in many cases the packing-houses probably were unaware of the practice. The delivery men found it a tempting opportunity to make money.

However, once the fat content in meat was controlled, the major packing-houses were not the source of the worst violations. Originally, several hundred major packing houses, dominated by the big four, controlled from 68 to 70 percent of the business. As time passed and the market became more disrupted–with new suppliers entering, some of them gangster connected–the percentage of meat flowing through the major packing houses decreased. In 1944–45 it fell to 58 percent. The decrease was much more marked for beef, a key product that caused most of the trouble. Most vexing was the control of the meat that passed through smaller slaughterers, ranging from established but small packing houses down to many thousands of butchers and farm slaughterers.

Violations at the slaughtering level inevitably led to violations at the retail level. Retail violations included excess charges, tie-in sales, short weight, upgrading, and selling without coupons. Retail stores could not stay in business if they sold meat bought at prices above the ceiling without charging prices above the ceiling themselves. Meat was in such demand that many stores maintained their meat counters as full as possible in order to attract trade to sell other groceries. Colossal economic pressure on retailers and the amount of violation at the wholesale level made considerable violation at the retail level inevitable. The demand for meat undoubtedly would have tempted retailers into overcharging even if the wholesalers had resisted all temptations. To avoid wholesalers' overcharges, some of the leading chain stores bought packing houses or established slaughterhouses.

The gangster element was moving into the meat business during this period, in part by buying or starting fly-by-night slaughtering houses, ransacking the country for cattle, and slaughtering and selling above the ceiling price. The gangster element also was counterfeiting or stealing ration coupons at a fairly high rate.

OPA's Enforcement Department made strenuous efforts to enforce the meat regulations. These regulations were the particular responsibility of the head of the Food Enforcement Division, Harry Jones, an extremely resourceful person [later professor of law at Columbia University]. Our efforts were not notably successful despite our concentration of manpower in meat enforcement. Our official policy was to allocate 40 percent of our manpower to food enforcement and of those, at least half were assigned to meat. Approximately 1200 regular investigators were assigned to food and about 500 regularly assigned to meat. Often investigators were borrowed from other divisions, so that usually more than 500 were working on meat regulations.

This impressive amount of enforcement activity was not adequate to bring the situation under satisfactory control. There were a number of reasons for this. In the first place, meat was supplied by numerous sources. We could manage that portion of the industry under the control of the 250 large packers, particularly since a high percentage of its production was handled by the big four. In 1941, 365 slaughtering plants each produced more than 2 million pounds of meat a year. What we found impossible to manage, however, were some 3000 local plants that produced anywhere from 300,000 to 2,000,000 pounds a year. Plus, in 1941 there were another 23,000 butchers slaughtering another 300,000 pounds. Controlling the small slaughterers and the two-bit butchers proved to be exceedingly difficult. Before our enforcement efforts could encompass them, the supply of livestock tended to flow to those slaughtering establishments that fetched higher prices. In addition, many new ones sprang up, so that slaughtering occurred more and more in a multitude of small plants. Even with 500 inspectors we could not–in fact, even if we had put almost our whole staff on meat, they would not have been able to–keep track of so many suppliers.

Second, the situation constituted an open invitation to black market operations. The intensity of the public desire for meat created an overwhelming demand. Enormous profits were possible by cutting into the meat business. Profits could be made quickly by a person with little capital or by the gangster type of capital. I do not mean to say that all violations were by speculating newcomers. Quite the contrary. The large packers had led off with deliberate violations on the fat trimming. Many of the smaller slaughterers who had been established for many years participated actively in the black market. But the point is that the demand for meat created a stupendous temptation for easy money and many succumbed to that temptation.

Third, we faced consistent opposition from many sources to adequate controls and more specifically to enforcement efforts. The Meat Institute was one of the most blatant of the industrial organizations opposed to OPA. The National Association of Manufacturers and other industrial organizations also participated in a campaign against OPA controls, particularly toward the end of the period. They contended that the only way to satisfy public demand for meat was to increase production, which would only be possible if OPA controls were lifted, and that the only way to reduce prices was to lift OPA controls. It was not that they wanted increased prices; they wanted lower prices for the consumer, which would be possible only with increased production. Their argument was clearly erroneous because it was not possible to increase the supply of livestock except over a period of years.

In addition, there were attacks from Congress. The agricultural bloc in Congress consistently opposed OPA regulations on meat. Congressmen attacked OPA investigators who were attempting to deal with the problem as "snoopers." The meat situation became most critical in the spring of each year; by the nature of the industry supplies were at their lowest then, and the pressures and violations were worse. The low point happened to coincide with the time that OPA appropriations came up or consideration was being given to amendments, so that meat regulation was especially called to congressional attention at the time when Congress was about to act on OPA problems. As a result, the opposition was able to make a better case before Congress than they would have at other times of the year. While the public supported controls abstractly, enough people condoned violations and were willing to buy black market meat themselves to set a general tone of disapprobation rather than support.

The fourth difficulty arose out of the very nature of the violations and the difficulty of applying sanctions. One of the most frequent forms of violation, payment of cash on the side by the butcher to his wholesaler, was difficult to detect. It did not appear on the records. It could be discovered from questioning retailers about purchases from wholesalers, but the retailers usually were unwilling to talk, knowing their supplies would be cut off. It was possible to send investigators around with shipments of meat once in a while, but obviously the regulation was not enforceable by having every shipment of meat accompanied by an OPA investigator. So cash on the side was difficult to uncover.

Grading violations, probably more frequent than cash on the side, were even more difficult. The large packers had the grade stamped on the meat under federal inspection. But the increasing volume of non-federally inspected meat had no grade stamped on it, and the determination of the grade was an abstruse process requiring an expert, and one on which experts could differ. Obtaining proof of upgrading was extremely difficult. Practically all the meat was sold as AA when only a very small proportion of AA was available, particularly in the kind of meat that these fly-by-night wholesalers were slaughtering. They would round up cattle from the local farmers, drive them into the slaughtering establishments, and although it was not by any means high-grade meat, it was sold as such. Upgrading at the retail level was also difficult to establish, unless an OPA investigator was present when the meat was bought from the wholesaler and sold to the customer. Tie-in sales and short weight were hard to establish, too.

In addition, applying sanctions had complications. The criminal sanction probably was the most applicable in this situation, but we had a particular struggle with the Department of Justice over the application of the criminal sanction. For long periods of time it was almost foreclosed to us. The next most valuable sanction was the suspension order, but after 1944 those could be used only for rationing violations, not price violations. The suspension order generally was applied only at the retail level. Treble damage was not particularly effective because it was difficult to prove enough violations to add up to a dollar amount that constituted a genuine penalty on a firm. The industry was consistently in violation and sufficiently disorganized that the books and records kept were wholly inadequate. Consequently, we might be able to prove an isolated violation here and there, but not the substantial number necessary. Injunction orders were useful, but we considered them too mild a response in this situation. So we met obstructions both in detecting violations and applying sanctions.

Another frustration arose from inconsistencies in the rationing program. When Bowles became administrator of OPA in 1943, one of his policies was to ease off on rationing in the hope of thereby obtaining greater support for price controls. The relaxation came in food rationing and particularly on meat. At the end of 1943 and the beginning of 1944, meat rationing was relaxed considerably, which gave the public the idea that the supplies of meat were greater than had been previously stated, and that the shortage of meat and the need for regulation was being overemphasized. This tended to cause the public to think previous restrictions had been unnecessary, and when stricter rationing was resumed, the public was more recalcitrant than before.

As if all these difficulties were not enough, by far the most important obstacle to meat regulation was the lack of adequate controls in two key areas: livestock ceilings and slaughtering houses. In establishing its original regulation for control of prices at the slaughtering, wholesale, and retail level, OPA had not instituted control of prices at the livestock level. This was due in part to technical difficulties, such as the need to anticipate what the grade would be while the animal was still on the hoof, which was the subject of informed guess by the buyers, and the fact that a substantial portion of the sales did not go through the major markets where they would be subject to ready controls. But political opposition from the farm bloc was the decisive factor in our not controlling livestock prices. And not controlling prices at the livestock level predictably resulted in an increase in livestock prices, which tended to put pressure on slaughterers and wholesalers, and thereby on retailers, to sell above ceiling prices. OPA always contended that the big four meat packing houses could control cattle prices. Assuming OPA was correct in this assumption, the big four were not above allowing cattle prices to rise as a means of putting pressure on OPA. In any event, some of the smaller slaughterers who did not make their profit from the by-products were under considerable pressure for a while. The big packers traditionally made little profit and sometimes lost money on the fresh cuts; they made their profit on the by-products. The small packers, not manufacturing the by-products, had to make a profit as best they could. Small packers ran a substantial risk of bankruptcy, even under the best of conditions.

When livestock prices rose, smaller slaughterers were squeezed harder than the large slaughterers. There was some indication that the large slaughterers may have permitted livestock prices to increase in order to bankrupt their smaller competitors. In any event, there was considerable outcry. Richard Gilbert, OPA economic advisor, testified before a congressional committee that the smaller slaughterers were taking a terrific shellacking, and that the failure to control livestock prices put them in a bind where it was difficult or impossible for them to comply with the regulations and make a profit. Prentiss Brown confirmed this testimony. As a result, the Department of Justice refused to bring any criminal prosecutions, contending that the OPA regulations were unfair and invalid, and they (Justice) would not enforce them. While this policy was not announced publicly, it was fairly well known in the industry, and for a long period of time we could not persuade the Department of Justice to bring prosecutions.

The Department of Justice's decision not to prosecute was the position taken by Francis Biddle, the attorney general, upon recommendation of the Criminal Division. We reported it to the OPA administrator at that time, Prentiss Brown. He, however, was not capable of arguing the position effectively in an appeal to President Roosevelt, so we had to live with the Department of Justice's inaction. Nothing was done until the subsidy program relieved the situation. To a large extent, then, it was a failure of leadership. Biddle's position was, "OPA itself says these fellows are getting a terrible shellacking. How can the Justice Department ever expect to win a criminal case, when all the defense attorney has to do is to read in evidence this testimony before the jury?" His argument had substance because our testimony had placed the Department of Justice in a vulnerable position. I think the lesser evil would have been to have proceeded vigorously anyway, but basically, the solution was up to the OPA and the Department of Agriculture.

The situation was somewhat relieved by paying a subsidy to the slaughterers. The subsidy served two purposes. One, it made up to the slaughterers for the increase in livestock prices presumably without increasing the slaughterers' price. Shortly afterwards, it was differentiated so that a larger subsidy was paid to the slaughterers who did not make the by-products. The subsidy also resulted in some control over livestock prices because it was not payable if the slaughterer had bought the livestock above a certain average ceiling. This operated as a livestock price control. However, as time went on the subsidy became less effective because black market profits exceeded the subsidy; withholding the subsidy because the slaughterer paid over-ceiling prices for livestock no longer discouraged the slaughterer from proceeding with his profitable business.

The lack of a ceiling on livestock plagued meat regulation until early in 1945, when a direct ceiling was put on livestock. By that time, however, the pattern of violation and disruption of the industry had proceeded to a point where enforcement remained out of hand despite the elimination of a basic cause.

Lack of control over the slaughtering houses was the other basic cause of the difficulty. The only way in which the movement of meat from the slaughtering houses to the retailers could have been regulated was by an adequate control over the amount of meat slaughtered in the packing houses, and an allocation of quotas in such a way that the established businesses would be able to obtain their share without bidding up the black market, and paying black market prices. Such control was difficult because the sources of supply of livestock were multitudinous. Although a substantial portion of the livestock came through the large markets in Chicago, St. Louis, and Omaha, livestock could be slaughtered anywhere. An elaborate system of slaughtering controls was attempted from time to time in various ways, primarily through the Department of Agriculture. Yet not only Prentiss Brown but even Bowles was unable to convince the Department of Agriculture to act effectively. Agriculture finally was straightened out, to some extent, through the Office of Economic Stabilization (OES; discussed in Chapter 14). OES could tell the Department of Agriculture to institute slaughtering controls, but it could not establish a division in the department to enforce such controls, nor could it change the day-to-day administration, by which dubious characters were granted licenses to slaughter in large quotas. OPA believed that the Department of Agriculture was not seriously interested in instituting its controls, and when it did institute them, administered them incompetently, so that the controls never worked effectively. In any event, controls on slaughtering houses were introduced at such a late point that the pattern had been established and the situation was virtually beyond repair.

In my judgment no application of traditional enforcement controls would have relieved the meat situation. Of course, I speak with some bias on this point because I was responsible for managing an unwieldy situation and have a natural tendency to blame some of it, at least, on others. Given the serious temptation to violate by both businesses and consumers, the large number of outlets involved, the difficulty in detecting violations, the available sanctions, the pressures that had been created, and the patterns that had formed, effective control was beyond the powers of any enforcement agency. I think we could have gained the upper hand only by relatively simple, readily enforced controls, such as whether a slaughtering house could operate or not operate, vigorously applied to the sources of supply. This meant livestock ceilings and slaughtering controls. Even then, the technical obstacles would have been substantial, but particularly the slaughtering controls could have saved the situation had they been applied early enough and vigorously enough.

## Poultry

As an example of the effectiveness of vigorous action, the poultry market challenged us at one time and we used somewhat unorthodox methods to handle it. A good deal of the poultry in the East came from the so-called Delmarva Peninsula, the peninsula that contains part of Delaware, Maryland, and Virginia. It was shipped to Philadelphia, New York, and other eastern cities, even as far as Cleveland, Ohio. The spring of 1943 saw a tremendous shortage of poultry. The army was finding it difficult to obtain a supply and there was an increasing black market by truckers who drove into the Delmarva area, paid cash to the farmer, carried the poultry out, and sold it above ceiling prices. In cooperation with the army, we instituted a system whereby the army applied its requisitioning powers to trucks leaving the Delmarva Peninsula. The system was possible because the number of roads leaving the territory was limited. The army stationed agents on these roads, stopped the trucks, examined the manifest, and if the driver could not produce a manifest, or if it appeared that the poultry had been bought above the ceiling prices, army agents simply requisitioned the poultry at the ceiling price, so that the shipper lost his load plus the amount he had paid above the ceiling. This practice was criticized as high-handed. Maybe it was. I have some doubts about it now, but it was effective in controlling the poultry black market in the Delmarva Peninsula. Later the poultry situation improved as the supply increased. The poultry supply is much more flexible than the supply of cattle, hogs, or lamb, as poultry reproduce and grow at a faster rate. We kept poultry, in contrast to red meat, under reasonably effective control.

It is interesting to note that Britain did not have this black market problem in meat as we did. Meat was one of their worst headaches, but it never approached the American predicament. The British imported a large portion of their meat, and the government had control of it from the beginning and was able to make direct allocations. Domestic meat was under strict slaughtering control, so that it was a violation for farmers to kill for their own use or that of their friends or perhaps their city relatives. An individual could purchase meat only from one butcher. Britain experienced nothing like the widespread violation and disorganization of the industry that occurred in this country, because they had price controls capable of being enforced.

## MAJOR HEADACHE II: GASOLINE

The other major headache of OPA enforcement was the gasoline black market. Here, again, there was a basically unfavorable public background. Many people originally doubted the need for gasoline rationing and doubt persisted in many quarters. As late as 1944, 49 percent of gasoline dealers and retail station operators indicated in a poll that they did not think rationing was necessary. A large part of the public remained unconvinced for a long time.

Like meat, gasoline regulation elicited strong feelings and markedly affected public morale. The subject of much newspaper comment, it was constantly in the public eye. The pleasure-driving ban in 1943, failing as we had been sure it would from the beginning, had tended to discredit the enforcement program. The public did not support enforcement, at least to the extent of reporting violations or in many cases to the extent of refraining from buying gasoline without coupons or at inflated prices. Against this background, the pressures on the supply became severe. Shortages had occurred on the East Coast all along; they gradually extended throughout the country. Whereas the average automobile chalked up 11,000 miles a year before the war, in 1944 enough gasoline was available for only 4300 miles. That required a substantial reduction in the driving habits of the public.

Violations were extensive almost from the beginning. The punchcard system was too loose to enforce satisfactorily. In 1943 and 1944 an extensive black market developed. Our estimates, perhaps wildly in error, were that 25 percent of the gasoline was being sold without coupons at prices above the ceiling. However, unlike meat, we finally obtained a substantial degree of control over the gasoline black market.

### Coupons

OPA and the Petroleum Administrative Board (PAB) were able to control gasoline supplies from the refinery to the wholesale distributing station. The number of wholesale distributing stations was sufficiently limited so that the supply could be controlled rather accurately to that point. Beyond that point were thousands and thousands of gasoline stations, industrial users, farmers, and others. The problem expanded dramatically. However, since we could control the wholesale point to see that supplies were not given without coupons, the thousands of distributors could not replenish their supplly for retail distribution unless they had coupons.

This meant that dealers who violated by selling without coupons had to obtain a supply of coupons somehow. As 1943 wore on and the system became more firmly established, the supply of coupons was obtained from counterfeiting, from theft of coupons from ration board supplies, and in some instances from excessive issuance of coupons by the War Price and Rationing Boards (due to mistakes, laxity, or corruption), old coupons which had expired, and so on. The business of supplying coupons to the gasoline dealers who wished to replenish their supplies became a monopoly of the underworld; underworld characters engaged extensively in counterfeiting, theft, and obtaining extra supplies from certain other sources. The gasoline dealers and to some extent the wholesale plants cooperated with the gangsters by serving as their market and buying the coupons from them. Illicit coupons rarely were sold directly to the consumer. The costs of distribution were too high to make that worthwhile. The illegal coupons were sold at 8 to 15 cents a gallon. A dealer might purchase a hundred or a thousand coupons to make up his supply. Gangsters did not find it worthwhile to peddle them in lesser amounts than that. A normal individual would not require enough gasoline that a gang would find it profitable to sell to him.

A dealer, in order to recoup the amount he had paid for the coupons, would have to charge above the ceiling price. Some upgrading (sale of regular gasoline as premium) occurred. Not only dealers but suppliers at the bulk plants engaged in upgrading as well as purchase of coupons and assistance to dealers by telling them where they could buy coupons.

Coupons for 31–37 million gallons were stolen in the single month of June 1943, mostly from local rationing boards. Bowles, testifying in the spring of 1944 before the House Appropriations Committee, gave the cumulative figures as 650 thefts, involving coupons for 300 million gallons. These thefts included breaking into ration boards and stealing their supplies, stealing from banks, stealing from centers where the extra coupons were stored, and sometimes stealing sheets on which the coupons had been pasted. In the last case, the thieves had to remove the coupons from the sheets. Originally, they steamed them off (we called those "steam-offs"), but that process left the coupons looking thin and bedraggled so they could be spotted fairly easily. Later, they froze the coupons off, using a quick freeze process that popped the coupons off (we called those "pop-offs"). Pop-offs were harder to detect, but with a special magnifying glass and light we could see some deterioration in the quality of the paper from the quick freeze.

Public disapproval of gasoline regulation affected the morale of local rationing boards and made them more willing to listen to hard-luck stories and distribute extra rations. On the other hand, most board members, understanding the situation much better than the general public, were so deeply convinced of the significance of their jobs that they got their backs up and tried to turn in a good performance. On the whole, I think they did. On rare occasions a board member would tip off an outside gang as to where the coupons were or when a large supply would be arriving. On the whole, the boards were more careless than anything else. At the beginning, hundreds of thousands of coupons were left around the corridors of federal court buildings or piled up somewhere behind a lock that could have been picked with a hairpin. The local boards failed to comprehend at the beginning how valuable the coupons were. But we rarely had to contend with actual corruption.

The counterfeiting of coupons became so profitable that the counterfeiting of money decreased during this period. If you had a coupon for four gallons of gasoline and you could sell it for 15 cents a gallon,

239

every coupon was worth 60 cents. You could carry around in your coat pocket a hundred thousand dollars worth of coupons. You could dispose of them to a fairly ready market, fairly easily. They were disposed of in the same way as dope, passed down the line to the peddlers, who would peddle them to the gas stations, obtaining their supplies from a middleman who in turn obtained his supplies from the top gang, each receiving a cut. Coupons were much easier to dispose of than was counterfeit money, easier to duplicate, and therefore more profitable.

At times rationing boards distributed substantially more coupons than the recipients could use and these extra coupons found their way to the black market. In some cases, the local boards were lax. Most of the surplus, however, came from issuance of coupons to trucks. This function, out of OPA control, was handled by the Office of Defense Transportation, which in our opinion did not have the rigorous kind of administration that we did, and passed out, at times, serious over-issuances of coupons to truckers—which also entered the black market.

### Enforcement

We consistently devoted a large portion of our manpower to gasoline regulation. In the East, about 37 percent of our investigators and attorneys spent most of their time on gasoline; in other parts of the country we allocated about 25 percent. As the gasoline black market was the one most in the public eye, regional and district directors pressed us to assign an even larger number of investigators to gasoline. At the top we perused reports from the field offices and concentrated on holding down the percentage of manpower allocated to gasoline. The head of the Fuel and Consumers Goods Division of Enforcement Department was Shad Polier, an aggressive, able lawyer, who devised what turned out to be an exceedingly effective program that in large part dissolved the gasoline black market.

Part of the program was the application of the normal sanctions to the black market operations. Up to January 1, 1945, a total of 15,095 sanctions were applied. Of these, 11,294 were suspension orders, 234 injunction suits, and about 3500 criminal cases. In the first five months of 1944, OPA arrested over 1300 peddlers of black market coupons. Furthermore, the sentences we were able to obtain in these cases were on the whole more adequate than in any other area. We also applied the other sanctions, the most effective being the suspension order. The injunction was not particularly applicable to gangster operations, as the gangster's reputation was not threatened by it; he already had made a decision to break the law and already was under threat of going to jail. Treble damage suits were not useful because most violations were at the retail level and involved sales without coupons, so the more effective suspension order could be used instead. Treble damage suits could have been brought against gasoline stations, but it was difficult to prove enough violations to make it worthwhile.

In addition to the normal application of these sanctions, the enforcement program in the latter part of 1943 and in 1944 involved other measures. First of all, we created a group of special agents in July 1944, to handle investigation of the gangster element in the gasoline black market. This unit was set up with the assistance of the Secret Service, trained by them, and supervised in part by one of their men loaned to OPA. It operated under control of the Washington office, as the gangsters operated a nationwide network.

These agents carried on their activities in the traditional undercover agent style. They were specially trained and had permits to carry pistols. In one case they got word from some underworld source that members of the Purple Gang of Detroit were bringing counterfeit coupons to Boston. Our agents met the gang members at the train, but these two individuals did not appear different from anybody else and there were insufficient grounds for arrest. The OPA investigators followed them to a restaurant. The two fellows insisted on sitting on their coats. On the basis of this evidence, the OPA agents made the arrest. They discovered 26,000 counterfeit coupons in the coat-linings. The gang members were intending to go to a prize fight and exchange coats with identical coats of the people who were to pick up the coupons. That kind of detective work was required in these situations.

In another case our agents arrested a gang in New York with plans to print 5 million coupons, worth $3.5 million. The agents had been tipped off and made the arrest just as the printing machines were about to roll.

Our agents had the various types of counterfeits coded, so that they could trace them down to the different sources in the different cities. On the whole, they were reasonably effective, insofar as this kind of operation could be effective in the detection and prosecution of counterfeiters. This approach by itself would not have been sufficient. OPA could have gone on forever, discovering counterfeiters or picking up peddlers of counterfeit coupons without making too much impression on the situation, but it was a necessary angle.

Another aspect of the gasoline problem was the protection of ration coupons. Originally coupons were left around under completely inadequate protection and large amounts were stored by ration boards. This system was completely revised. A system of guarding the coupons from the very beginning was undertaken. Earlier, a special paper easily recognizable under infra-red light was developed and used. All this paper was manufactured at one plant in Fitchburg, Massachusetts. Beginning at that plant, the coupons were thereafter continuously guarded, right down to the issuance by the ration boards. In fact, in one case we were able to prevent a good deal of counterfeiting by recovering a huge roll of this special paper stolen from the Fitchburg plant. The paper was loaded on a truck, covered with a pile of junk, and driven out of the plant. The truck driver hid the paper under his woodpile at home, ready for pickup by a gang of counterfeiters. The OPA agents discovered the paper at the house of this fellow and were able to recover it, thus preventing millions of coupons from reaching the black market.

The protection of ration currency involved also the printing establishments. Most printing was done in the government printing office, but some was contracted out to private establishments. It was necessary to assure that both the paper and ration coupons as printed were protected against possible theft in the printing plant. This involved a system of plant protection that was not different from other systems of a similar nature.

One of the most important aspects was the protection of ration coupons in the course of distribution from the printing plants to the local board and the ultimate consumers. Originally, coupons had simply been shipped back and forth across the country, stacked in almost any place of storage, and subject to rather easy theft. The OPA enforcement staff worked out much more careful regulations providing for the establishment of distribution points to which the ration coupons were originally sent. These distribution points were kept under careful guard and protected by other usual methods. Coupons were then shipped from the distribution center to the local boards on order of the local board, and stored and distributed by the local board. Protection was necessary at every point along this route.

In addition, we needed to work out methods by which the local board did not have on hand a larger supply than was necessary for the minimum period of time. Originally, the boards had ordered and received huge quantities of coupons, enough to last them for months. This stock of coupons would be stored by the local board and in many cases was an easy prey for thieves. Since the protection afforded coupons at the local board was necessarily less than that available at the distribution centers, where the material could be fairly well protected, regulations were issued requiring that the local boards could not order or have on hand more coupons than would last for, say, two weeks. The effect of these regulations was to cut down the amount of ration coupons available at the boards and also thereby cut down substantially the amounts that were stolen.

Other provisions tightened up the whole gasoline rationing system. One important revision was the printing of ration coupons in rolls, rather than in the form of books, and adding serial numbers to each coupon. By a system of record keeping indicating to which board certain numbers were sent and to which individuals certain numbers were allocated, coupons could be traced.

In addition to this, we required that the vehicle license number of the motorist be written on the back of the coupon at the time that he submitted it for gasoline. This had the effect of establishing proof that a particular individual had used a particular coupon. A person was less likely to use coupons not his own knowing there would be written evidence by which the coupon could be traced.

As a result of these two changes, the gasoline dealer could choose to protect himself against accepting counterfeit or stolen coupons if he wanted to. The serial numbers issued to any individual were recorded on the outside of his coupon books. By comparing the serial number of the coupon given him with the serial numbers recorded on the outside of the book and checking to see that the license number of the individual using the coupon was recorded on the back of the coupon, gasoline dealers could be fairly certain that they were not accepting invalid coupons.

Perhaps the most important measure against the gasoline black market, a device synthesizing some of the other provisions, was the establishment of the Regional Verification Centers and the debiting system in the second part of 1944.

The Regional Verification Centers examined all ration coupons used by consumers and submitted by dealers seeking additional supplies of gasoline. An elaborate system determined how many and which coupons were counterfeit and which were stolen. Ultraviolet light revealed most brands of counterfeits. The special paper used by the government appeared a particular color under infrared light, and by using a machine that circulated the coupons under an infrared light a worker could spot which ones did not have the true color and were counterfeits. The special paper included a chemical that responded to some sort of chemical test. The chemical and the formula for making the test were both secret, known only to the Government Printing Office and the company that prepared the paper. By using these chemicals it was possible to run coupons through a process that would show quickly which were counterfeit. Other methods determined which coupons had been steamed or frozen off the "bingo" sheets. Delicate scales weighed the coupons in a particular envelope to determine whether approximately the proper number were there. Workers checked the accuracy of the statements by the dealers as to how many coupons they had turned in.

This checking process was merely the first step. It showed how many invalid coupons were being used and the extent to which dealers were misrepresenting the number of coupons they were turning in to their ration "banking" accounts. That, by itself, would merely have been an informational process, important for indicating the trend, but not solving anything. The aspect of this procedure that had the greatest impact on the black market was the debiting process.

Under the debiting process, any invalid or short-weight of coupons was debited against the dealer who had turned them in by notifying the bank and debiting his ration banking account. If we found a thousand counterfeit coupons among those submitted by a particular gasoline station operator, his account at the ration bank would have a thousand coupons deducted. This would mean that he could not replace his supplies of gasoline to the amount represented by those thousand coupons. If he continued to accept counterfeits or stolen coupons, he gradually would be driven out of business because he could not replenish his supply. Thus, we had devised a method of almost automatic enforcement against the gasoline dealers.

We encountered considerable opposition to the debiting of accounts. The industry howled strenuously. Even some of the OPA staff outside our Enforcement Department protested. The Enforcement Department insisted from the outset that it was essential. Enforcement contended that the procedure was fair because gasoline station operators would know whether or not they were accepting invalid coupons. Furthermore, Enforcement pointed out that the black market in gasoline was almost entirely the result of the sale of the invalid coupons to the gasoline station operators, sometimes to the wholesale distributors, who passed them on to the gasoline stations, but almost never was there a sale to individual motorists.

After some argument, the system was accepted and rather strict debiting was implemented. A certain amount of leakage from the tank occurred. Once in a while a dealer might accept a few invalid coupons without being able to detect them. So we thought it unfair to impose a completely rigid system, as by declaring: "You're entitled to so many gallons. You must turn in coupons in order to replenish your supplies. Under no circumstances will you be given additional supplies without valid coupons." We permitted a certain leeway to "bail out" gasoline dealers from time to time. The Rationing Division allowed a certain percentage for leakage and granted bailouts under certain circumstances. That meant that the system had some degree of laxity, but the net result of the Regional Verification Centers and the debiting system was to tighten up enormously the whole flow of supplies and to keep it substantially within the framework of the rationing system.

The actual operation of the debiting proved successful. In November – December 1944 the Regional Verification Centers retrieved 3.3 million counterfeit or otherwise illegal gasoline coupons. As the system took effect, the number of invalid coupons dropped rapidly. By February 1945, only 333,000 illegal coupons were detected. By July of that year, the number had decreased to 78,000. Within six months after the system was established, the volume of illegal coupons had dropped to the point where they were no longer of any great significance. In other words, the system was a raving success. It proved, incidentally, that the Enforcement Department had been correct about the dealers' being aware that they were turning in invalid coupons.

### Public Relations

Another important aspect of gasoline rationing enforcement was industry relations and public relations. The Enforcement Department, largely through Shad Polier, head of the Fuel and Consumer Goods Division, persuaded the Petroleum Industry War Council to cooperate with OPA in its efforts to eliminate the gasoline black market. The Petroleum Industry War Council was an association of oil companies organized to contribute to the war effort. We were able to work out a program with this council that had a considerable effect on the whole picture. The council set up in each district a committee whose function it was to educate the distributors and dealers in the rationale and procedures of gasoline rationing. These district committees carried on an ambitious program of information and education. To some extent also, although this was entirely informal, they conducted a program of pressure. As the members of the council in each district were the main leaders of the industry in that district, they could exert considerable economic pressure on the dealer, and to some extent on the wholesaler at the bulk plants, to conform to the regulations. How much of that activity went on is not entirely clear, but there were indications that at times the council's efforts at persuasion became powerful enough to amount to economic coercion.

The petroleum industry had not started out to cooperate with us. The secret of their cooperation was that they were persuaded, in part by what we divulged to them, that there was a risk that the entire gasoline distribution system would fall into the hands of gangsters and would be run by gangsters when the war was over. We pointed out the extent to which their dealers were becoming part of an underworld system and the dangers that would represent for the industry, not only in wartime but in peacetime. Persuaded that the situation was getting out of hand, they were motivated to cooperate.

The oil companies also mounted a prodigious $0.5 million advertising campaign explaining OPA regulations and attacking the black market, pointing out its implications to the economy and the war effort. Of course they could deduct these advertising costs from their income taxes, but nevertheless, the campaign indicated that they were seriously interested in cooperating with OPA. This does not mean that they cooperated at every point. They constantly opposed us in terms of price regulations and the whole system of distribution. They insisted on following the pre-war patterns of distribution. In other words, we had not converted the petroleum industry to pursuing public interest above profit–it was simply that they feared a rival power springing up in the industry.

We ourselves conducted a public relations campaign against the gasoline black market. We polled public opinion to assess what information the public knew and how they reacted to various aspects of the program. On the basis of polls we fashioned a systematic educational and informational campaign. We also consistently issued press releases about enforcement measures. Some of these were stories about how we had broken up a counterfeit gang or brought proceedings against particular individuals. Others were stories showing the number of cases that had been brought in the first three months of the year, or in the last six months, or a relevant period of time.

How much the industry cooperation and the public relations programs affected the outcome is difficult to assess, but certainly they must have had some effect. As a result of all these measures, OPA was reasonably successful in bringing the gasoline black market under control. By the end of 1944/beginning of 1945, the problem had been substantially licked. Our figures show–and in this case they must have been reasonably accurate–that by the end of 1944 the black market in gasoline had declined very substantially, and the problem was under control. However, many people never relinquished the impression they held from the first part of 1944 that there were widespread violations of gasoline rationing.

It is illuminating to compare our success with gasoline and our failure with meat control. Success in gasoline was due only in part to the application of conventional legal sanctions against immediate violators. We used all the sanctions that were available to the extent of our manpower, but that was not the turning point in the campaign against the gasoline black market. The turning point came when we took measures to dry up the source of illegal coupons. The establishment of the special agents, the various measures used to prevent counterfeiting, and the coupon protection devices were important aspects of this. However, the most important were the Regional Verification Centers and the debiting process, which finally tipped the scale. Success was attributable to an administrative system that operated almost automatically, one that could be managed by careful monitoring at the bulk plants and control of the dealers through the debiting program. In other words, administrative machinery of a preventive rather than a punitive nature enabled us to maintain a reasonable amount of control over the gasoline black market.

Our administrative success occurred in the context of relatively favorable public support. Most of the people we targeted under our enforcement program were not respectable businessmen engaged in white collar crime, but regular gangsters. No one openly supported the black market. Congressmen were no exceptions to that: if they took a public position, it was to denounce the black market. Rather, the attack was mounted indirectly. People would attack OPA investigation policies, charging that OPA investigators were snoopers. Congress would refuse to appropriate sufficient sums to carry out the program. People openly objected to the debiting process, but that operation was so rapidly successful that there was not much time for congressional repercussion.

Few people appreciated the complexities and the difficulties we had. Our polls indicated the public did not grasp the operation and ramifications of the gasoline black market. Congress, a surprising segment of the Roosevelt administration, and even other OPA departments were not appreciative of our difficulties. Our problem became fairly technical toward the end and was solved by technical devices. Although we did our best to disseminate information, our priorities naturally tended to be direct enforcement measures.

I do not recall any pressures from the administration with respect to the political implications of the black market, one way or another. The White House was concerned with the black market as tending, among other things, to discredit the whole war program, and to break down adherence to other wartime regulations. I would say, insofar as there was any pressure from the administration, it was pressure in support of our efforts and expressions of concern at the extent of violation. I recall nothing in the way of pressure to hold off or to go easy on the grounds that it would antagonize people and have adverse political repercussions. That came later on the meat issue under the Truman administration. At this time, however, the administration's attitude was one of support.

I suppose we had as full support in our efforts on the gasoline black market as we had on any phase of OPA enforcement, probably more. The amount of the industry cooperation, for instance, was unusual. We were unable to solicit that degree of cooperation in almost any other area. So we did have the most favorable conditions in terms of support for gasoline control.

## PRICE PROBLEMS IN VARIOUS FIELDS

In enforcing President Roosevelt's "Hold the Line" policy, OPA's Enforcement Department had to work out separate techniques for the different sectors of the economy. There were some common problems, but by and large the problems differed, and we needed to have an appropriate program to meet each particular difficulty.

### Lumber and Scrap

One of our troublesome areas illustrating this diversity was the lumber industry. Widespread violations occurred at times in many parts of the lumber industry. The worst offenders were the southern pine producers, who at one time came close to 100 percent violation. Some violations were straight overcharges with payments of cash on the side, but the major form of violation was up-grading. For example, lumber that was largely or entirely No. 2 grade would be shipped as No. 1 grade. Statistics would reveal that enormous quantities of No.1 grade had been sold, a much higher percentage than had ever been produced before. Those figures were explicable only by postulating up-grading. However, to prove up-grading in a particular case was impractical. Once the shipment had been stockpiled or used, there was no way of telling whether or not it had been No. 1 or No. 2 grade. The books and records would show a shipment of No. 1 grade lumber at ceiling prices. Violation was also hard to prove because an expert was needed to determine the grade and it was not easy to find an investigator who had the qualifications to assess the grade of lumber. Our technique in the lumber industry tended to center around these two issues.

To solve the grading problem, we trained investigators in methods of grading lumber and also used graders supplied by the trade association in the lumber industry. The trade association was willing to make available inspectors on their staff who were acquainted with the industry and who would be able to distinguish the two grades. To keep track of particular shipments we had to coordinate the activities of our enforcement staff in the place of shipment with our enforcement staff at the place of marketing. The enforcement investigators in the lumber-producing areas would inspect a carload of lumber about to be shipped out, obtain the number of the car and the particulars about the invoice, and telegraph that information ahead to the point at which the car was to be received and used. That was about the only way to prevent the invoice for that car from being rewritten in the course of passage from No. 2 grade to No.1 grade. By these devices we were able to maintain some control over the lumber industry. The situation was not so far beyond the realm of solution, as was the meat debacle. The degree of compliance tended to correlate directly with the number of staff we could devote to the lumber industry. We did not have sufficient investigators or attorneys to bring the situation under complete control, but we improved compliance and prevented a complete collapse of controls.

The main sanctions we invoked were the injunction and to some extent the treble-damage suit. We had particularly bad luck with the Department of Justice on criminal cases involving the southern pine industry. The industry dominated those areas of the country where it operated sufficiently so that the U.S. attorneys had difficulty securing grand jury indictments, convictions, and sentences in the rare cases where they did obtain convictions. That obstacle prevented us from using the criminal sanction to the extent we would have liked. The treble-damage suit was the most effective and the injunction the quickest and easiest to use.

The situation in the scrap industry was similar to lumber. Periods of extensive violation occurred as shortages of scrap increased. Violations consisted primarily of up-grading. As fewer ultimate outlets for scrap existed than for lumber, the solution was a little easier. Steel scrap was used primarily by the large steel mills; by concentrating on the shipments to those mills, we could keep the situation more or less under control. If the mills paid legal prices, that tended to reinforce legal prices back down along the line to the wholesale dealers and the retailers. Controlling the price paid by small junk dealers would have been impossible. Since the steel companies as major buyers created a bottleneck, we could eliminate the competitive bidding-up process by posting enough investigators at enough plants. Again our success was related to the amount of manpower available. Usually the level of control proceeded in cycles, because we could not afford to put much manpower on the scrap industry; whenever we relaxed, violations would increase and we would have to commit more staff and toughen up again.

The lumber and scrap situations were difficult because we had to bring several different offices into close cooperation. Organizational red tape tended to create obstructions. There were always problems between Washington and regional offices, between Washington and district offices, between regional and district offices, and so on. The serious difficulties arose when you had to have two different offices in two different areas attempt to pull together in a very precise way. Then you got into trouble.

## Clothing

Another important area in which we experienced unique challenges was the clothing industry. Clothing was a major item in the budget of the consumer. In addition, clothing was necessary for the army, workers in defense plants, and other workers who wore uniforms or special outfits on the job. Extensive violations occurred from the very beginning and continued throughout the entire war period in the clothing industry.

Some violations were straight overcharges with cash on the side, but most violations took the form of evasion of the regulations. In fact, the dividing line between violation of the regulations and an action that was not strictly a violation but that nevertheless increased the price of clothing was at times hard to draw. Whenever clothing changed in style or the kind of fabric used, a new commodity was being produced under OPA regulations and therefore determining the price ceiling became more complicated than if the companies had continued producing the old styles and types of product.

The most serious form of evasion was the highest-price-line strategy. The clothing manufacturers would concentrate on making products in their highest-priced lines, from which they derived a higher profit. The result was that low-cost items disappeared from the market. For all practical purposes, clothing prices escalated. To some extent the same thing was happening in the sources of supply of the clothing industry. Textile mills also made a higher margin of profit on their higher-priced lines. Consequently, in response to price controls they shifted production to the higher-priced lines. The result was that garment manufacturers could not obtain fabrics from the mills for their lower-priced lines. Supply problems thus tended to force the clothing industry to move into the highest priced lines.

Other violations arose from the complexities of the price formula. Originally, clothing prices were frozen under the General Maximum Price Regulation, but we soon realized that this was not feasible because of frequent product modifications, so the General Maximum Price Regulation was replaced by various types of formula regulations. These tended to be complicated, and there was abundant opportunity for manipulation in the application of the formula, in terms of deciding which factors should be included in the cost, calculating depreciation, selecting the nearest comparable product, and other matters. Some of this was in violation and some not, but again the effect was an increase of prices.

Enforcement in the clothing industry focused on tightening the regulations. The enforcement staff that dealt with clothing spent a substantial portion of their time making suggestions and arguing with the Price Department about revisions of the regulations that would make enforcement possible. We pointed out that the General Maximum Price Regulation was totally unenforceable in the clothing industry. We were instrumental in drafting special regulations applicable to the various parts of the industry. However, as these special regulations were a formula type, they tended to be difficult to enforce, particularly as most of the formulas were complicated. We persuaded the Price Department to simplify the formulas, to write rules that would take into account a minimum number of factors, and factors which could be established readily by legal proof. Where that was done, it helped. The enforcement task then became first of all a matter of enforcing the record-keeping requirements, since everything depended on records of costs. One simply could not calculate the price ceiling unless companies maintained adequate records for the various costs that went into their products. Hence OPA's first endeavors were to see that the companies complied with the record-keeping provisions. We mainly used the injunction for this purpose.

Enforcement of the record-keeping provisions alone enhanced compliance because the companies became more aware of their own price setting practices and because violations, now involving an open type of misrepresentation, became more hazardous. Following up the record-keeping measures, we moved mainly into the treble-damage area. We initiated some criminal suits, but the complexity of the regulations made criminal prosecution dubious. The treble-damage cases, however, seemed to be quite influential. A number of important ones were brought in the clothing industry, some against major manufacturers. We filed one that was the subject of particular controversy against Munsingwear, for instance. Word of these suits quickly spread around the industry, and this seemed to have a genuine deterrent effect.

In addition, we encouraged the Price Department to establish dollars-and-cents regulations whenever possible. This was feasible only in those areas where it was possible to specify standards to which the garment had to conform, such as the work clothing industry, where there was practically no question of style, and where we could require standardized production. It was also feasible in the hosiery industry, where standardization was much more possible. Where dollars-and-cents prices were in effect, the number of violations automatically dwindled.

The Price Department gradually worked out other techniques, such as pre-ticketing. They would require manufacturers to attach a label or ticket to the garment indicating the retail price. This was useful in checking the manufacturers' compliance, but even more valuable in ensuring that the garment reached the ultimate consumer at a reasonable price. Pre-ticketing curtailed arrangements whereby garments would be sold back and forth among a series of wholesalers, each taking a mark-up. The establishment of price charts also helped enforcement in clothing. These devices, like dollars-and-cents prices, tended to be almost automatically enforceable, and made the job of the enforcement staff much easier.

The most persistent problem was the highest-price-line strategy. OPA faced opposition from a number of sources in attempting to resolve this issue. The industry's opposition was reflected in substantial congressional opposition to OPA's highest-price-line provisions. We quickly realized that the problem could be solved only by vigorous action by the War Production Board (WPB). OPA's authority to standardize products was limited by the statute, and became more limited as Congress passed amendments prohibiting the highest-price-line provision and other provisions. However OPA's powers, even if fully confirmed by Congress, would not have been sufficient, because OPA had no authority to control production at the textile mills, the source of the difficulty. The solution required an elaborate WPB program, fixing the kinds of cloth the textile manufacturers could produce in various quantities and various percentages, allocating them to the various manufacturers who needed the low-cost cloth, requiring the manufacturers to make them into certain standard products, or at least comply with some degree of standardization, and, in other words, setting the stage for a structure to which the OPA could apply a price scale. This was the only way in which a successful program of price control would have been possible throughout the clothing industry. Even then it would not have been possible in some areas, but at least in the major areas this could have been done. The WPB was unwilling to do this. Reflecting mainly the industry point of view, the WPB would not undertake the far-reaching controls that were indicated.

This dispute between two agencies in the stabilization field was brought to the OES, the coordinating agency. It actually came before me when I had transferred to the OES (see Chapter 14). Prior to my arrival, however, the OES under Fred Vinson, largely at the instigation of Edward Prichard, had issued a general order requiring the WPB to establish a system of controls of the nature I have indicated. It was one of those situations where a super agency issues a paper directive and the operating agency to whom it is directed fends it off by raising questions and delaying action. So, although some progress was made, no full-scale assault on the problem ensued with the use of WPB powers. As a result, we recognized that the regulations were inadequate, but we could not do much about it in certain areas. Consequently, we confined our activity largely to those areas where the regulations were most enforceable, as in work clothing, where dollars-and-cents regulations existed, and in those sectors where simplified formula regulations existed. We never were able to bring a large part of the clothing industry under control.

### Consumer Durables

Other areas of the manufacturing field also proved troublesome. In regard to canned foods, for instance, we encountered great difficulty in grading. The determination of price depended on the grade. OPA originally attacked this problem by drawing up standards for grading and making them enforceable through a system of grade labelling. Then Congress prohibited grade labelling and actually restricted the degree to which OPA could apply standards; we could only apply standards that had previously existed in the industry. The pricing of canned foods remained partial and difficult to enforce. The canners had an active lobby in Washington and a number of vocal congressmen used to sound off about the terrible plight of the canning industry. The congressional controversy also involved the agricultural bloc. Thus, we contended with political difficulties in the processed food field.

The other major area of manufacturing was consumer durable goods. Here the problem was that many restrictions had been imposed on the production of automobiles and other consumer durables, so the main issue was control of secondhand sales rather than original sales. Few original sales took place. Control of second-hand sales was unwieldy as the products resisted standardization, each item having developed idiosyncracies while in the hands of its previous owner or owners. Enforcement of the used car ceilings was a backbreaker. No regular channels of business were involved. We could establish ceilings over which no car, no matter what its condition, could be sold, but how could we stop consumers from paying on the side? Most violations took place at the retail level. We required much more manpower, much tighter controls, and a much greater degree of administrative control of some sort. Something might have been done through a licensing system, a useful way to control car problems, but no action was taken. We had neither the time nor the manpower; used car sales were not sufficiently important to divert the necessary resources.

The remainder of consumer durables quickly escaped the confines of the General Maximum Price Regulation. Companies marketed many new models. Shortages requiring substitution of another material, plus WPB orders reducing (but not eliminating) the use of scarce materials in various types of consumer durables exacerbated the normal practice of frequently introducing new models. The constant change of the product meant that various formula-types of regulations had to be worked out. On the whole, however, control of consumer durables was passable. While we could deploy little manpower, favorable factors, such as the fact that in some areas there were relatively few producers, buttressed our efforts.

## Rationing in the United States Versus in Britain

It is interesting to compare enforcement problems in these fields I have mentioned in the United States with what happened in Britain. Britain, fighting for national survival, had few of the problems that we did. In the food field, for instance, much tighter controls existed in Britain. A large percentage of their food was imported, which brought it into the government's hands from the beginning. The rest was subject to direct, far-reaching, stringent controls. Gasoline was hardly a problem because no gasoline was available except for what amounted to official business. The scarce supply was distributed under strict controls; the British did not have to combat pleasure driving or any general driving at all. In clothing, the utility clothing program under which a large percentage of clothing was produced, provided a high degree of standardization. Specifications were defined, prices were fixed, and there was little opportunity for violations. The government ignored the remainder of the clothing industry, the luxury items. In consumer durables, here also there was a high degree of standardization. Many consumer durable products, even dishes and china, could be made only in accordance with certain fixed specifications. Where that was true, the price could be readily fixed and pre-ticketed, so enforcement was simple. By virtue of a much more far-reaching set of controls–made necessary by the British position in the war–their enforcement problem was much less serious. Possibly the British people were also more disposed to comply with the law. At any event, there was considerably less violation, and considerably more success, in Britain with enforcement of wartime economic distribution.

## Wholesale

In the wholesale field prices continued to be fixed by the General Maximum Price Regulation in most instances throughout the war. Those prices tended to become out-of-date fairly rapidly, however, because manufacturing products were constantly changing. Not only were new items produced, but as the manufacturing prices increased, wholesalers tended to be squeezed. It was not a satisfactory arrangement. We needed to write wholesale regulations covering particular products.

Formulating regulations in this field involved answering questions such as "What is a wholesaler?" and "What function does a wholesaler perform?" No one came up with satisfactory answers. From a strictly economic point of view, the functions performed by wholesalers often appeared to be of little value. If OPA attempted to formulate the definition of wholesaler by his economic function, we would invalidate middlemen whose existence was accepted practice in various industries, even though they did not appear to perform a significant economic function. On the other hand, if we defined wholesaler in any other way, we condoned practices by which a long string of wholesalers simply took mark-ups on the products as they passed them along. Once we discarded the General Maximum Price Regulation and introduced individualized formulas, the formula had to be framed in terms of the mark-up. The wholesaler was allowed a certain margin over what he paid for the goods from the manufacturer in setting his price to the retailer. It would, on the face of it, be legitimate for any number of wholesalers to take a mark-up before the product finally reached the retailer. Preventing price increases by multiple sales before the product reached the consumer taxed our ingenuity.

The Price Department never made much progress in formulating sound wholesale regulations. Our inability to enforce the existing regulations discouraged us from operating in the wholesale field. Only a small amount of staff were assigned to wholesale. In the allocation of manpower, manufacturing and wholesale were considered together; retailing was separate. So, if we allocated 40 percent of our manpower to food enforcement, most would go to food manufacturing. The same group was supposed to handle wholesaling, but in practice we de-emphasized that. Not that wholesale controls completely disintegrated; it was similar to the consumer durables situation in that we did not have the time and staff available to work out a comprehensive program that would have kept wholesale prices under fairly tight control. Had the attempt been made, we might have encountered opposition.

### Retail

Retail enforcement was quite different from enforcement of regulations at the manufacturing and wholesale levels. An enormous number of retail outlets engaged in a staggering number of retail transactions. Furthermore, OPA received many more complaints about violations at the retail level than at the other levels. Pressure from approximately 140 million consumers bombarding our field offices could not be ignored. On the other hand, allocating our entire staff to handling the complaints rather than the affirmative enforcement programs would have resulted in chaos. In response to figures disclosing that a high proportion of our manpower currently was being assigned to the retail field, the Washington enforcement staff would exert as much pressure as they could on the field offices to channel the manpower in other directions.

Another difficulty in the retail field was that each transaction was so minute in terms of the overall enforcement problem. The purchase of a can of tomatoes was a trifle in most people's budget, and the over-ceiling price probably would not exceed two or three cents per can. However, the law was framed in terms of individual transactions. Consequently, it was hard to enforce a law based on assumptions that seemed to conflict with common sense. Retail regulations framed in terms of pricing policies or profit levels might have helped.

## ENFORCEMENT OF RENT CONTROL

One of our four divisions was devoted to price control of services and rent control. Services included barber shops, beauty parlors, laundries, repair shops, and other retail outlets where the product was a service rather than a tangible object. The service area, with its extensive and exasperating problems, was the orphan of OPA's Enforcement Department. It was in this area that we probably attempted the least. Services were not as crucial to economic stabilization as most other areas, yet they were too important to be as neglected as they were. As many small outlets, but few large operations, were involved, the staff that could be allocated to services could not accomplish much.

In contrast, we placed notable emphasis on rent control. Next to food, rent was the largest single item in the consumer's budget. If food be considered as a series of separate purchases, rent was by far the most important single item in the consumer's budget, representing anywhere from a normal expenditure of about 20 percent of the person's income, up to as high as 50 percent. Rent was also significant because it was relatively inflexible. A person could postpone buying a new suit of clothes, a new car, or a new washing machine until after the war, but he could not postpone finding a place to live.

Rent control was a gigantic test because of the enormous number of units involved. The final maximum figure of the dwelling units subject to rent regulation was 15.6 million. Of these, somewhat under 500,000 were hotels and rooming-houses, which presented a special problem. Those remaining 15 million units meant that the percentage of the 3,200 investigators that could be allocated to rent control would not cover much ground. We had some 500 or so area rent offices and never more than several hundred investigators available to handle the entire rent field. This area was comparable to the retail field, and had to be handled similarly.

One factor favoring enforcement was that the rent was clearly fixed in practically all cases. There was no dispute or doubt, as there was in most other areas, about what the ceiling price of the rent should be. Some efforts were made to get it changed, but by and large landlords, tenants, OPA, and the public could know precisely what the rent was. That was a tremendous starting advantage. Registering all dwelling units with OPA and the practice of sending the tenant a copy of the registration, which enabled the tenant to know what legitimate rent amounted to, was a tremendous help. It meant that the most interested person, the tenant, knew the rent ceiling and was in a position to object if he were overcharged. Many tenants, disposed to regard their landlord suspiciously, were primed for battle about overcharges. Others, because of the scarcity of rental accommodations, desired to retain cordial relations with their landlord. Unwilling to join battle, they tended to conceal violations rather than report them. Even so, consumers offered more support here than in almost any other program. Not only were they in a frame of mind to object to the landlord's actions, but protest was financially rewarding because the actual sum involved was markedly higher than in most particular purchases.

We found substantial public support for rent control. A large proportion of the population paid rent, so the need for keeping rents down was fully appreciated. Even members of Congress, who generally criticized OPA, tended to favor the rent program. Indeed, the first legislation Congress passed in the price control field was a bill to control the rents in the District of Columbia. Opposition arose mainly from the organized elements among landlords, the Association of Real Estate Dealers and others, and infected some congressmen, but there was more congressional support for rent control than in any other field.

Moreover, the courts on the whole were friendly. Courts have a tradition of objecting to landlords' attempting to evict tenants. Fairness usually is interpreted as favoring the tenants' position, and courts have placed more and more technical obstructions in the way of eviction. The general tradition of the judicial system to give tenants a break worked to the advantage of OPA, particularly in connection with the key aspect of threatened evictions.

Finally, the scarcity of rental accommodations, although adding to the pressure for rent increases, simultaneously operated as a favorable factor in one respect. It meant that the vacancy rate declined to an extremely low point. Landlords had no difficulty finding tenants and hence losses through vacancies dropped to a minimum. This and other factors enabled landlords to maintain themselves in a reasonably satisfactory financial position, so that we did not need to bail them out in order to relieve financial hardships. Some landlords genuinely needed a rent increase, but most did not.

On balance, we had a favorable situation for obtaining compliance. Adequate results certainly could have been achieved if we had had sufficient personnel.

Some violations were simply overcharges, the landlord asking more than the ceiling rent and the tenant paying it. The consumer treble damage action, however, worked particularly well in rent cases. Furthermore, a tenant could continue to pay the rent until the statute of limitations was about to run out and then sue for the entire back period, when the amount involved would be substantial enough to warrant a lawsuit. The percentage of violations through actual overcharge probably was not high. Those that did occur were fairly easy to handle once they were reported.

Violations by unfairly evicting tenants were prevented relatively easily by the administrative device of requiring a certificate in advance before an eviction proceeding even could be brought. Consequently, it was not possible for a landlord to attempt an eviction proceeding without prior OPA approval. This meant that practically the only enforcement problem in eviction cases was the initial establishment of the validity of the certificate requirement, which we accomplished at a fairly early point, and from then on complaints about unauthorized evictions were readily handled by injunction proceedings.

The more difficult forms of violation revolved around other practices. One violation we never were able to handle satisfactorily was the reduction in the services that the landlord provided. Under the regulation the landlord was supposed to provide the same services as he had in the past. These services included redecorating, janitorial service, heating, garage space, timely repairs, and other services commonly provided by landlords. The most common violation of the rent regulation was a failure to keep up the services. The services that the landlord was required to perform were included on the registration statement, so that the tenant knew what services he was entitled to. However, as services were of peripheral concern to tenants, frequently they did not complain and as a result landlords got away with considerable violation. The landlord would omit redecorating for a year when he had been doing it annually. Accommodations would be rented to a new tenant with an extra charge for the garage or the garage would no longer be included. In some respects services were not as definite a proposition as the actual rent price. Heating might be required, but whether the setting had to be 65 or 70 degrees might be a debatable matter. Or the frequency and extent to which janitorial service was performed might be debatable. Landlords and tenants might argue about whether needed repairs were completed in a timely fashion. In many cases service violations were trivial matters, hardly the subject for criminal prosecution. Injunctions were cumbersome and treble damage suits were tricky because the amount of the overcharge depended on estimating the value of the service, a debatable matter. So service violations were less specific, less important, and OPA could not afford the time to handle them unless the circumstances were unusual.

Other evasions that occurred concerned tie-in sales, security deposits, and fictitious sales. In a tie-in sale the landlord would rent housing and require a tenant to buy the furniture at outrageous prices, or tie in some other payment with the rent. Requiring a security deposit (a sum deposited with the landlord to cover possible property damage and failure to pay rent) where none had been required previously and failing to return the deposit when the tenant moved out were evasions of the rent regulations. Fictitious sales were pseudo-sales under which the tenant would undertake to make monthly payments higher than the rent ceiling, purporting to be payments of the sales price, but actually being rent, the terms of the sale being such that if any minor deviation occurred, the landlord cancelled the arrangement. At times these violations became serious and OPA would make an effort to control them.

The main factor in rent control, however, was the lack of personnel.

The problems could have been handled on a reasonably effective basis if sufficient personnel had been available, with one exception: hotels and rooming houses.

Hotels and rooming houses had a rapid turnover of tenants compared to other rentals. Transients were unlikely to file complaints. If complaints were filed, evidence was difficult to obtain because the tenant had departed. Furthermore, hotels and rooming houses were likely to be business enterprises much more than individual housing accommodations or even apartment houses were, and the business world's willingness to violate OPA regulations tended to pervade this area, too. In addition, the amounts involved were normally smaller because the tenants did not stay as long or rented a smaller space. Some of the most prestigious hotels in the country accumulated outrageous records on violations. In Enforcement we eventually decided to concentrate a substantial portion of our rent manpower on the hotels and rooming houses.

In some areas, the southside of Chicago for example, violations were rampant. Violations usually were more prevalent and more serious in slum areas than elsewhere. Enforcement tended to concentrate on geographical areas with flagrant violations as well as on hotels and rooming houses.

Since so many units were involved, and for the same reasons that prevailed in the retail field, we had to obtain assistance from outside the enforcement staff for handling rent compliance. We sought that assistance mainly from the Rent Department of OPA. Almost from the beginning a jurisdictional controversy had existed between the rent staff and the enforcement staff as to who was to handle complaints of violation in the rent offices. The rent staff was extremely anxious to obtain jurisdiction over the handling of these violations. They originally had a staff of investigators who investigated rent values, that is, when the OPA rent director was required to make a determination of what a particular rent should be, he would need an appraisal of the housing accommodations for that purpose, and various facts. These investigators could also function easily as investigators to obtain data with respect to the violations. For this reason, as well as others, the Rent Department insisted from the beginning that the handling of complaints at the rent offices should be their task. I have already mentioned how Paul Porter stole several hundred investigators from me and assigned them to this work in the rent offices. In general, the enforcement staff definitely accepted the proposition that the rent staff investigators should be used to handle complaints at the local office level, and we functioned under a loose system whereby complaints were handled there, and the serious cases referred to the enforcement staff.

It was not until the middle of 1944 that we finally negotiated a full-scale compromise with the Rent Department, embodied in an instruction from the Enforcement Department to the Rent Department officials in the field. Under this agreement, the Rent Department was given jurisdiction to handle complaints. They would make investigations either in response to a complaint or on their own initiative as a spot check. The rent staff was authorized to negotiate the settlements where violations were found, to compromise cases on the basis of a payment to the tenant or full payment of the treble damage claim. The serious cases involving flagrant or persistent violation were referred to the Enforcement Department for action. In other words, the agreement was somewhat similar to our arrangement in the retail field. The rent staff, however, was much more professional than the price panels. No volunteers were used and the rent staff tended to become experts, and were in a position where they could do a more effective job.

The enforcement attorneys and investigators operated mostly from the district offices. In a few situations, such as the New York City rent office, we could assign a full-time investigator or a full-time attorney to handle enforcement cases. Generally speaking, however, rent cases were handled by Enforcement from the district offices, so that practically all the 500 rent offices had no enforcement staff assigned. This led to some friction because of the distances involved and the difficulties of communication. Enforcement had to operate on that basis, however, because we simply did not have enough manpower to do otherwise.

A large number of rent cases were handled. The collected figures do not show the difference between claims for adjustment and complaints for violation, but in the three years from June 1942 to June 1945, OPA received a total of 2.6 million tenant complaints and adjustments. The majority were complaints of violation. Of course, many proved to be without foundation, but adjustments or settlements were made in some form in 784,000 of these cases. Some 20,000 of them were referred to the enforcement staff for enforcement action, and in 4600 cases sanctions were actually applied by the enforcement staff.

On the whole, the enforcement of the rent regulations was satisfactorily carried out. There were, as was to be expected, a large number of violations, but by and large the situation was kept under control. A fairly high number of sanctions was applied and the problem did not get out hand. We could have accomplished even more if we had had more personnel.

# 13

# ORGANIZATIONAL ISSUES
# AND DEVELOPMENTS

*The Executive/Legislative balance.*

I would now like to discuss the relationship of my Enforcement Department to the rest of OPA, particularly to indicate the support we had and the pressures brought to bear on the us.

## SUPPORT FROM OPA STAFF

Of course, it was essential that the rest of the organization back the Enforcement Department, particularly the office of the OPA administrator and his staff. The number of staff members allocated to Enforcement would depend on the administrator's decision as to what proportion of the budget we should have. Unfriendliness to Enforcement would show up first of all in a small budget, or in refusal to approve budget increases and ad hoc funding requests. The support of the administrator also was important in dealing with other departments of OPA. Points of difference constantly arose between Enforcement and other departments. As a matter of prestige in carrying on negotiations and pressing for solutions, it was important that the Enforcement staff was known to have the general backing of the administrator and his staff. The same was true of changes in the regulations. Enforcement's views with respect to the necessity of reframing the meat and clothing regulations carried much more weight with the administrator's backing, or if in negotiations the administrator was placing a good deal of emphasis on enforcement.

If the administrator had been unfriendly to Enforcement, it would have been difficult to maintain adequate morale. If he had gone so far as to repudiate Enforcement action, morale would have deteriorated rapidly. Any situation where the top official stepped in and took a case away from the Enforcement staff, and compromised or settled it himself on some basis they did not think was right, would tend to ruin the whole spirit of the department.

Generally, Enforcement did have the strong backing of all three administrators during my period there. At certain points the administrator was unaware of certain problems, or at least we thought so in

259

Enforcement, but in general we had support for a strong and determined enforcement policy. A considerably different atmosphere prevailed in the War Production Board, where enforcement was seriously neglected. Most emphasis was placed upon voluntary compliance, and there never existed the firm attitude toward enforcement that prevailed in OPA. Our first administrator, Leon Henderson, was relatively inexperienced in the enforcement field, but he gave enforcement work strong support. At an early stage he realized the necessity of vigorous enforcement measures as a basis for OPA price work. His general friendliness toward the Legal Department extended to enforcement problems. He made no compromises of any individual cases or any situation through refusing to back up the Enforcement staff. However, the problems and techniques had barely developed in the Henderson regime. We were just beginning to move into operation when he left.

Prentiss Brown was also sympathetic. Although on the whole an ineffective administrator, he recognized the importance of enforcement activity. He gave it his general backing–although his general backing was not notably effective. Inwardly blocked from taking any initiative, he settled problems as they came up to him, but failed to offer us active support. He never settled any cases contrary to the Enforcement Department's views or put any pressure on us to settle an enforcement case. I cannot say the same regarding some of his subordinates. Some of the men he brought into OPA were basically hostile to enforcement. They tried to moderate and curb our programs. They also occasionally interfered in individual cases. However, when Enforcement refused to agree to their proposed disposition of any particular case, the matter was dropped.

The position of Chester Bowles, our third administrator, changed as time went on. He originally came in with the theory that everything could be settled by competent public relations, relegating enforcement to a somewhat minor role. He recognized its importance as a last resort, but believed that practically everything could be handled without actual enforcement procedures. He became increasingly aware, however, that strict enforcement action was imperative, and moved gradually from a position of acceptance to one of positive support. He devoted his weekly radio program to enforcement problems fairly frequently, was active in the attempts to obtain additional staff from congressional appropriations, and supported Enforcement in many of its controversies with other departments. I think Bowles' final acceptance of the basic enforcement policies and programs actually did not happen until January 1945, when he wrote a strong memorandum to the regional directors reviewing the entire enforcement program and adding his strong affirmation. Actually I drafted most of the memorandum, but he added to it, in all cases strengthening it. That document carried great weight throughout the organization, particularly with regional and district administrators.

Bowles also never made any attempt to call off the Enforcement Department in any enforcement case. He received an increasing number of complaints about enforcement activities in one area or another. He would look into them but would never substitute his judgment for the reasoned judgment of the Enforcement staff, and he certainly never made any effort to modify enforcement activities against any particular company because that particular company might be involved. Bowles's assistant, Jim Rogers, Jr., at one time became concerned about a case involving the Lipton Tea Company. I guess some business friend approached Jim Rogers and told him the OPA Enforcement Department was acting unreasonably. Jim talked to me about his friend's objection, but he never used any improper pressure on me, nor did any of the other members of Bowles' staff.

I remember one case that typifies the support Enforcement received from successive administrators. The Enforcement staff had begun proceedings against the Overseas Trading Corporation, represented by Brien McMahon, at that time in private law practice in the District of Columbia. McMahon had been assistant attorney general in charge of the Criminal Division under Homer Cummings (a powerful Democrat figure in Washington) in the early days of the New Deal, and he later became senator from Connecticut. For some reason McMahon seemed desperate, willing to take almost any measures to induce OPA to drop the case. He put formidable pressure on us from all sources he could tap, and he was an important figure in Democratic politics in Washington. McMahon came over and conferred with George Burke, who was then general counsel. When that failed, he mobilized various political pressures. McMahon even spoke to Gardner Jackson and promised that if he, Gardner, would use his influence on me, he would support some of the legislative measures that the CIO was interested in. Both Prentiss Brown and Bowles refused to make any concessions. McMahon's contention was that OPA did not have any jurisdiction over sales abroad. He was clearly wrong and OPA had taken the opposite position. There was no ground for calling off the case except to do a political favor, but neither Brown nor Bowles would consider it.

We did not fare as well with other departments of OPA. Early in the game, the Price, Rent, and Rationing Departments were not convinced Enforcement should play a major role. Occasionally a staff member was friendly to some industrial interest and obstructed enforcement by giving interpretations that let the company off the hook. We also had jurisdictional controversies with other departments. In general, however, the other departments did not obstruct us; as time went on, they rallied more and more to the active support of the Enforcement program. The Information Department was particularly friendly to us, despite their constantly shifting leadership. They assigned one of their members, Elizabeth Baker, to work exclusively with the Enforcement staff. She handled most of the enforcement public relations and supervised enforcement public relations in the field offices.

We experienced some difficulty with some of the regional administrators. Dan Woolley of New York became embroiled in a controversy with the head of the enforcement attorneys, and the regional administrator in Chicago clashed with the regional enforcement attorney there. Both of these cases were somewhat unusual. The objections seemed to be somewhat irrational and more psychologically motivated than representing a reasoned position. The result, however, was a pitched battle between the administrator and the enforcement staff in those regions.

Bowles was not adept at resolving intrastaff conflict and these issues tended to drag on. The Chicago dispute, which came up first, I thought he handled rather weakly. Our man, Alex Elson, was one of our best enforcement attorneys. There was no question about his honesty and reliability. The facts plainly revealed that the regional administrator was suffering from job strain and was on the verge of a nervous breakdown. Bowles stalled and stalled on rendering a decision and we eventually lost Alex Elson as a result. The New York dispute arose later, mainly after I had left the agency. Bowles handled that conflict much better, although there was less ground for support of the enforcement attorney there, perhaps, than in Chicago. Neither of those incidents, however, seriously compromised our enforcement work. Occasional flare-ups in district offices also had to be handled. On the whole, however, the frictions did not jeopardize the enforcement program.

## RELATIONS WITH THE EXECUTIVE BRANCH AND CONGRESS

The administration did not wholeheartedly support the enforcement program in that it let us fight our battles for more appropriations with Congress pretty much on our own. It tended to play a passive role. The White House certainly was concerned about price control, gravely perturbed about the gasoline black market, and apprehensive about the meat situation. Even though presumably worried about the possibility of a general collapse of price enforcement, the White House never committed itself to a public, vigorous backing. On the other hand, the Roosevelt staff refrained from affirmative action to obstruct enforcement and did not attempt to interfere in particular cases. David Niles (a presidential assistant) at the White House telephoned once or twice to call my attention to certain situations where people had complained to him and to ask me to look into them. These calls were not followed up with any further pressure. Aside from that, I remember no instances in which the White House or other agencies in the executive branch attempted to intervene in individual cases. This was quite a different atmosphere from that which developed in the latter days of the Truman administration, when considerable personal and political influence apparently was wielded in various enforcement agencies. In the Roosevelt era pressures may have been exerted on other people that I did not know about, but so far as I personally was concerned in OPA enforcement, I cannot recall now a single instance in which even any suggestion of pressure came from the administration.

My experience of the lack of political pressure applies to all the New Deal agencies I worked in, and I believe it was characteristic of the Washington scene at that time. I know of no effort to influence the decisions of the NLRB, nor did I hear of any regarding the Securities and Exchange Commission. Political maneuvering occurred from time to time, but it was very rare in my opinion. I can not recall any cases where it happened. Certainly no case came within my immediate jurisdiction and I think I would have heard about others had the practice been widespread. I would correlate the prevalence of political favors with the low calibre of the administrator. One of President Truman's greatest weaknesses was his personnel appointments. Although he had to contend with a general exodus of talent from Washington, Truman appointed to top rank positions individuals who had been considered third or fourth rank. During the preceding five or ten years they never would have held any position of significance. He also appointed individuals more prone to employ political favoritism. Once that practice starts at the top, it tends to accelerate rapidly through the ranks.

At OPA we had to watch continuously not only for outright corruption but also for the dispensation of small favors. It was a constant problem that was likely to arise in any organization. Only if the firmest measures are taken at the top and agency heads provide the most immaculate example can the practice be minimized. Because Truman appointees did not take the strict stand against political favoritism that Roosevelt appointees had, corruption spread rapidly. President Roosevelt was not opposed to playing politics, but he had a reputation for not playing politics with individual cases. He played politics with broader issues, and he played politics with judgeships, public works projects, and similar matters. But in regard to administrative agencies such as the NLRB or prosecution for violation of OPA regulations, he played no politics at all. He was strong enough to maintain his own position rather than make peace with Congress at the expense of the agencies.

The situation was quite different in regard to Congress. I cannot remember a single instance where congressional influence was exerted in behalf of stricter price control or prosecuting someone. To the contrary, even Rep. Mike Monroney of Oklahoma complained about our vigorous enforcement campaign in the defense rental area of Norman, Oklahoma. The congressman believed we had gone too far in various methods we used. In our long discussion with Monroney about the matter he was quite reasonable, but the net effect of his concern was to put pressure against a strict enforcement policy. Certainly that was the overwhelming impact of our relations to Congress.

Opposition took various forms. The earliest, systematic attacks were by the Smith Committee, which continued throughout its existence to snipe at OPA enforcement. I have mentioned the congressional attacks on OPA snooping. Other aspects of enforcement received concerted attacks. Isolated attacks on enforcement such as the one by Rep. Fred Busbey accusing me of subversive activities occurred as well.

We had considerable trouble over appropriations. Rep. Clarence Cannon of Missouri, chairman of the House Appropriations Committee, was reasonably friendly, except insofar as he was a member of the farm bloc; so he was inclined to oppose us on food and agricultural issues. Rep. John Taber, the ranking Republican member of the committee, was extremely hostile. He objected so strenuously to OPA operations, and he seemed to us so emotional and off-balance about it, that we never took him seriously. He seemed to us to be on the lunatic fringe of Congress. (I thought I had always maintained a polite attitude, but the other day I was informed that Taber had written a letter objecting to some action of mine and recalling my performances before the Appropriations Committee as "surly and insolent.") We were more concerned with the Democratic majority than with the Republican minority in the Appropriations Committee. The Democrats were not wholly unfriendly; they occasionally would listen to reason and recognize our problems, although they never granted us all the investigators or staff we thought we needed. On the other hand, the Bureau of the Budget never gave us everything we needed either. In sum, we never received overwhelming support from Congress or the House Appropriations Committee. The Senate Appropriations Committee was more favorable, with the exception of Chairman Kenneth McKellar.

Congressional opposition also emerged in the form of amendments. When the Price Control Act came up for renewal in the first half of 1944, the controversies over enforcement were considerably outweighed by controversies on other matters. When I testified at the hearings on renewal, I was not seriously challenged on enforcement policies by the members of the congressional committees. Senator Chandler of Kentucky made a considerable stir over his proposals for amendment of the treble damage provisions, the passage of which curtailed seriously the effectiveness of those provisions. On the other hand, we were able to obtain passage without serious opposition for our amendments in the treble damage provisions that authorized the administrator's action in retail cases. Opposition increased as time went on, so that the subsequent renewals involved additional enforcement issues' being resolved contrary to our wishes.

I have already alluded to one experience with the Senate Agricultural Committee that indicated the extent of congressional opposition in the early months of 1945. The Senate Agricultural Committee was making an investigation of the meat situation and requested me to testify. A week or two earlier I had left OPA for the OES, but the matter related to OPA enforcement. I found the committee hostile, irascible, and completely unwilling to listen to what I had to say. A government employee before a congressional committee is in an unenviable position because he cannot answer back and can hardly defend himself. He is obliged to remain polite in the face of the most extreme provocations lest congressmen retaliate against his agency or against him. Sen. John Thomas of Idaho was chairman, but the major thrust of the attack was carried by Senator Wherry. To my surprise, Wherry suggested that I was not interested in strict enforcement at all, but on the contrary was weak and temporizing, and was playing favorites with the various companies that were in violation. The principal way he conveyed this was in connection with a particular case involving the meat black market. A reporter for one of the Hearst magazines had started out to write a story about the black market. He came to us and told us that for journalistic purposes he had represented himself as a cattle buyer, purchased cattle, and then had sold them above the ceiling. He also had acted as a wholesaler and purchased meat above the ceiling. He had all the information and could identify one of the major violators. He offered us all the information that would enable us to make the case against this firm if we would keep him informed of the progress of the case so that he could write it up. I was not inclined to make any deal with a Hearst reporter. Further, I would not make a deal with a person who had participated in illegal transactions. I had no idea whether illegal entrapment might be involved, and so forth. Finally, I refused to participate on terms that required us to reveal confidential information to someone outside the government. We thought we knew which company the Hearst reporter was alluding to and had already instituted an investigation. So, for all these reasons, I turned down the offer. The reporter apparently took my refusal to Senator Wherry. By a series of statements and questions, Senator Wherry tried to make it appear that I was not interested in prosecuting black market violators or else that I had some particular reason for favoring the firm fingered by the Hearst reporter. I was astonished that Senator Wherry's insinuations, which so fantastically distorted the situation, made some impression on his audience. We also disputed the extent of violations. He claimed that 95 percent of the retail stores in the country were violating the meat regulations. I challenged that figure. Neither of knew beyond an educated guess, because it was almost impossible to tell. Certainly there were very extensive violations at that time, but I doubt they were anywhere near 95 percent.

In addition to these more or less official attacks on OPA and obstructions and interferences with its operations, there were a surprising number of individual instances in which members of Congress intervened in particular enforcement cases. One of the most outrageous interventions was by Senator McKellar. We had instituted a rather large treble damage case against a lumber company in Tennessee. Senator McKellar called the enforcement staff member who was handling the case into his office, berated him, shouted at him in the presence of officials of the company and their attorneys, and attempted to bludgeon him into withdrawing the case. We refused. Without attempting to present a rational argument, McKellar insisted that we should not have brought the case for some reason of his own; perhaps some political supporter of his was threatened. Over a long period of time McKellar persisted in exerting drastic pressure on us to drop the case.

Another senator who consistently pressured us was Scott Lucas of Illinois. We had brought a series of gigantic treble damage cases against the liquor industry. The liquor industry had been one of the most flagrant violators. One subterfuge was to sell the same old liquor under new brand names for excessive prices. Liquor violations involved millions of dollars. A number of times Scott Lucas called me or some other member of my department on the telephone and tried to convince us to drop the cases. He sent lawyers to see us and exercised persistent pressure on us to drop the cases or settle for insignificant amounts. Senator Lucas never forgave us for resisting.

It was not at all unusual for a congressman to call up and ask us to come to his office–less often they came to our office–and pressure us to compromise or abandon a case. Even more frequently a congressman would call us to make appointments for people who were interested in the case. Nothing was particularly wrong with that in itself, but often the pressure went considerably beyond that.

Exerting pressure in particular cases was not confined to unfriendly congressmen or to those who did not support the OPA in general. I suppose Republican congressmen anticipated no favors from OPA, so they did not create as much fuss as the Democrats did. Rep. Emanuel Celler of New York, one of the strongest supporters of OPA, engaged in some of the most flagrant pressure tactics. In fact, he brought to my office on several occasions persons whom he introduced as clients of his and discussed the settlement of the cases with me. This was a violation of federal law, which provides that no member of Congress or anyone attached to the government can represent a private client in a matter involving the government. John Lord O'Brian told me that when Celler came to his office on such missions, O'Brian would throw him out of his office. I did not have the nerve to do that, but I should have, I suppose. I never did anything for Celler, but he never held it against me later, in connection with his work on the House Judiciary Committee.

Even New Deal senators such as Claude Pepper attempted to bring pressure on OPA. Senator Pepper approached our Florida office on behalf of the Florida race tracks. Apparently beneath his liberal New Deal position was some of the mud and money of the Florida gambling interests. When we proceeded against Florida race tracks, Senator Pepper put tremendous pressure on our Florida office to abstain. We did not respond to the pressures, but they were always there. I found it discouraging that congressmen lobbied a federal agency for private interests without so much as a pretence of considering the merits.

We also had interchanges with senators on matters of personnel. By and large, in the Legal Department at least, and pretty much throughout the OPA, the Washington staff was selected without regard to political patronage. Often we would ask some person we were hiring to obtain his congressman's endorsement. Occasionally, preference would be given to a candidate of a particular congressman. That happened more frequently in the regional offices. From the beginning the regional and district offices had been more of a patronage area. Furthermore, a congressman would be particularly resentful if his political enemies were in charge of the local office in his own territory, so more clearance of field appointments with congressmen occurred. In general, however, the situation was simply one of clearance on some of the jobs. A man the congressman strongly opposed probably would not be considered, but it was not by any means a situation where a person could not be hired unless he first had a congressional endorsement. Congressmen perhaps took more interest in the lawyers than other OPA personnel, but pressure was concentrated on regional offices.

Despite these limitations, pressure from congressmen on personnel appointments was constant. We ducked the barrage of letters and dodged around telephone calls to avoid creating antagonisms by our refusals to capitulate. On the whole we did evade the pressure. It remained a constant factor in personnel selection, however. Sen. Tom Connally called me up one time and wanted me to appoint a particular man as regional attorney at the Dallas office. This candidate seemed wholly incompetent to me and I intimated that I did not intend to comply, whereupon Senator Connally became enraged. While he berated me over the telephone for ten minutes, I hung on in silence, trying not to make him more angry than he was and not give him cause to say that I had been impertinent. He gave me a terrible lacing up and down and made it perfectly clear that OPA would suffer if his man was not appointed. We finally compromised by appointing his man to an inconsequential position where he did not do much harm. That was the most extreme case of congressional pressure on appointments.

### The Executive/Legislative Balance

Political opposition was growing. Opposition tactics concentrated on congressional investigations and cavilling when our budgets came up for appropriations. The New Deal lacked a majority after the 1938 elections, so there was, to some extent, a stalemate. The Republicans, southern Democrats, and other conservative Democrats had enough power to prevent further expansion of the New Deal, but not enough power to enact an affirmative program.

This imbalance between the executive and legislative branches had destructive consequences. As to whether congressional bitterness was directed toward OPA or the purposes for which OPA was designed, or more toward Roosevelt, that is hard to distinguish. Of course, attacks on OPA often concealed attacks on the president. OPA was more vulnerable and a safer target. But I believe that they were not assaulting us merely to wage war on the White House and the New Deal. At least, it seemed to us at the time that they were genuinely concerned with the immediate issues for which they castigated us.

## CONCLUSIONS OF THE OPA EXPERIENCE

It is hard to evaluate the effectiveness of OPA enforcement. It is almost impossible to know the actual extent of pricing violations that occurred, and even if one knew that, it is not easy to weigh the impact that the Enforcement Department had, or to separate the enforcement activities from other factors that figure in the situation. However, I would say that on the whole, OPA enforcement was successful in that OPA accomplished its basic purpose. Despite areas where there was a serious lack of enforcement and other defects, such as virtually unenforceable regulations in the meat and clothing fields, the objectives of OPA were accomplished, at least in the period prior to V-J Day, and without injustice to any large number of individuals.

## Price Controls Worked

The principal evidence of this is the Bureau of Labor Statistics' CPI, which, as I have pointed out, rose only two points in the period from the "Hold the Line" order in April 1943 until April 1945. In May 1945, when I left OPA, it stood at 127.1. Considering that in the period immediately before this it had been rising at the rate of one point a month, this was an extraordinary record.

The evidence resting on the CPI requires some qualification because it did not necessarily reflect an accurate picture of prices in certain areas, i.e., where the black market was important. By its nature, the black market involved concealed prices that would not be reflected in government statistics or in reports made to the government as to what the prices were. Nevertheless, the index was not excessively far off, and although it may be subject to some discount, on the whole it reflects reasonably well what the price level actually was.

An analysis of the figures also shows that prices increased less in those areas where the looseness of the regulations or the failure to cover sufficient territory made the regulations difficult to enforce. For instance, the prices of products fixed under dollars-and-cents ceilings rose less than prices in the clothing field, where determining the price ceiling was more complex. In those areas where enforcement was possible, the prices held better than in other areas.

In addition, the figures show that prices rose rapidly as soon as OPA controls were lifted. In August 1945, the month in which V-J Day occurred, the CPI stood at 129.3. Immediately after V-J Day there was extensive decontrol and slackening of the whole effort at price control. By June 1946, the CPI had gone to 133.3. At that point the price control legislation expired and there was no renewal for a period. When it was renewed, a good deal of ground had been lost and amendments had greatly weakened it. Finally, in October 1946, just before the congressional elections, President Truman abandoned practically all price controls. The result was that by November 1946, the month after the abandonment of price control, the CPI had risen to 150.7. It is quite clear that as price controls were lifted, and to the extent that they were lifted, the price index rose rapidly.

Another possible measure of the success of OPA enforcement is the figures on its activities. It is fairly clear that OPA enforcement at least did a large volume of work. The number of investigations conducted, the number of cases disposed of or settled, and the number of court cases brought indicate indefatigable activity. Enforcement work was carried on aggressively.

The amount of money deposited in the federal treasury as a result of OPA enforcement always considerably exceeded the budget for the Enforcement Department. In other words, the fines, treble damage judgments, and settlements of treble damage cases amounted to a sum considerably larger than the sum spent on the enforcement operation. We used to point this out to the appropriations committees, arguing that additional investigators and attorneys would result in additional income for the government, without making much of an impression.

Another possible measure of enforcement competence would be the percentage of decisions won in court. An average of 96 percent of the cases brought by OPA ended successfully. OPA enforcement was successful in persuading the courts to its point of view on all major issues. Some cases were lost on less significant issues, but the major issues pressed before the courts were all victories for OPA. So, the record of the agency in the courts was impressive.

While judging OPA to be a success in terms of price control, I came to some other conclusions both about how the OPA experience was valuable in additional dimensions and the sobering implications of its limitations and failures.

We were impressed by the limited role of conventional enforcement sanctions. The notion of enforcement as simply the investigation of cases and the application of court sanctions was superseded entirely in our experience. We soon discovered that at least equal importance must be attached to public relations, the general situation in a particular industry, and most important, to administrative devices designed to prevent violations before they occurred. The injunction, criminal prosecution, and treble damage suit were only one string in our bow. Our task was broader and more complicated than a police operation of detecting violations and applying sanctions.

OPA developed a substantial advance in the techniques of governmental administration, a substantial accumulation of information and methods of handling problems of governmental regulation. The OPA administration was incomparably superior to NRA. In OPA we were committed to governing by general principles, as opposed to the ad hoc or whimsical basis that an individual case happened to strike a particular person in NRA. OPA developed procedures for collecting information, for the hearing process, for a limited type of court review, all of which worked effectively and did not exist in NRA. The OPA staff had markedly more information available and created new methods for obtaining information. This development of sound administrative process was one of the important contributions made by OPA.

OPA conducted a remarkable experiment in terms of decentralization and the democratic participation of citizens in governmental operations. The extent to which local offices were permitted to function independently and assume responsibility was greater than in most other governmental agencies. The experiment with the participation of individual citizens in the War Price and Ration Boards was unique. Perhaps that degree of voluntary citizen participation may have been possible only in wartime.

However, it provided a model for a broadly based democratic program for managing public matters significant to everybody.

Turning now to observations about the nation that our task sensitized us to, we shared the amazement of the entire country at the performance of the nation in the war period. We applauded the tremendous productive capacity of the country. With eleven million of its most able-bodied citizens in the armed forces throughout most of the war, and producing prodigious quantities of military supplies, the United States nevertheless was able to maintain and even increase the level of production for civilian consumption. Unemployment had, of course, disappeared. We realized that the recovery was due to the war effort, but nevertheless it was impressive. The question in everyone's mind was: what part of this could be carried over to peacetime? Would it be possible to organize the economic forces of the country under peacetime conditions so as to maintain the level of material progress elicited by the war?

Another observation was the seemingly great power of individual pressures on a congressman. In regard to OPA we mainly saw business pressures reflected in congressional action. I suppose the influence on the congressmen was due in large part to possible campaign funds from these sources. Courting of direct votes is ruled out because many more votes were available from affected consumers than from the business enterprises. In any event, congressmen seemed amazingly responsive to local pressures and almost without exception to lack a national interest viewpoint on OPA issues. I constantly was perturbed at the apparent inability of Congress to formulate basic policy. Overwhelmed with the urgencies of immediate local pressures, they ignored many of the broader issues. They did not seem to be performing their function of weighing and considering questions from a national point of view and making a decision as to what the issues should be.

This parochialism is both a source of weakness and a source of danger to Congress. Ultimately the issues must be resolved, if the nation is to survive, in terms of the general welfare. For a congressman to fail to understand the problems of the nation as a whole and work toward the common solution means that his actions are almost irrelevant, that he will exert little influence, and that in the long run he and his colleagues forfeit the power and prestige that Congress otherwise would have. Fragmented into diverse and local interests, the intended role of Congress is frustrated and Congress becomes subordinate to the executive branch which may take a more national viewpoint. The potential subordination of Congress is a real danger. I have always believed, as I suppose all persons interested in the democratic process have, that Congress as the direct elected representatives should play the foremost role in formulating policy. Danger to democracy exists when the formulation of policy devolves too much into the hands of an executive or bureaucratic group.

**Mitigators of Success**
*Profits, greed, and complexity*

Perhaps the major issue that arose from my OPA experience was the strength of the individual drives toward maximizing profit and pleasure. As I have indicated, we were discouraged by the high degree of noncompliance in many areas of industry. It seemed to us that there was a serious weakness in business ethics and an unusual readiness for business to violate the regulations. That was due, I suppose, to the whole theory of business operations, which is based on the principle of buying or producing at the lowest possible cost and selling at the highest possible price. I suppose it is hard to throw off that whole attitude. The extent of violation was due in part to the competitive system, in that the violation of selling above ceiling prices by one group in the industry frequently put serious pressure on competitors, and self-preservation to some extent required violation by the rest if once started by any important segment of the industry.

In any event, we were impressed by the degree to which business firms, including leading business firms, succumbed or engaged in violations. We were concerned also by the lack of an individual's willingness to sacrifice in the interests of the general public. While most people were willing to make sacrifices during the war period, there was a tremendous readiness to cut corners at certain points and to be led into noncompliance with the regulations if others were doing it.

I think this attitude has serious implications for an effort at an economy partially controlled by the government, or an effort at any form of mixed economy. It makes it enormously difficult to impose economic regulations in such a way that firms and individuals still retain a reasonable degree of the power to make decisions. This atmosphere of willingness to evade regulations and the general attitude that such evasions are not unethical, but are rather to be expected, will make any attempt at control of the economic structure through a regulatory process difficult. In other words, a democracy aimed at a mixed economy or at a control that still leaves in the hands of business and individuals many important decisions must have at its base a strong commitment to the collective welfare on the part of those who are being regulated. People must have a sense of restraint, a willingness to make concessions or even to sacrifice for the common good, and a sense of responsibility. The OPA experience raised doubts as to whether the moral fiber of the economic interests in our country exists to form the basis for a successful regulation under a democratic process.

A corollary issue is that it became clear, as time went on, that economic regulations inevitably became extremely complex. This was due in part to the great diversity of business practices and industrial operations, in part technical, in part geographical, and so on. It was also due, however, to the constant and ingenious efforts that were made to avoid the impact of the regulations. OPA was constantly amending regulations to deal with a particular method of evasion that was a response to the original regulation. There was a constant process, then, of refinement and increasing complexity of the regulations as time went on.

Again, the implications of this seem fairly serious. At a certain point the effort to control from the outside will collapse if the task becomes too complicated. Those subject to the regulations cannot understand them, the courts cannot understand them, and they become much too technical for practical operations. The only alternative would seem to be some simplification in terms of government ownership or direct government operation. That raises other problems, but at least it is much simpler. I think there is some question as to whether a system of more remote control, leaving the ownership and many of the decisions in the hands of private enterprise, can work effectively or whether it ultimately will break down and require the simpler (in this respect) operation of the system by complete government ownership or operation.

The answer to the lack of business support for regulations and to the violation and evasion of regulations inevitably became a greater degree of regulation, not only in the complexity which I have mentioned, but also in the extension of control to other parts of the industry. For example, in the attempt to control meat prices, where black market operations tended to disintegrate controls and channel meat through new black market distributors, the only solution was an extension of government control into the slaughtering establishments by the placing of quotas on the amount that could be slaughtered, the licensing of slaughterhouses, and so on. Or in gasoline enforcement, as black market operations developed through the dealers and some bulk stations buying invalid coupons from gangsters, the solution depended on increased governmental control through the Verification Centers. The same solution was true of clothes, a problem that was never solved because the controls were never imposed: an elaborate set of additional controls that would include a system of standardization of clothing and allocation of textiles to particular garment manufacturers. Britain's success with price control and the fewer enforcement struggles it had compared with the United States was based largely on the fact that its controls were much more far-reaching.

Again, the OPA experience has general implications as to the difficulties involved in governmental regulation of the economic structure. Can a problem be solved by fairly simple regulation of one aspect of the structure, or will the complications and the evasions, and the consequent need to escalate controls, press to a point where it is difficult to find a middle ground, where it is difficult to find anything short of complete ownership and control? That presents a crucial problem for this country at the present time.

## OPA to OES

In concluding my observations on OPA I will say a few words about my resignation. In March of 1945, William H. Davis had been appointed director of the Office of Economic Stability (OES). I had known him somewhat before, primarily through NRA. He looked around for a lawyer to act as his general counsel and decided to ask me to take the position.

I was inclined from the beginning to accept, but talked with Bowles about the matter first. Bowles expressed himself as being unhappy to have me leave, but agreed that the job in the OES was more important. He also said it would be strategic to have someone from OPA or someone who understood and sympathized with the OPA point of view in the OES. Bowles had experienced some difficulties in his relations with Vinson, the previous director of OES. He and Vinson had not gotten along well together. They tended to distrust each other, and Bowles believed that OPA's point of view had not received sufficiently sympathetic consideration at OES. Eager to place one of his people in that office so that OPA would receive more favorable attention, he raised no objections to my leaving OPA and taking the OES position.

The main reason I transferred to OES was that it was a position on a higher policy level. That agency dealt with the whole problem of stabilization, was on the next higher level than OPA and would entail more contact with the people who were making the decisions at the top.

When I resigned, Bowles wrote me a letter expressing his regrets:

Dear Tom,
Your leaving is going to make a very definite hole in the OPA organization, and I only hope you have some understanding of the good wishes which go with you in your new work.
There are plenty of hard jobs in OPA, but certainly none that has ever been any tougher than yours. Working with totally inadequate resources, you have had to organize a department that would make these ceiling prices stick. The records in organization training and tangible achievement which you have run up in the two years you were in charge of enforcement have been nothing short of remarkable. I have admired the way you have organized your operation, as I have told you on many occasions, but I am sure you have no idea how much it has meant to me personally to know that I could completely trust the basic integrity and honesty of our enforcement work, and of you and the other people who were heading up our enforcement. In the area of your operations, frequent compromises would have been easy to rationalize, and yet I don't believe there is anyone in the organization who has compromised any less.

Then he discussed my appearance before the Senate Agricultural Committee, and continued:

In any case, Tom, we are going to miss you, tremendously. It is good to know that you will still be working on the same program, and that we can from time to time call on you for help. I hope that the personal relationship which you and I have developed over the past year and a half will be extended beyond the war in whatever work we may both be doing. Certainly our interest in public questions run along very similar lines.

Sincerely,

(signed) Chet

Senator Wherry, my nemesis from Nebraska, issued a statement or made a speech claiming that I had been fired by OPA, and that impression was also prevalent in some other parts of Washington. Bowles issued a special press release denying Wherry's statement, explaining that I left OPA only because Mr. William Davis' agency requested my services and reiterating his praise for my enforcement work.

# 14

# THE OFFICE OF
# ECONOMIC STABILIZATION

*From merely regulating prices to trying to manage the economy.*

I went over to the Office of Economic Stabilization as general counsel around the first of April 1945, just before President Roosevelt died.

## PERSONNEL AND FUNCTIONS

The background of the Office of Economic Stabilization was this. Upon the passage of the Stabilization Act in October 1942, President Roosevelt had issued an executive order establishing the Office of Economic Stabilization (OES). The order gave the office broad authority to formulate and develop a comprehensive national economic policy relating to the control of civilian purchasing power, prices, rents, wages, salaries, profits, rationing, subsidies, and all related matters. The head of the office was authorized to issue directives on policy to the various federal departments and agencies concerned with stabilization problems.

James Byrnes, who was then a Justice of the Supreme Court, resigned to become the first head of the OES. The office operated as a general coordinating authority in the field of economic stabilization. The April 1942 "Hold the Line" order conferred further duties on the director of economic stabilization: to exercise all the powers and duties conferred on the president by the Stabilization Act, and generally to take such actions and issue such directives as the director deemed necessary to stabilize the economy and to maintain production and aid in the effective prosecution of the war.

Shortly after President Roosevelt issued the "Hold the Line" order, he created the Office of War Mobilization and Reconversion (OWMR) by executive order. This top coordinating office was to handle all problems pertaining to the war effort, other than problems of the operations of the armed forces or foreign policy. Stabilization was one of its functions. It was contemplated, however, that the stabilization function would be left to the OES, although the OWMR had ultimate authority if it wished to exercise it in that field also.

## Personnel

James Byrnes was promoted to head the OWMR and Judge Fred Vinson became director of OES. Vinson resigned from the Court of Appeals for the District of Columbia in order to accept the position. The office continued under Vinson until March 1945, when Byrnes resigned as chairman of the OWMR and Vinson replaced him. William H. Davis, who was then chairman of the National War Labor Board, was appointed director of the OES. The general counsel of the OES under Vinson, Edward Prichard, moved with Vinson to the OWMR, and consequently there was a vacancy as general counsel at the OES. It was that position that William H. Davis offered me.

As director of OES, Vinson was essentially a politician, although a rather superior politician. A shrewd operator with many friends, he had served in Congress for many years, was one of the best known members of Congress, and remained on very friendly terms with them. He was "one of the boys" and was very well liked in Congress. Vinson's point of view was that of a moderate liberal, considerably influenced toward the liberal position by Ed Prichard, his chief assistant throughout this period. Vinson was one of the relatively few persons who enjoyed the support of both the liberal and conservative wings of the Democratic Party. He was liked and trusted by the southern Democrats and the other conservative groups in Congress. At the same time, primarily through Prichard, his liberal outlook procured the confidence of the liberals. I think that his liberal point of view was primarily based on political considerations rather than any firm convictions. He wanted to obtain the support of the various elements of the Democratic party. Or rather, put another way, his natural tendencies were on the conservative side, but he maintained a liberal attitude to elicit support from labor and the liberals.

While Vinson was not an original thinker or an intellectual, he was a person of considerable ability. He had the ability to delve to the heart of a problem quickly. He was an excellent negotiator and mediator. He performed best in handling a conference at which a large number of varying viewpoints were represented. I attended a number at which he presided. They were called to discuss difficult and intricate problems involving three or four or even more agencies. The very fact that the matter was being considered by Vinson meant that sharp conflicts were involved; if the question could have been decided by the agencies without his intervention it would have been. On all these occasions Vinson handled himself skillfully. He would listen carefully to the various points of view, see what the basic issues were, and stimulate a discussion so as to get some feel of the possible options. He would let it go on for a certain period of time and at the crucial moment he would suggest some proposal for a compromise. His proposals would very often be acceptable, or after some debate and some modification would be accepted. Then he would summarize it clearly, and the conference would be over and the matter settled. He was much more willing to render an opinion and to make a decision than Byrnes was. Of course, some matters required further consideration. He would take them under advisement to think about further or obtain further information, and they would drag on over a long period of time. He was an excellent mediator among the different agencies, though, and accomplished a great deal in that capacity.

Vinson's general counsel and chief assistant was Ed Prichard. Prichard came from a well-known Kentucky family, had racked up an impressive record at Harvard Law School, served as law clerk to Justice Frankfurter on the Supreme Court when he first went to Washington, and collaborated with Frankfurter in an article for the *Harvard Law Review*. Prichard was one of the most brilliant of the younger New Deal group. A person of amazing intellectual capacity, he had a broad point of view and comprehended the implications of problems, piercing through the surface of issues and understanding what was actually occurring in practice. His extremely sharp tongue and brilliant wit resulted in many sayings being attributed to him. For instance, when he was drafted into the army he weighed 250-300 pounds. Everyone had assumed that this would disqualify him from army service. However, the army—perhaps leaning over backwards because of his position—accepted him. He remarked at the time that the selective service system had said that they were scraping the bottom of the barrel, but now they had taken the barrel itself! Actually, Prichard did not last through basic training. He developed a back ailment and was hospitalized and discharged within a couple of months.

Prichard was fairly aggressive and confident of his own ability. On the other hand, he could see other points of view and compromise. He was able to handle himself in almost any situation. Prichard was very bold in his thinking. He did not refrain from advancing audacious ideas or advocating daring positions. When it came down to an actual settlement of an issue, though, he was entirely reasonable, and was extremely effective on the whole. As a close friend of Ben Cohen, Bob Nathan, and other major New Deal brain trusters, he was constantly in the thick of things, knew everything that was happening, and was pulling strings all over Washington and elsewhere to accomplish things.

Vinson's staff consisted primarily of Prichard and himself. Vinson also had an assistant named Paul Kelley, who had been his clerk previously, on the Court if I remember, and maybe in Congress. Prichard had an assistant, a young lawyer who was exceedingly able and carried a certain amount of the work. The office contained only six or eight people aside from the clerical staff.

William H. Davis was much more of an intellectual, interested in philosophical problems and broad intellectual issues, and not political. He was a member of a well-known firm of patent lawyers in New York. He had participated in NRA and was experienced in mediation. Well known in the labor field, Davis was recognized as an extremely intelligent, able, public-spirited lawyer cognizant of the realities of labor-management relations. I think he boasted that he was one of the few people who understood Einstein's theory of relativity. His probing mind was constantly at play. He was unwilling to accept prevalent cliches and was always thinking things through in his own terms. For instance, he was constantly challenging assumptions—such as that a wage increase necessarily resulted in an increase in costs, and therefore would require a price increase—reiterating that a wage increase had practically no relation to the problems of cost, that very often it resulted in management redoubling its efforts at efficient operation, and might actually lower costs. Davis was rather dogmatic in his views. A competent person who was sure of his position, he would listen to arguments, but rarely changed his mind. As a mediator he was extremely resourceful. He had a good feel for problems and could actually suggest a workable solution that offered something to both sides. He was a very pleasant, attractive person. At times he could be moved to anger but was usually very pleasant in his relationships with people. Getting along in years, he was rather garrulous and often tended to reminisce. Sometimes I had difficulty bringing him down to the point. I also thought that his mind was essentially not very precise; he thought in broad but somewhat fuzzy terms, even though he usually held the right position. Not a good administrator, he had no particular interest in the day-to-day operations of the office or in following channels of authority. Davis was such a staunch individualist that working as part of an organization was not his forte.

Davis also maintained a small staff. When I arrived, he and I were about the only ones in the office. He had an assistant who handled some of the more routine matters involving wage problems and several other minor officials were around, but he and I practically carried the entire load ourselves. At my suggestion we hired an economist to help us, as many of the problems involved economic issues. We brought Walter Salant from the OPA research staff, one of Dick Gilbert's chief assistants. Salant became a sort of third member of our triumvirate, although Davis tended not to grant him as full a status as I think Salant deserved.

## THE OES

The OES was set up to settle disputes and to determine basic policy. Its function was primarily to coordinate and supervise operating agencies, including OPA, the War Production Board, the War Labor Board (WLB), the War Food Administration, the Federal Reserve Board, the Reconstruction Finance Corporation, and other agencies concerned with economic stabilization.

In addition to the staff, the executive order had established an economic stabilization board to advise the director of the OES. This board consisted of the secretaries of the Treasury, Agriculture, Labor, Commerce, the chairman of the Federal Reserve Board, the administrator of OPA, the chairman of the WLB, the director of the Bureau of the Budget, and two representatives each from labor, industry, and agriculture. Jim Patton of the Farmers Union and Ed O'Neal from the Farm Bureau Federation were the agricultural representatives. I believe William Green and Phil Murray were the labor representatives. Thus, the board was composed of high-ranking officials, with Davis as chairman. Under Vinson the board had not operated extensively, but Davis believed it was possible to use the board more effectively, and he attempted to revive it.

Meetings were held about once a month, but the board never contributed much. The high-powered issues on the agenda could not be handled by the members of the board without extensive prior preparation and briefing. Consequently, no real decisions could be worked out on detailed matters. Broad questions of policy were considered with few concrete results. The OES was third in the hierarchy of decision makers on economic policy, with OWMR and the president above it. Consequently, board members, many of whom were cabinet officials, were reluctant to attempt any general settlement of policies in the board meetings. After the first one or two meetings, which did not produce many results, the top people more or less stopped coming and began sending assistants to sit in for them, so that eventually the board pretty much dropped out of the picture.

The operations of OES put me in contact with a considerably higher level of the government hierarchy than my work at OPA. We dealt with the OWMR frequently, and with Vinson. Our interchange with other agencies sometimes involved the top officials of those agencies or if not, usually officials pretty high up.

**OES as Referee**

In general, the functions of the OES were of two varieties. First were specific matters involving activities of the operating agencies, which were presented to the OES for a referee's decision. For example, under the price control legislation, the prices of agricultural commodities or products processed from agricultural commodities could be fixed only by joint action of OPA and the secretary of Agriculture. Where a difference of opinion between OPA and the Department of Agriculture could not be resolved, the matter was submitted to the OES.

Another instance arose under the price executive orders, concerning proposed price increases to be made by OPA on cost-of-living commodities where the increase was above the minimum required by the standards and the law could be made by OPA only with the approval of OES. These were situations where price increases were requested for the purpose of increasing production.

A third matter of this kind arose when there were differences of opinion between OPA and other agencies concerning requests by other agencies for price increases that they contended were necessary to stimulate increased production. These would come to OES for a decision.

The OPA subsidy program also was within the jurisdiction of OES. I think any subsidies granted could be done so only by OES. The subsidy regulations were actually issued directly in the name of OES. In that sense OES was almost an operating agency. However, the details were worked out by other organizations. In cases where the WLB recommended a wage increase and OPA found that such an increase would require a price increase, the wage increase could be granted only if approved by OES. A number of such cases were constantly coming before us.

Finally, cases in which the WLB was unable to secure compliance with its orders were referred to OES for enforcement action. A continual flow of specific matters came to OES for decision.

## OES as Policymaker

The second main function of OES was the broader one of developing basic programs and policies, including the whole thrust of the stabilization program, the handling of new issues such as whether the "Little Steel" formula should be revised, reconversion pricing, and matters of decontrol of stabilization measures. It was the function of OES to anticipate these issues, to study them, and to lay down the basic policy. The operating agencies were required to carry out these policies.

## OES in Operation

Those issues that took the form of our giving approval to some action another agency wanted to take usually came before OES in the form of elaborate memoranda with supporting documents outlining the measure that was contemplated and enclosing a draft of a directive or order necessary to put it into effect. Our job was to check through the material and see whether anything looked suspicious. If not, it would be approved by the director. If there seemed to be any question, most likely a conference would be held with the submitting agency. Sometimes we would ask for further data and there would be discussion on the data that was submitted and some effort made to probe the background of the action in a meeting.

Cases of disputes between the agencies were handled primarily by setting up a meeting with representatives of all the agencies involved. The agencies usually had submitted memoranda or documents representing their point of view. If the issue was important, our director, William H. Davis, would preside at the meeting. If it were less important, I or someone else would attempt to handle it. The meeting included a discussion of the various points of view, exploration of possible compromises, and an effort to reach some agreement. Sometimes Davis would simply send the parties away and tell them to talk it over some more and try to agree. Sometimes he would propose solutions and at other times he would simply take the issue under advisement.

Longer-range projects also were pursued largely through meetings. We might start out with individual conferences with technical experts in various agencies and continue at the technical level for some time until recommendations were forthcoming. In other cases we would begin with a meeting at the top policy level. Again our process was to bring representatives of operating agencies into a meeting place, encourage them to express their views, and attempt to find some reasonable program of action that met with as much agreement as possible.

Before making a decision on a seriously disputed issue, OES sometimes took the precaution of clearing it with OWMR or President

Truman. We also had some responsibility to check whether the decisions were carried out. However, we did not have much time to follow through and had to rely on other agencies to file complaints if the policy was not being carried out.

Much of what I did at OES was not in the legal field at all. I worked almost entirely in the fields of economics and government administration, and dealt almost entirely with policy issues that were not legal policy issues. The work was quite a change from my days at OPA. It was much less arduous in many ways. I spent more time sitting around and listening. Others did more of the hard work and presented it to me in a memorandum. I had relatively few personnel or administrative problems. I was dealing with a staff of half a dozen people instead of a staff of some thousands. That allowed me considerably more time to concentrate on a few basic issues.

On the other hand, the work was less within my range of knowledge or experience, and less within my range of competence, than it had been before. I was dealing with issues that required considerable skill and information beyond questions of law or legal administration. Questions arose about the economics of the clothing industry, or problems in accounting, or issues of labor relations in connection with a strike, which were beyond my field of experience. I often felt frustrated because I was uncertain whether the decision I was making was the proper one. No one could have had adequate training for the job because it covered such a wide variety of problems. No one could possibly have been an expert in all the areas involved. A lot of it, however, was pure shooting in the dark. I might have an intuition that something was wrong with a memorandum presented by an agency, but as I was not an expert in the relevant field, I could not tell what was amiss. When an agency insisted something could not be done, I could not be sure whether it really could not or whether the agency just did not want to do it. I was operating beyond my depth, as anyone holding the job would have been.

Human relations were not difficult between OES and other agencies. No antagonism or bitterness toward OES appeared in the open. However, beneath the surface much opposition existed to various policies of OES and few had any inhibitions about attempting to thwart our policies. Perhaps that opposition was preferable to the agencies blindly following OES policies. It did make our job difficult, though, because we could never be sure whether an agency was doing the best it could or was opposing us. I would say that no agency really cooperated with us. No agency would accept an OES directive they opposed and attempt to implement it with full force. The modus operandi of government officials under these conditions would be to stall or obscure or appeal to somebody else. However, everyone recognized that the various operating agencies overlapped sufficiently and had disagreements to a sufficient extent that a coordinator was imperative. Therefore, no one attacked the basic design or the basic objective of the agency: to furnish a dispute-settling and coordinating organization. None of the operating agencies, however, was willing to yield to a decision contrary to its views without a fight.

So despite the less arduous nature of my work, I still could not sleep peacefully at night, satisfied that I had done a perfect job that day and could breeze through tomorrow's problems as well. The fact that we were a coordinating agency meant that I did not have the same relationship to the other people as I had in OPA. In OPA I was head of the department with authority to hire, discharge, discipline, and promote. When we settled a problem and I had approved an order or memorandum implementing our solution, I had some confidence that my subordinates would make a substantial effort to carry it out. Of course, even subordinates hold back on their bosses, but in OPA I had direct authority to require certain things to be done, and direct control over the people who would do them. In OES, on the other hand, I had the authority to require that certain things should be done—but no authority over the people who were doing them. The result was that people had more opportunity to resist whatever measures I was attempting to take.

I will postpone until the last chapter, on OWMR, an appraisal of the accomplishments and difficulties of OES as a coordinating agency. Actually, the OES was in effect a subdivision of the OWMR. There was need for coordination in economic stabilization, but stabilization needed to be coordinated with other aspects of the war program that were not directly matters of stabilization. That is to say, the problems of manpower, postwar settlement of contracts, dividing available products between military and civilian needs, and other issues of that sort, which were not strictly stabilization issues, nevertheless had to be pulled together. The coordination of stabilization was only one aspect of the total problem of coordination, and therefore although OES at this period was set up separately, it had to function as a division of OWMR. Being technically a separate agency had some advantages. One was that we could take some of the load off OWMR. Many of the details that OES handled would have been a burden to top policymakers at OWMR. Many of the smaller issues and inter-agency disputes were effectively disposed of by OES without requiring the attention of OWMR. Another advantage was that by being a separate agency, it was possible to get a more powerful personality in charge. The position of director of OES was a position of honor and responsibility that would attract men of a higher caliber than it would have had it simply been a division within the OWMR. On the other hand, the effect of being a separate agency but ultimately subject to OWMR was to lessen the prestige of OES. It meant that people could appeal our decisions to OWMR as well as to President Truman. Actually, people usually had a single chance of appeal because Truman would normally refer matters to the OWMR. That people could easily go over the head of OES, however, resulted in a lack of prestige.

## SIGNIFICANT EVENTS AFFECTING THE AGENCY
*Five bells on the ticker. . .*

Two major events circumscribed the whole operation of the OES during my tenure: the death of President Roosevelt on April 12, 1945, and V-E Day the following month.

### FDR

The death of Roosevelt came as a stunning blow to Washington. I was sitting in my office when I heard five bells ring on the ticker. By that time I had reached the point where I depended on the ticker instead of the newspapers, or at least I was operating at such high levels of government that I had to know what was going on five minutes after it happened, so that my secretary constantly placed the long yellow sheets from the ticker on my desk. The ticker was in an outside office. The door was open and I heard five bells ring, signaling some sort of extraordinary announcement, so I went out and watched as the ticker typed out that President Roosevelt had died in Georgia.

Most of us had not contemplated the possibility of the president's death. In retrospect, it was obvious that he had changed tremendously in physical appearance. Pictures taken of him at the last conference indicated that he had aged tremendously, and from time to time there were rumors that he was in ill health, but the possibility that he might die was one that none of my friends, so far as I know, had ever considered. It was a tremendous shock to Washington and to the whole country. Many of us had hardly known any other president. Roosevelt certainly was a "father image" to a great many people and his death had a distressing impact.

Some of the implications of his death were fairly clear as soon as we had time to pause and think about them. No other outstanding leader had emerged in the Democratic Party who could in any sense take his place. No other individual or group had anything like the prestige or the hold on the country that Roosevelt had. We realized that it would be exceedingly difficult, if not impossible, for anyone else to hold together the various forces composing the administration or the Democratic Party.

It was clear also that the emerging domestic and foreign issues were ones that a person of less prestige than President Roosevelt could scarcely handle very well. Although V-E Day was not to happen for another month, we nevertheless realized that the end of the war must be near and that the postwar problems were about to descend upon us. As I said, there had been very little discussion of all this. Obviously, virulent differences of opinion would develop. It was clear that the absence of Roosevelt's leadership would make the solution of those problems, both domestic and foreign, extremely difficult.

Almost immediately we glimpsed the nightmare that views held by the extreme right-wing groups in Washington would gain wider acceptance. Until then government employees had been fairly well protected from the

Dies Committee (subsequently the House Committee on Un-American Activities). The "lunatic fringe" of Congress, such as McKellar, Bilbo, and Rankin were able to generate a commotion, but were not able to affect appreciably the standing of an individual in the executive branch of government. President Roosevelt had been powerful enough to shield his administration from such attacks. We feared that that protection would now be withdrawn and glimpsed the possibility that these ideologues might come to represent a stronger and perhaps even a dominant force. We also realized that the southern Democrats of a more respectable nature–Senators George, Russell, and Tom Connally–would carry more weight and perhaps determine ultimate policies. We even began to visualize the prospect of a Congress controlled by the Republican Party, speculating on the effect of a committee on Appropriations headed by Representative Taber or a Committee on Government Expenditures headed by Representative Hoffman of Michigan, and on what would happen if some of the Republicans who had hitherto been confined largely to spouting off should now assume control.

At the time I was struck by the speed with which the Roosevelt myth developed. His supporters immediately adopted the concept of Roosevelt as a person who could do no wrong. I suppose the solemnity of his funeral procession influenced the myth. As his body was transported from Union Station through the streets of Washington I could feel the emotions emerging to surround his name and his administration. When Roosevelt was alive we had been quite critical at many points. We told each other that he did not know what he was doing here, that he was yielding too much there, that he was weak in this regard, that he did not step in energetically enough to make decisions in disputes between agencies, and so on. We were always complaining about the president, although everyone realized the significant role he was playing. All criticism disappeared almost overnight, however, and his supporters almost deified him. Of course, Roosevelt's enemies continued to hold their views as strongly as before. The Roosevelt myth as a man who operated beyond reproach and who could have solved all future problems of the country seemed to grow up almost overnight, however.

Nobody visualized Truman as able to occupy the shoes of "FDR." Truman himself shared the prevalent view. Changes developed gradually, however. At first the momentum of the administration carried it along to a large extent as it had been going before. Truman's position and the kind of administration that he would head appeared somewhat gradually. However, certain signs disturbed the Roosevelt loyalists almost from the beginning. One was Truman's appointments. Members of the Roosevelt cabinet resigned rather rapidly. In May 1945 Senator Schwellenback replaced Frances Perkins as secretary of labor, Representative Anderson replaced Claude Wickard as secretary of agriculture, and Tom Clark replaced Francis Biddle as attorney general. In July, Byrnes became secretary of state. The change that concerned us most was the appointment of Tom Clark as attorney general. At the same time Bennett Clark and Wilbur Miller were appointed to the Court of Appeals for the District of Columbia. We were shocked and extremely discouraged at these first indications of Truman's incompetence in making appointments, particularly to positions related to law. This key weakness in the Truman administration was manifested quite early.

## V-E Day

The other major event of my early days at OES was V-E Day. V-E Day came as no surprise. In fact, many had expected that V-E Day would occur considerably before this. As early as the late summer of 1944 many people in Washington thought that the war in Europe was practically over. Then came the Battle of the Bulge and the realization that more fighting remained. By the time of V-E Day, however, it was clear that the war in Europe was finished. Washington celebrated, but the tone was restrained by the feeling that a long road lay ahead. Most of the military prognosticators were indicating that the war in Japan might go on for another two or three years and would involve enormous casualties.

V-E Day did produce a substantial change in the situation. A number of economic problems immediately arose. The possibility of reconverting some industry to civilian production raised the possibility of removing some of the wartime restrictions–a "program of decontrol," as it was called. There was the possible cancellation of government contracts for ships and other materials no longer needed. Ending the war in Europe also created the problem of keeping the energies of the country geared to still fighting a war and not permitting a letdown to occur. We were concerned that if the Japanese war should end at the same time as the war in Europe, an overwhelming economic depression, or at least dislocation, would result. Therefore, we admitted that a continuation of the Japanese war would have the advantage of permitting a more gradual readjustment of the economic situation. But a major postwar adjustment would undoubtedly be necessary in any event.

## British Labor and Hiroshima

Two further significant events occurred in the latter part of my work with OES. One was the victory of the Labor Party in England in the elections of July 1945. These elections had considerable impact on the American picture, at least in Washington. The regulars in the New Deal had been fighting a rearguard action for so long that we were somewhat taken by surprise when the British Labor Party achieved a substantial victory over the grand old conservative, Churchill. It seemed to indicate that people were beginning to think that a certain degree of government control and planning would be acceptable if it produced the kind of full employment and high prosperity that had occurred during the war. Hence, it bolstered the morale of what remained of the New Deal in Washington, and gave promise of a future for New Deal policies and ideas.

The other major event was the dropping of the atomic bomb on

Hiroshima August 6, 1945. Again I recall first learning of this event from the ticker. The account on the ticker was somewhat confused, but it was clear that something significant had happened. The report referred to dropping an "atomic bomb" with the capacity of 20,000 tons of TNT, with the explanation that it was the same energy that comes from the sun. I knew very little about the scientific background of the atomic bomb. In addition, the secret of the bomb's manufacture had been extremely well kept. I know of nobody then or since who claimed to have any information about the development of the atomic bomb. A few of us inside the New Deal had heard that there was a large, secret project operating in Oak Ridge, Tennessee, and that large sums were being appropriated for some mysterious purpose. But nonscientists, at least, in the government had no awareness whatsoever of the impending use of the atomic bomb. Nor did I ever hear rumors of secret weapons. We all were taken completely by surprise and failed to understand the implications for weeks and months. The significance in terms of military strategy, the problems involved in attempts at international control of atomic energy–all these implications dawned on people rather slowly as more information on the bomb came to light and as the problems developed.

## OES POLICIES

I will describe some of the major issues that came before OES during this period.

### Southern Pine

One illustration of a specific decision was a request for price increases in the southern pine industry. The WPB was frantically striving to obtain increased lumber production. They came to OPA with the proposition that there would be more lumber production if the price was increased. OPA, either because it agreed with the proposition or because it was willing to pass the buck to OES, acquiesced. (Since it was a price increase not required by OPA standards but designed to exceed those standards for purposes of obtaining increased production, the request had to be submitted to OES.) I had some information about the southern pine industry as a result of my OPA enforcement activities. We looked over the proposition, and both Director Davis and I agreed that the price increase should not be granted. We turned it down on the theory that it would not have resulted in an increase in production, as the prices were sufficiently high to create as much production as was feasible. This was an example of a clear-cut problem with a clear-cut solution.

### Meat

We were head over heels in meat problems. Just before I had come to OES, Vinson had laid down a ten-point policy for the meat industry that included regulations dealing with slaughtering, subsidies, and so on. This new policy was supposed to enable OPA to successfully enforce the meat regulations. The main difficulty was that this workable policy had come too late, and also that those parts of it administered by the Department of Agriculture were not being seriously enforced. The meat problem was not solved, and it repeatedly returned to haunt us. We issued revisions of the meat program from time to time, including revisions in the subsidy program, but nothing we did was notably successful. By that time the problem had gotten out of hand; it would have required considerably more time to have gotten it back under control.

### Clothing

Another problem that occupied a good deal of our time, one intermediate between day-to-day issues and broader policy issues, was the clothing industry. In the fall of 1944 OES had issued an elaborate directive requiring WPB to set up certain controls to facilitate handling of the "highest price line" problem in the clothing industry. Prichard had developed this directive and convinced Vinson to issue it. The WPB resisted it strongly and in effect failed to carry it out. Part of the program under the Prichard directive had been put into operation but that part was working badly. The OPA requirements for producing lower-priced lines were hard to meet because the WPB was not providing the low-cost materials necessary to produce the low-cost items. The garment industry was in great turmoil about the program; delegations from the industry frequently traveled to Washington to protest the way it was operated. Consequently, when I joined OES the clothing problem still needed urgent action.

OPA, with WPB disagreeing, developed a system whereby WPB would issue so-called "set aside" orders requiring a manufacturer of textiles to set aside a certain portion of his product for low-cost producers. In other words, this system allocated raw materials to producers who were required to produce certain types of products. By this time a decline in the production of textile products had become one of the basic sources of the trouble. Hence, increasing the volume of textile production would contribute to the solution. WPB, and to some extent OPA, claimed that textile production would not rise unless price increases were granted. Also, the textile industry had been having trouble maintaining its labor force. Some thought this was due to low wages, with the solution being an increase in the wage scale. The ramifications of the issue–prices, manpower, and wages–began to encompass the entire stabilization problem.

Our office tossed around this problem, one of the most difficult and frustrating ones we had. Director Davis called a number of meetings to discuss it and sent it back for further consideration. Then Davis went on vacation and the problem landed in my lap. I had no idea of what to do about it. It was one of those situations where I could not be sure that the program suggested would accomplish the results. The industry was screaming louder and louder. WPB finally declared openly that it would not follow the proposed program unless directed to do so by President Truman. WPB's position was that it did not want to impose, as a matter of principle, the kind of controls we believed necessary to solve the problem. WPB thought the issues could be solved by price increases, and that it was worthwhile making a price increase rather than attempting the elaborate government controls that would be necessary to resolve it without price increases. WPB was pretty much taking the textile and clothing industries' point of view. OPA was willing to grant some price increases, but on the whole was anxious to hold the line, and OES was determined not to make any price increases unless they were necessary.

Who knows what eventually would have happened? Before any resolution occurred, the situation was definitively changed by V-J Day.

## Price Policies

Another major problem before OES was the consideration of some basic price policies that arose out of conditions subsequent to V-E Day. One issue was pricing reconversion goods. This problem continued to be a serious one, extending not only to goods that had not been produced during the war but also to model changes and adaption of goods from military to civilian purposes. Since our ideas on this issue were similar to OPA's, we could generally leave the matter to OPA and follow its recommendations.

A second aspect of price policies during this period was the problem of decontrol, that is, the suspension or exemption of commodities from price control. OES issued a broad directive authorizing OPA to suspend price controls in those situations where this would not result in an increase in prices above the general level then existing. Any suspension of price controls on commodities affecting the cost of living had to be submitted to OES before being issued. OPA was authorized to suspend controls without specific OES approval if a commodity did not significantly enter into the cost of living or into business costs, or the control of the commodity involved administrative difficulties disproportionate to the effectiveness of the control, or suspension of the control presented no threat of destabilization through diversion of materials and facilities. This directive made a bow to the forces calling for decontrol, but actually permitted OPA very little leeway to remove price ceilings except in insignificant areas. This policy on decontrol was satisfactory to OPA, as it was worked out largely on the basis of OPA recommendations.

However, OPA was pressing for change in two areas. One was that they wanted to increase the number of individual adjustments. Previously, individual adjustments had been granted only where it was necessary to secure the added production for war purposes. With the end of the war in Europe and the beginning of reconversion, OPA was suggesting a relaxation of the adjustment policy, and proposed a program for extending individual adjustments to many other cases where manufacturers could not carry on under the ceiling prices. As OES did not believe a relaxation of the adjustment policy was necessary, we stalled until V-J Day. OPA also was pressing for the establishment of policy under which it could grant price increases above the minimum required by law for the purpose of obtaining increased production. It had had some power to do this with OES approval, but OPA was requesting a general statement of policy from OES rather than case-by-case approval. Again we judged it inadvisable to write them a blank check about that, and as I recall we took no action.

**Wage Policy**

In this period wage policies were also coming to the fore. The WLB was considering whether the "Little Steel" formula, still the basic formula for determining whether wage increases should be allowed, should be revised. They were also discussing whether labor should be compensated for the loss of wages due to the lessening of overtime as the result of V-E Day. Should normal pay rates increase to compensate for this loss in take-home pay and also for certain other alleged downgradings? If the War Labor Board granted wage increases, could they be absorbed by the manufacturers without price increases? Pressure grew for a restatement of the entire wage policy and those aspects of price policy that would depend on wage policy. After considerable study OES decided not to take action at the time. Davis, an expert on wage policy, had firm ideas about the matter. It might have become necessary to revise the wage policy at some point, except that V-J Day changed the whole picture.

OES also proposed an amendment to the Fair Labor Standards Act. The act still contained the $.40/hour minimum wage. Most hourly rates were far above $.40, but certain unorganized and low-wage areas would have been helped by an increase of the minimum. OES recommended a minimum wage of $.50, with a provision for raising it to $.65 on a recommendation of an industry committee. The Department of Labor under Schwellenback, succumbing to more urgent labor pressure, was recommending a minimum of $.65 with authority to increase it to $.75. Again, no resolution of the issue occurred during the period that OES was in existence.

Another problem we were confronted with was the inflation in the value of capital goods. The prices of real estate, farms, and securities had all increased rather rapidly. The economists believed that measures should be taken to control this increase. The Economic Stabilization Board considered this issue in some detail and finally gave their approval. OES proposed a four point program: 1) an executive order authorizing the Federal Reserve Board to limit the use of credit in purchasing farms and real estate in cities; 2) the Federal Reserve Board should increase the margin requirements for the purchase of securities; 3) the period for computing long term-capital gains under the federal income tax be extended from six months to three years (in other words, a gain would be considered a long-term type of gain and therefore subject to the lower tax only if the capital goods had been held for at least three years); and 4) an educational campaign stressing the need for caution in purchasing farmland, urban real estate, and securities. OES spelled out this proposal in some detail. We worked out an agreement with the Federal Reserve Board and the SEC. We had an executive order and a message to Congress already drafted. These documents were submitted to OWMR when Vinson was there. A little doubtful, Vinson sat on the proposal for a while. When he left and John Snyder came in, Snyder was not doubtful at all and rejected the proposal.

We were also concerned with the problem of the construction industry. The economists pointed out that the best source for capital investment and employment in the postwar period would be the construction industry, with the backing of civilian construction projects constituting an important expansion in civilian production where returning veterans could be employed. We held a number of meetings and considered various projects for speeding up construction, housing programs, and related matters. Our planning was in the elementary stages when V-J Day occurred. The program was later carried on by Wilson Wyatt and the Housing Administration.

We were also concerned with the full employment program, a matter affecting many other agencies including OWMR. Walter Salant and I did a substantial amount of work on the proposed Full Employment Bill. Davis was also interested. I will postpone any further discussion of that, however, until I describe my work at OWMR.

Another aspect of OES work involved legislation. The major piece of legislation pending in Congress that OES was concerned with when I was there was the renewal of the Price Control Act. It expired again at the end of June 1945 and came up in the same month for renewal. Actually, OES did not play a significant role in the renewal of the OPA legislation; OPA itself carried the major burden. OPA had the staff to prepare data for the hearings and technical knowledge about the details of amendments, as well as the most direct interest in the outcome. Top level pressures had to come from OWMR and President Truman rather than OES. Consequently, I observed more than participated in the struggle over the renewal of OPA. The bill that passed Congress was not so emasculated that operations were impossible. By and large members of Congress realized, as they had the year before, that the legislation was still essential. At that time it was uncertain when the war with Japan would end. I expect most people believed it would last another two or three years. It was evident that pressures on the economy made it impractical to continue the war without price controls. Recognition of this abstract principle, however, did not prevent massive lobbying for modifications to benefit individual industries or particular sections of industries. In addition, this time there was much more pressure for modifications that would have weakened the entire structure of OPA. Sen. Robert Taft led the fight for relaxation of the general policies under which OPA had operated. He was particularly concerned with the operation of the "generally fair and equitable rule," the industry earnings standard, and the individual product standard. The dangers of rather serious modifications seemed imminent. In the end, however, the renewal did not so qualify the price provisions that the administration of the act was impossible.

### Enforcement of War Labor Board Orders

One aspect of OES activity of some importance was more in my line than some of those policy matters: enforcement of WLB orders. While WLB regulations affecting maximum ceilings of wages and similar issues were enforceable under the Stabilization Act, decisions of the board settling disputes that did not involve ceilings on wages were not enforceable by any statutory provision. In most of those cases the employer and union complied voluntarily, but in a certain number one side or the other became recalcitrant. Typically, employers became recalcitrant, as usually the employer was called upon to make a change in the wage scale. Occasionally, a recalcitrant union would strike. As a result, it became necessary to devise some method of backing up the WLB's decisions. If nothing were done about the few recalcitrant cases, the virus would spread and other decisions of the board and its regional offices also would be ignored.

An executive order was issued authorizing OES to take measures for the enforcement of WLB orders. Three measures could be taken. One was to recommend to the president the seizure of the plant involved. A second was to direct procuring agencies to cancel contracts. Both of these devices were directed against the employer except when a plant was seized during a strike. One method of bringing the employees to terms was a directive to the War Manpower Commission ordering the cancellation of draft deferments.

In the course of OES's existence, I suppose about thirty or forty cases involving refusal to comply with WLB orders came before it. In all except two or three of those cases it was the employer who had refused to comply. Our usual remedy was to order seizure of the plant under the Smith-Connolly Act. We determined whether seizure was justified and the proper solution to the problem; if so, we recommended to the president that the plant be seized. We prepared the executive order and had all the papers ready for the president's signature. It was also our job to select the particular government agency that was to take charge of the seized plant. Government agencies hated that assignment. For one thing, word had spread around that the individual government officials who took over were liable if the company lost money during the period of the seizure. I kept assuring them that they were reasonably safe on that, and if they did get sued for millions of dollars, Congress would reimburse them--but that did not seem to make them feel any better. It was our job to require an agency to take over a plant. During my period at OES I suppose we must have seized 10-15 plants. Probably 25-30 were seized altogether. The seizure was almost entirely a paper transaction. Notice was posted that the plant was under government supervision. A government official would enter the plant and occupy the president's office, and that was approximately all that would happen. The management continued to run the plant. The funds coming in were kept within the business and when the plant was returned any profits were turned back with the business. In every case the WLB's decision was put into operation. With that exception, one could not tell the difference between a plant that had been seized and one that had not.

In two or three cases a plant was seized while a strike was in progress and the employees were refusing to comply with the WLB's decision. The strikers returned to work when the government seized the plant. Again the seizure was purely symbolic; the government did not actually operate the plant. For some reason, however, the piece of paper proclaiming that the government was now running the property had the effect of inducing the employees to cooperate.

In a few instances the symbolism did not have this magical effect. The most notorious, of course, was the Montgomery Ward case, in which Sewell Avery strongly objected to the government seizure and was carried out by soldiers into the street. That had happened before I came to OES. There the government became involved in plant operations because the company was unwilling to cooperate and one or two problems came before OES in connection with government operation of Montgomery Ward.

A more systematic method of handling the seizures would have evolved if we had continued the procedure and I suppose that ultimately the seizures might have been used to exert more pressure. The procedure was haphazard, however, and was never fully considered. It was as if everyone were afraid to face the problem of government seizure. It was acceptable as an emergency matter, but not appropriate for more systematic treatment. In addition, serious conflict potentially existed on government policy: whether the government should keep the profits earned while the plant was in the government's hands and so on. None of those issues came to the fore.

The other method of dealing with recalcitrant employers was to direct the procurement agencies to cancel government contracts. It was at this point that OES met almost universal resistance from the operating agencies. Actually, the sanction was normally not available because in most cases the production of the company was urgently needed and it would not have been feasible to cancel the contracts. A few cases involved firms that held nonessential war contracts and the goods could be procured from other sources. Under Vinson OES had never used this sanction. Davis and I ordered the procurement agencies to cancel contracts in one or two cases. The agencies stalled and refused, so, as I recall, in no case was the sanction actually implemented.

We also attempted to direct the WPB to cancel allocations. The WPB was completely rebellious. Its director, Jacob Krug announced that he would not do that unless the president ordered him to. We submitted the matter to President Truman through Snyder's office [as director of OWMR] and heard nothing further.

The Petroleum Administrative Board (PAB) rather than the WPB controlled gasoline allocations. The PAB apparently *was* willing to curtail allocations in response to OES directives. In litigation designed to test the validity of OES action in withdrawing allocations, the Wentworth Bus Company brought suit to enjoin curtailment of their allocation. This litigation generated controversy among Department of Justice staff, who expected difficulty in the courts. OES insisted on the importance of success in the suit and arrangements were made to defend the OES action. The litigation was postponed because of some proceedings before the National Labor Relations Board, and was set for argument in the district court in the early part of September 1945. However, V-J Day intervened, gasoline rationing was abandoned, and the suit became moot–so the question never came to a formal decision.

## Racial Policies

In one other area OES attempted to exercise its directive powers to compel operating agencies to curtail government contracts or allocations as a means of obtaining enforcement of other government action: in connection with the Fair Employment Practices Committee (FEPC). The FEPC had no legal authority to enforce its orders dealing with matters of discrimination against Negroes in employment. Most of its decisions were complied with voluntarily or through persuasion. However, matters occasionally arose that could not be settled on a voluntary basis. It was important for FEPC to obtain compliance with these decisions because of the effect on its prestige and subsequent influence. Consequently, in accordance with the terms of its executive order, which provided that where there was noncompliance the FEPC should refer the matter to the president, the FEPC referred one or two cases to OES with the request that recommendations for action be made to the president. This was actually the first time that FEPC had undertaken to back up its orders with any potent sanctions. It was clear that there would be difficulty in persuading any other government agency to champion the FEPC on this problem. I was supportive of FEPC enforcement, and I guess the only reason the FEPC referred the matter to OES was that they knew I was there and knew of my interest in the matter. OES Director Davis was also concerned and wanted to test the matter.

In view of our experience in attempting to enforce WLB orders through withdrawal of contracts or allocations, we assumed that we would have even less success with FEPC orders. We therefore decided that before attempting directives of any sort we should obtain clearance further up the line. We wanted to prepare those above us for the controversy that would ensue and we wanted assurance that we could get some backing if we undertook to issue a directive to another agency. The matter was referred to OWMR and possibly reached President Truman. Again, we heard nothing further about it, and no further action was taken, nor was there anything more that OES could do in the matter. The result was that no effort was made along this line to obtain compliance with FEPC orders.

This outcome was hardly surprising to us. We knew from the beginning that the cards were stacked against us and that it would be very unlikely that anything would ever happen. I do not mean to imply that the Truman administration was entirely opposed to the FEPC or to Negro rights. As a matter of fact, during the New Deal administration considerable progress had occurred on discrimination. When I came to Washington in the early days of the New Deal, for instance, there were practically no Negroes in government posts beyond the purely custodial ones–janitors, messenger boys, and elevator operators. I cannot recall now a single Negro who occupied any post of responsibility in the government in any department–there may have been one or two, but it certainly would have been most unusual. The armed forces had a rather rigid policy of segregation at that time. Many of the government projects, such as restaurants, maintained that segregation policy.

The change was very gradual. I recall that David Niles, who was President Roosevelt's assistant on minority problems, made quite persistent efforts behind the scenes to obtain jobs for Negroes in various agencies. To some extent he was successful in this. He spoke to me several times about hiring Negro lawyers at the NLRB. I would have been perfectly willing to do this and interviewed one or two, but no sufficiently qualified Negro lawyers applied. Very few Negroes were being educated for the law. However, we all recognized that it would have been exceedingly risky to have hired one; in addition to all the objections to our legitimacy, we would have been taking on a substantial controversy with Congress if we had hired Negro lawyers. That would have been even worse for our relations with Congress than to have ten women lawyers on the staff. However, we would have done it had we been able to find anybody. I suppose that in all fairness I must admit that I did not make affirmative efforts to search for Negro lawyers.

I think it was the war that changed things most. There had been gradual change prior to the war, but the shortage of manpower during the war created a situation where it became essential to use Negro labor, including in the more skilled positions. Gradually there began to be appointments–in some agencies, at any rate–of Negroes to more responsible posts. The War Labor Board was one of the most advanced in this respect, but there were Negroes in many of the government agencies–not on the basis of full equality, but nevertheless treated as equals when they were in there. Of course, they did not hold government jobs in proportion to their numbers in the population. The FEPC was created largely in response to this demand for labor and the effort to use Negro labor in more skilled jobs and on a non-discriminatory basis.

In addition to the war the position of Negroes in the government also improved for a political reason. As the New Deal tended to lose many of its supporters, it began to rely more heavily on the Negro vote. The Negro vote became more important in many key areas of the country. As time went on, then, even though the New Deal administration turned consistently more conservative, the status of the Negro in the government tended to improve. However, this incident with the FEPC indicates that things had not reached the point where one was likely to find overwhelming public or agency support. We knew from the beginning that we could not get backing for the FEPC from the WPB or the other war agencies unless there was a clear mandate from President Truman himself. I am not sure that the issue ever reached President Truman. I suspect it never reached him personally.

## MOVE TO OWMR

Fred Vinson, head of OWMR, had been appointed secretary of the Treasury and John W. Snyder was appointed as director of OWMR. Vinson's general counsel, Ed Prichard, accompanied Vinson to the Treasury Department. (Shortly afterward Prichard retired from government service and returned to Kentucky to practice law and politics. Planning to run for governor of Kentucky, he thought the time had come to shift his activities back to Kentucky.) Prichard's transfer left a vacancy in the position of general counsel at OWMR.

At the time, the end of July or the beginning of August, 1945, William Davis was on vacation in Maine, and I was acting director of the OES. Not much was happening in the late summer months, but the office was reasonably active. Hans Klagsbrunn, who was John Snyder's principal assistant, invited me to lunch. Klagsbrunn was a lawyer from the class behind me at the Yale Law School. He asked me to come over and serve as general counsel of OWMR. (I will return later to why Klagsbrunn's invitation surprised me.) I immediately felt that it was a substantial promotion and that I should take the job. However, I could not give an answer while Davis was away. When Davis returned within the next day or so, I talked it over with him, and he agreed that it was only fair that I should take the job at OWMR. I checked into the character and methods of operation of Snyder and got a fairly lukewarm but not too damaging report. Since the position was clearly one of advancement, as it was dealing with top level policy questions, I decided it would be more interesting and more important, and I did not hesitate about the choice. I went over to talk to Snyder and told him I would start after I had had a chance to take a vacation. Just as I was ready to leave for my vacation, V-J Day occurred, which thwarted my vacation plans. I had learned the lesson at the time of Pearl Harbor that such events created economic dislocations and opportunities for new solutions, so my work urgently demanded attention and I could not leave town. I transferred to OWMR approximately the middle of August 1945.

The problems of economic stabilization that OES was dealing with were becoming more difficult and frustrating. After V-E day controls were relaxed. On the other hand, it was imperative that the controls be maintained on an effective basis. This was becoming more difficult because of pressures from industry and Congress, and the general decline in public support. Nevertheless, there was still a vital and challenging job of stabilization to be done. The job, so far as I could see at the end of July, when the question of my leaving arose, would continue for a considerable period of time. It would have been more difficult, more frustrating, but still would have presented an interesting challenge. On the other hand, I anticipated that increasingly, particularly as we tackled reconversion problems, OWMR would be the key agency. OWMR would run the show and OES was bound to be a second-string affair. This hierarchy was becoming more and more recognized, and OES's prestige was tending to decline. William H. Davis did not wield the power that Vinson had. Vinson's relations with Congress, his position on the court of appeals, his relations with President Truman and his political backing, all made him a towering figure in the Washington power scene, compared with Davis. Vinson was one of the major figures in the Democratic party, a possible candidate for the presidency, probably Truman's chief rival at the time. Perhaps there were other reasons for the declining prestige of OES. I did not have the capacity for maneuvering that Prichard had, so I was not able to generate as much support as Prichard had for pet projects in all quarters of the administration.

The task at OWMR obviously would be much broader. It would include not only the stabilization effort but all problems of the conduct of the war apart from military policy and foreign policy. It also would include a much broader field in terms of reconversion. Finally, it was the chief economic planning agency of the government. Apart from the work the Bureau of the Budget did in connection with the annual budget, OWMR was the one place in the government where basic planning on economic and political issues took place. This planning, which was beginning to get under way, had a special appeal for me. I thought that in the postwar period the most vital spot would be the agency that studied projects and events from the long-term point of view, attempted to predict future trends, and formulated policies to keep the economy on an even keel. This was not the express purpose of OWMR, but it was a function that OWMR was gradually beginning to assume, largely under Robert Nathan, the chief economic advisor there. The possibility of getting in on the ground floor of that very fundamental and exciting function attracted my particular interest.

My OES experience, and in part at OWMR as well, was frustrating in that the broad problems seemed no longer within my grasp. In the NLRB, OPA, and the other agencies I was dealing with much more concrete issues. I could observe results and measure my success. Here I was dealing with much more complicated issues, issues that were primarily economic rather than legal, and success very often depended upon forces that were completely outside my control. On the other hand, the broader issues were more exciting and significant. Furthermore, I was dealing with the top hierarchy of the government. My job was to attend meetings at which cabinet members or under secretaries would normally be present, to work rather closely with them–in other words, to operate at the very top level of the government. To watch those people in operation, to get to know them and to read the ticker tape on what each one of them was doing day by day was a tremendous experience.

### Personnel at OWMR
*As I prepared for my next career move, to the OWMR, I considered the people I would be working with*

I was quite impressed by Robert Patterson, the secretary of war. Many of the others disappointed me, though. Marriner Eccles struck me as a garrulous fellow without too much to say. In fact, it was hard to keep him from monopolizing the conversation at every meeting. Claude Wickard, who was secretary of the Department of Agriculture, was a second-rater, a very pleasant but weak and untalented person. I was puzzled as to how he stayed in, or why he stayed in, or how he got appointed, as he did not seem to have backing of any sort. The Reconstruction Finance Corporation people seemed to be among the most bureaucratic of all. I suppose that agency had been running longer, but they were all tied up in red tape and seemed to have a very narrow point of view.

I saw something of Admiral Leahy at that time. He seemed to me a senile old man who could not possibly know what he was doing. I was somewhat impressed by Eric Johnston, who was the industry representative on the OES board and the OWMR board. He was obviously a slick fellow, not profound, but intelligent, quick, and reasonable, with considerable charm. Ed O'Neal of the Farm Bureau Federation was a foxy old man who would not look at anybody; he knew his own strength and was willing to exercise it. I had the impression that he was a pretty intelligent and shrewd individual, but I did not see much of him. I was very much impressed with Jim Patton of the Farmers Union. Patton was a highly intelligent person who could take technical advice. He seemed to have as firm a commitment to the public good as any individual inside or outside of government that I met at that time. George Mead, the industry advisory representative, seemed to me a relic of better days with nothing to offer in this situation.

I was greatly impressed with Harold Ickes. He was an irascible fellow with tremendous energy and tremendous gifts of expression. He had exceedingly sound instincts. Almost every time he seemed to be on the right side and if he was there you could count on a big gun firing in the right direction.

Jacob Krug of WPB never seemed to fulfill his potential, although he had moved up rapidly. He was a very intelligent individual, but seemed to lack a solid core, shifting with the winds rather than having a basic philosophy about what he was doing. Although he began as a liberal public servant in the Donald Richberg tradition, he was pushed rather quickly into becoming an apologist for big business. He was a person of great ability who seemed to use it for other people and for other purposes, rather than for some independent purpose that he had figured out as the right one.

I had not found the same kind of talent and willingness to take risks and move forward in OES as I had in my earlier experiences. I found it again at OWMR. Many of the army people that I came across in OES seemed to be persons with no spark or flair, persons who had obtained their present ranks by outlasting others. I also struck a good deal more timidity.

It is very hard to say why persons with a flair for innovation disappeared from the New Deal government. Nathan and his group in OWMR were rather quickly defeated; after six months or so the group had lost its power. A Madden or a Henderson or a Ginsberg were rather rare figures. Only a limited number of highly talented people like Ickes and Patterson were available. Perhaps the basic explanation was that the temper of the times was shifting. During the war period there was a united front among all forces in the administration and a build-up of potential backing for New Deal methods and policies, largely based on fear of another depression. World War II had ended the depression and people feared that when the war ended we would be plunged right back into it. On the other hand, during the war effort they had seen the possibilities of what could happen and had had a glimpse of the kind of leadership that might continue and carry forward the economic prosperity. If anything could accomplish that, it appeared rather clearly that it would be a New Deal kind of planning. And so a possibility built up in the last days of the war that gave new life and new significance to the New Deal group. Of course by this time many New Dealers were casualties to the political trends. Henderson had no public or political prestige. Madden had retired to the court of claims. Jim Landis was on the periphery. While many of the original crowd were no longer available, many remained, particularly on the secondary level. New Deal spirit and power flared up briefly in the last days of the war and until the first part of 1946. But by that time it was clear that the trend was definitely in the opposite direction.

# 15

# THE OFFICE OF
# WAR MOBILIZATION
# AND RECONVERSION

*How much of the New Deal could-should-would continue into posterity?*

The Office of War Mobilization was created by an executive order issued in May 1943. James Byrnes, who had been head of OES, was promoted to become director. The War Mobilization and Reconversion Act of October 1944 established the agency on a statutory basis as the Office of War Mobilization and Reconversion (OWMR), and Byrnes continued as director after the legislation was passed. The main functions of OWMR were to make plans and determine policies in regard to all aspects of the conduct of the war with the exception of military policy and foreign policy. OWMR was intended to formulate basic policies, anticipate developments, study trends, be prepared with policies on emerging issues, and also to establish policy for issues urgent at the moment. In addition, it was to coordinate the day-to-day operations of the line agencies by settling disputes and ruling on issues that arose among them.

## FUNCTIONS AND PERSONNEL
*Snyder, Klagsbrunn, Nathan*

OWMR had the power to issue "directives." These directives were executive orders, except that they were issued by OWMR rather than by the president. Theoretically binding on the other agencies, these directives were a device by which OWMR could make its decision effective.

The offices of the agency were in the East Wing of the White House. This location conferred great prestige, which enhanced the agency's effectiveness. Byrnes was known as "the assistant President." This informal appellation caused some difficulty, and Byrnes did not encourage the title, but he was generally considered that way, and his duties amounted to that. Under Byrnes the office operated primarily on a one-man basis. Byrnes had three or four assistants who handled particular problems for him. Benjamin Cohen was his general counsel. Major General Lucius Clay had the title of deputy director for war programs. John B. Hutson handled agricultural problems for Byrnes and his principal assistant was Donald Russell. Byrnes, Ben Cohen, and Russell conducted most of the operations. Clay and Hutson had a significant influence. It was a very small office, though, where Byrnes made practically all the decisions himself. He participated personally in all negotiations of any importance. To a large extent he operated by telephone and small face-to-face meetings. He issued very few directives. He operated mainly behind the scenes; very little of what he did was made public. Byrnes made no effort to obtain publicity for his office or to enhance public relations.

Byrnes concentrated on settling disputes between agencies. Operating on a day-to-day basis, the agency did some important work, particularly in resolving disputes between the military and civilian supply agencies and in keeping the military demands for scarce materials from running wild. The office did very little broad policy formulation while Byrnes was there. No economist of any rank was on his staff. The only planning accomplished by Byrnes was farmed out to Bernard Baruch, such as the responsibility for preparing a report on postwar problems of contract settlement and surplus property disposal, resulting in what was known as the Baruch-Hancock Report.

Byrnes resigned as director of OWMR in March 1945, and Fred Vinson moved up from OES to succeed him. Vinson brought Edward Prichard with him. They conducted operations somewhat differently from Byrnes. Robert Nathan was brought in from the War Production Board as one of the major members of the staff. Gradually, largely under Nathan's leadership, a staff operation rather than a one-man operation began to emerge. In other words, the top coordinating office was becoming an institution. Various divisions were established and a much larger staff was brought in.

In many ways this transformation made OWMR that much more important and more effective. For one thing, the agency could put its fingers into many more pies. With more staff, we could compile more information about what was happening, accomplish more work on our own, and generate more specific proposals. Inasmuch as OWMR permeated the operations of the executive branch substantially more, it was more influential. Now we had the staff and technical assistance to engage in more long-range planning. Transcending the mere settlement of disputes, we could operate affirmatively, by discovering problems that should have been the subject of dispute but that no one was bringing to our attention officially. We could begin to plan an affirmative program, short-term as well as long-term. We could follow up to see that the policies we had enunciated were carried out.

However, other consequences of this transformation also served to decrease the agency's prestige, resulting in diminished effectiveness. Many decisions now were made at lower levels of OWMR. Vinson himself could not possibly have participated in all that went on. The decisions that Byrnes had made, he had made personally, making them much more likely to happen. Now many decisions that Vinson took responsibility for actually were made by a subordinate. Information about who actually made a given decision is quickly available in Washington; when people know a subordinate has made a decision, they will appeal to the agency head to block the decision. That, for instance, is what happened in the attempt to exert some federal control over the clothing industry, which was largely the work of Prichard and some of the economists, and which Vinson himself undoubtedly never really understood. On balance, the institutionalized OWMR covered more ground, but not with as powerful a punch as under Byrnes.

John Snyder was appointed director of OWMR when Vinson became secretary of the Treasury in July 1945. Snyder had been a banker in St. Louis. During World War II he worked in Washington with the Reconstruction Finance Corporation and then served rather inconspicuously as head of the Defense Plants Corporation. Snyder was head of the defense plants when Truman suddenly became president. If Snyder had not been a close friend of Harry Truman for many years, it is doubtful he would have risen to any significant position in the government. The two of them had served in World War I together and had maintained close relations since then. The story was that when Snyder came to Washington and was invited to a formal party, he would borrow Senator Truman's dress clothes. Or was it the other way around? Anyway, Snyder was one of President Truman's closest friends and they were extremely loyal to each other.

Snyder's intense loyalty to Truman induced him to take positions with which he did not personally agree but which he believed were necessary for Truman's political success. One instance was his position on the Full Employment Bill, which he supported in its original form without understanding it, for had he understood it, his inherent conservatism would have led him to strongly oppose it. However, where he believed that maintaining President Truman's grip on power required compromise with the forces of evil, he was willing to do so. He did so reluctantly, and he did it more at the beginning than toward the end. As the scene shifted and the liberal forces declined, Snyder's position tended to become more outspokenly conservative.

Snyder was not a person of any great native ability. He had a fairly quick mind and was fairly shrewd in his thinking, but his level of talent was generally mediocre. His outstanding characteristic was narrowness. He was completely uneducated, with no interest in intellectual or cultural issues; in fact, nothing outside the immediate area in which he was operating intrigued him. His point of view was almost entirely that of a small-town banker. He seemed never to have been exposed to any other point of view. He was ignorant and inexperienced about labor problems and consequently suspicious and afraid of the topic. He knew that labor caused trouble by striking, or caused trouble on the political scene, and his response was hostile. Toward consumers he was disdainful.

Snyder usually was rather glum, sharp-faced, and mean. He had no sense of humor and was quite impatient and irascible. He had no respect for the feelings or dignity of his subordinates. He would fly into a rage without justification and give a tongue-lashing to a subordinate. As a result he was not particularly liked by his staff. Perhaps in his private life he was different. I never saw him socially. We clashed pretty much from the beginning. It may be that in his contacts with President Truman he was much more charming than he appeared to the office.

Snyder's principal assistant was Hans Klagsbrunn. Klagsbrunn had worked as an attorney for Snyder in the Defense Plants Corporation and had gone along with him to OWMR. Snyder trusted Klagsbrunn completely and relied on him heavily as a general troubleshooter and chief assistant. Klagsbrunn did a certain amount of work for President Truman. He came to participate in most of the presidential speechwriting and worked with Truman as Truman revised a draft and polished it up.

Klagsbrunn had been in the class behind me at Yale Law School. I was considerably surprised when he offered me the job as general counsel in OWMR because of the background of our relations at law school. Klagsbrunn was a very industrious and intelligent student who led his law school class. By tradition he would have been elected my successor as editor-in-chief of the *Yale Law Journal.* However, some of the more aggressive and colorful figures on our Board of Editors got the notion that Klagsbrunn was totally without imagination or flair, and they opposed him as editor-in-chief. Beyond that, they judged his contributions to the *Journal* dull and highly conventional, and they thought he should not even be elected to the board. I reviewed Klagsbrunn's contributions carefully; while it was true that they were uninspired, one could not say they were incompetent. But I was finally persuaded not to oppose the move to exclude him. Not receiving an appointment was a major shock to Klagsbrunn. I am sure he must have thought I had treated him very unfairly, and since that time I had run across him only very casually. So I was startled when he offered me a position as general counsel of the agency in which he was second in command. I took it as an indication of his mature perspective and willingness to forgive.

As I worked with Klagsbrunn at OWMR I became more favorably impressed than I had been in law school. There was no doubt about his ability at handling legal and general issues. He was a keen lawyer who grasped things very quickly. He still was prosaic and conventional. If he had had much flair, I suppose he would never have reached his level of success in combination with John Snyder. Many of Klagsbrunn's friends were in the liberal New Deal group, so that he was somewhat oriented in that direction–but not committed to it. His conservative outlook earned him the full confidence of Snyder. As time went by he came to split more and more with the New Deal crowd in the office, although he remained a bridge between the New Deal group and Snyder. Often he could be persuaded to a point of view and could in turn persuade Snyder, whereas the direct approach to Snyder would be destined to fail.

Klagsbrunn had one assistant, and Snyder had a couple of assistants, but essentially Snyder and Klagsbrunn were the chief members of the office, apart from the remnants of the Vinson staff, an aggressive New Deal group headed by Robert Nathan. Nathan held the post of deputy director, as I recall. He had been hired by Vinson and Prichard to supply the economic technical advice that had been lacking at OWMR. Nathan had been chairman of the Policy Planning Commission of the War Production Board. In that capacity he had served as the focus for opposition to big business and the military. As head of the Planning Commission he had fought vigorously to reduce the demands of the military for supplies. He had argued strenuously–and successfully to a very substantial degree–that the military was planning on producing more military equipment than they could use.

Nathan had tremendous energy and an extremely fertile mind. He was one of the leaders in the younger New Deal group, a friend of Ben Cohen, Prichard, Dave Ginsburg, Landis, and Frank. He knew the entire New Deal group and was one of the main brain-trusters. To some extent he was naive; at least he was not the consummate political manipulator the Prichard was. He occasionally thought in too grandiose terms, but on the whole he was extremely effective. He had the capacity for innovation, daring moves, unconventional positions, and an unwillingness to be bound by conventions and red tape that had characterized the early days of the New Deal. At this time he was only in his early thirties.

On Nathan's staff was Charles Hitch, one of the most brilliant economists in the government. Everett Hagen, another very able economist, was on his staff. About the time I came, J. Donald Kingsley was a member of the staff. William Haber, a somewhat older man, professor of economics at Michigan, was there. Another member was William Remington, a rather reserved and unsophisticated person who was considered too timid to be a real liberal. Remington was fairly capable but nowhere near the caliber of most of the others I have just mentioned.

A member of Nathan's staff who later was appointed as assistant to Nathan and who is now [1953] one of my best friends was James R. Newman. Newman was a lawyer by training but an amateur scientist by inclination–not so much a practicing scientist as a scientific theorist. He had graduated from Columbia Law School about 1929 at the age of twenty or twenty-one. While in law school or shortly thereafter he had written a book called *Mathematics and the Imagination*, of which he was co-author with Professor Edward Kasner of Columbia's Mathematics Department. Newman had practiced law in New York for about ten years, apparently a straight legal practice in which he did a considerable amount of trial work, mainly representing insurance companies. He came to Washington during World War II and for a time was assistant to Robert Patterson in the War Department. He served in Britain for a period during the war. Newman had returned to the United States and transferred to the OWMR staff just a short time before I arrived there.

Newman had one of the most brilliant minds I have ever come into contact with. Extremely widely read, with a phenomenal memory, he was a walking encyclopedia. He had as wide a scope of interests as anyone I have ever known. A brilliant conversationalist, he could zero in on the essence of a topic. A keen political analyst, he was primarily interested in science. He followed the latest scientific developments in each branch of the natural sciences, and was widely acquainted with the social sciences and other fields.

At OWMR Newman worked on various issues relating to science. To a large extent he created the job himself. One problem was the release of scientific information that the government had accumulated during the war. The government held considerable amounts of information that had been kept secret for military reasons: scientific developments in the United States, and German scientific material seized after V-E Day. Newman wanted to get as much of this information into the hands of the public as possible so that it could be used for nonmilitary purposes. His task was delicate because certain security requirements still existed, and he had to deal with the War Department and the Navy Department, both of which were reluctant to release much of the information. Newman was also the major draftsman of the Atomic Energy Act. Although his duties related primarily to science, he also participated generally in the work of the OWMR.

Another member of the office staff was Harold Stein. At one time a teacher of English at Yale, he had given up the academic profession and gone to Washington in the early days of the New Deal. He had been with the staff administering the Fair Labor Standards Act and then had worked in various war agencies. He was a very capable person who seemed to have numerous contacts, to get around Washington a good deal, and to be well informed on what was happening in various places. He was one of the chief sources of inside dope on what occurred in various government agencies and in the making of various decisions. He had no particular specialty. In OWMR he was concerned mainly with problems involving surplus property disposal and international or economic problems.

Shortly after John Snyder assumed control of OWMR, he reorganized the office and created three deputies: Klagsbrunn was made the first deputy director and Nathan was designated deputy director for reconversion. Colonel Campbell, the deputy director for production, was supposed to facilitate the shift from production of military goods into production of peacetime goods. He and his staff of eight or ten army officers operated practically entirely apart from the rest of the office. Nobody knew what was going on over there, although we suspected nothing much was happening. Whatever he did was not of long-term significance and did not affect the rest of the office's operations.

In effect, then, Nathan was head of the rest of the staff that I have mentioned so far, which was the main nucleus of the office. In addition, there was an Information Division, which was rather large in relation to the rest of the office. There were four other lawyers in addition to my staff. My general assistant was a lawyer named Byron Miller, who had worked for me in OPA. Another was Carl McGowan, who later became one of Adlai Stevenson's chief advisors. A third was Creekmore Fath, who served primarily as liaison with Congress. The fourth was a very recent graduate of the Harvard Law School named Charles Ewing. The total staff of OWMR while I was there, counting the clerical and other support staff, must have been in the neighborhood of 130 or 140.

In addition to the staff there was an advisory board consisting of representatives of the public, industry, labor, and agriculture. Most of these had also been on the OES board. The chairman of the advisory board was O. Max Gardner, who had been governor of North Carolina and who subsequently became under secretary of the Treasury. The industry representatives included Eric Johnston, who had been president of the Chamber of Commerce but who at the time was president of the Independent Motion Picture Producers Association. George H. Mead and a businessman named Nathaniel Dyke, Jr., who was a consultant to the smaller Defense Plants Corporation, were supposed to express the small businessman's point of view. The labor representatives were William Green, Phil Murray, and T.C. Cashen, who represented the Railroad Brotherhoods. The representatives of agriculture were Ed O'Neal of the Farm Bureau Federation, Albert Goss, head of the Grange, and Jim Patton, head of the Farmers Union. Public representatives, in addition to the chairman, Gardner, were Anna Rosenberg and, originally, William H. Davis. When Davis became head of OES, he was succeeded by Chester Davis.

Snyder and Klagsbrunn had their offices in the East Wing of the White House; the rest of us had offices in the RFC building about two blocks away. I moved into an office that had just been vacated by General Clay, the most magnificent office I had occupied up to that point, with plush furniture and a private bathroom.

## Snyder's Consolidation of Power at OWMR

As soon as Snyder had pulled his organization together, he set up a staff committee composed of the three deputy directors and myself. The staff met every morning, or sometimes three times a week, at 9:15, and then met with Snyder at 10:00. Snyder participated in the meetings with President Truman at 9:00 and came to our meeting afterward. Truman conferred every morning at 9:00 with his "kitchen cabinet": Matt Connelly, his private secretary; Snyder; Harry Vaughan, his aide; John Steelman; George Murphy, his counsel; and a group that worked directly with him. They would talk about the problems of the day and make tentative decisions on what to do. Sometimes they would meet again in the afternoon. Snyder would then come to our meeting and pass on to us whatever decisions had been made that affected our work, and discuss our decisions with us.

A general staff meeting of the main OWMR personnel took place once a week. Bob Nathan used to hold informal meetings once a week with the chief economists of the major federal agencies, to coordinate economic policy by learning about issues that were arising within the purviews of the various agencies, exchanging information about developments, and predicting trends. I sat in on those luncheon conferences. We met in Nathan's office and ate dank ham sandwiches, bad for the digestion, but the discussion made it worthwhile. Occasionally a legal problem would come up on the periphery. At times we would get into political discussions. But most of the talk was in rather technical economic terms. By this time I had picked up a fair amount of economics from my government career, but this capped it with an exposure to highly technical discussions of what the economists saw as the major economic problems facing the country. It was quite an education for me, despite the fact that these economists were far from accurate in their predictions. For example, most of the government economists predicted unemployment at around 8 million within a few months after V-J Day. They turned out to be completely wrong, of course, although their prediction had some effect on government policy and public opinion for awhile.

### The OWMR Advisory Board

The advisory board met twice a month in the conference room of the East Wing of the White House. These meetings usually occupied two days. The major OWMR staff members sat on the sidelines, occasionally presenting a report or responding to a request for information. The advisory board was pretty much of a failure. Particularly as time went on, it did not seem to serve much purpose, except to occupy the time of the board members and the OWMR staff members for these two days every two weeks. Part-time persons from outside government could not possibly accumulate sufficient information with respect to various issues requiring decision to form a carefully reasoned, detailed opinion. They might hold opinions about general policies, but as soon as an issue broached technical matters or the implementation of policy, the public members of the board simply did not have enough information. Usually, someone from OWMR familiar with the problem reported to the board on the facts, but that was apt to be a one-sided presentation that did not express other points of view current in the government, and thus provided only a smattering of the necessary information. In addition to that, all of these board members were exceedingly busy people in their own right. They did not have sufficient time for their work on the advisory board. So far as I know, none participated in any work for the board, apart from their presence at the meetings. Very often they would skip meetings. Only a few attended regularly.

The board members represented different points of view: industry, labor, agriculture. The board did not make final decisions; it merely made recommendations to Congress, OWMR, or other parts of the government. Consequently, none of the representatives of the various interest groups could make concessions, because it would constitute a concession before the real bargaining started. Instead board members simply restated the basic viewpoint of the interest that they represented, without attempting to reach an agreement. On certain issues they were able to agree. They would agree on extending the OPA legislation, for example, but the industry and farm representatives would be in considerable disagreement with the others as to details. Thus they could do nothing more than address a general letter to Congress indicating, in this case, that they thought the act should to be renewed.

I do not recall that the advisory board made any significant contributions throughout this period. Their discussion was sometimes helpful to the OWMR staff in learning other points of view, but the staff usually already knew the basic position of the Farm Bureau Federation, for example, on a particular issue. The three major interest groups may have had the satisfaction of being represented inside the counsels of the administration, but even that is doubtful because as time went on they tended to do less and less. The board meetings continued, but clearly the whole concept was not working out. Phil Murray and William Green seldom appeared after the first few meetings. Cashen, the other labor representative, attended fairly regularly, but he could not speak for the AFL or the CIO. Jim Patton used to attend fairly regularly, but Ed O'Neal came very seldom. Eric Johnston attended fairly frequently, but the others from industry came rather seldom. Ann Rosenberg was frequently present. The board was clearly unsuccessful in offering basic advice from the major interest groups of industry, labor, and agriculture.

I saw no real evidence of a willingness to be convinced of the soundness of another person's point of view in that group. On general policy each of these groups had normally committed itself publicly. And since the board was purely advisory, it was too early to make concessions because it was too far removed from the point at which the actual decision would be made. A certain camaraderie occurred before and after the meetings, but I saw very little exchange of ideas or influence of one on another.

The meetings themselves did not afford the possibility of publicity. In fact, there was no publicity whatsoever. It was an entirely private meeting within the White House itself. Once in a while the board would ask any OWMR staff to leave the room, but usually, with the exception of three or four OWMR staff members, there was no one else present. Nor were there any newspapermen outside, waiting to ask questions when the meetings broke up, as newspapermen were not admitted to that part of the White House. As a result the board meetings were entirely unpublicized–but even that atmosphere did not help to promote the free exchange of ideas.

This was not an unfamiliar kind of advisory board to me or the others. The New Deal had appointed advisory boards from the very beginning. (I recall the NRA advisory boards and my experience with the OES advisory board, mentioned earlier.) This confirmed my general experience that advisory boards failed to perform any significant function, by and large. Occasionally–perhaps once every two months–they would visit President Truman and talk to him. I did not attend those meetings, but they were so short and formal, to some extent a one-way conversation by the president and the rest a restatement of general positions by the various interest groups, that it was impossible to believe that anything could possibly have come out of them.

I suppose that having this board was partly psychological from the point of view of the government, intended to demonstrate to the various interest groups that they had an opportunity to voice their ideas. However, as the board was not composed of technicians, it did not serve the purpose of a technical advisory committee, able to give detailed information about how a particular proposal would affect industry, for example.

The board was useful to some extent, I suppose, as a pressure group on Congress, but even there it did not work well, because only on those issues where there was consensus was it of any value. A board communication to Congress in which the three labor members dissented would have served no purpose, nor would one in which the three agriculture members or the three industry members dissented.

## V-J DAY

V-J Day had a major effect on the operations of OWMR. The announcement of the request for an armistice came on August 15, 1945. The event was not a surprise once we knew about the atomic bomb, but until the announcement that two atomic bombs had been dropped, few people in Washington thought that the war with Japan would end anytime that year. A tremendous celebration spontaneously erupted in Washington and other parts of the country. My family was vacationing at the beach for the month of August, and I had planned to join them for the last two weeks, but V-J Day prevented me from leaving Washington. I have never seen such crowds or more hysteria on any occasion before or since. I took a streetcar to downtown Washington about 11:00 that night. The streets were crowded with people simply walking up and down, shouting rather hysterically. Some people were guzzling alcohol. Ordinary manners were completely abandoned; at times the scene approached a sort of orgy. A girl stripped off all her clothes on the corner of 14th and F Streets in front of the old *Washington Post* building. Another girl and man stripped off all their clothes and exchanged clothing in front of the Washington Hotel. A great deal of heavy necking was going on on the lawns in the parks. Others told me afterwards that some people engaged in public acts of sexual intercourse. These were mainly soldiers and WACS, who seemed to take the news with particular abandon. Practically anything went. Streetcars were crowded and people were jumping on and off, but nobody was collecting fares. The police did not interfere with anything. I never would have believed such an orgy was possible.

For most people V-J Day was a complete relief; the war was over and their job in the war was completed. As I had only recently joined the staff of OWMR, my job was just beginning, or this part of it was, and I would not even be able to take my vacation because urgent questions would need immediate attention. My responsibilities for postwar problems dampened my spirits sufficiently so that I could look on this scene with detachment. I did not immerse myself in the mood of the mobs. All I could see was a long day's work staring me in the face the next day and the day after.

Of course, V-J Day did change all the problems. It solved some long-standing ones, but created many new ones, which obviously would demand much attention.

### A Change in Philosophy

To summarize the basic developments in OWMR, the conservative Snyder became head of the agency, bringing Klagsbrunn as his chief assistant and taking over the Vinson organization led largely by Bob Nathan and consisting primarily of young people with a New Deal outlook. I was brought in as general counsel and built up a small legal staff that shared the viewpoint of Nathan's staff. From the beginning Snyder dragged his feet on issues that Nathan, Jim Newman, I, and others were pressing hard. The latent conflict between Snyder and most of this staff was manifested in differences over immediate issues. In the beginning Snyder seemed to be either unaware or unconcerned with the basic disagreement, and accommodated his point of view to the New Deal staff, but fairly soon fundamental political differences emerged as a crisis. Nathan's relations with Snyder deteriorated and Nathan lost his influence with Snyder. I no longer had any influence with Snyder by December or January. Nathan resigned in December 1945, signaling the complete defeat of the New Deal element in OWMR. The New Deal element had never succeeded in getting many of its ideas put into operation. It had been influential in persuading Snyder or President Truman to take certain positions, but not influential enough to get those positions carried out where they were contrary either to the views of Congress or to the pressures of industry or other forces.

**Winding Down at OWMR**

The public attitude had changed rather noticeably by the end of 1945. Around August, in the fall of 1945, there seemed to be potentially large public support for a policy of planned postwar action. This support was based on the prognostication of 6, 8, or even 10 million unemployed, and on the fear that the depression would immediately return once the major military expenditures ceased. As time went on it began to be clear that such fears would not be realized. Unemployment rose somewhat as the result of the shift from war production to civilian production and as a result of the demobilization of the armed forces, but it neither reached significant figures nor lasted long. Reconversion came with such rapidity that plants were open and unemployment did not last long for any particular individual. As the threat of a depression evaporated, pressure generated by public opinion on Congress and industry for New Deal-type controls disappeared. As the economy maintained a reasonably prosperous level, with rapidly inflating prices cushioned for the consumer by equally rapidly increasing wages, the New Deal group in the government lost its influence. In addition, President Truman's appointments tended to substitute for the capable and rather experimentally minded New Dealers a collection of second- and third-rate administrators who simply did not have the talent, even if they had had the inclination, to do more than liquidate the New Deal measures. This was becoming fairly apparent by the end of 1945.

When Nathan resigned, his division was split into independent units reporting directly to Klagsbrunn. While virtually all personnel who had been there under Nathan remained, it was understood that the New Deal outlook would not prevail under normal circumstances. The New Deal element could achieve results only incidentally by selling a particular project to Klagsbrunn or Snyder. Nathan was replaced by Richard Bissell as an economic consultant. Bissell was a Yale graduate who had taught economics at Yale for a number of years. He had gone to Washington fairly early in the New Deal period and had worked mainly, I think, in the War Shipping Administration. Bissell was an economist of considerable ability. His point of view was conservative on the whole, not reactionary but cautious. In many ways he reminded me of Blackwell Smith. Bissell's influence definitely buttressed Snyder.

I resolved to leave OWMR as early as January 1946, and had accepted an appointment to the Yale faculty in January. I would have left then except that I wanted to remain until the full employment bill had passed or failed in Congress and until the Atomic Energy Act had finished its legislative progress. I actually stayed until June.

The branch of the OWMR under Colonel Campbell was supposed to be expediting the transition to civilian production by providing methods by which key producers could obtain scarce materials, by eliminating bottlenecks, and so forth. I have no idea what they did or whether they did anything. I am sure whatever they did had no substantial effect on the picture. Gradually they disappeared from the scene. A second problem the office dealt with was contract cancellations and contract settlements. This was handled by a special division, with the OWMR at this point acting as an operating agency. Any legal problems there were rather routine, and I did not get into any of that work. A third problem was that of surplus property disposal. The office did considerable work on this. Again the legal problems were technical and of a minor nature. One of my assistants from the office was assigned to handle them and I did not get very much into it. The major issues of surplus property disposal, including the disposal of government-owned plants, and involving anti-trust questions, for example, arose at a somewhat later stage. Another issue was the question of credit control: the relaxation of federal reserve controls over credit and restrictions on consumer credit. Again the legal problems that came up were not particularly serious.

### "Planning" Becomes a Dirty Word

One important aspect of the OWMR operations was the extent to which the office would engage in long-term planning. There was no other agency in the government mandated to plan on a broad scale and to lay down policies based on that planning, except possibly the Bureau of the Budget. In planning the budget each year, the Bureau of the Budget made studies of the economic situation in order to base its policies on assumed economic trends. The bureau exercised its planning functions in a quiet, unobtrusive way and only with respect to its decisions in the area of government appropriations. Other agencies had members of their economic staffs who concerned themselves with long-range planning, but they did so more or less as individuals or incidentally with respect to other functions they were performing. No agency was assigned to come up with an overall plan based on economic trends of what would be necessary in order to maintain a high level of prosperity.

The OWMR was set up in such as way that it could have performed that function. It would have been only a slight expansion of OWMR operations with respect to planning war policies and programs to take care of problems arising during the war. OWMR's mandated function was to deal with reconversion, and the underlying problem of reconversion was whether the economy could operate on a peacetime basis at as high or nearly as high a level as it had operated during the war. So it rather clearly fell within the sphere of action of OWMR to operate as a long-term planning agency. The New Deal staff under Nathan had realized these possibilities. They had also realized that planning agencies in Washington had had rough going in previous years. The National Resources Planning Board, which was perhaps the only prior agency that had undertaken any long-range planning, had been abolished by Congress in 1943. It was generally understood that Congress was opposed to anything that smacked of planning or even involved use of the word "planning." We realized that the issue would have to be approached cautiously. Nevertheless, we believed that OWMR should operate as a long-term planning agency. We hoped that in this way OWMR would obtain experience and establish a precedent so that when the war was over, this function would be assumed by some successor agency.

We attempted to carry out long-term planning by the device of the quarterly report. Under its enabling statutes, OWMR was required to make a report every three months to Congress on the progress of the war or reconversion and on OWMR policies. These reports tended to take on a propaganda aspect instead of aiming for balance. They contained a good deal of factual material, but they were slanted in an attempt to educate Congress, business, and the public generally as to what OWMR was doing and to secure approval for OWMR policies. The Nathan staff intended this quarterly report to be used as the medium for making public a program of long-range planning.

The staff then drafted a tentative and rather elementary effort at prognostication of economic events. It was a study of what the prospects were for business in the next few years, where the weak spots would be, what places needed attention, and what kind of government programs might be used to secure a high level of employment. The possibility that the housing industry could absorb large numbers of unemployed, for example, and contribute to an increase in the gross national product was stressed.

This planning analysis was put before Snyder to go into the quarterly report to be published early in January 1946. It was the practice for the staff to draft the reports, submit them to Snyder for his suggestions or revision, and then have them printed. Snyder simply said that he thought it better not to have that sort of material in the report and it was removed rather quietly. That was all that happened. There was no full-scale battle over the question. Nathan did not press the point or elaborate the significance of what he was doing or attempt to institute a major battle. The decision of Snyder not to go into such matters was simply accepted without further controversy. However, that ended any effort at long-range planning on the part of the executive branch. From then on our functions were limited to the more immediate problems of the postwar reconversion period. This low-keyed maneuver of Snyder's was one of the important factors in Nathan's decision to leave OWMR.


## BOWLES vs SNYDER

In September 1945 President Truman fired William H. Davis as director of the OES. Davis had given a press conference in which he had made some statement with respect to wage policies that Truman judged irresponsible. I think the statement Davis made was that it would be possible to have substantial wage increases without additional price increases. It is possible that he urged an amendment to the Minimum Wage Act to establish a minimum wage of $.75. In any event, his statement was at variance with Snyder's policy, and President Truman summarily dismissed Davis. That was an example of Truman's personnel policies—not that he usually treated people as abruptly as he did in this instance. However, whenever an issue arose in which one of the Roosevelt supporters took a view differing from Snyder's, the Snyder group would prevail and the other fellow would be fired.

The OES was transferred to the OWMR on September 20, 1945. I became acting director of the stabilization administration within the Office of War Mobilization with all the perquisites of office, including a government car. After three weeks, Truman appointed John Caskie Collet as the permanent director.

A typical Truman appointee, Collet was utterly unsuited for the job. He was a federal district judge in Missouri on leave of absence to take this post. Although he was a pleasant person, he had no competence in economics, administration, or even in law. He had no idea what the issues were. They were totally beyond anything he had ever thought about before. He was completely lost in the job, never knew what he was doing, and operated purely as a figurehead. The net result was to replace Davis, a person of considerable ability and great experience, by a nonentity with no capacity. Until February 1946, when he resigned to return to the district court, he had no influence. Later Truman rewarded him by an appointment to the circuit court.

In February 1945 Chester Bowles was shifted from administrator of OPA to become director of the OES. In order to give Bowles greater prestige the office was reestablished as separate from OWMR, and Bowles was kicked upstairs. Although Bowles still maintained theoretical control over price policies in OPA, WPB, and other agencies, and Paul Porter, a strong believer in price control who had been deputy administrator for rent in OPA, replaced him, Bowles was removed as active administrator of the OPA statutes. Snyder probably engineered this arrangement; at least it had his support and encouragement. Whether the idea was originally Snyder's or not, I do not know, but President Truman relied on him almost entirely in the domain of OWMR.

By this time Bowles had become very unpopular with Congress and most of the top officials in the Truman administration. He had tangled with Vinson when Vinson headed OES. Snyder cordially disliked Bowles and Snyder influenced President Truman so that Truman also was cool toward Bowles.

Snyder's opposition was based on two issues. First, he disagreed with Bowles' policy of attempting to maintain firm price controls. Snyder took the industry point of view that allowing industry to expand without price controls would increase production to such an extent that the resulting increase in supply would keep prices down. Second, and perhaps more importantly, Snyder believed that Bowles was playing a long-term political game to the detriment of Truman. Snyder told me directly that he thought that Bowles was anticipating a revival of liberal and New Deal sentiment and was attempting to establish himself as a leader of the liberal group, at the expense of Truman. Snyder believed that Bowles' theory was that the Democrats would be forced to nominate a liberal because if they nominated a conservative they would be "out-conservatived" by the Republicans, and Bowles was running for president. I think Snyder's assessment was correct. I believe Bowles was taking his positions as a matter of intellectual conviction rather than political expediency. However, the net effect of what he was doing was pretty much as Snyder had analyzed it.

I do not know whether Bowles himself was aware of being kicked upstairs. I did not see Bowles at the time, at least not in circumstances that permitted me to discover his assessment. My guess is that he more or less realized it, but believed he still could accomplish a great deal as director of OES. Technically, it was a promotion. Only those insiders who understood the situation would have viewed it otherwise. Bowles probably realized that he was in a similar position to that of Leon Henderson at the end of 1942: persona non grata to so many congressmen that he would have trouble with the coming appropriations and renewal of the legislation, and that the interests that he supported would be more successful if he accepted the "promotion."

The dislike between Snyder and Bowles was mutual. I would not say that Bowles disliked Truman, but he believed that he was incompetent and that the future of the Democratic Party depended on finding someone else to assume leadership. In the period before the 1948 convention Bowles openly said that Truman should be replaced because he was not qualified for the presidency. When Truman was nominated there was a reconciliation, presumably for political convenience: Truman was running for president and Bowles was running for governor of Connecticut, and they needed each other. Later Truman appointed Bowles ambassador to India, but he probably was influenced as much by the desire to get him out of the country as by anything else.

## THE END OF PRICE CONTROLS

One of the first major issues that confronted OWMR was what to do about production, allocation, and manpower controls that had been in effect during the war. One ramification of this issue was consumer rationing. As head of OPA, Bowles thought that all or practically all consumer rationing should end immediately, with the possible exception of certain aspects of food rationing. (Since there was a tremendous shortage of food worldwide, the rest of the world would need considerable assistance from the United States to survive the coming winter, and food production and distribution were highly disrupted.) But Bowles judged it more important to demonstrate to the American people that President

Truman was acting in good faith in withdrawing controls as rapidly as possible. He visualized maintenance of price controls as the only prime necessity. His theory that it would be essential to maintain price controls for some time was based on a different assumption than that of the economists, who anticipated long-term deflation instead of inflation, but everybody agreed that a temporary continuation of price controls would be necessary to avoid serious inflation in the short term. Bowles' approach was to lift the rationing regulations, reasoning that in order to obtain public and congressional support for continuing price controls, it was essential to show good faith by abandoning the more unpopular rationing regulations. OPA immediately ended rationing of gasoline, fuel oil, processed foods, and stoves. In the next few months all consumer rationing ended except on sugar.

A drastic cut in OPA's staff was called for. On V-J Day OPA had more than 62,000 employees. By the end of September 1945 that number had been reduced to 44,000. The rapid liquidation of the OPA rationing program, however, turned out to be premature, at least in the food field. The tremendous worldwide food shortages made the United States appear to be consuming excessive quantities of food without any rationing system, while the rest of the world starved. There was some talk of President Truman's restoring food rationing. But the situation was out of hand by the winter and spring of 1945–1946. Restoring rationing was impractical both in terms of public opinion and technically: a whole new set of rationing currency would have to be printed and distributed, for example. One measure taken as a substitute for rationing was to increase the price of grain for export, so that grain that was exported would be sold at a higher price than grain that remained on the domestic market, an incentive for the export of grain. The U.S. government also took various other measures to relieve and reorganize the world food situation.

The War Production Board (WPB) also moved quickly to liquidate most of its wartime controls. Some controls were retained to channel supplies into civilian production, but even there, in many instances where controls would have been useful, they were abandoned. The main example was the WPB position on the order known as L-41, which limited the use of building materials for certain kinds of construction. Both before the war and as a result of the war, an extreme shortage of housing existed in the country. A reasonable housing program would have required that supplies of raw materials that were still in fairly short supply be channeled into the building of houses rather than the building of theaters, racetracks, or other nonessential construction. That was what L-41 accomplished during the war. WPB, however, was so anxious to dump all controls that it insisted on dumping L-41. That was one of the first controversies between the remnants of the New Deal and the conservatives in the Truman administration. Bowles opposed the removal of L-41, but the conservative groups won: WPB eliminated it.

I spent a good deal of time on price and wage controls because that was the area with which I was particularly familiar. Economic pressures requiring the continuance of price controls included a huge backlog in civilian demand, a scarcity of many supplies, and a large increase in personal savings. An enormous volume of money was being held, essentially involuntarily, in personal savings, ready to flow into the market for hitherto scarce products. Industry was unable to supply these products as rapidly as consumers would have liked. Without intervention, an inflationary spiral would result from a rapid increase in prices, accompanied by corresponding demands for wage increases. Such a development might choke off the pent-up demand and cause a recession or depression more quickly than otherwise might be expected. All the administration's economists, even those who were predicting temporary, widespread unemployment, thought that price and wage controls, or at least price controls, were necessary. On the other hand, industry exerted tremendous pressures for the elimination of controls. The National Association of Manufacturers carried on a tremendous publicity campaign, arguing in advertisements—paid for out of tax deductions—that as soon as restrictions were eliminated, production would step up enormously, resulting in abundant supplies and a huge period of national prosperity. They said that prices could decline only with increased production, and increased production depended on an abandonment of price controls. The meat industry carried on similar campaigns, as did a number of other industries. As public support for governmental controls receded, the general atmosphere contained little support of the continuation of strict controls.

One of the important aspects of postwar economic stabilization was the prices that OPA had set for products that had not been made during the war but that were beginning to be produced again for civilian consumption. The price of automobiles became a key problem. No automobiles at all had been manufactured during the war, so the postwar demand obviously would be enormous. The automobile industry was one of the most important industries producing for civilian consumption. Fixing prices for automobiles involved many factors that could not be accurately calculated. A fair price would depend in part on the speed with which reconversion to civilian production took place, that is, how long before the industry was producing at a sufficiently high rate so as to keep its unit costs down. Labor and industrial costs were other factors. What percentage of profit both manufacturers and distributors should make and whether the percentage should be the same on high- and low-priced products had to be considered. OPA issued prices in January 1946, allowing some increase for the manufacturer and cutting the distributors' margin by 2.5 percent. A 2.5 percent cut was a victory for the distributors because they would be selling cars like hotcakes and earning as much or more than ever. The conflict over car prices resulted in a standoff. OPA maintained its position fairly well without putting across all that it would have liked. Snyder was behind the scenes, in general favoring the point of view of the automobile companies, but I do not know of any attempt by Snyder to use his influence to go for higher prices.

Meanwhile, the wage issue had come to the fore and was perhaps the key factor in the pricing picture. The cost of living was rising all through that period and labor was exerting tremendous pressure for wage increases. The coal miners had obtained some higher rates and the rest of labor wanted increases too. Wage increases were bound to increase price pressures. There had been few price increases during the war period, in spite of some real cost increases, so some manufacturers were operating on a narrow margin in some instances. However it still remained the case that an increase in wages would provide a justification for an increase in prices.

Shortly after V-J Day the War Labor Board cancelled approximately 85 percent of its regulations. However, the board retained the provision that wage increases would be permitted without securing prior government approval only so long as they were not used as the basis for price increases. Where wage increases were to be the reason given by the employer for price increases, the wage increase had to be approved by the board, and the price increase needed the approval of OPA. Firms had to wait six months to see how the wage costs affected prices before OPA would give approval. The effect of this was to remove governmental pressure against wage increases while allowing overwhelming pressure for increased prices. Many industries refused to approve wage increases as large as labor demanded, and a series of strikes took place during that period. The General Motors strike that started in November 1945 and continued until March 1946 was the first major strike. By January 1946 the United Electrical Workers were striking the electric plants, including General Electric, meatpackers were out, strikes were occurring at other automobile plants, and a strike was pending in the steel industry.

**Letting Steel Raise Prices**

Meanwhile the National Wage Stabilization Board replaced the WLB. The principal function of the Wage Stabilization Board was to rule on those wage increases that would be reflected in price increases. The situation was in considerable turmoil through December, January, and February. In January 1946 the conflict in the steel industry came to a head, providing a test of how far the government would go in granting wage increases and resisting price increases. Labor wanted a wage increase. Industry was willing to give an increase of 18.5 cents/hour, but only if it received about $10/ton in price increases. The economists in OPA and OWMR agreed that the industry could absorb the 18.5 cents with a price increase of not more than $1-$2/ton. Some of the economists believed that no price increase would be necessary and others thought that a price increase on certain products rather than across-the-board might be advisable. The profits of the steel industry had been higher than at any previous period; they could have paid the wage increase and still operated at a profit that was within the range of what they were making during 1936-1939. At OPA, Bowles resisted the price increase. It ultimately came up to OWMR. Snyder took over negotiations with the steel industry, calling them into his White House office. I believe Klagsbrunn was there, and perhaps Richard Bissell.

Just before this negotiation took place I had talked with the OPA lawyers about whether $5/ton, which was the figure purported to be what the steel industry would settle for, was valid under the price legislation. It could be argued that the price increase was invalid, unnecessary to meet the requirements of being fair and equitable, and so on. On the other hand, if OPA wanted to do it, no one would have been able to challenge it successfully in any important proceeding. The legal issue was really subordinate. However, Richard Field, Henry Hart, and I concurred that it exceeded OPA's legal power as it had been exercised up to that point. I prepared an opinion for Snyder, telling him that the $5 increase was illegal and presenting the general reasons. I took this short memorandum over to Snyder, gave it to him, and told him the gist of it. He glanced through it and then handed it back to me, saying, "I don't want to receive this memorandum. If it is ever stated that I received this memorandum, I will deny it." Shortly thereafter it was announced that Snyder had granted the $5 price increase to the steel industry.

This decision forced OPA to greatly modify the stringency with which it was attempting to hold the price line. The Wage Stabilization Board also modified wage policies so as to conform to the pattern of the steel case. In effect, the decision was to sanction the first spiral of wage-price increases in industry.

The steel settlement had the effect of ending most of the strikes, although some of them continued. The General Motors and General Electric strikes were ended in March 1946. The coal strike in April resulted in the seizure of the mines by the federal government and litigation over the refusal of the miners to return to work. Then, in response to the railroad strike in May, Truman called on Congress for special legislation. It seemed fairly clear that, prior to his submission of the message, Truman had been advised that the railroad workers were willing to call off the strike. Truman, however, disclosed an ominous impatience and lack of understanding of the labor problem by asking for extremely drastic legislation, which would have set an extremely anti-labor pattern. Congress was on the verge of passing it when it was stopped, primarily by Senator Taft, who said that the matter was being considered with too much haste. It appears that John Steelman, chief labor advisor to Truman, had given the president very poor advice. This was surprising because Steelman had been a conciliator for the Department of Labor for many years. Unfortunately, Steelman had extremely limited ability. He struck me as very stupid and rather conceited.

After the steel settlement, the number of OPA price controls steadily declined. The Bureau of Labor Statistics index continued to advance in spite of the deflationary pressures caused by the temporary shutdown of industry for reconversion and the flood of manpower from military discharges. Prices promised to escalate rapidly if controls were removed.

Chester Bowles resigned as director of OES in June 1946. He believed that the situation was either already out of hand or rapidly getting there and that he could not associate himself with it any longer. Taking a leading part in the liberal wing of the Democratic Party no longer seemed possible to him from a position within the Truman administration. He returned to Connecticut to enter politics. He thought that the tide had turned against him for the time being, but that after he had been in state politics and had handled local problems he might have another opportunity on the national level. Bowles obtained the Democratic nomination for governor of Connecticut in 1948.

Also in June 1946, Congress ripped to pieces the bill renewing OPA. Led primarily by Senator Taft, Congress had included many destructive provisions, including one proposal by Senator Taft that would have required OPA to set prices under which each company could make a profit on each item it produced. OPA contended that this proposal was administratively impossible and that it would result in serious price increases, even if it could be administered. The act was to expire on June 30, 1946, but nevertheless Truman vetoed the bill, saying that it was so bad that even though OPA would expire, he could not put his name to it. I think President Truman was probably correct in rejecting that particular bill. OPA told Truman, and Snyder did not object to this, that the OPA renewal bill in its present form would in effect have meant virtually no price control. The steel decision had greatly weakened price control, but not nearly to the extent that this bill would have done. Truman would have accepted responsibility for the price increases if he had signed the bill, whereas if he did not, he could put the burden on Congress.

For almost a month no price control legislation existed. OPA operated under an executive order and continued its function, but no legal enforcement was possible in price control. About the only prices that OPA could hold down were in the area that perennially took the brunt of effective price control, namely the landlords. Most courts stayed eviction cases during this period, waiting to see if the price control law would be renewed, so that rents changed very little. Other prices shot up enormously and it was never possible to bring them down again. Congress passed a somewhat better bill on July 26, 1946, which Truman signed, and an effort was made to reestablish a price control system, but it never operated successfully.

By September 1946 an effort to reestablish an effective form of price control over meat was met by an out-and-out strike on the part of the meatpacking industry. The major packers simply did not buy cattle, immediately creating a tremendous shortage of meat. Cattle were flowing into Chicago but were not being bought by the packers, and as the stockyards filled with cattle, word got back to the farmers and they held out.  Farmers were probably holding back cattle anyway, waiting for the OPA price to break so that they could get a better profit.  At any rate, the meat industry made a deliberate effort to put the squeeze on the administration by refusing to operate under price controls.  The meat industry filled the newspapers with advertisements to the effect that if OPA price controls were removed, there would be plenty of meat and at lower prices.  The congressional elections of 1946 were imminent, and Truman saw that the meat situation was going to be damaging to the Democrats.  In October he announced dramatically over the radio that all meat controls had been removed.  It was a complete surrender to the meatpacking industry. As soon as price controls were removed, beef prices, contrary to the predictions of the industry, shot up very sharply.  Cattle prices at Chicago moved from $20 to $27 a hundredweight within a very short period.  The elections came soon afterward, so that whatever effect the meat prices produced–and probably that was very important in the elections–the damage had been done.

Shortly after the elections Truman ordered practically all price controls removed.  Only controls on sugar, syrup, rice, and rent remained.  Paul Porter resigned and OPA was completely liquidated.  In November the Bureau of Labor Statistics' Index stood at 150.7.  The rapid elimination of many controls in the earlier months, and particularly the policies fashioned by Snyder in the steel settlement, ultimately led to the collapse of OPA.  Of course many forces were moving in that direction, but these events showed that the administration was not prepared to take a firm position in the face of strong pressures from some industries for relaxation of controls.

**Housing**

During the OWMR period one serious attempt was made at maintaining and to some degree extending government controls.  This was in the housing field.  A tremendous housing shortage had developed because little new housing had been built during the war.  The administration hoped the housing industry would absorb many of the workers who were being laid off from the war industries.  Consequently special attention was paid to the housing industry in the immediate postwar period.

Wilson Wyatt took charge of the housing program.  New to the Washington scene, Wyatt had been mayor of Louisville, Kentucky.  He was a young, rising star in Kentucky politics, known to the Kentucky Democrats such as Alben Barkley and Paul Porter.  As a friend of Vinson and Prichard, he must have been appointed to the position through them.  Wyatt was a lawyer, a very energetic, able, effervescent person.  He had the reputation of being a real go-getter, with real executive ability.  In other words, he was considered exceptionally well-qualified for the job.  In the early days of his administration Truman was anxiously looking for people to help out, and consequently Wyatt was in a good bargaining position. Thanks to the warnings of Paul Porter and other friends in the administration, when he accepted the position he insisted on having complete authority and not being subject to limitations in carrying out his program. He was determined, I assume, not to be under Snyder or some other official who could veto what he was doing. He also wanted to have authority to direct other agencies to take actions within their jurisdiction that he considered necessary. Truman agreed to these terms, and Wyatt was generally referred to as "the housing czar." Technically he was in the Office of War Mobilization, but it was understood that he had complete freedom to operate on his own. I suppose he was able to obtain that freedom because he had stipulated as the condition of taking the job that he be given complete powers to direct other agencies and to report directly to the president. Snyder was reluctant to accept Wyatt's independence but did not make any real fight over it. Housing was such a vital area that it was of extreme importance to have the job successfully accomplished, and therefore Truman and his henchmen were willing to make concessions.

Wyatt went to work in a way that was reminiscent of the early days of the New Deal. He gathered a small staff and started off working practically day and night. They all went at a terrific pace. He had some help from OWMR. I worked with him to some extent. I was not in physical or psychological condition to devote the time and energy that Wyatt himself did. He did not have any other legal counsel, in the beginning at least.

Wyatt drew up an elaborate program for housing that included allocation controls to channel lumber and other scarce materials into housing rather than into other types of building, proposals for credit for persons who were constructing houses, daring ideas about prefabricated housing (at that point Wyatt had to negotiate with the building trades union, or at least to make an effort to placate them), proposals for legislation to supply government funds for public housing, and government guarantees of loans made in private housing.

Unfortunately, this comprehensive program was largely if not completely a failure for a number of reasons, none of which was attributable to Wyatt. Wyatt simply did not receive the support for the program that he had calculated on and that was necessary for successful operations. His czardom was almost entirely on paper; he lacked the actual backing of officials in certain key spots. The general and well-meaning support of Truman was never translated into very active support; Truman did not understand what it would take to put the program across. In spite of the earlier arrangement, Snyder became a key figure in the program. Wyatt was a coordinator or expediter; he did not have the power himself to carry out operations, but merely to direct other agencies. The other agencies did not move, or did not move quickly, or raised objections. On the whole they were unwilling to accept the Wyatt program. That meant that Wyatt had to find a way to enforce his directives. He could not take every issue to the president.

The issues tended to get very technical. For instance, Wyatt was pressing the Reconstruction Finance Corporation (RFC) to loan large sums of money to Lustron, Kaiser, and several other firms that would undertake to manufacture prefabricated housing. The RFC objected on technical grounds, such as that the companies had not solved the engineering problems and the loan was inadvisable from a banking point of view. This was not the sort of issue that Wyatt could take to the president for a decision on whether RFC should go ahead. Perhaps he could have taken one issue like that, but not many. The president had to rely on subordinates for advice as to whether Wyatt or the RFC was correct; Wyatt's only recourse, therefore, was to take his problems to White House subordinates, of which Snyder was the principal one. Snyder was not sympathetic. Snyder originally had been for the program but did not understand the implications of what it would take, that is, the extent to which he would have to fight business and congressional opposition. When the chips were down, Snyder was unwilling to pay the necessary price. Also the program was based on predictions about levels of unemployment and recession that turned out to be erroneous, so that much of the pressure for doing the job evaporated. It soon became known that Wyatt did not have any real backing from the White House. Certainly he had no backing from Snyder, and Snyder stood between him and the president at most points. The resistance of the other agencies increased and Wyatt's prestige fell. The end result was that relatively little was accomplished.

Wyatt began with tremendous energy. The initial phase was mainly planning. He had to explore the various possibilities and make up his mind what his program was. After working exceedingly hard at first with a small group of devoted assistants, he was able to work out his program—and then came the problem of putting it into effect. In the the the beginning the RFC, for example, was very cordial; they understood the emergency and were anxious to work as rapidly as they could. Only after six or eight weeks had gone by with nothing accomplished did Wyatt begin to realize what he was up against. Wyatt had to find some official in Washington who would resolve the dispute between himself and the RFC. Theoretically Wyatt could tell the RFC what to do, but in practice Wyatt could not go over and vote at the board of directors of the RFC and tell them to grant a loan.

Another factor in this situation was that the concept of an affirmative government program was contrary to the current trends. In every other area government controls were being lifted. Wyatt was definitely operating against the trend of the times. The result was that he had no congressional or popular support either. A substantial part of his program depended on legislation from Congress. A bill was passed, but it was a rather weak version of what he had in mind; it did not include any federal funds for public housing or government-financed housing, for example. He was a very intelligent person, and he realized soon enough what was happening. He continued for a time even though he felt frustrated and discouraged, but eventually he resigned.

## THE END OF THE NEW DEAL
*Truman's famous 21-point plan for carrying on the New Deal, and my plan for how to implement it*

The other major area in which I worked at OWMR was on the legislative program. This involved long-range planning, except that I focused on legal rather than economic issues. The government had no agency mandated to coordinate and affirmatively press for the administration's legislative program. In the early 1900s Congress was insulted if the president actually drafted legislation himself and submitted it to Congress. By the time of Franklin Roosevelt, however, the leadership in formulating and pressing for a legislative program had passed to the president. Each cabinet department handled the relevant measures. Someone in the president's office might follow many of the measures, but the only central authority on the executive legislative program was the Bureau of the Budget. Under existing executive orders every agency wishing to propose a piece of legislation had to clear it with the Bureau of the Budget. If a congressional committee requested an agency to comment or called agency personnel to testify on pending legislation, the agency's answer or testimony had to be cleared with the Bureau of the Budget. In theory, the bureau had considerable control, but in practice it was much less. Rigid control was impossible, particularly in the spirit of Washington. The bureau could clear the formal presentation of a cabinet officer or other agency personnel, but it could do nothing about the questions that the congressmen asked the witness when he was before the committee. Nor could the bureau prevent an agency from suggesting to a congressman that he ask certain questions and thereby raise issues that did not appear in the advance copy of his testimony. Nor could the bureau prevent individual contacts with members of Congress or chairmen of key committees. Furthermore, the bureau could refuse to approve certain actions of the other agencies, but the bureau was not empowered to undertake any affirmative coordination or to press for any particular legislative program. The head of the division that cleared the legislation was an oldtimer who was rather crusty in his relations with people and made no effort to use the potential powers of his position in a broader way. His office confined itself to doing what had been done in the past with no elements of assertiveness or imagination, and so legislative clearance tended to be a formality.

Right after V-J Day President Truman called a special session of Congress because it was clear that many legislative proposals would need to be considered. Some members of the OWMR staff, I in particular, became interested in what legislation would be proposed initially because many reconversion problems demanded legislative attention. The OWMR advised President Truman on what legislation was necessary and what he should ask for. OWMR drew up an elaborate program encompassing 21 different legislative issues. The New Deal element in OWMR initiated this program in consultation with other groups within the government; for example, the War Department was responsible for the selective service and universal military training provisions. I drew up a one-page list of projects for Snyder to present to President Truman, first those things that were necessary, and then at the bottom certain other recommendations that could be postponed if the president did not want to thrust that much on Congress. These were policies we were not sure either Snyder or Truman wanted to press, such as the full employment legislation. We all realized it would be extremely difficult to get the program through Congress.

I remember being astonished at the time that Snyder accepted the program. We had not realized the full extent of his conservatism then, but we recognized that he was not a flaming New Dealer. I think that at the time Snyder simply did not comprehend the implications. There was great pressure for action, great public concern about unemployment, and no real crystallization of conflicting forces yet. There had been a good deal of talk about postwar planning, even on the part of congressional committees such as the Colmer committee in the House and Senator George's committee in the Senate. People generally assumed that the government had a definite responsibility for leading the transition from war into a prosperous peacetime.

Snyder took the list, carried it to President Truman, and returned with the word that Truman wanted everything in, including the additional recommendations at the bottom of the page. Our staff then wrote up the details of the message. Truman went over the draft with great care and made revisions. He understood what was being asked for and he clearly endorsed it. He did not realize what resistance the program would encounter, but he proposed it in good faith. Later he must have realized that the chances of getting Congress to pass this legislation were not only remote but impossible, and then he persisted for political reasons.

At the opening of the special session of Congress on September 6, 1945, Truman presented this program. What they could not finish would be continued in the new Congress in 1946.

The program, which became known as President Truman's 21-point program, contained a substantial number of far-reaching and important measures. It proposed to expand the unemployment system in order to meet the anticipated unemployment. It proposed a revision of the Fair Labor Standards Act in order to increase the minimum wage and maintain purchasing power. It requested that Congress enact full employment legislation (a bill had been drafted already and was pending in Congress). It called for enactment of legislation setting up the Fair Employment Practices Committee on a permanent basis. It called for legislation dealing with labor disputes and wage stabilization, primarily a procedure for fact-finding boards. It contained important measures relating to agriculture, including price supports, revision of the crop insurance program, the school lunch program, and conservation of soil and forest resources. It included a provision for continuing the Selective Service, and one for universal military training (as requested by the War and Navy Departments). It included a proposal for the housing bill in line with the housing program. Jim Newman was largely responsible for a proposal to create a federal science foundation that would promote scientific research. There were measures for tax revision, both short-term and long-term, some proposals dealing with small business and with veterans. There was a strong recommendation for the development of public works for national resources, particularly a proposal for additional river valley projects modeled on the TVA, a proposal for highway construction, for appropriations for UNRRA, and a proposal for increasing congressional salaries.

The program also included some technical points, such as the extension of the Second War Powers Act, the question of whether the United States Employment Service should be located in the Department of Labor or the Social Security Board, and other matters of that sort. A program of health legislation was submitted in a subsequent message, as well as the extension of social security generally and the development of the St. Lawrence River Valley.

This long-range, comprehensive legislative program, formulated largely by New Deal groups within the administration, was designed to continue the New Deal. The program was put forward mainly as necessary for a high level of economic prosperity and secondly as an improvement in the particular areas covered by the legislation. But it was clearly a major effort by the Truman administration to press forward along lines that had been originally mapped out in the New Deal period but that had been interrupted by the reaction against the New Deal beginning in 1938 and by the war.

On September 19, 1945, I sent a memorandum to Snyder in which I said,

> It is clear that the legislative program outlined in the president's message will not get itself automatically enacted into law. Concerted and continuous effort on the part of the president, OWMR, and the various interested government agencies will be required to put the program through. In order to coordinate the entire program and to assign definite responsibility for its various parts, the following procedure is recommended.

I then proposed that the various aspects of the program be specifically assigned to particular agencies. The job of each agency was to make the necessary studies, to obtain the material that was essential to carry through the legislative program, to prepare that material, to assist in drafting legislation, to present testimony to congressional committees, and in general to follow that particular legislation in Congress. Each agency would also cooperate with the other agencies interested in the same problem, but one particular agency would have responsibility for affirmatively pressuring or carrying through, so far as the executive could, each part of the legislative program.

I also proposed that OWMR, in cooperation with the Bureau of the Budget (a bow to the bureau because of its technical jurisdiction in the field), undertake to coordinate the program by following the course of the legislative proposals, resolving difficulties between interested government agencies, assuring that the agency assigned responsibility for carrying out parts of the program was indeed doing so, and generally assisting in the achievement of the program. In other words, OWMR was to function with respect to the legislative program as it had on other issues during the war–that is, act as a coordinator and resolver of disputes and affirmatively follow through on the program. I recommended that one or more persons act as legislative liaisons between OWMR and Congress or between the president and Congress, to assist in presenting the administration's point of view. In other words, we were suggesting the appointment of a couple of high-powered assistants to the president who would work with OWMR to enact the program.

I recommended that OWMR maintain contact with Hannegan and his staff at the Democratic National Committee in order to coordinate our program with their work. The theory behind this was that the Democratic National Committee should arouse public support for the program. This was a considerably different concept of political parties and of the Democratic National Committee than had existed heretofore; until then they had not advocated specific legislative proposals. A final proposal was that OWMR should prepare for the president each week prior to his Monday conference with Senate and House leaders a brief report on the status of the program, with suggested actions that the president might desire to take. I attached a chart to the memorandum, listing each legislative proposal, indicating the agencies that were concerned, recommending an agency to handle it, and indicating the present legislative status, as most of the measures were already pending.

Snyder accepted the proposals and discussed the memorandum with Truman. He reported that Truman was enthusiastic and OWMR would be designated as the coordinating agency. OWMR was authorized to designate the other agencies that were to be assigned particular responsibility for a specific aspect of the program. Truman also welcomed the weekly report before his meeting with congressional leaders. No action was taken on the recommendations that required action outside OWMR: the appointment of liaison representatives on the president's staff to deal with members of Congress or the proposal to make the Democratic Party into an advocate for the program. However, OWMR did have a mandate to carry forward those aspects that it could perform itself.

Actually, what was accomplished depended mainly on my efforts, with some help from Nathan and his staff. I took responsibility for implementing our proposals. We wrote letters, which Snyder signed, to each agency that we had tentatively designated to handle aspects of the program. These letters informed the agencies that they were responsible for whichever aspect of the legislative program and outlined the actions they were expected to take. The letters asked the agencies to report to OWMR periodically what they were doing to forward the legislation, what the status of it was, and what problems needed attention by the president or by OWMR. We determined who in each particular agency would be the key person who actually was going to do the job. In November 1945 and again in January 1946 we circulated charts to all the agencies involved, showing the exact status of the legislation. Snyder gave copies of the charts to Truman. We sent memoranda to Truman before his Monday meetings with the congressional leaders. By these measures we attempted to make OWMR the agency with affirmative responsibility for carrying through the legislative program.

The 21-point program was a complete failure. By January 1, 1946, no more than two or three of the most minor aspects of the program had been passed. Long delays were in prospect even before consideration would be given to many of the other aspects of the program. None of the important measures was close to passage, with the exception of the Full Employment Bill. Revision of the unemployment compensation laws, the Fair Labor Standards Act, FEPC, the river valleys, and so forth were clearly bogged down. In January when the new session of Congress opened, Truman delivered his State of the Union message. OWMR prepared much of that message, reiterating the legislative program, but that did not help. As time went on, it became perfectly clear that no important parts of the 21-point program would be enacted. Some technical problems received attention, but none of the projected measures unrelated to the technical liquidation of the war effort, with the exception of the Full Employment Bill, were ever passed.

**The Reasons for Failure**

The reasons for the failure of Truman's 21-point program to be passed in Congress were similar to those I have indicated in the housing program. The forces in the country that supported action of this sort tended to lose interest when the economic situation did not develop as predicted. Public support for the program did not materialize. The opposition came from organized pressure groups, mainly the business groups. Opposition to government controls had been accumulating because of dislike of the restrictions imposed by the rationing and allocation programs. In addition, Congress could actively oppose as well as silently obstruct. Moreover President Truman did not have Roosevelt's ability to obtain public backing for his measures. He had none of the dramatic flair for radio speeches, nor the ability at a press conference to put across ideas, nor the capacity of instilling public confidence that

Roosevelt had. He did not understand the major struggle required to arouse public support, educate public opinion, and thereby force Congress to accept his program. Another factor was the caliber of Truman's appointments. The persons who were then taking over the major departments were not capable of persuading Congress or the public of the necessity of these measures. The effort of OWMR to act as a coordinating agency came to nothing, as well. After a while no further reports came from the agencies on the status of legislation and there was no point in my office drawing up reports showing the status of the various proposals.

This failure was devastating to the morale of the New Deal element of the agencies. It indicated that the possibility of progressive action on the part of the government was ended for the indefinite future, and this contributed substantially to the exodus from Washington of a number of persons, such as myself, who had been there almost from the beginning.

## LAST DAYS OF OWMR

That the liberal viewpoint in the administration would not prevail became clearer by the end of 1945. It was confirmed by Nathan's resignation in December and subsequent events: the modification of the Full Employment Bill, the complete failure of the legislative program as a whole, and the failure of the housing program. When I was offered a position teaching at the Yale Law School I decided to accept. In January 1946 I notified Snyder that I planned to take the position at Yale. I did not choose to leave immediately because I wanted to see through both the Full Employment Bill and the Atomic Energy Bill. Furthermore, it was convenient to start at the beginning of the fall term. My decision was agreeable to Snyder. We were still on speaking terms, but my influence was minuscule and shortly afterward we engaged in a controversy over the steel measure that left me with virtually no influence in the office.

As the months of 1946 passed, demoralization spread throughout the office. By May, Newman was persuading me to go to weekday afternoon ballgames from time to time. On one occasion I was watching the game when I suddenly remembered that Truman might want to issue an executive order taking over the coal mines that day. The order had been drafted, approved, and was being held on standby. I hoped that I would not be found at a ballgame when the crucial time came to get the order ready for Truman's signature. Fortunately, I escaped that. It was not that I had nothing to do. The possibilities were so limited, though, that we could not do much except let things roll along as they were going. Most of the staff were discouraged, feeling that they were not accomplishing very much.

By March or April the task of OWMR had narrowed almost exclusively to liquidating the war machinery, with the exception of the Atomic Energy Bill. At the beginning of June, Vinson became chief justice and Snyder was appointed secretary of the Treasury. John R.

Steelman took over about the middle of June as Snyder's successor, just about the time I left the organization and went away for a summer vacation.

In summary, I would say that OWMR was fairly successful in its function of planning, determining policy, and coordinating the war effort. It was not always able to accomplish what it wanted, but on the whole it functioned reasonably effectively. As an agency to plan and formulate policy for peacetime, however, OWMR collapsed completely. It is not clear, of course, that Congress had ever intended it to have any important function in that respect. It was created to handle the reconversion period, but it was always considered a purely temporary agency. Nevertheless, OWMR offered obvious possibilities in influencing the postwar period, and at one time some of its staff served in that capacity, but in that connection it was not able to accomplish anything; its functions came down merely to liquidating the war machinery.

## From the Perspective of a Professor at Yale

On the Yale faculty I specialized in the field of political and civil liberties. I was particularly interested in that field for two major reasons. First, during my years in Washington I was struck by the importance of working out the relationship of the individual to government in modern society. I had seen that process from the point of view of the government for a number of years. I had seen how the government operated and brought to bear its powers and pressures upon the individual citizen or private group. It had always seemed to me equally important to look at that process from the point of view of the individual who was faced with the power of the government being brought to bear against him, or of a minority faced with pressures from a majority or larger group. I was drawn to that field to comprehend both sides of the picture and perhaps to make some contribution to the ultimate resolution of the problem, which was, of course, a central problem of the times.

Second, my experience in my later days in Washington left me convinced that there was little possibility of making any substantial advance in terms of government measures to solve economic or social problems. I have concluded from my New Deal experience that progressive thinking on the part of the people is really "crisis thinking," without necessarily any awareness of the forces loose in the world or even of the nature of the problems. That interpretation was prevalent among New Dealers in Washington by the middle of 1946. Only another war or depression would spark further major changes in government programs, we thought. In periods of economic prosperity and in the absence of war, the general citizenry is not eager to undertake novel government projects. The possibility that problems exist that may come to the fore as soon as another year does not influence ordinary people much. The problems must stare them in the face.

After World War II the country was not forced to face the economic issues because military expenditures resumed. Conservative forces in this country are able to prevent important changes for the general welfare unless faced by overwhelming demand from the public. Conservative groups control the mass communications media, support congressmen through campaign funds, and exercise control over so many aspects of the economic situation that by and large they have things well under control [1953]. The forces needed to overcome that resistance will accumulate only in a period when the problems become urgent, and not in a period of apparent prosperity, even though serious problems are lurking below the surface.

I had seen a tremendous advance in forward thinking during the New Deal, but with the end of the Roosevelt administration the forward movement stopped, and it seemed unlikely that the government "of the people" would take on additional functions in the next few years, with the possible exception of atomic energy. Consequently, it seemed to me that the emerging problems were less likely to revolve around governmental attempts to solve issues such as unemployment, use of natural resources, or extension of social welfare programs. My hunch turned out to be correct; the emerging issues concerned civil liberties and the preservation, maintenance, and advancement of the democratic process. I turned, then, to that field as the major focus of my attention.

# INDEX

# INDEX

liberals after 1938, 186
liberal viewpoint, 17, 329
Liberty League, and unconstitutionality of National Labor
Relations Act, 57
"Little Steel Formula," 194, 280, 289

MacChesney, Brunson, 174
Macy's department store, 10, 27
Madden, J. Warren, 53, 85, 91-94,
101-102, 107, 123-130, 297
–*background*, 91
–Chairman of the NLRB, 53
–not reappointed to NLRB, 129
Magruder, Calvert, 37, 48
–and bill establishing new NLRB, 50
McCarthy, Joseph, 113
Millis, Harry A., 36
Muir, Malcolm, 18

Nathan, Robert, 302
National Defense Advisory
Commission (NDAC) 142
National Industrial Recovery Act, 8,
9, 14, 25, 30 33
–codes, 10*ff*
–invalidated, 26
–section 7(a), 9, 34, 36
National Labor Relations Act, 29,
33, 51-52, 61, 70, 74, 82, 153
–amendments of 1939, 108; AFL bill,
108; Chamber of Commerce bill,
110; employer bill, 111
–constitutionality of, 71
–Section 12, 70
–test cases, 54; and Emerson, 57;
Fruehauf Trailer case, 72; Jones &
Laughlin Steel Company case, 72
–unconstitutionality, 77, 80
–violations, 66
National Labor Relations Board, 33-
36, 84
–[original], 28
–powers, 37
–1940, end of an era, 121
–and Appropriations Committees,
106
–assessment of young lawyers in
Washington, 131
–bill establishing new NLRB, 49, 50
–"cease and desist" order, 52
–Chief Trial Examiner, 106
–Emerson's assessment of, 94
–Fruehauf Trailer case, 72
–injunction proceedings, 78

–Jones & Laughlin Steel Company
case, 72 [new], 37, 47, 51, 57

–Pennsylvania Greyhound case,
71-75
–procedures, 141
–record in the courts, 95
–regional offices, 54
–Review Division, 118
–Secretary's Office, 99, 100, 105, 118
–test case: Pennsylvania Greyhound,
71
–the "red" issue, 122
–vulnerable to attack, 97
National Lawyers Guild, 179, 184,
186
–and Roosevelt's Court packing
plan, 84
National Recovery Administration, 6,
7, 12, 14, 26-30, 33
–administration of, 12; and business
interests, 31
–advisory boards, 12
–attorneys
–Blue Eagle, 14-15; not respected, 15
–code authorities, 11-12, 22
–codes: continual revision, 11;
problem of enforcement, 15
–collective bargaining provisions, 10,
29
–constitutional test, 24
–Consumers Advisory Board, 13-14
–Enforcement section, 15
–Industry Advisory Board, 13
–Labor Advisory Board, 13
–lawyers, 21-23
–lawyers' influence, 23
–Legal Division, 18-24
–liquidation, 28
–opposition, 31
–President's Reemployment
Agreement, 14
–Section 7(a), 13, 29
–wages and hours provisions, 10
Nazi breakthrough into France, 142
Nelson, Donald, 143, 157
New Deal
–accomplishments, 97
–administrative agencies, 141
–Congressional strength in 1938, 113
–election of 1936, 82
–judiciary, 37
–lack of majority after 1938
elections, 267
–lawyers, and Roosevelt's Court
packing plan, 83
–second term, 96
Newman, James R., *background*, 305
Newport, R.I., 45
Niles, David, 7, 262
Nixon, Richard, 175
NRA, *see* National Recovery
Administration

334